Broadsides

&

Boarders

Marvin H. Albert

Broadsides

&

Boarders

Appleton-Century-Crofts, Inc.
New York

Copyright, © 1957 by Marvin H. Albert

Library of Congress Card Number: 57-8847

PRINTED IN THE UNITED STATES OF AMERICA

To my father, Bernard Albert,
who first stirred my imagination,
and
To the memory of my beloved
mother, Tillie Albert, *who believed in me,*

I dedicate this work

CONTENTS

CONTENTS

PART VI   A FEW FIR-BUILT THINGS

ILLUSTRATIONS

(Following page 50)

The Capture of Briel by de la Marck's "Sea Beggars"

The Invincible Armada Set Upon by the English

Admiral Blake Before Tunis, 1655

The Four Days' Fight, 1666

The Explosion of the *Orient* During the Battle of the Nile

The Death of Nelson

Stephen Decatur Fights Off the Algerian at Tripoli

The Engagement Between the *Constitution* and the *Guerrière*

The Battle of Lake Erie

Perry Carrying His Pennant to a New Flagship

INTRODUCTION

The Glorious Captains

One of history's shortest and most stirring chapters tells the story of sailing ship warfare. Although it looms large in the romance of our past, warfare with cannons-under-sails lasted from start to finish less than three hundred years. It did not begin until almost a hundred years after Columbus discovered America, and before the American Civil War it was forever ended. But in this brief, bloodstained time, sailing ships-of-war changed the course of history, creating a balance of power that has shaped much of our modern world.

This book attempts to re-create those three hundred years of sailing ship warfare through the handful of sea captains who gave the period its peculiar glory. This small succession of audacious men, employing sails and wooden hulls, broadsides and boarders, may have varied in bravery, brains, and bombast. But the same spirit was in each of them: the spirit that chanced everything—personal honor, their ships, their country's fortunes—to beat the enemy.

One spirit resounds down through the centuries, echoing in Dutchman van Heemskerck's "Hold your fire till you hear the crash!" . . . in Englishman Nelson's "No captain can do very wrong if he places his ship alongside that of an enemy" . . . in American John Paul Jones' "I have not yet begun to fight!"

Nelson, of course, was the greatest of them all—but only because the genius he brought to bear on this spirit was afforded by his time the opportunity to express it in complete measure. The spirit itself, they all had. And in the same measure.

PART ONE

Dutch Sea Beggars

There were sea battles before sail. But these were essentially battles between opposing armies that used ships only to bring their troops together. Once face to face, the men fought across the decks as they would on land. If ships themselves were used as weapons at all, it was solely to ram into other ships. Ram, grapple and board were the tactics of oarship battles.

This continued to be the case long after sails came into use. Merchant ships were propelled by sail for centuries before the last great sea battle between oarships, the Battle of Lepanto in 1571. But up until that time, sail was used in warfare only to bring an army to the point of battle. Or to carry it away. Thus, when the Greeks spoke of "hoisting sails," they referred to running away from a fight.

Rowed galleys remained the basic instrument of sea fighting, even after the introduction of cannon and other related types of heavy guns to sea warfare. This was chiefly because rowed galleys were considered far more maneuverable than sailing ships in a close fight.

But a sailing ship could carry to the scene of battle much more than a galley's maximum load of about three guns. Long rows of guns could be mounted along the sides of sailing ships; on galleys that same space was taken up by oars and rowers.

In 1538, during the battle of Prevesa between the Turks and

1

the allied Christian forces, the Christians brought into action a 128-gun sailing ship, a galleon. As luck would have it, once this galleon arrived on the scene, it was becalmed. The Turks, under the misapprehension that immobility meant defenselessness, gleefully rowed their galleys out to seize it. But the galleon's superior firepower not only held them off all day, but also sank dozens of the attacking galleys. The galleys in turn could do little against the gunners protected behind the galleon's higher wooden sides. In the end, none of the galleys got to the becalmed sailing ship, which during the night was towed out of danger.

But this encounter was considered, insofar as it was considered at all, a freak. None of the Mediterranean sea commanders drew from it the obvious conclusion that despite their relative lack of maneuverability, sailing ships were both more effectively defensible and better able to inflict damage on opponents than were galleys.

It was in the cold, choppy waters of Europe's North Atlantic seacoast, where galleys fared poorly in rough weather, that sailing ships finally came into their own as weapons of war. The change began with the arming of merchant vessels against piratical attacks. Once this had been done it was only a short step further to the converting of merchant vessels into ships intended almost solely for fighting. It was the Dutch who first made effective use of these.

Why the Dutch? Cardinal Bentivoglio explained it, long ago: "Of their ships the Hollanders make houses, of their houses schools. Here they are born, here educated, here they learn their profession. Their sailors, flying from one pole to the other, practising their art wherever the sun displays itself to mortals, become so skillful that they can scarcely be equalled, certainly not surpassed, by a nation in the civilized world."

1

The Duke of Alva's Spectacles

THE STRANGE CAREER OF WILLIAM DE LA MARCK

A little before eleven o'clock on the morning of June 5, 1568, a man whose short, strong figure was dressed in a severe black doublet and whose hard face was a mask holding back fury, shouldered his way through the crowds of Netherlanders packing the huge Brussels square. When he reached the inner edge of the crowd, where three thousand Spanish troops formed a barrier around a newly erected scaffold, he halted and stood waiting, still and tense. His name was William de la Marck.

Like the rest of the Netherlanders, he had been drawn to the square by the shocking news that his cousin, the Count of Egmont, and the Count of Horn were to be beheaded that morning. Although certain Netherlands groups had banded together under the Prince of Orange against the tyranny of Spain, the nation that ruled them, neither Egmont nor Horn had taken part in the revolt. To the contrary, they had behind them years of military service on behalf of Spain. As fervent Catholics, they had supported Spain's religious persecutions in the Netherlands. Their sole indiscretion had been to point out quietly that some of the latest

Spanish measures of oppression, if not corrected, would squeeze the lifeblood out of their country. Yet these two noblemen were to die, sentenced to death by the Duke of Alva as a warning to other Netherlands noblemen not to grumble at the harsh edicts from Spain.

Reluctantly, William de la Marck looked at the place of death which had been raised in the middle of the square. A huge black cloth was spread over the entire scaffold, upon which were a table with a silver crucifix, two velvet cushions, and two tall iron spikes. The executioner was not yet in sight.

A murmur swept through the crowd. A tall, thin man in his sixties had appeared at a balcony window, wrapped tightly in a black cloak. His long, thin face, decorated with a gray-streaked beard, was expressionless. It was the Duke of Alva, come to watch the execution he had ordered.

Alva, the most famous military leader of his day, had been sent here by Philip II of Spain to crush the rebelliousness of the Netherlanders; to punish all who protested against the heavy taxes, to destroy all heretics who had turned away from the Roman Catholic church. He had entered the Lowlands with his army at his back, had beaten the three Netherlands armies that tried to stand against him. Their leader, the Prince of Orange, had fled the country, gone into hiding in Germany.

Now Alva was free to get on with his reign of terror. This execution was only part of the beginning. Before he was done, he would be able to boast of having executed almost nineteen thousand people. When he finally departed, he would urge his king to burn every single Netherlands city and town to the ground, along with the people in them.

The murmuring of the mob below Alva's balcony was suddenly stilled. On the edge of the crowd, a company of Spanish troops was shoving back the Netherlanders to form a passage, through which came Egmont, walking slow and erect, the Bishop of Ypres, and a company of Spanish guards. Egmont's red-rimmed eyes fixed on the nearing scaffold and his lips moved ceaselessly: ". . . Hear my cry, O God, and give ear unto my prayer . . ."

De la Marck watched his cousin mount the scaffold and look upward to the window from which the Duke of Alva was observing the proceedings, his face cold and pitiless as stone. Egmont's face flushed with rage. Unfastening the cords of his robe, he hurled it aside to show that he had himself removed the collar of his shirt and doublet to bare his neck for the execution blade. Then he knelt on one of the velvet cushions and recited the Lord's Prayer with the Bishop, kissed the silver crucifix, and stood erect again for one last look at the upraised faces of his countrymen. He took off his plumed hat and replaced it with a small cap which he pulled down to cover his eyes. Then he knelt once more on the velvet cushion and bent his head forward, waiting.

The executioner appeared upon the scaffold, the sword of execution in both hands, and advanced across the black cloth to where Egmont knelt. The executioner raised the sword high above his head. Egmont cried out suddenly in a voice that carried across the entire square: "Lord, into Thy hands I commit my spirit!" The sword flashed down, severed Egmont's head from his body.

For a moment, De la Marck thought he had been struck deaf. It was the absolute silence of the square stuffing his ears. Then the silence was broken with sobs and shouts of hatred. De la Marck did not shout with them. He could not take his eyes from the headless body of his cousin, over which a black cloth was being placed.

The Count of Horn now mounted the scaffold and stood for a moment staring down at the shrouded body of Egmont. At last he raised his eyes to the faces of his countrymen. "Pray for my soul!" he shouted, and an answering cry of grief and anger rose from the massed crowd. As the executioner raised his sword and slashed it downward, striking away Horn's head, they could be held back no longer. The crowd pushed past Alva's soldiers to dip their handkerchiefs in the blood of Egmont and Horn.

Marck watched soldiers impale the heads on the long iron stakes and raise them high for everyone to see. He watched the blood stream down the stakes from the severed necks. And as he stood there, that blood began to work a change in him. He looked up once again at Alva's stone face, swore an oath of horrible revenge, and strode away.

That was how it began. Thereafter Marck lived on the run and in hiding, a man of the shadows—striking suddenly, killing, looting, then vanishing. He was called an insane, bloodthirsty pirate; he called himself an angry, vengeful patriot. Both descriptions have their truth. For the oath that he swore was this: "I shall not cut my hair or nails or beard until I have avenged the death of Egmont." He kept that vow, and it changed him into a monster.

Before the execution of his cousin, Marck, a man of wealth and high family name, had been wild, aggressive, eager for a fight. He came from a long line of such men; one of his ancestors had seized by force the castle of Godfrey of Bouillon and earned himself the name of "The Wild Boar of Ardennes." As a boy Marck had led a band of ruffians in roistering and pilfering, and in manhood he became known as a dangerous agitator against Spanish oppression. Yet before the death of Egmont, his wildness had been kept within certain bounds; he had remained a man.

Now, however, ruled by the lust for revenge, he became a monster. He soaked his hands deep in the blood of his victims; his face became vicious; his hair and beard grew long and wild. His followers called him "Longnail."

This was the man who would lay the cornerstone of the Dutch Republic, and give his people their first taste of liberty from Spanish oppression, a man driven to lead an outlaw's life by the calculated cruelty of an evil ruler.

That ruler, Spain's King Philip II, launched the two greatest fleet battles of the sixteenth century: the Battle of Lepanto in 1571 which ended in Spanish victory, and the Armada's attack against England seventeen years later which ended in utter defeat.

The Battle of Lepanto, the last great oarship fleet action, occurred three years after the beheading of Egmont and Horn in the Netherlands. With the victory of Philip's Christian fleet over the Turkish fleet in the Mediterranean Spain became the most powerful military nation on land or sea, a power no other nation or group of nations could withstand. Yet the same year that seemed to prove Spain's invincible power also saw the beginning of the destruction of that power. For in 1571 William de la Marck found an outlet for his oath of vengeance: he joined the Sea Beggars.

The Sea Beggars had taken their name from a Spanish jeer. Back in 1566, when a group of Dutch nobles petitioned the Spanish authorities to ease taxation, the Spaniards had called them "beggars." The Dutch, furious, accepted the word as a challenge. By the next day, "Long live the Beggars!" was the rallying cry of all who refused to knuckle under. Those who became outlaws and hid in the marshes and forests called themselves Wilderness Beggars. Others were Mountain Beggars. But the most dangerous enemies of Spain were the Sea Beggars. For the Dutch knew the sea and lived off it. And in those days a merchant voyage across the oceans often required as much fighting as trading. Pirates infested every coast. The governor of each port was a law unto himself. Sometimes a merchantman would be welcomed for peaceful trading. At other times, vessels would shoot out from the harbor and try to seize ship and cargo, kill the crew and send any survivors into slavery on the galleys. The Dutch had long ago armed their merchant ships and learned how to fight on the sea.

Now thousands of exiled Netherlanders had taken to the sea and turned to piracy. The Prince of Orange, realizing their usefulness, issued letters of marque to their ships, thus giving them the dubious respectability of privateers, fighters for freedom, instead of pirates. But the name under which they fought meant little. Their motives—revenge and livelihood—and their methods —piracy and looting—remained the same. So did their victims: Spaniards and Netherlanders who supported Spanish rule. It was this ragged band of freebooters that was to confound the most powerful military nation on earth, fighting guerilla fashion, harrying the Spanish at isolated points along the coast, terrorizing wealthy Dutch families that were friendly to Alva, raiding commerce, seizing ships that carried troops, munitions, food and gold from Spain.

During the storms of winter they holed up in the German ports of Emden and Hamburg and in English ports like Dover and Plymouth. But with the coming of summer, they sailed out to sea— and to war. Each summer they ranged farther. The names of the most daring of these raider captains—Roobol, Jan van Troyen, Jan Abels, Dirk Duyvel—were known and feared by all who lived along the North Sea coasts. And the most famous—or infamous— of all was William de la Marck.

When Marck decided to buy and equip two merchant sailing ships for fighting, he had no difficulty finding crews for them: exiled Netherlanders flocked to him, begging for the chance. He picked carefully from among them crewmen whose savagery nearly matched his own, and sailed out to join the Sea Beggars. In the months that followed, the revenge-obsessed nobleman with the wild beard, tangled unshorn hair, and long nails ravaged the coasts of the Netherlands. When he seized a ship or sacked a town, he left not a single Spaniard behind him alive. Priests were a special target for torture and death. Priests had come to symbolize Spanish rule—even to Catholic Netherlanders—for when anyone was tortured or executed by Alva, a priest was always present. Netherlanders whom Marck suspected of being partial to Spain were tortured into revealing the hiding places of their gold; their wives and children were carried off and held for ransom.

Other Sea Beggar ships began to follow him, to act under his direction; for most could find something in him to follow. As brave as the best of them, more cruel than the worst, he was both cunning and successful. Within a year the Prince of Orange, against the advice of many of his followers, chose Marck as the new admiral of the entire Beggar fleet.

For some time the Prince of Orange had been trying to weld the Sea Beggars into an organized, disciplined fleet. But the Sea Beggars had no home port of their own; and the individual ships or groups of ships that slipped in and out of dozens of foreign ports could not be successfully directed and controlled from his distant exile inside Germany. He had made a first step when he issued letters of marque to them, commissioning them to "seize violently and to make war against the enemies of the Prince, their ships and goods. . . ." The next step had been to persuade a large group of Beggar captains from Zeeland to sign a contract to the effect that ". . . during the past years, the greater part of the nobility of Friesland as well as of Holland and this country, have been driven away from their fatherland, leaving behind goods, wives and children. . . . We agree to assist one another . . . for the purpose of damaging, destroying and annihilating the Duke of Alva and his blood-thirsty adherents." The contract stipulated that one half of all the loot acquired by the captains of Zeeland was to go to the Prince of Orange to help him war against Spanish rule. The Prince of Orange appointed an admiral over them all. And a new navy—a navy composed entirely of sailing ships—was born.

But the first admiral used the fleet thus handed to him for his own ends and none of the wealth he seized reached the Prince. He was dismissed; the Prince of Orange tried again. The second admiral was not strong enough to force the individual captains, each used to acting on his own, into a fleet answering one man's orders. Units of the Spanish navy began catching Beggar ships and destroying them. The Prince of Orange tried a third admiral. This time he appointed a man on whose complete loyalty he could depend, and a man strong enough to bend all the others to his will: William de la Marck.

Using the English port of Dover as his base, Marck was able to prey upon shipping in the English Channel and along the European coasts beyond. Under him, the Sea Beggars became a fighting navy. And with this navy the bloody toll of Marck's revenge increased a hundredfold.

He found it easy to dodge Spanish warships. Spanish merchant ships, poorly convoyed, or not convoyed at all, were burned, their cargoes taken, their crews drowned or murdered on deck. Those who dwelled along the Netherlands coast shrank in terror from Marck's approach. His forays ashore sent families who collaborated with Alva scurrying into the protection of the walled cities. The Beggar fleet slashed through the northern waters, an ever-growing danger to the Duke of Alva and Philip of Spain.

Finally, the Spanish began to realize that something must be done. They turned pressure upon neutral countries to stop sheltering the Beggar ships.

Late in March, 1572, England's Queen Elizabeth bowed to this pressure, ordering all the Sea Beggars out of her ports immediately. It was a staggering blow; for Marck, without a port of his own, now had no place to land.

The Duke of Alva assumed that now the homeless Beggars would quickly disintegrate as an effective fighting force. But the blow, far from killing the Sea Beggars, instead brought about the birth of the Dutch Republic.

For Marck's fleet, thrown out of England so suddenly that they had been unable to provision, had nowhere to go but home. At sea, hunger reigned aboard his ships. If no foreign port would take them in, Marck decided, the Sea Beggars would have to seize the shelter and provisions they needed—in the Netherlands.

It was the wind, not Marck, that chose the town of Briel to be "the cradle of Dutch liberty." Originally, Marck headed his fleet toward the wealthy North Holland port of Enkhuizen, on the Zuider Zee. But the wind shifted to the north and Marck, seeing that his smaller vessels were faring badly in the heaving waters, turned his fleet about and let his ships fly south before the wind.

He sailed along the coasts of Zeeland that thrust out like huge separate fingers into the sea, until he reached the island of Voorne in the massive mouth of the Maas River. At two o'clock on the afternoon of April 1, 1572—April Fools' Day—the startled citizens of the small city of Briel on the island of Voorne looked over their walls and saw the Beggar fleet, twenty-five ill-assorted vessels, dropping anchor beyond the dike that kept the ocean from their north wall.

From the poop of his flagship, Marck stared at the walls of Briel and debated his next move. Those walls were high and strong; the guns of the city would be more numerous, heavier, and of greater range than his own. He had no idea of the size of the Spanish garrison inside the walls—nor even whether the Netherlanders of Briel were favorably disposed toward the cause of the Prince of Orange.

Marck had only about seven hundred men aboard his twenty-five vessels. Hungry men. His was as motley a fleet as had ever been assembled. His largest vessel was a bare 160 tons, and carried twenty pieces of artillery. Only a few of his ships had been designed for fighting; the rest were converted coasters and fishing vessels: caravels, schooners, tiny sloops. From their mastheads streamed all manner of flags and banners: the crests of individual nobles, flags of various cities, the colors of the Prince of Orange, blood-red flags on which were painted ten pennies as a reminder of the harsh "tenth-penny" tax, white flags with red crosses, banners bearing mottoes such as "Regain Or Die," "For Country," "Long Live the Beggars."

The men of this strange fleet had been hacked and molded into the best sea fighters of the day. But could they fight well enough on land to capture a fortified city?

At this crucial moment a quick-witted Briel fisherman named Peter Koppelstok stepped into history. On this afternoon he was ferrying a few people across the river in his fishing boat when they spotted the Beggar fleet. The passengers panicked and demanded to be put ashore at once. Koppelstok obliged them and then decided to row out to the Beggar fleet and see what they wanted. As he neared the fleet, the banner floating from the masthead of one ship caught his attention. It was the banner of Treslong, a nobleman of Briel, known to everyone. His dead father had once served as the city's governor. With mounting excitement, Koppelstok rowed to Treslong's ship.

Treslong quickly took the fisherman to his admiral's flagship. There Marck anxiously questioned him concerning the strength of the town. Koppelstok replied that the Spanish troops that garrisoned Briel had left for another post just the week before. Now the taking of Briel was a possibility.

Marck designated Koppelstok as his special messenger to carry the Sea Beggars' demand for the surrender of the city to the magistrates of Briel. There was no time for the writing of a message; Koppelstok was to tell the magistrates that a delegation must be sent to the jetty to work out the terms of surrender with the Beggar admiral. Koppelstok set off eagerly in his rowboat, carrying with him Treslong's signet ring, which, known as it was to the citizens of Briel, would prove his authority to speak for the Sea Beggars.

The gates of the city had been locked at the first sight of the Beggar fleet, but they were quickly opened to him. Inside the walls, he pushed his way to the city hall through crowds of frightened people, and announced himself to the magistrates who had assembled to discuss the defense of their city. He showed them Treslong's ring, and gave them Marck's message. "Have no fear," Koppelstok told the magistrates. "The Sea Beggars will harm no one. They are here to save Briel from Alva's tyranny and his tenth-penny tax."

But although most of the citizens of Briel were either for the Prince of Orange or at least against the Duke of Alva, the magistrates were afraid. If they resisted the Sea Beggars, Marck might burn down the whole city. If they did not resist, and opened their gates to the Beggars, Alva was sure to punish them. Jan Nicker, the governor of Briel, at last asked Koppelstok a practical question: "How strong are the Beggars?"

And Koppelstok ended the magistrates' indecision by lying blandly: "There are more than five thousand of them." Whatever will they might have had to resist collapsed. While the delegates went out through the North Gate to meet Marck and delay him, hundreds of the well-to-do citizens of Briel rushed to their homes, crammed valuables into carts, and began to stream out of the city's South Gate, rushing inland to hide.

Marck, unaware of the exodus, demanded of the two delegates, who stared with terrified eyes at the cruel face framed in its un-kempt tangle of hair and beard, that the city be unconditionally surrendered to his forces within two hours. The delegates hurried back inside the North Gate—which was immediately closed and

barred—and joined their fellow burghers as they streamed out of
the city through the South Gate.

Marck remained on the jetty, waiting. With him were the men of
his fleet, their hunger showing in their faces as they eyed the high
walls of the city. The two hours passed but the North Gate did not
open.

Sensing at last that he was being duped, Marck sent Treslong
with a body of armed sailors around the city to the South Gate,
while with the rest of his men he stormed the North Gate. The gate
was stout. But Marck ordered a mast used as a battering ram
while some of his Beggars scaled the walls. A few of the burghers,
sympathetic to Alva, fired at them from the tops of the walls, then
fled in terror. There was no real resistance, however, and at 8 P.M.
—a moment that is now considered the Dutch birthday—Marck
broke into the city of Briel.

Meanwhile, Treslong and his men reached the South Gate just
in time to catch the city treasurer fleeing with 6,000 guilders in
city funds. Treslong took the money "in the name of the Prince of
Orange." The South Gate was slammed shut as Treslong approached it, but was quickly opened again when he threatened to
set fire to it. He led his men inside and met Marck in the center
of the city. Briel was theirs.

But now Marck must make another decision—and make it
quickly. He had Briel—what was he to do with it? News of its
capture would soon reach Alva and a huge force of Spanish troops
could be expected to descend on them within days.

Marck's first instinct, prompted by over a year of constant
killing and looting, was to take what they needed from the city
and then set it afire and sail away before the Spanish army
arrived. And yet . . . once they left Briel, where would they go?
English ports were closed to them; German ports nearly so. Briel
had a fine harbor for the Beggar fleet. He was the first man to
succeed in tearing a part of the Netherlands out of the iron hands
of Spain. Must he give it back so soon?

Marck moved into the city hall, called his captains together there,
and put the question to them: Should they sack and burn Briel—
or stay and defend it? His captains were united in their answer.
The taking of Briel had transformed them from pirates pretending
to be patriots into real patriots, from wandering exiles to freedom
fighters standing on their own soil for the first time in years.

Marck took Briel in the name of the Prince of Orange, ran the Prince's colors up on the towers of the city, and sent word of his conquest to the Prince in Dillenburg, Germany.

For the first time, Marck restrained himself. The Sea Beggars did not molest the citizens remaining in the city—no matter what their affiliation. They took as much food and clothing as they needed, and moved into the homes of people who had fled. Marck contented himself with sacking the Catholic churches (the only churches, since Alva permitted no others to exist) and murdering thirteen monks to slake the edge of his bloodthirst.

Hundreds who had fled the city returned as soon as they learned that they would not be harmed. Working side-by-side with the Sea Beggars, men, women and children helped strengthen the fortifications; the unaccustomed smell of freedom was in their nostrils.

News of the liberation of Briel swept through the Lowlands to Alva. A rhymed jeer was on everyone's lips. Since Briel had been taken on the First of April, and Briel meant "spectacles" in Flemish, the Dutch were happily chanting:

"On April Fools' Day,
Duke Alva's spectacles were stolen away!"

When the news of Briel reached Alva—and with it the infuriating rhymed taunt—he ordered a huge body of troops to sail to Briel, retake it, sack it, slaughter everyone in it, and burn it to the ground.

Four days after Marck captured Briel, twenty-five ships carrying thousands of Spanish soldiers reached the island of Voorne and anchored in the Bornisse stream a few miles from the city. Marck made no effort to oppose their landing. His seven hundred men, even bolstered by the citizens of Briel, could not stand against such an overwhelming force. Remaining inside the walls of the town, behind rows of ready big guns and muskets, he sent a party of men under Treslong and Roobol out through the woods to circle the Spaniards.

The Spanish troops advanced on Briel with flags flying and drums beating. So confident were they of defeating the small pack of ragged Beggars that they had brought no artillery with them. But as they marched along a country lane leading to the city, they suddenly ran into a barrier of felled trees and tangled branches. Before they could pull apart the barrier, a hail of musket balls and arrows rained into their massed bodies from the thick woods on either side of them. Startled and confused, with comrades falling all around them, the Spaniards broke and rushed to shelter in the low land below the Niewland dike. There, as they hurriedly re-grouped for an organized attack on the northern walls of the city, they suddenly saw a man carrying an ax emerge from Briel. He leaped atop the dike and began running along it.

The man was Rochus Coninck, the city carpenter. Before the startled Spaniards could fire at him, he disappeared over the side of the dike into the water. With his ax between his teeth, he swam to the Niewland sluice and began to chop away at the sluice doors. Minutes later the sluice broke open and the water rushed in over the low land.

The Spaniards, horrified by the sight of the flood advancing on them, clambered up on top of the dike for safety, only to see that the onrushing waters had cut off all approaches to the city—except by way of the inland South Gate, behind which Marck had massed most of the city's big guns and his own musketeers.

As Marck had anticipated, the Spanish troops now rushed along the dike to attack the South Gate. He waited till the Spaniards were almost up to the gate. Then his shout rang across the walls. The big guns and muskets fired point-blank into the massed uni-forms of the oncharging Spaniards.

Hundreds of Spanish soldiers died on the spot. The rest turned and ran for it, a panicked, completely disorganized mob. They scurried to the shelter of the dike—only to find that the flood let in by the broken sluice was already up to their chests. Throwing away their guns in their terror, they waded through the surging waters toward the inland paths that led back through the woods to their ships. Many drowned before reaching the woods. Many more were killed from ambush by the Beggars. Those that reached the ships found them burning and sinking. Treslong and Roobol had set fire to the Spanish fleet while the soldiers were marching on Briel.

Some of the Spaniards managed to get aboard vessels that were still afloat, put out the fires, and sail away. But more of them were left behind on the island of Voorne. With no way to get off the island, they tried to hide in the woods and marshes. Marck's Sea Beggars hunted them out, shot them down, beat them to death, stabbed them, impaled them on pikes, drowned them. By nightfall, there was not a single live Spanish soldier left. The despised Sea Beggars had defeated the pride of military Spain.

The reaction to this victory swept through the Netherlands like a raging fire—and nothing that Alva or Philip II did from then on could put it out. Town after town along the coast rose with the help of the Sea Beggars, overthrew their Spanish garrisons, and prepared to defend their walls against Alva's retribution. Before long the entire country was being rent by a bloody revolution that was to go on and on, year after year, until the Dutch were entirely free of the Spanish yoke.

Through it all, the Sea Beggars continued to lead the fight. For the freeing of Briel changed their character, as well as the character of their country. They were no longer pirates, but men dedicated to a single purpose: the liberation of their people. And this dedication ennobled them.

It ennobled them all, that is, except William de la Marck, the man who had struck the first blow for liberty. He had felt what the rest felt, but only briefly did it deflect him from his primary purpose of revenge.

When the Prince of Orange, seeking to unite the country behind him and looking toward the day of freedom, spoke out for toleration of all religions, Marck ignored him. To Marck, any Catholic church or churchman remained a special prey. Soon he became a liability to his master. Catholic Netherlanders held off from siding with the Prince because of the depredations of the Sea Beggar admiral. When finally Marck tortured and murdered the seventy-two-year-old Father Cornelius Musius, a man universally beloved, even the non-Catholic Dutch could stomach him no longer. The Prince stripped Marck of his position as admiral of the Sea Beggars.

Marck swore revenge. He swore to raise his own private rebellion. He swore many things, but he never got a chance to carry them out. He was killed, quite appropriately, by the bite of a mad dog.

The leaders of the rebellion breathed easier—and went on without him.

2

The Too-Bitter Heart

It took the Duke of Alva a long time to understand that the center of the Dutch revolt was on the sea. For years he regarded the Sea Beggars as a mere annoyance. But when this "annoyance" began tearing away parts of the Netherlands' coastline from him, and became so strong that it set up a virtual blockade against all commercial shipping in and out of Amsterdam, Alva realized his mistake. He set about destroying the Sea Beggar fleet.

A Spanish fleet of thirty ships was equipped for battle in Amsterdam. On October 3, 1573, Admiral Bossu, with three thousand soldiers and sailors aboard these fighting ships, set out to find the Beggar fleet and wipe it out at one blow.

Bossu found his quarry on the Zuider Zee: twenty-four small ships carrying fewer than one thousand men and ammunition sufficient for less than two hours' battle. He hurled his thirty big vessels at the Beggars, confident of the outcome. His flagship, the *Inquisition,* alone carried 380 men and thirty-two big guns— more than a match for any five of the Beggar vessels, which were mostly little fishing schooners and sloops carrying artillery which he ridiculed as "wooden cannons." He planned to smash the Beggars quickly with his long-range cannons and return in triumph to Alva. It was a practicable plan, except for one thing. Bossu's vessels were not only big, they were also clumsy. In order to get within gunnery range—and still not allow the enemy to get close enough to be able to board—his fleet must outsail the Beggars. But the Beggars' little vessels were faster and more maneuverable than his own.

The commander of the Beggar fleet, Cornelius Dirkzoon, eyed the oncoming Spaniards and swiftly laid plans of his own. His men, though fewer than the Spaniards, were superb seamen and vicious fighters. (It was a Spaniard who, after seeing the Beggars in action, wrote that "they excell the Turks in inhuman fury.") He might not have many guns, but his ships could move and his skippers knew these waters with their treacherous shallows far better than the Spanish captains. As Bossu's Spanish fleet approached, Dirkzoon's Beggars dodged into a stretch of these shallow waters, hoping to lure Bossu into following. The light little Beggar vessels with their flat bottoms skimmed easily over the shallows, where the big, deep-keeled Spanish ships would go aground. But Bossu refused to be drawn into the trap.

Dirkzoon began maneuvering to close with the Spaniards. Once he succeeded in this, his Beggars would be able to grapple the Spanish ships, board them, and settle matters in hand-to-hand combat on the decks. Bossu, at the same time, began maneuvering for a long-range artillery duel in which his big guns could pulverize the Dutch patriots.

For two days and nights the two admirals circled each other, feinting and retreating. Each time the Spaniards got the range with their guns, the tiny Beggar vessels darted into the shallows. Each time the Beggars rushed back in an attempt to grapple and board, the Spanish fleet turned tail to keep the distance and hit the Beggars with their guns. The winds were light and changeable, not allowing either fleet to achieve its objective against the will of the other.

Several times, individual ships managed to clash. Dirkzoon saw one of his captains, Jacob van Til, dart in against a big Spaniard, the *Ape*, and get his grappling hooks on it. Til boarded the *Ape* in a wild man-to-man struggle, killed sixty Spanish soldiers, and began shifting the *Ape's* guns to his own vessel. But at that moment another Spanish ship got within gunnery range and let go at Til's craft. Til was forced to flee back into the shallows.

Another Beggar vessel had just managed to grapple a Spaniard when Bossu's big *Inquisition* sailed up and fired a broadside that killed fifty men, almost the entire Dutch crew. The Beggar ship was barely able to limp back to the shallows.

At last, the wind began blowing strong to the southeast, from behind Bossu's ships toward the Beggar fleet. Dirkzoon, realizing he hadn't a chance with the wind against him, fled across the shallows close to shore, and settled down to wait for the wind to shift. Bossu, watching Dirkzoon's Beggars in flight, assumed that the Dutch had had enough and were quitting. He began to celebrate a Spanish victory.

Five days later the wind suddenly shifted. Bossu was interrupted in the middle of his noonday meal by the startling news that the Dutch fleet was in sight again, approaching at full speed with the wind behind them. Quickly donning his light fighting armor and buckling on his sword, Bossu rushed out on deck. It was true. There came the Beggar ships across the shallows, all sails taut with the wind that hurled them onward.

Bossu barked his orders: The Spanish ships were to remain anchored so that there would be no chance of going aground in the ensuing battle; they would destroy the oncoming Beggar vessels with their artillery as they came within range.

Moments later, every ship in Bossu's fleet was belching smoke and iron in thunderous broadsides. But Dirkzoon's Beggar ships came in too fast and were too widely separated for his barrage to do much damage. Before the Spaniards could reload for another barrage better-aimed—an operation that required between eight and ten minutes with the best of gun crews—the Beggars were in among them, closing for the kill.

The decks of the Beggar vessels swarmed with battle-eager Dutch fighters, their hands clenched around knives, swords, axes, pikes, hammers and clubs, their eyes fastened on the bulwarks of the nearing Spaniards. Up in the rigging were more Beggars, holding pots filled with fiery coals, burning pitch, boiling oil—waiting.

Behind the Beggar cannons the gunners, knowing the poor quality of their weapons, held their fire for the last moment. As the two fleets clashed together, the gunners fired at stone-throw distance. One Spanish galleon, holed at the waterline by three different Dutch ships, sank while the roar of the guns still echoed against the shore. Other Spaniards, when they saw this, slipped their cables, against Bossu's orders, and tried to maneuver against the Beggars.

It was too late. The Beggars, with the wind in their favor, drove in and scattered them. Five Spanish ships, trying desperately to evade the grappling hooks, were forced aground in the shallows. A dozen Beggar vessels closed in around them. The men high on the Beggar masts hurled their fire-hoops, burning coals and pitch down on the Spanish rigging and decks. Screaming Dutchmen leaped wildly over the bulwarks and hurtled into the Spanish defenders through the fires, slashing with their knives and swords, striking with their hammers and axes, jabbing with their pikes—until the Spanish decks were cleared of the enemy. Those Spaniards who could, swam ashore, leaving the blood-spattered Beggars to loot their burning vessels.

The rest of the Spanish fleet, unnerved by the sight of six ships lost in the first clash, slipped their cables, lightened their ships by throwing their cannons overboard, and fled across the shallows back to Amsterdam. All but one. Bossu's great *Inquisition*. Trapped, it was fighting for its life.

When the Beggar ships had first attacked the anchored Spanish fleet, Dirkzoon had chosen the big Spanish flagship as his own victim. Its very name, *Inquisition*, was an enraging taunt flung in the face of the Dutch. As his own little flagship darted into the Spanish fleet, Dirkzoon ordered his helmsman to steer straight for the *Inquisition*.

Bossu, standing beside the *Inquisition's* mainmast in his armor, his big sword held in his powerful right hand, watched Dirkzoon's little vessel close in. He yelled an order and the deck shuddered as sixteen of his cannons let go at the Dutch admiral. As the massed iron balls hurtled toward Dirkzoon's flagship, his helmsman, terrified, veered the vessel away in an attempt to flee. The furious Dirkzoon whirled on him. But another of his seamen, Jan Floriszoon, was quicker. Knocking the helmsman aside, Floriszoon grabbed the tiller himself, and set them back on course towards the *Inquisition*.

Bossu's next shots smashed across Dirkzoon's deck. One of the dozen men killed was the frightened helmsman, struck by an iron ball as he huddled against the bulwarks. Before Bossu could reload to fire again, Dirkzoon's ship was against his side. Within minutes, three other Beggar ships had joined his battle with the overtowering Spanish flagship.

But the *Inquisition's* number of men and big guns was greater than that of all four Beggars combined, and its side loomed too high above their decks for grappling. One of the Beggar vessels got under the *Inquisition's* stern in an attempt to shatter its helm with gunfire, but burning pitch dropped from the high poop of the Spanish flagship set the Beggar afire and drove it off. Now there were only three Dutch vessels hemming in the *Inquisition*—and the Spanish big guns and fire-throwers were more than a match for them.

Dirkzoon, his decks being smashed apart by iron balls, his sails on fire, still saw one way to win. Slipping his little craft close under the *Inquisition's* overhanging wall, he cut the Spanish flagship's anchor. Bossu, directing the fight from his mainmast, suddenly felt his big ship drifting toward the shallows. Before he could do anything about it, the *Inquisition's* keel shuddered over the rocks and stuck fast. The three little Dutch vessels closed in again.

The sun set on the one big ship and the three little ones locked in their death struggle. The enemies pounded each other point-blank with their guns. Up in the burning rigging, Beggar sharpshooters exchanged musket shots with Spanish soldiers, and hurled fire. Down on the low Beggar decks, grappling hooks were hurled up to catch at the Spaniard's rails. Howling, soot-smeared, blood-streaked Dutch seamen swarmed up boarding ropes to fight their way in through the Spanish gunports.

All night long the fight continued, and the people who lined the shore watched it by the light of the flames consuming the spars, sails and rigging of all four ships. Down under the roaring fires, men fought across decks slippery with blood and choked with the bodies of the fallen. Time after time, Dirkzoon and his Beggars forced their way to the center of the *Inquisition's* deck, only to be beaten back by Spanish soldiers led by Bossu. The Spanish commander stood like a great rock in the midst of the tempest, his armor deflecting musket balls, arrows and pike-thrusts, his powerful arm swinging the long sword in unflagging arcs of destruction.

Dawn came, and still the battle went on. The savage Beggars, attacking again and again across the *Inquisition's* waist, managed to hack down more and more of the men standing with Bossu. At last, after twenty-eight hours of steady battling, Bossu found himself with only fifteen of his men at his side. Less than eighty of his 380 men were still alive. He knew it was useless to fight any longer. Exhausted and stunned by the totally unexpected defeat, he ordered the white flag run up, and surrendered his sword to Beggar Admiral Dirkzoon.

Thus ended the first sailing-fleet battle—between the glory-covered old Spanish navy and the brand-new Dutch navy. A complete victory for the Dutch.

The hated Duke of Alva was recalled to Spain. Because of the Sea Beggars, he had failed in his task of subjugating the Netherlands. All that land was now in active and effective revolt against Spanish rule.

In Alva's place, Philip II sent Don Luis de Requesens to be his new governor-general over the Netherlands. The fact that Requesens had served for a number of years in the Spanish navy had much to do with his choice. For Philip now realized that despite the power of his army, the Sea Beggars were loosening his hold on mile after mile of coast. Requesens arrived at his new post knowing that his main job would be to tackle the new Dutch navy.

The first task Requesens set for himself was the relief of Middleburg, the capital of Zeeland. Middleburg was in Spanish hands, and all attempts by the Dutch armies to take it had failed. But Middleburg was also on an island—and for a year and a half the Sea Beggars had turned back all ships trying to supply the Spanish garrison. Inside this blockade, the Spanish position in Middleburg was becoming shaky. Unless they could get supplies, food and reinforcements, they would not be able to hold out much longer.

Requesens immediately began to ready a great fleet of 115 ships to strike the Sea Beggars' Zeeland fleet, defeat it, and relieve the Spanish garrison at Middleburg. Forty of the Spanish ships were at Antwerp, seventy-five at Bergen op Zoom. Requesens gave orders for these two groups to join together at sea, and sail to Middleburg.

But these two groups were destined never to meet. A man named Louis Boisot, commanding a fleet of Dutch ships, saw to that.

The total Zeeland Beggar fleet was sixty-five ships. Like the Spanish, they were divided into two groups: twenty-five stationed off

Flushing, forty hovering off Bergen op Zoom. These forty were commanded by Louis Boisot, who knew the fleet of Spanish ships were getting ready in the port of Bergen op Zoom and was waiting off the coast of Tholen Island, just outside, for it to come out and fight.

On the cold, rainy morning of January 29, 1574, seventy-five Spanish ships sailed out toward Boisot's fleet of forty. The Spanish admiral, Romero, his vice-admiral, Glimes, and every one of their officers looked forward cheerfully to the battle. Aboard the ships bands played merry tunes. Governor-General Requesens hurried out to Tholen Island and stationed himself atop a dike to watch his superior fleet defeat the Beggars. He smiled and swelled with pleasure as each of his ships fired a salute to him in passing.

Word of the approach of the Spanish sped to the Dutch fleet. Louis Boisot ran up the blood-red Beggar flag and fired a cannon to signal attack on the approaching enemy. The commander of his flagship, Captain Schot, rushed up on deck from a sickbed and insisted on taking back his command from his lieutenant. Boisot, remembering how Schot's son had died beside him in a previous sea fight with the Spaniards, understood Schot's eagerness and let him stay. This was going to be different from the battle of the Zuider Zee: no more darting away from long-ranging Spanish artillery this time. Boisot's fleet carried hundreds of excellent guns —cannons, demicannons, culverins and other big pieces—all captured from the Spanish.

Boisot, his face wet with the fine cold drizzle, led his forty ships through the choppy waters toward the enemy. The two fleets clashed with an explosion of gunnery, and then pounced on each other for close action. For neither had yet discovered the best way to use a sailing ship carrying cannons. Instead of dueling, employing their big guns in shattering broadsides, they fired off their guns merely to stun the enemy, then closed for a boarding fight.

Boisot headed straight for the flagship of the Spanish admiral. Romero started to dodge out of the way, but suddenly changed his mind when he got a good look through the rain at Boisot's deck. Most of Boisot's wild Zeelanders were eagerly jammed in the waist, ready for boarding. Romero swiftly brought his flagship around, got within musket distance, and poured a full load of iron balls and chains across the Dutch waist.

The result was devastating. Boisot saw half his crew torn apart before something struck him in the face and sent him reeling. When he seized the mainmast to steady himself, he found that blood was streaming down his cheek and he could see out of only one eye. He touched the shattered part of his face. The other eye was gone.

Shoving himself away from the mast, Boisot looked around at his wrecked ship. Captain Schot, one arm torn off, was still on his feet, yelling at what remained of his men, trying to get the ship out of the way as Romero came about to hurl another salvo from his other side.

Somehow, Captain Schot succeeded. Romero's shots were less effective than the first batch had been. But a moment later, the ship of the Spanish vice-admiral, Glimes, emerged from the cold mists on Boisot's other side and crashed against him. Spanish grappling hooks swung out and caught Boisot's rail. Spanish soldiers swarmed over to attack the depleted, disorganized Beggars. Boisot and Captain Schot, ignoring their maiming wounds, rallied their men out of the confusion and led them in a swirling counter-charge against the Spanish boarders.

Glimes' soldiers reeled back before their fury, then surged forward again. The fight seesawed back and forth on Boisot's deck until another Beggar ship appeared through the rain and struck at Glimes' ship. Glimes hastily recalled his soldiers to the defense of their own vessel. His ship and the other Beggar vessel drifted away through the battling fleets, locked together.

For a moment, Boisot's flagship was free. Then Admiral Romero's ship closed against it and grappled a tight hold. Romero's soldiers came leaping over the bulwarks as Boisot's men turned to face this fresh enemy.

But once on the Dutch deck, the Spanish soldiers hesitated, waiting until enough of their fellows joined them to dare attack such notorious fighters as the Beggars. Boisot, seeing their in-decision, rasped orders to several of his men, who swiftly dis-appeared into the hold. Then he shouted at the rest of his men to fall back away from the Spanish soldiers gathering on one side of their deck.

The Spaniards, surprised, hesitated a moment longer, looking at the withdrawing enemy across the expanse of wrecked, corpse-strewn deck. There were about sixty of them now, enough at last to attack. Boisot yelled down to the men he had sent into the hold. An instant later, just as the Spaniards braced for their rush, the deck under their feet exploded upward in a roar of fired gunpowder, hurtling them into the air and killing them all.

Admiral Romero, who had been on the point of joining his boarders, leaped back and stared, stunned, at the place where his sixty soldiers had been, where he himself would have been a moment later. In that one moment, the odds had almost been evened. Romero shouted for his men to cut off the grappling hooks and get his flagship free.

But Boisot understood the changed odds just as well as the Spaniard. Quickly, his remaining eye scanned the other ships in the smoke-filled rain. Spanish ships were adrift in flames, some being boarded, others trying to get out of traps formed by clusters of Beggar vessels working together. Off in the distance, Vice-Admiral Glimes' ship was aground and burning to the waterline. Boisot turned back to Romero's flagship, still caught fast to his own, and screamed: "Boarders!" His men rushed over the rails with him. Now the battle was fought on Romero's ship—on the deck, up into the rigging, down under the deck among the big guns. Other Beggar ships closed in to join the assault, cannons pounding the Spanish flagship. More boarders swarmed over the bulwarks to follow Boisot's howling Zeelanders in slaughtering Spanish soldiers and crewmen.

Romero, realizing his flagship was lost, slipped away from the hacking, wrestling mob, sneaked down to a dark corner under the deck, and hurriedly got out of his fighting armor. Wriggling through a gunport, he dropped into the sea and swam ashore to Tholen Island. Once on the beach, he lay exhausted for a few moments—listening to the pound of guns—until he saw the legs of someone standing before him. Raising his head, he saw that the legs belonged to Governor-General Requesens, who stared aghast, from his waterlogged admiral to his shattered navy out on the rain-swept ocean.

The battle had lasted two hours. The Beggars had captured or destroyed fifteen Spanish ships and killed twelve hundred Spanish fighting men, including Vice-Admiral Glimes. The rest of the Spanish fleet, beaten, was fleeing toward Antwerp, pursued by the savage Sea Beggars. The Spanish garrison at Middleburg received news of the defeat and knew that all hope of relief was gone. They pulled out and left the Zeeland capital to the Dutch.

Boisot's winning of this battle was more a triumph of savagery than of superior naval science. Tactics peculiarly suited to sailing-ship fighting were still in the trial-and-error experimental stage. What Boisot's Zeeland Beggars had proved was that under proper conditions, tough sailors could outfight seasoned soldiers on the water. These same sailors next demonstrated that they could even best the Spanish soldiers on land—given very special circumstances exploited properly.

The Spanish armies, entrenched in southern Holland, were well on their way to bringing the Dutch-defended cities of that whole area to their knees. On May 26, 1574, the Spanish had clamped an unbreakable siege around the walled city of Leiden, setting up sixty-two fortified positions which blocked every road in or out of the city. No attempt was made to attack Leiden. Instead, the besieging Spaniards settled down to starve its fifteen thousand citizens into surrender.

By September, after four months of siege, it seemed certain that Leiden could hold out no longer. The people inside the walls had eaten everything in the city, including the dogs and cats. They were down to living off pigeons and rats. Then Louis Boisot and his Zeeland Beggars entered the picture.

On September 10, Boisot set out from Rotterdam with over two hundred Beggar-crammed, gun-carrying little vessels to lift the siege of Leiden. Leiden was an inland city. But the land between the city's walls and the water was interwoven with miles of dikes, which alone kept the water beyond the view of the city. Boisot's plan was to break through each dike as he came to it, let the water flood through, and thus sail the Beggar fleet all the way across the land to the walls of Leiden.

But to break through an earthen dike took long hours of hard work with shovel, ax and pike. And the thousands of Spanish troops cutting off Leiden rushed to defend each dike as the Beggar fleet neared it. The Beggars met them with salvos from the big guns on their vessels, then fought them hand-to-hand on the dike. At each dike they must fight—and win—a battle.

The dikes were broken, one by one. Boisot advanced with his flotilla across the slowly flooding land between the sea and the city, battling every mile of the way with guns, pikes, boiling oil, burning pitch, knives, clubs, and bare hands. It took his men almost a month to reach Leiden.

That the Spaniards, equal to any fighting men in the world, were beaten, is a tribute to the intensity of the Dutch passion for liberty. For it was this passion alone that kept Leiden from sur- rendering. Before Boisot's men could break the seige, hundreds inside the walls died of starvation. The survivors, waiting out the endless weeks of watching for a glimpse of the nearing Beggar fleet, swore to cut off their own arms for food rather than surrender.

It was this same near-mad passion that won the Beggars dike after dike as they advanced across the flooding land. One recorded scene of their wild fury comes down to us: A Zeeland Beggar stands atop a dike from which the Spanish defenders have just been driven. Still boiling with the rage of the encounter, he cuts the heart out of a dead enemy, bites into it with his teeth. Then he flings it away with a grimace and cries, "It is too bitter!"

Before this kind of man the Spanish finally fled from the walls of Leiden. Boisot sailed up to the city with dozens of vessels piled high with food for the starving survivors. And another large chunk of the Dutch homeland was ripped from the grasp of Spain.

Within another two years, the inability of Philip II's tremendous land and naval forces to put down a handful of Sea Beggars would break the Spanish government in the Netherlands. The Dutch then formally united and set about the task of hurling Philip's armies out of their country.

3

"Do not tell the men till after..."

HEEMSKERCK IN THE DRAGON'S LAIR

There was nothing of the fighter in Jacob van Heemskerck's look or manner. Even as a slim youth working in the countinghouse of his father, an Amsterdam merchant prince, you could see it: Jacob was a dreamer.

His long, thin face was gentle. The large eyes below his high forehead were warm and soft, clouded with visions. But a "soft" man of vision can become the hardest fighter of all if his vision is opposed—as the young Jacob was to grow up and prove.

Jacob van Heemskerck grew up during the fight of his country to throw off the yoke of Spain. He was only five when William de la Marck struck the first great blow against Spanish rule. By the time he was twenty-nine, the Spanish armies had been cast out and the Netherlands Republic was a sovereign nation. But Spain refused to admit that she had lost. A state of war continued, year after year. Spain might be unable to invade the new Republic and retake it, but her huge navy continued to hamper the growing commercial success of the Dutch on the oceans.

Young Jacob sat erect on his tall stool in the countinghouse, copying figures in a ledger—figures that represented rare goods, long and desperate voyages, magical distant lands. He listened, breathless, to tales told by the skippers of his father's far-seeking vessels. His father expected him to remain in the countinghouse to learn its ways, and eventually assume control of the business. But Jacob's eyes were filled with limitless, heaving oceans. His head was stuffed with the immense idea of finding a new way to the fabled Orient.

A new way was certainly needed. The Spanish navy blocked the old route. To reach the rich ports of the East, Dutch merchants had to sail south around Africa. But the Spanish navy stood in their way, increasing the risks of a voyage already made hazardous by length, storms and pirates. The rewards of such voyages, when successful, were so great that Dutch skippers continued to run the risk of trying to slip past the Spanish warships. Some made it; more did not. Spanish harbors claimed scores of captured Dutch vessels. Torture at the hands of the Inquisition or a horrible lingering death as a chained galley slave claimed hundreds of captured Dutch seamen.

All this Heemskerck read in the profit-and-loss statements he jotted in his father's ledgers and heard from the skippers who got back. He knew that the Dutch could become the greatest commercial nation in the world. Fluits, a new type of long, narrow merchant vessel designed by Dutch shipbuilders, were proving easier to sail, and thus more economical, than the vessels of any other country. But because of the depredations of the Spanish navy, a voyage south and east to the Orient was more likely to put loss than profit on a Dutch merchant's books. The route west, around the bottom of South America to the Orient, was so long that most companies which tried it were ruined.

There was only one other possible way to reach the Orient, a way no one else had ever found, though some had tried. Jacob van Heemskerck looked north, toward the cold, unknown world of polar ice, and decided that somewhere there must be a route through the ice-choked ocean—a route that would allow ships to sail east over the top of Europe to the Orient.

At last, in 1595, when he was twenty-nine, Heemskerck's dream freed him from his father's countinghouse. On a clear, warm morning in July, he launched an expedition seeking the northeast passage to the Orient. Heemskerck sailed as captain of one of the ships, giving command of the expedition to Captain William Barendsz, a man who had himself once sought the northeast passage, only to be turned back by ice.

The expedition reached Greenland, and could sail no farther against the massive blockade of close-packed ice. They were forced to return home, the expedition a failure.

Heemskerck refused to accept his defeat as a final one. For a full year he talked and cajoled, until he persuaded other merchants to help him finance another expedition.

Heemskerck sailed with two ships in May, 1596. This time he commanded the expedition; the two ships were captained by Barendsz of the first try, and Cornelius Ryp. They ran into dangerous drifting ice before they reached the Arctic Circle. As they progressed north, huge mountains of ice gathered around the two tiny ships, threatening to crush them between their gigantic teeth or to close behind them and cut off retreat. At last Captain Ryp could keep his nerve up no longer; he took his ship and sailed back home.

Heemskerck and Barendsz pushed forward in the remaining ship, sailing deeper and deeper into the freezing channels, through that white, dazzling maze gleaming in the perpetual sun. Again and again they would sail into a promising stretch of water, only to find it was a cul-de-sac from which they must sail quickly back before they were trapped.

After they had been in those waters for three months, the thickening ice of winter closed in, seized the ship, and held it fast. Helpless, Heemskerck stood on the deck of his imprisoned ship and watched the long arctic night descend upon them. All through that winter he waited in darkness, knowing his dream had failed him. When Captain Barendsz died in his arms of the cold, Heemskerck's dream died with him.

At last the sun returned, and the ice all around the ship began to melt and break apart in the summer thaw. Heemskerck managed to maneuver his vessel out of the Artic Ocean and back to Amsterdam, one and a half years after setting forth from it. He had failed, but his herioc attempt and his success in lasting out the arctic winter had made him a national hero. It had done something else—to him. The long months trapped in the arctic had convinced him that he would find no northeast passage. But nothing about Heemskerck had really changed. His eyes were still warm, his face thoughtful. He had always possessed a stubborn, fearless determination. But where before this determination had been directed north, against the ice, now it was directed south, against the Spanish navy. If the ice could not be navigated, the Spanish navy must be destroyed.

When Heemskerck sailed again, it was as the commander of two fighting ships. With these two small vessels, carrying between them a total of two hundred men, he fought, beat and captured a great Spanish war galleon defended by over eight hundred soldiers and sailors. Yet the new fighting man was still gentle when the fight was won. His Spanish captives afterwards formally thanked him for treating them with a kindness completely unexpected from a man who had inherited the mantle of the savage Sea Beggars.

He was now the leading seaman of his country. His belief that the Spanish navy must be destroyed so that the Dutch could sail unmolested to the Orient was voiced everywhere. At last, the Dutch government agreed.

In April of 1607, Jacob van Heemskerck sailed out of Texel in command of twenty-six small, swift, low-decked warships. He went down through the English Channel, past the shores of France, along the coast of Portugal—a tall, lean, dignified figure erect on the poop deck of his flagship—toward the stronghold of Spanish naval power.

Off Cape St. Vincent, a Dutch merchant vessel appeared on that horizon, slicing through the swells toward Heemskerck's fleet under full sail. Her skipper, a seaman from Flushing, was rowed to the Dutch flagship, *Æolus*. Heemskerck was waiting for him in the waist as he climbed the rope ladder and stepped onto the deck. The Dutch admiral's first question was precise: Had the Flushing skipper seen anything of the Spanish navy? The skipper nodded; he had seen too much of it for his own comfort. A Spanish war fleet was in the Straits of Gibraltar, lying under the guns of their rock fortress in wait for any Dutch vessels that tried to enter or leave the Mediterranean. His ship had barely managed to slip past the Spanish fleet in the night. There were dozens of Dutch vessels in the Gibraltar harbor, reminders of other skippers who hadn't been so lucky.

Looking around him at Heemskerck's low-decked little fighting ships, the skipper added a warning: The Spanish warships were much larger and better armed than this.

"That," Heemskerck answered quietly, "does not trouble me in the least."

No sooner was the skipper down the ladder and into his boat again than signal flags raced up Heemskerck's masts. The Dutch fleet headed straight for Gibraltar.

The blue sky above Gibraltar was warm and cloudless on that morning of April 25, 1607. Not a breeze disturbed the languid air or rippled the smooth sheen of the harbor. A fleet of twenty-one mammoth Spanish warships rode at anchor under the great guns of the overhanging rock fortresses. Aboard the flagship of this fleet, the galleon *St. Augustine,* the Spanish admiral, Don Juan, stared out at the fleet of little Dutch ships that had appeared in the distance and seemed to be moving slowly in his direction.

Don Juan, the winner of history's last great galley fight, the Battle of Lepanto, was puzzled. For weeks he had been at the dull work of snaring Dutch vessels unwary enough to venture within his reach. Now an entire fleet seemed to be offering itself up to him. He knew that it must be that Dutch fleet's intention to fight him. Yet he couldn't quite believe the Hollanders were that foolish. Not here, not under these conditions. They couldn't really intend to sail right up to the strongest Spanish coastal fortress, impregnable Gibraltar, and attack an organized fleet of such might and under the command of himself. . . .

Don Juan looked around him at his fleet. Eleven huge eighty-oared, three-masted galleasses. And ten of the biggest galleons ever built—ornate monsters with four-storied castles towering high above their massive decks, each mounting more artillery than five of those tiny Dutch ships combined. As for manpower, his own flagship, *St. Augustine,* alone carried over seven hundred soldiers and crewmen. In all probability that entire Dutch fleet didn't carry many more.

Don Juan suddenly snapped an order to one of his officers. From deep in the hold of the *St. Augustine,* a ragged, dirty man, weighed down with manacles, was shoved up onto the quarter-deck before the Spanish admiral. He was a recently captured merchant skipper from Rotterdam, named Govert. Don Juan pointed a finger, heavy with jeweled rings, at the distant Dutch fleet. "What do those little vessels want here, do you suppose?"

At first Govert could only stare dully across the water, blinded by the sunlight after the complete darkness of the hold. With grimy fingers he wiped the tears from his smarting eyes and looked again. Then he saw them, and a glitter replaced the dullness of his eyes. "If I know my countrymen," he growled, "they have come to give you a battle."

Don Juan's laugh was filled with genuine contempt. "Battle? I and this flagship alone can send all your countrymen out there to the bottom!"

And he meant it. He didn't even bother to up anchor. There was no wind to maneuver with, anyway. Let those Dutch fools come to him as best they could and be destroyed right here where all of Gibraltar could watch and enjoy the spectacle. . . .

Aboard the Dutch flagship *Æolus,* Heemskerck had all his captains assembled on the quarter-deck before him. He looked them over with affectionate satisfaction. There was his vice-admiral, Lambrecht Hendricks—nicknamed Handsome Lambert—who had shown the stuff inside him some time ago by tearing into a Dunkirk pirate fleet and smashing it to bits. And the others were of the same metal: "Long Hank" Janszoon, Harpert Tromp, Alteras, Bras, and the rest—all tough-grained captains who would fight joyously to their last breath as long as they were fighting the hated Spaniards.

Since there was no wind, Heemskerck told them, they would let the current flowing from the Atlantic into the Mediterranean carry their ships through the Straits to the fleet awaiting them in the harbor. One of them remarked that without a wind, they would be unable to maneuver once inside the harbor; the far more numerous and heavier guns of the Spaniards could blow them apart if they just drifted in like sitting ducks.

Heemskerck pointed to the south. There, heavy black storm clouds raced low over the coast of Africa. Those clouds were moving north toward the Straits. By the time the Dutch fleet reached the harbor under Gibraltar, they would be overhead—and so would the wind pushing them.

Quickly now, Heemskerck told them his plan. Once inside the harbor, with the wind filling their sails, the Dutch were to hit the Spaniards in pairs—two little Dutch vessels striking a single big Spaniard together. As soon as a pair destroyed its victim, it was to find a fresh prey or join any other pair having a hard time of it. Heemskerck left the details of the attack to the proven ferocity of Dutchmen in a fight. He doubted that the Spaniards would maneuver at all. The Spanish fleet, he expected, would remain at anchor because of the lack of wind and rely on their heavier weight of artillery fire against the slowly drifting Dutch. If they did, they would be caught that way when the wind from Africa reached the big harbor. If the Spaniards did up anchor and try to maneuver against his little fleet, Heemskerck could depend upon the superior sailing quality of his smaller ships, and superior seamanship of his sailors, to carry through his plan anyway.

Heemskerck dismissed his captains. "The safety and sanctity of our homes, the freedom of our native land, the honor of our nation," he told them softly, "has been entrusted to you and me. The eyes of Europe and Africa are upon you. It is yours to deserve, with the blessing of God, the gratitude of your country and of all posterity."

They went back to their ships, these captains, each carrying with him a love for his gentle, resolute fighting admiral, a love that was felt by every man in that fleet.

Aboard each ship the orders rang out. Slowly, the Dutch fleet slipped into the Straits current and drifted toward the fortress harbor. The cannons, culverins, periers, mortars, sakers and other varieties of artillery were loaded and run out. Men with pikes and grappling irons waited at the bulwarks. Others with muskets and kettles of pitch ready to be set afire climbed the masts and perched on the yardarms. The sails, dangling uselessly now, were nonetheless open and ready.

Their progress throughout that morning and into the early afternoon was almost imperceptible. But gradually the massive rock loomed higher and nearer, the Spanish warships grew larger and more dangerous. Rigid with tension, Heemskerck stared fixedly at the so-slowly nearing enemy in the harbor. He felt something cool move against his cheek. For a moment, in his single-minded concentration on his objective, he did not identify it. But then it came again, stronger—a breeze.

He turned quickly and looked up at the sails. They were beginning to stir listlessly. The main-topsail flapped, hung still, then flapped again. Up in the sky, the black clouds from Africa were almost upon them. The surface of the water rippled, stirred by a slowly, steadily increasing wind. All the sails of his fleet began to catch it and spread.

Heemskerck spared one quick glance at the enemy. Their anchors were still down; the sails of the galleons were still furled. His heart swelled. His voice was unusually loud as he gave the order that sent the red flag of the Sea Beggars racing aloft to signal the attack to his captains.

Bugles and drums sounded thinly across the water from ship to ship as masts began to strain and shrouds to creak with the force of the ever-increasing wind slapping into the sails, sending the Dutch bows slicing through the whipped-up water toward the anchored Spaniards. The whole force of the African storm was now pushing his little ships onward. They raced so swiftly that when the Spanish fleet let go its first ear-shattering, bay-rocking barrage of broadsides, little of the hurled metal found its mark. Not one of the Dutch ships was stopped.

Before the guns of the overhanging Gibraltar fortress could fire, the Dutch fleet was in amongst the big Spanish ships. And it was too late. The Gibraltar guns had waited a moment too long. From now on they could not fire down for fear of hitting their own ships.

Heemskerck, a look of intense joy transfiguring his wind-burned features, sighted the *St. Augustine,* Don Juan's flagship, and headed straight for it with his *Æolus.* Close behind him raced Handsome Lambert on his *Tiger,* in accordance with the two-against-one orders. Off to his left, Heemskerck saw Captain Alteras' *Red Lion* and Captain Bras' *Black Bear* pairing off against the Spanish vice-admiral's ship, *Señora de la Vega.* Other pairs of Dutch ships darted through the anchored enemies to find their own prey.

The fury of the attack told almost immediately. The Dutch ships, obeying Heemskerck's orders to save their ammunition until they reached point-blank range, blasted their victims only seconds before they closed, grappled and boarded. Spanish ships slipped their cables and reeled back clumsily. Off to one side of the bay, two Dutch ships caught a mammoth Spaniard between them and pounded it into the water with broadsides. One great galleon, its high castle-structure aflame, drifted without a helm against the shore and burned to the waterline.

Captain Alteras' *Red Lion,* closing in on the Spanish vice-admiral, suddenly found itself caught between two big enemy ships that had slipped their cables and unfurled their sails. Alteras traded gunfire with them both, darting between and around them, hitting them and avoiding their shots so competently that both finally turned and fled. He pursued them, caught one and sank it before the other could swing around to join the fight. Then he drove the second aground and set it afire.

As dusk slowly settled on the bay, Heemskerck pursued Don Juan, who had slipped the cables of his *St. Augustine* and darted away behind his other warships. With every sail straining under the storm wind he closed in on his quarry, Handsome Lambert's *Tiger* still at his heels. The near side of Don Juan's flagship vanished suddenly in a roaring cloud. Heemskerck felt the rush of spar-slashing, deck-gouging metal fly through his ship. The *Æolus* dove straight into this barrage toward the side of the *St. Augustine* as Heemskerck's wild cry reached his eager gunners: "Hold your fire till you hear the crash!"

The next moment, the *Æolus* rammed full-tilt into the *St. Augustine* just forward of the mainmast—and simultaneously the Dutch guns roared, slamming a broadside into the overhanging hull of the Spanish admiral's ship, tearing great holes in the water-line. The combined effects of the crash and broadside brought the *St. Augustine's* yards, sails and rigging toppling down on the Spanish decks to add to the devastation. Don Juan, hero of Lepanto and scorner of the Dutch sea fighters, fell with the first Dutch barrage. A moment later, Handsome Lambert's *Tiger* grappled hold of the *St. Augustine's* other side and joined the *Æolus* as it pounded the Spaniard in preparation for boarding. But the huge Spanish galleon gave as much as it got; its guns fired down again and again from their greater height onto both Dutch decks.

Yards away, three Dutch ships, grouped around the Spanish vice-admiral's ship, battered it to a pulp with their guns, boarded it, and then set it adrift, its rigging aflame, consuming first the masts and then all the rest.

The Spanish on shore watched with mounting horror and disbelief as one after another of their great vessels caught fire, erupted in explosions of gunpowder that hurled bodies, chunks of wood, webbed rigging, tattered sails high into the air, and sank under the waters of the bay.

Night closed in, but those ashore could still watch the destruction of their fleet by the light of those immense torches that had once been Spanish warships.

Heemskerck himself saw little of his triumph. Minutes after his *Æolus* crashed into the *St. Augustine,* the Spanish flagship had let go a broadside across his deck. Heemskerck had seen a whirling cannon ball fly in his direction, hurl aside a smashed seaman, and rip off the hand of a gunner. Then, all at once, Heemskerck found himself face down on the deck, stunned, hardly understanding what had happened. He saw Verhoef, his flag captain, bending over him, his face twisted with shock. Heemskerck looked down at his body. His entire right leg had been shorn off. There was no pain—seeing the way his blood gushed out of the wound, he knew there would be no pain. He laid his head back on the deck and did not feel its hardness. "Verhoef," he whispered. "Do not tell the men till after . . ." Seconds later, he was dead.

Dazed, Captain Verhoef rose to his feet and looked around him. Heemskerck had been afraid that knowledge of his death would take the heart out of his men—but already they were crowding around, looking down at the dead man on the deck. The news was racing across the deck, up into the rigging, down to the gunners. Verhoef looked at the faces of the others. Dishearten them? No! Rather, he saw in their eyes what he felt himself. His next order was a cry of pure rage: "Boarders! Boarders!"

The men of the *Æolus* scrambled up the boarding nets, into the *St. Augustine's* gunports and over its bulwarks, charging into the defending Spanish soldiers with a madness nothing could stop. They slaughtered a path across the deck and there met Handsome Lambert and the men of his *Tiger* coming up the other side. When Lambert was told that Heemskerck was dead, the fate of the *St. Augustine* and its defenders was sealed. Even the raising of a white flag by the Spanish aboard could not stop the men led by Lambert and Verhoef. Heemskerck would not have tolerated their vengeance; but Heemskerck was dead. The *St. Augustine* had more Spanish fighters aboard it than any other ship in the fleet, and it was the last ship to go down. But down it went, down to the bottom of the harbor.

When the moon rose and cast its pale glow over the harbor, there was not a single fighting ship left for those on shore to see. Both fleets were gone. The Spanish fleet—every last ship of it— had been wiped out. The remains of the Dutch fleet had sailed away.

Jacob van Heemskerck's job was done. Now his fleet carried

home the body of its admiral, to be buried with honors and tears in his own city of Amsterdam—where long before he had first dreamed a boy's dream of greatness. That dream had come true. Not as he had thought it would, perhaps, but in another way— through a violence he could not have foreseen and with a result more lasting.

Heemskerck had dreamed of opening the rich ports of the Orient to his country by finding a northeast passage over the top of the world. Instead, he had achieved his goal by giving the Spanish navy a fantastic beating. For the defeat of the Spanish fleet in its own lair, under the most imposing coastal fortress in the world, lowered Spanish prestige so drastically that Spain was forced to come to terms with the Dutch a short time later. The Dutch victory earned its navy a reputation that would afterwards assure Dutch merchants the right to trade anywhere in the world without interference. The Netherlands Republic grew into the wealthiest commercial nation in Europe.

PART TWO

English Sea Dogs

While the Dutch Sea Beggars were challenging Spain's rule along the coasts of Europe, the English Sea Dogs of Queen Elizabeth sailed across the oceans to mock Spanish might by snatching at the riches of America—which King Philip II considered his own God-bestowed property.

Like the Dutch, the English sea fighters evolved from merchant sailors. And like them too, they altered history with fighting vessels smaller than today's harbor tugboats.

The Dutch, pioneers though they were in the new science of sailing-ship warfare, had still depended on the ram-grapple-and-board tactics of rowed galley fleets. It was the English who gradually developed a method of sea fighting that utilized and depended upon the particular qualities of sailing ships: the stand-off cannon duel between carefully maneuvered vessels. It was a method that declared itself—and proved itself—finally in the battle against the Invincible Armada. The Spanish sailing fleet went to its destruction clinging vainly to a faith in the efficacy of the formations and tactics of its victorious galley fleets of the past.

The sail-fighting strategy of the Sea Dogs was not discovered in a flash of inspiration. It evolved gradually—with the change of merchant-vessel masters into battleship captains.

And a sailor named Francis Drake—fashioned by the tough, turbulent, grasping land and time that produced Elizabeth, Bacon and Shakespeare—emerged to personify this change.

39

4

"I have brought you to the treasure of the world..."

FRANCIS DRAKE ON THE SPANISH MAIN

Young Francis Drake was barely aware of the heat of the fierce July sun under which his ship, the *Pascha,* rode before the stiff Caribbean breeze. His attention was concentrated beyond the dip and lift of the bow on the distant line of white fringed with green that had appeared on the western horizon. There the blue expanse of the sea ended upon the thick-forested shore of Central America.

He stood with an attitude typical of him: feet planted wide apart, his thick, rope-scarred sailor's fists on his hips. His blue eyes gazed possessively upon the nearing land. An English seaman who dared venture upon these waters faced the constant threat of death by Inquisition rack and fire. But it was not for death that Drake, then in his late twenties, had made his seven weeks' crossing of the ocean. With him were two tiny, well-armed ships and seventy-three men as young and eager for a profitable fight as himself. He had come for the only things that made life worth living, to his way of thinking: wealth and fame.

Both seemed as good as in his grasp when he looked at that

distant white line of surf. The hot sun beat against his blunt, impudent face, flamed in his reddish hair and short-pointed beard. He looked like the devil that the Spanish were soon to believe him to be.

A yell from the lookout in the mast brought his spyglass up. He scanned the shore until he spotted two great rocks that seemed to rise from a solid barrier of jungle-hemmed shore. Between those rocks lay the entrance to a small bay. He knew, because he himself had discovered it the year before—and had prepared it as a secret taking-off place for his next move, clearing an area around the sheltered beach and burying supplies.

He had named this hidden harbor Port Pheasant, because the jungle surrounding it abounded in pheasant. It would be the perfect place to put together the three disassembled pinnaces in the hold of his larger ship. And those swift, sleek little vessels would be essential to his next move.

The *Pascha,* and its smaller companion, the *Swan,* slipped easily across the water toward their fast-approaching destination. Drake, on his quarter-deck, still stared at the lush, green land, tense with excitement and conscious of all that depended upon him. He was responsible for his two ships, for the large investment of the men backing this venture, for the seventy-three men—two of them his own brothers—for whom he served as admiral, navigator, general, minister, and physician. But these were all responsibilities for which he was ready. Sometimes he felt he had been born ready. He had the shoulders and strength made to carry burdens. And the inner determination. He was a man of solid, stubborn ambition—a man with the experience, wit and nerve to succeed. And he knew it.

The *Pascha* and *Swan* had reached the bay's small entrance when Drake ordered both vessels hove to. Long ago, he had learned to temper his daring with precaution. Lowering a boat, he climbed down into it and was rowed through the stone pillars.

As the boat entered the widening curve of the little bay inside, Drake's keen eyes studied the sheltered beach. There was little wind in here, and without it the tropic heat engulfed them, as intense as the silence between the oar splashes. Drake saw that the jungle was already moving down over the beach area he had cleared last year. Vines and . . .

"Hold your oars!" he hissed.

The oars rose out of the water and hung, dripping in the harsh sunlight. Drake's gaze was riveted on a spot at the edge of the jungle, where a thin trail of smoke rose in the still air. His blue eyes were cold as he slowly surveyed the jungle on all sides. There was no sign of anything moving. Yet that was smoke. No mistaking it for the heat mist that clung to the jungle. "Back to the *Pascha*," he ordered softly.

The oars made less sound rowing out than they had coming in. On reaching the *Pascha,* Drake ordered another boat lowered quickly. The men in both boats were armed before they rowed back into the bay.

Drake stepped from his boat to the beach, his sword drawn. As he strode slowly toward the smoke, he saw that it rose from the smouldering stump of a burned tree. Ordering his men to spread out through the surrounding jungle, he advanced to the smoking stump.

As he reached it, a flash of light to one side made him whirl, sword leaping up. Then he relaxed slightly. The sunlight reflected against a sheet of lead nailed to another tree. He stepped up to it and read the message cut into the metal:

Captain Drake! If you fortune to come to this Port, make haste away! For the Spaniards which you had with you here, the last year, have betrayed this place and taken away all that you left here. I depart hence, this present 7th of July, 1572. Your very loving friend,

John Garrett

July the 7th! That meant that Garrett had left this message just five days ago.

Drake remembered Garrett well: A Plymouth seaman like himself. He also remembered "the Spaniards which you had with you here last year." Those would be the prisoners he had been forced to take off the little Spanish vessels he had seized to replenish his food supply. He had kept them here and then released them before sailing back to England. It had been a foolish gesture of generosity.

Well, the damage was done now. When his men returned from the jungle and reported that they had found no one, he set them to work digging in the spot where he had hidden his supplies the year before. Garrett was right; the supplies were gone.

Ordering the *Pascha* and *Swan* into the bay, he set his men to work building a strong log fort at the water's edge—just in case. His thoughts were far away as he strolled to the shore that evening and gazed out across the darkening sea that reached back to England. Garrett's message did not alarm him unduly. He was not afraid of violent death; nor on the other hand unusually brave about it. He merely accepted it as a companion, a hazard of his trade. He was familiar with death. Life was apt to be harsh and short in his day. Men on land died of mysterious fevers, wars, starvation. Seamen died of all these—plus thirst, scurvy, drowning, and the tortures of the Spanish Inquisition or galley slavery.

If he died on this venture, there were few who would miss him, fewer who would mourn. He was unknown to the large world and to most of England. Those who did know him thought of him for the most part as a poor sailor, burdened with debts. But if he succeeded now. . . . His pulse quickened at the thought of it. Wealth and fame were not his only motives for being here. . . .

Drake stared across the dusk-shrouded sea. He had come a long way to this—the beginning of his private war with Spain. The knowledge that Spain was his enemy reached back to his earliest memories; he had been all but born with the seeds of it inside him, as had most of the Sea Dogs of England.

Drake had been born when England was going about the bloody business of breaking its official ties with Rome and Catholicism, changing into a Protestant nation. At the same time Spain, growing richer and stronger each year on the wealth it dug out of America, had decided that, as the mightiest Catholic nation, its duty was to protect its religion throughout the rest of the world. With Spain actively—and often openly—supporting the Catholic cause in England, internal religious wars threatened to rip the island kingdom apart. Protestants persecuted and slaughtered Catholics, and the Catholics responded in kind. It only depended on which group was stronger at any particular place and time.

Since Drake happened to be born during this turbulence, and since he happened to be born a Protestant and further happened to spend most of his youth with English seamen nearly all of whom were also Protestant, he grew up with a horror of Catholics and a hatred of Spain.

He could barely remember fleeing his Devon birthplace with his parents and a mob of other Protestants running for their lives from the fury of aroused Catholics. He had been only a few years old at the time. He had some little, nightmarish recollection of huddling with those Protestants on the temporary safety of Plymouth harbor's St. Nicholas Island until it was safe to leave.

Those childhood memories were later made more vivid for him by his father, Edmund Drake, who told him the story of what had happened many times—told it in bloodcurdling detail, and with a vehemence of which he was a master. For Edmund Drake was a sailor turned preacher. And a passionate preacher he made.

Francis Drake could always hear, across the years, the thundering voice of his father reciting with fierce pleasure from the New Testament: ". . . Being filled with all unrighteousness, fornication, wickedness, covetousness, maliciousness; full of envy, murder, debate, deceit, malignity; whisperers, backbiters, haters of God, despiteful, proud, boasters, inventors of evil things. . . ." And so on, down the list of those worthy of death in the judgment of God. There was no doubt that his father was thinking of Catholics when he recited that list, and of Catholic Spain.

Francis Drake's early memories were of this—and of the sounds, smells and feel of ships. He was a small boy when his father obtained a job reading the Bible aloud to the crews of navy ships in the Medway River. The job paid barely a living wage, and the best home Edmund Drake could manage for his family was aboard the hulk of a dismasted wreck floating in the harbor.

Young Francis loved it. Except for occasional bouts of hunger, the life he led was a boy's dream of paradise. He spent his days exploring the ships around him, learning their ways, listening to their crews. At night the movement of the water rocked him to sleep. With dawn the sounds of a busy harbor awakened him.

From his father he acquired an avid taste for Bible reading and sermonizing. But everything else he learned came from the ships and water and seamen around him.

After the throne of England passed into the hands of Catholic Mary, Edmund Drake was dropped from his position as Navy Bible-reader, and Francis, not yet in his teens, was apprenticed to the master of a bark trading between England and the Netherlands. He eagerly accepted his new life. The sea was already in his blood. So well pleased was the bark's master with his young apprentice's application and intelligence that when he died several years later, he left the bark to Francis.

Drake, still in his teens, found himself the owner and master of his own merchant vessel. For a time he plied his trade and carefully pocketed the profits, all the while absorbing every speck of information and know-how that might be of use to him in the future. He perfected his skill as a seaman, navigator, trader, and doctor to his small crew. He had no need to perfect his fighting skill; he had loved to fight ever since he was a small boy. But after a time he grew tired of his bark, and decided to sell it. He was ready to invest the profits—and himself—in a larger, more hazardous venture of which he had heard interesting rumors. A trader named John Hawkins was promoting it, and Hawkins happened to be a distant relative.

When his young relative, Drake, showed up eager to join him, Hawkins explained that what he had done was to find a way to trade in the New World. No English merchant was supposed to have access to America. The Spanish had considered the continent of America their own ever since it had been discovered by Columbus almost a century before. The riches from this new land financed Spain's wars and its control of other countries. Fantastic amounts of gold and silver were extracted each year from the Spanish mines in the New World. Wondrous quantities of precious stones were to be found there. Because of this, Spanish settlements had sprung up in Central and South America, and among the islands of the Caribbean, long before the English ever ventured near the new land. Spanish planters soon found the raising of sugar there another means of wealth.

Most of this Spanish activity depended on slave labor. The native Indians, however, refused to become slaves. They fought to the death rather than be captured, and those who were captured managed to die before they got much work done. The only alternative for the Spaniards was to import Negro slaves from Africa.

A brisk slave trade soon grew up between Africa and the Caribbean coasts of Central America. King Philip II of Spain, confining this trade to Spanish and Portuguese merchants, decreed that only merchants licensed by him were allowed to sell slaves to his Spanish settlements in America. The price he charged for a license, however, was so high that only a few merchants could afford it, and before long there was a serious shortage of slaves in America. The Spanish planters saw themselves heading for ruin.

John Hawkins knew of this situation. And though it was illegal for the Spaniards to buy slaves from an English trader, he decided that the planters might be amenable to some carefully unofficial business.

In 1562, John Hawkins sailed to Africa, picked up a load of slaves, and carried them to the islands of the Caribbean. As he had anticipated, the Spaniards offered him token resistance by day, and then got together with him secretly by night. He left all his slaves behind, and returned to England a rich man. His next voyages were even more profitable.

Hawkins was preparing another expedition with three ships, in 1566, when Francis Drake showed up and asked for his right, as a relative, to invest his meager savings and himself in the venture. Hawkins, pleased by the tough, eager look of the young man, agreed.

The voyage began without Hawkins, who was prevented from leaving at the last minute, after Spain, having learned of what Hawkins was about, demanded that Queen Elizabeth prevent him from sailing. Hawkins officially severed his connection with the voyage and appointed a Captain John Lovell to lead it in his place. Drake, all his money invested in the venture, sailed under Lovell as a subordinate officer. They arrived off the Spanish Main in 1567 with a load of slaves, and began to trade. But Lovell turned out to be no match for the Spaniards. The governor of Rio de la Hacha persuaded Lovell to land most of his slaves before payment was in Lovell's hands. Then, once the slaves were ashore, he refused to pay for them. Lovell looked at the port's fortifications, and sailed away to England without either slaves or profits.

Drake was equally furious at Lovell's stupidity and the Spanish cupidity. Every cent he had worked for years to earn and save was gone. But Hawkins was already preparing another slave-trading venture, his biggest to date. And he agreed to take Drake along as an officer—his pay to be a small share of the profits.

They sailed in October of 1567, with six vessels. Before they reached America, Hawkins, impressed by his young relative's seamanship, gave Drake command of one of the ships, the little *Judith*. When they arrived in the West Indies with a huge cargo of five hundred slaves, the Spanish planters, whose plantations were all but ruined due to the lack of field workers, were more than ready to trade—and willing to pay high prices for what they needed.

By the time they were ready to turn homeward, Drake realized that he was returning to England a very well-to-do man.

Then the storm struck. Hawkins' fleet was passing the western end of Cuba when a furious gale smashed into them. All the vessels managed to weather it, but when it was over few of them were in any condition to cross the Atlantic. Hawkins had no choice but to sail into the nearest port to repair his fleet for the long homeward voyage. That port was San Juan de Ulua, on the Mexican coast. No Spanish port, of course, was officially open to them. Hawkins made his ships' guns ready and advised the authorities of the port that he would do them no harm so long as they refrained from attacking him. Then he set to work patching up his fleet.

All would have gone well—except that one morning thirteen big Spanish ships appeared, heading straight for the port. It was the treasure fleet from Nombre de Dios, on the Isthmus of Panama, coming to San Juan de Ulua on its annual collection of gold taken from Mexican mines. With the treasure fleet was the Viceroy of New Spain, Don Martin Enriquez.

As soon as the Spanish fleet sighted Hawkins' ships inside the harbor and his guns commanding the entrance they hove to. The entrance was narrow and they could not get in if Hawkins chose to keep them out. This left the first move to Hawkins, who found himself neatly trapped. If he refused to let the Spanish enter their own port, he would be committing a flagrant act of war. On the other hand, once he let the Spaniards inside, they could, if they chose, easily destroy him.

From Viceroy Enriquez came assurances: Hawkins would not be molested. If the treasure fleet was allowed to enter, he promised to allow Hawkins to get on with the repair of his ships and depart peacefully. Reluctantly, Hawkins accepted the Spanish Viceroy's solemn word and permitted the treasure fleet to enter the harbor. But as he had feared, the Viceroy had no intention of keeping his word. Under cover of night, the Spaniards attacked in force.

Only two English ships managed to escape: Hawkins' *Minion* and Drake's *Judith*. The men they left behind were either put to death or chained to row-benches in galleys for the rest of their lives. A few managed to escape years later, and returned to England to set other seamen aflame with tales of the horrors they had survived.

Though Queen Elizabeth and King Philip continued to play at

peace, from San Juan de Ulua on, every English sailor considered himself at war with Spain. And none more strongly than Francis Drake. The Spanish treachery at San Juan de Ulua not only wiped out the profits of the venture and robbed him of the wealth his share would have brought, but also left him deeply in debt. He took this personally. Mighty Spain had chosen to fight with him, and he had never backed away from a fight in his life. The power of Spain did not overawe him. He had already spotted a flaw in it: it was spread too thin; it was riddled with weak spots.

There was some bad feeling between Drake and Hawkins upon their return to England. After escaping from San Juan de Ulua, Drake had sailed away alone back across the Atlantic, not waiting for Hawkins' overloaded vessel. Hawkins had accused him of deserting him. But in time the two captains became cordial again and undertook many ventures together.

Fantastic amounts of gold, silver, pearls and precious stones annually crossed the Atlantic from America to bolster the strength of Spain. They were carried by treasure fleets too well armed and guarded to be seized by a few English vessels. But the towns in America where the treasure was stored until the fleet could pick it up were vulnerable; Drake and Hawkins had learned that when they seized San Juan de Ulua to repair their storm-damaged ships.

Drake wanted to sail back to America quietly, learn the details of the Spanish treasure movements, and then go back in force and extract payment. The English government could not, of course, openly allow such actions. England and Spain were not officially at war. But they were sufficiently close enough to war—with Spain making preliminary threatening gestures—so that Queen Elizabeth might look the other way if Drake returned with enough loot from a venture which would also have the virtue of lowering Spanish prestige.

Hawkins and a few other merchants agreed to take the chance. They backed Drake. And two quiet trips to America in the little *Swan* brought Drake more knowledge about the Spanish settlements and treasure movements than was possessed by any other Englishman.

He learned that Spain's greatest gold and silver mines were located on the Pacific coast of South America. There the precious ore was loaded on great galleons. But these ships did not attempt the long and hazardous trip down the west coast of South America, through the storm-beset Straits of Magellan, and across the Atlantic to Spain. Instead, they carried the treasure up the Pacific coast to the narrowest portion of America, the Isthmus of Panama. There the treasure was put ashore and transported by hundreds of mules across the Isthmus to the town of Nombre de Dios on the Caribbean coast, where it was stored in a treasure house until, when the treasure house became full, a fleet arrived to pick it up, and complete the final lap of the journey to Spain.

The town of Nombre de Dios slumbered soundly on the night of July 28, 1572—unaware of the three armed pinnaces and the longboat which rode the calm waters just outside the harbor, hidden in the darkness. Drake, sitting erect and tense near the tiller of the middle pinnace, peered through the starlit gloom at the near shore. Relishing his own excitement, he listened for any sound of alarm from the land. There was nothing beyond the lapping of water against the sides of his tiny vessels, the nervous whispers of the men packed around him, the rattle of a pike against a musket.

The three pinnaces—the low, sleek little sailing vessels he had assembled in the bay of Port Pheasant—carried fifty-three of his men. The one to his left was commanded by his brother John; the other by John Oxenham. The longboat was manned with twenty men supplied by Captain Ranse, an English seaman who had chanced into the hidden bay of Port Pheasant just as Drake was leaving, and asked to join Drake in whatever he was up to.

The presence of Ranse seemed unfortunate to Drake, but the man had been with him and Hawkins at San Juan de Ulua. Drake had had no choice but to accept his longboat and men, leaving Ranse himself at a nearby island to guard the *Pascha,* the *Swan,* and his own vessel.

The moon was rising. Drake felt the nervousness around him grow. The men had heard that Nombre de Dios was a big town —perhaps as big as Plymouth; that fresh Spanish troops had recently been garrisoned there. Drake had planned to launch the attack with dawn. But now he realized that his men, most of them untried in battle, were not standing up well under the strain of waiting. The longer they were forced to sit out here on the water, the more their enthusiasm would cool. Changing his plan suddenly,

The Capture of Briel by de la Marck's "Sea Beggars"

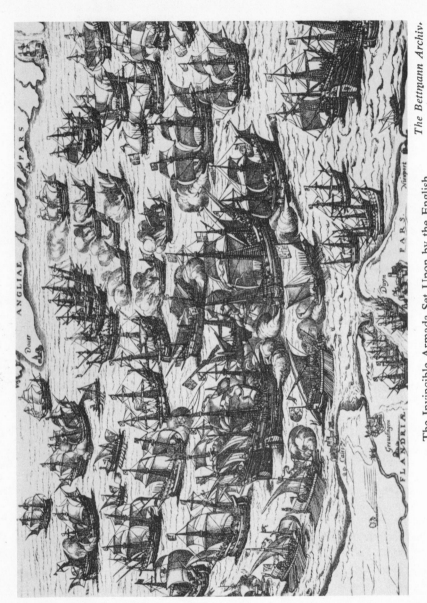

The Invincible Armada Set Upon by the English

Admiral Blake Before Tunis, 1655

The Four Days' Fight, 1666

The Explosion of the *Orient* During the Battle of the Nile

The Death of Nelson

Culver Service

Stephen Decatur Fights Off the Algerian at Tripoli

The Engagement Between the *Constitution* and the *Guerrière*

The Battle of Lake Erie

Perry Carrying His Pennant to a New Flagship

he stood up in his pinnace and called toward the other vessels: "Dawn is near. Out oars! Give way!"

The moonlight glistened on his rowers' bare, sweaty shoulders as they strained at their oars. Drake's pinnace curved around the jut of land and shot into the bay ahead of the others. The blade of his sword rasped out of its scabbard. With his other hand he snatched a cumbersome wheel-lock pistol from his belt. His eyes swept the nearing shore until he made out the high darkness of a hill back from the beach on the west side of the harbor. Atop that hill, according to his information, was a battery commanding the bay. If the Spaniards manned those heavy guns after the town took alarm, they could blow his flimsy craft to splinters with a volley and cut off his retreat. "Steer for that hill," he told his tiller man.

The splash and drip of the oars seemed unusually loud. But the dimly seen buildings emerging beyond the beach remained dark. The town was so silent he could hear the screeching of nightbirds in the jungle behind it. The keel of the pinnace skidded on the bottom and the little boat stopped with a jerk. Drake caught his balance. The next instant he was over the side, out of the water, and heading up the beach toward the hill battery. He heard the others, most of them barefoot, padding through the sand behind him.

He was halfway up the hill when the dark, thin figure of a man popped up between the outlined muzzles of two guns above him. Drake dug his toes into the earth and surged up the rest of the way, pulling back his sword for the swing. The sentry vanished. When Drake reached the edge of the battery he was gone. And there was no one else there among the six guns.

Glancing back the way he had come, Drake saw the other vessels grounded alongside his, the men streaming across the beach and up the hill with their swords, pikes, muskets and longbows. By the time a dozen of them had reached his side at the battery, the frantic yells of the vanished sentry began to sound in the dark streets of the town below.

Drake put his shoulder to the first of the six guns with his men. One by one, they sent the heavy guns spilling and crashing down the hill into the sand below. A moment later, a church bell in Nombre de Dios began to bong crazily. Its alarm was taken up by the blare of a trumpet, the rattle of drums.

Down the hill went Drake. Twelve men were left to guard his little fleet at the beach. Twelve more he sent with John Oxenham and his brother John Drake in a dash along the beach to slip into the other end of town. The rest of the men, Drake led directly off the beach into the main street of Nombre de Dios. Two men on either side of him beat drums and sounded the charge on trumpets. Lights were being brought to windows all around them. By the time they reached the market square, a crowd of hastily aroused soldiers blocked their path.

Drake charged straight toward them. He was halfway across the square when scores of Spanish muskets crackled. He saw their flash, heard a scream beside him as one of his trumpeters crumpled, blood streaming from his face. Then he felt the shock and burn of something tearing through his right thigh. He stumbled. Pain radiated along his right side. There was a hot wetness running down his ripped leg. Behind him, he heard the curses of other men nicked by the volley, felt the rest hesitate. He straightened and roared an order at them, pulling them back from their impulse to panic. Before the Spaniards could reload, English musket balls and arrows poured into their close-packed ranks.

The screams of the enemy gave the attackers new courage. Setting his teeth against the throbbing pain of his wound, Drake led the charge, firing his heavy pistol and slashing with his sword in tight, murderous arcs that bit deep through the leather jackets of the Spanish soldiers. On both sides of him, his men shouted defiance and drove the sharp points of their pikes into the defenders. The Spaniards rolled back, then hesitated, striving to hold and fight. All at once, out of a narrow alley behind them, Drake's brother and Oxenham with the rest of Drake's men charged into the square. At the same time, Drake and his group drove into the Spaniards again. The defenders, with no way of knowing the size of the second attacking force, broke and ran, leaving their dead and wounded behind on the cobbles.

Drake braced his weight on his good leg as his men gathered jubilantly around him. He knew better than to make any attempt to staunch the flow of blood from his wound. The excitement of his men could too easily shift back to nervous fright once they realized he was hurt. Moving carefully to avoid the appearance of limping, he led the small force to the home of the governor, hoping to hold him as insurance against a counterattack. For the

Spanish officers would soon have their panicked troops in check. The door of the big house was open. The English crowded inside, searching. The governer was nowhere to be seen, but the men made another discovery. Their shouts of joy brought Drake, who found them clustered in front of a storeroom filled with bars of silver.

Angrily, Drake told them to forget the silver. He was after something more valuable: gold. Leaving the governor's house, he led them through the deserted streets to the massive bulk of the King's Treasure House.

Off in another part of the city, drums began to beat and trumpets to blare again. The Spanish soldiers were being reassembled. Drake set his men to work battering at the thick, heavily barred Treasure House door. The hinges were beginning to give way when he felt drops of cold water splash against his face. A second later, they were engulfed in a sudden tropical downpour. Gasping against the sudden force of it, Drake ordered his men away, led them back down the street and under the shelter of an open, lead-roofed shed. Choked with frustration, he peered through the torrent at the looming Treasure House. The gold was almost in his grasp. Yet he must stay here, yards away from it, and wait. For the rain would wet the powder of his muskets and make his bowstrings slack. And he knew the Treasure House was guarded inside by well-armed troops.

The storm was soon over, though it seemed interminable to Drake. The rain stopped as abruptly as it had started, revealing a clear sky beginning to gray with the light of dawn. From the direction of the beach, where he had left his vessels with a dozen guards, came the sound of sporadic musket fire. There was no time at all to be wasted.

Drake started out of the shed toward the still-barred entrance of the Treasure House, forgetting his wound in his haste. His leg collapsed under him with the first step. He fell to his hands and knees in the mud, dropping his sword. He was up again quickly, steeling himself against the agony in his leg, trying not to sway with the dizziness which engulfed him. But he had been seen. His men crowded around him, anxious. It was nothing, he snapped at them; he had merely stumbled. The growing light of dawn revealed the truth to them, however. The cloth sticking to his leg was soaked dark. They saw the trail of blood that followed him. Drake tried to rally his failing strength, pushing away hands that reached to support him. His strength was gone. He leaned against a shed pillar to keep himself upright, yelling at his men to hurry about breaking into the Treasure House.

But they had forgotten the gold. All they wanted now was to carry him back to safety. And at that moment one of the men he had left with the pinnaces came racing up with word that Spanish soldiers were grouping on the beach, preparing to cut off their escape. Drake saw the fight go out of his men and made one last desperate attempt to bring it back: "I have brought you to the treasure of the world," he pleaded with them. "If you want for it, you will have no one to blame but yourselves!"

For a moment, he thought he might still hold them to their purpose. Then the dizziness swept through him. Their faces blurred and he felt himself fall, tried to drag himself up out of his faint, but could not.

When he came to, he was stretched out in one of the pinnaces. He stared up at the gold-streaked sunrise and listened to the creak and splash of the oars speeding his tiny fleet across the water to the little island where they had left Captain Ranse with their ships. Accepting the defeat calmly as God's will—a temporary setback— Drake shoved himself to a sitting position in the pinnace, ripped his shirt into strips, and began to apply a tourniquet to his wounded leg.

The attack on Nombre de Dios had failed. The town henceforth would be too well guarded and alert to be worth attacking. Captain Ranse shrugged off his disappointment, upped anchor, and sailed away. But Drake was stubborn. As he slowly recuperated from his wound, his mind dwelled on Spanish gold. There was more than one way to do anything worth doing. He had come here for Spanish gold. He was not leaving, alive, without it.

Some months later, Drake was deep in the dense jungle of the Panama Isthmus. Four days behind was the Caribbean, three days ahead the city of Panama, the Pacific terminal of the treasure ships from Peru. With him he had brought eighteen seamen, the pick of his crews—and thirty-one dark, near-naked Cimaroons.

A strange, savage race, the Cimaroons. The Spanish treated Indians and African slaves with the same horrible cruelty. The Cimaroons were a mixture of both—the offspring of slaves who had escaped into the jungles and interbred with the natives. Their hatred for the Spanish amounted to monomania. It was this hatred that Drake had counted on when, as soon as his wound had healed, he had made contact with them. He had told their leaders exactly what he wanted to do: ambush a Spanish treasure caravan carting gold across the Isthmus. Drake had decided that if he could not seize the gold in Nombre de Dios, he would seize it before it got to Nombre de Dios. The Cimaroons cared nothing for gold. But, as Drake had hoped, they were eager to do anything to harm the Spanish—and were willing to join anyone who was at war with their hated enemies. At Drake's request, they scouted across the Isthmus to Panama and returned with word that the next gold caravan from Panama to Nombre de Dios was still five months away. This didn't discourage Drake, however; he settled down to wait out the five months.

But the way he settled down unsettled the entire Caribbean. He knew that he could not afford to keep his men idle; they would grow stale and quarrelsome. So during the next five months, he and his little force darted in and out of ports to snatch food, clothing and supplies, and preyed upon Caribbean shipping. Spanish warships were sent out in search of him. They raced to areas he had stung, stole up on little bays where he had lately rested. But they never found him. He was always away by the time they arrived.

Drake's force did not get through those five months unscathed. His brother John and another seaman were killed in an attack on a well-armed merchant vessel. His brother Joseph died—along with almost thirty others—when an unknown tropical sickness swept through Drake's ships. By the end of the waiting time, less than half of the seventy-three men who had left Plymouth with him were still alive.

But those five months made Drake the most famous name in the Caribbean. Everyone talked of him. Everyone wondered where he would strike next. Some thought he was preparing for another attack on Nombre de Dios. Others suggested San Juan de Ulua—or any one of a dozen other ports on the coast. No one ever considered the interior of the Isthmus of Panama. . . .

They were out of the marshes now, crossing a range of low mountains topped with tall forests. It was February, and though the jungle behind them was steaming, it was pleasant marching up here in the cool shade of the trees. Drake was moving along at a steady pace when he noticed the Cimaroon leaders up ahead halt by a tremendously tall tree at the top of a hill. As he strode up to them, he saw that steps had been hacked in the tree's thick trunk.

The Cimaroons urged him to go to the top of the tree. Drake climbed the trunk's steps with the agility of a seaman to the top, where he found a platform. The view that stretched away beneath him was breath-taking. From the summit of this mountaintop tree, he could see both the Atlantic and the Pacific oceans. He looked back at the Atlantic, the sea from which he had come. Then he turned and gazed at the other ocean for a long time, praying to God to let him sail an English ship upon it.

Three nights later, Drake crouched in darkness beside a trail outside Panama—one thick-muscled hand tight around the hilt of his drawn sword, the other braced against the soft, springy earth—listening to the tintinnabulation of distant mule-bells drawing nearer from the west. He could not see the men of his crew and the Cimaroons hidden in the tall grass on both sides of the road; but he could feel them there, crouched and waiting.

The tinkling mule-bells drew closer. Eight of those mules were weighted down with packs of gold, according to his Cimaroon spies; and one carried jewels. His fingers itched for battle. He had told his men to wait until the last mules were passing the last men before springing the ambush. Then they would fall upon the poorly guarded caravan from both sides of the road.

His attention was suddenly caught by the sound of a horse's hooves. A lone horse and rider were outlined against the star-filled sky, trotting toward them along the road—a Spaniard riding far ahead of the mule train. Tensely, Drake watched him come. It didn't matter. The Spaniard would ride past, see nothing, and the . . .

A flash of white moved in the grass to Drake's left. One of his sailors, forgetting the orders, leaped up prematurely as the horseman rode past. For an instant, the white of the sailor's shirt shone in the night. Then a Cimaroon rose and yanked him back down into the grass.

Too late. The horse shied, frightened. The Spaniard wheeled his mount and raced down the road sounding the alarm. The treasure mule train did an about face and scurried back toward the protection of Panama. All Drake was finally able to catch were mules carrying food and baggage.

He had failed again.

But Drake was a man whose stubbornness grew with frustration. He led his men back across the Isthmus, beating aside a Spanish attempt to stop him, and sailed away. He resumed his gadfly darting about the Caribbean, annoying Spanish shipping. All the while, his Cimaroon spies kept watch on the city of Panama. When the Spanish at last had assured themselves that Drake was far away and busily occupied, the gates of Panama were opened. Out streamed almost two hundred mules loaded with gold, silver and precious stones. Off raced the Cimaroons, across the Isthmus, to speed the news. For Drake was waiting. And this time he had company as he went ashore and headed into the jungle. While sailing along the coast, he had run into a French privateering vessel under a Captain Testu. Drake, with only thirty-one men left of his original crew, half of whom he would have to leave behind to guard his vessels, told his plan to Testu, and the Frenchman eagerly agreed to join him on the inland foray with twenty of his own privateers.

The mule train this time was guarded by forty-five well-armed and mounted soldiers. Alert for attack as they left Panama, they became less so the nearer they got to Nombre de Dios. They could not know that Drake lay in ambush so close to Nombre de Dios that he could hear the sounds of vessels being repaired in the harbor at the same time that the tinkle of mule-bells reached his ears. He watched from his jungle hiding place as the treasure caravan moved slowly up the road toward him. This time no one made a hasty move. The lead mules were passing Drake when the Cimaroons, Frenchmen, and his own sailors closed the trap.

At Drake's shout, a flight of English arrows struck the mule train, followed by the crackle of muskets. Drake leaped up with the others and charged into the Spanish soldiers, who desperately fired at them as they came on. The attackers slashed into them with pikes, swords, knives and clubs, drove them away from the mules, and sent them running down the road to raise the troops in Nombre de Dios.

By the time Spanish reinforcements arrived, the attackers were gone, having staggered off through the jungles toward their waiting ships under the weight of all the treasure they could carry. It had cost them two men—a Cimaroon and Captain Testu. Drake divided the loot equally with the French ship, bade a warm farewell to the Cimaroons, and sailed for home.

He had entered the Caribbean the year before, a poor young

sailor pitting his puny weight against a mighty nation not even aware of his existence. He left it rich, famous—and a respected enemy of Spain.

One night, early in 1577, three strikingly different people met secretly in a small, locked room in the palace of Hampton Court: Drake; the forty-year-old Queen of England; and sickly, fanatical Sir Francis Walsingham, the Queen's secretary.

Walsingham, his feverish eyes aglow in his intense face, watched the two whom he had brought together this night take the measure of each other in the candlelight. Queen Elizabeth obviously liked what she saw. Walsingham had told her of Drake's exploits. They perfectly matched the rare solid-yet-daring look of this short, thickset fighting sailor with the bright blue eyes and reddish hair and beard. Drake was the instrument she wanted for her purpose.

Drake stared at this regal, lean-faced woman with the steady, challenging eyes. He found it hard to believe that he, Francis Drake from that hulk-home in Plymouth harbor, was actually in the presence of the Queen. That he had been summoned here to meet her at her request.

He had come home from the Caribbean at a bad time. When he had left Plymouth for Nombre de Dios, England and Spain were at each other's throats. But by the time he returned, King Philip was making peaceful gestures; and Queen Elizabeth, anxious to avoid war with a nation far stronger than her own in military power, was pretending to believe those gestures.

Aware that the presence of Drake in England with loot seized from his raid on the Isthmus might prove embarrassing, Hawkins and the other merchants who had secretly invested in him quietly took their shares of Drake's loot and advised him to disappear. Drake did this as he did all things, to the hilt. He vanished for two years, and to this day, no one has discovered where he went or what he did in that time.

He only returned when he sensed that England and Spain were resuming their more normal state of open enmity. As war seemed to grow closer, he began making contacts with important officials of the English government, feeling them out. A few of the men close to the throne felt that England had better find a way to strike a hard blow at Spain and set Philip II back on his heels. Philip was letting it be known that he would be pleased to see someone other

than Elizabeth on the throne: a Catholic monarch closely attached
to himself. There were reports that once Philip's armies in the
Netherlands managed to get his troublesome subjects there under
control, Spanish troops would next be thrown at England. Plots
to assassinate Elizabeth, all originated or supported by Philip,
were unearthed.

Sir Francis Walsingham was one of the small number of influential men who felt the time was ripe to bring Philip to his senses
with a show of violence. But most of those close to the throne,
led by Lord Burghley, the Queen's treasurer, were against any gesture of strength. England was too weak, they felt, to do anything
that could bring on a ruinous war with mighty Spain. It was because of Burghley and those with him that Walsingham brought
Drake and Elizabeth together in secret.

The candlelight gleamed on the Queen's jeweled hands and
elaborately sewn dress as she leaned toward the sailor before her.
"Drake," she told him directly, "I would gladly be revenged on the
King of Spain for divers injuries that I have received."

Then she sat quietly, nervously fiddling with the rings on her
thin fingers, never taking her shrewd eyes from Drake's face as he
told her exactly how she could be revenged for those injuries.
In his view, Spain's ability to make war rested squarely on the base
of treasure that streamed into its coffers from America. Weakening
that base would lessen Spain's strength. At one and the same time,
Spain's prestige could be lowered and England's raised.

It was true that Spain's Atlantic treasure fleets were well armed
and convoyed. But not so its Pacific fleets. For Spain felt quite
safe: no Englishman had ever yet ventured into those waters.
According to Drake's information from the Cimaroons, the Spanish
had not bothered to station a single warship in the Pacific. There
were hardly any guns aboard the transport vessels there.

But Drake had seen the Pacific—from a treetop on the Isthmus.
It could be sailed as well as any other ocean. And he was the man
to sail it—and make off with a goodly portion of the treasure with
which Philip expected to replenish his treasury, near-bankrupt now
from his costly attempts to put down the Netherlands revolt.

When Drake had finished speaking, Queen Elizabeth looked at
Walsingham and smiled. He had been as taut as a drawn bow-
string up to that moment, but now he relaxed, flushed with victory.

Elizabeth agreed to back Drake's venture—but in deepest secret.

Nothing was to be in writing. Spain must never learn that she sanctioned Drake's depredations. Nor must the timid officials close to her. "Of all men," she told Drake emphatically, "my Lord Treasurer, Burghley, is not to know it."

The saga of Drake's voyage to the Pacific, and then across it and back to England, encircling the world, is not one of naval warfare. As he had foreseen, he never once had to fight to take what he wanted. The Pacific treasure ships were unarmed and unguarded. He ranged that ocean as though he owned it, seized loot without struggle, treated his prisoners graciously, and sent them on their way with his good wishes once he had transferred their ships' cargoes to his own hold.

But the voyage, and his conception of it, serve as a magnificent testament to his daring imagination. It took him almost three years, and he reached home his decks nearly awash, with enough treasure to pay the costs of running all England for an entire year.

The most important thing that happened on that voyage, as far as naval history is concerned, was Drake's pioneering of a revolutionary change in the status of the men aboard a fighting ship. There were two distinct groups aboard a ship of war in those days: the sailors and the soldiers. The soldiers were the important class, and they never lowered themselves to help the crew in handling the ship, even during dangerous storms. The gentlemen who commanded the soldiers were the real rulers of a fighting ship; the vessel's captain took his orders from them. But Drake, though now the military commander himself, remained basically a sailor—and considered himself as such. When the soldiers—or "gentlemen"— and the sailors began to feud shortly after leaving England, Drake decided the situation, though traditional, was ridiculous. He conceived that the best fighting ship would be one on which all men joined together and acted as a unit. Just before entering the Pacific, Drake assembled all of his men and laid down the law. "By the life of God!" he roared at them. "It doth even take my wits from me to think on it. Here is such controversy between the sailors and the gentlemen, and such stomaching between the gentlemen and the sailors, that it doth make me mad to hear it! My masters, I must have it left. I must have the gentlemen to haul and draw with the mariner, and the mariner with the gentlemen."

Having thus with one stroke begun the rise of sailors to an equal status with soldiers in the military organization of his nation,

Drake looked meaningfully at the "gentlemen" and said softly: "I would know him that would refuse to set his hand to a rope."

No one spoke. And the idea of a united discipline aboard a navy ship was begun.

Drake returned to England with a vast amount of treasure. He quietly anchored behind St. Nicholas Island—the same island to which his parents had fled with him during the Catholic uprising when he was a child. In time, it was to be given a new name: Drake's Island. Then he made discreet inquiries ashore. The news was bad. Spain was demanding his head, and the return of all the treasure taken by him. Most of the Queen's advisors were urging her to comply at least with the latter request, to avoid an open conflict. Elizabeth seemed uncertain. Drake went back to his ship, the *Golden Hind,* and waited.

He kept in touch with Walsingham until a message came from the Queen. She wanted to see him. Drake hurried to London, and with him he took an eye-popping assortment of pearls, precious stones and gold—a precautionary token of his esteem, and a suggestion of what still lay waiting in the *Golden Hind.*

On a cool, sunny day in April, 1581, the most elegant, important personages in Queen Elizabeth's court crowded the decks of the *Golden Hind,* now at Deptford. But Drake had eyes only for his Queen. She stood before him, her lean face stern, but humor quirked the sides of her firm lips and there was affection in her eyes. In her hand was a jeweled sword. A hush spread across the ship as her eyes left Drake's and moved over the faces of those around them.

"The King of Spain has demanded Drake's head," Elizabeth cried out harshly. "Here I have a gilded sword to strike it off."

Her clear, steady eyes returned to him. "Kneel!" she ordered.

There was a ringing in his ears as his knee touched the old, familiar deck. Such pride and joy surged through him that he could scarcely breathe. The blade touched his shoulder.

And then the voice of Queen Elizabeth again, ringing loud across the ship for all to hear—including those who would speed word of it to Philip of Spain:

"I bid thee rise, Sir Francis Drake."

5

"Prepare in England strongly, and most by sea"

THE DEFEAT OF THE INVINCIBLE ARMADA

The die was cast. Philip of Spain had at last set his course: the invasion of England, annihilation of the Protestants, seizure of the island nation. It had been a long time in coming. In 1583, the admiral of Philip's navy, Santa Cruz, had come to him with plans for an "Invincible Armada" to be sent against England. But Philip had hesitated. He was busy conquering Portugal, and still vainly trying to bring the Netherlands back under his power.

More important, as long as Queen Elizabeth's Catholic cousin Mary Stuart, Queen of Scots, lived—even though imprisoned in Sheffield—there was little to be gained by a treasury-emptying expedition to conquer England. Elizabeth might die (Philip had a hand in several plots to hasten her death) and Mary become Queen without Spain having to risk bankruptcy. If he did conquer England for Mary, he might gain nothing more than her thanks; for all she was Catholic, she was not likely to accept Spanish domination of England.

So Philip held off, even when Elizabeth unleashed that devil

Drake against his possessions in the Caribbean—even when Drake sacked Cartagena and San Domingo, and returned boasting that "there is now a very great gap opened, very little to the liking of the King of Spain."

In 1586, an English trial declared Mary Stuart guilty of having taken part in a plot to assassinate Elizabeth; and in the following year the Queen of England executed her cousin. Now Philip had every incentive to invade England. With Mary dead, there was no chance of England's becoming a Catholic ally through peaceful means; with Mary dead, a conquered England could become a Spanish province.

Philip called for Admiral Santa Cruz and told him to go ahead with his preparations. Soon, word trickled back to England of fighting vessels and transports gathering in Spanish and Portuguese harbors and being provisioned, and of new ships being built and armed.

This great force of ships was scheduled to sail against England in the summer of 1587. But on the nineteenth of April of that year, Drake appeared with twenty-three ships off the entrance to Cadiz.

"The wind commands me away," had been Drake's last message to Walsingham as he led his squadron out of Plymouth two weeks earlier. But it was not the wind that had commanded him. Queen Elizabeth herself, alarmed to action by the frightening news of the mighty Armada preparations, had ordered her favorite admiral "to impeach the joining together of the King of Spain's fleet out of their several ports, to keep victuals from them . . . to distress the ships within the havens themselves."

The last part of his sovereign's command was especially to Drake's liking. As his ships rolled through the swells toward Cadiz he could not know it, but it was this same part of her message that Elizabeth had regretted at the last moment. After Drake had sailed, the Queen had sent an urgent order countermanding it. The vessel which bore the revised order belonged, however, to Hawkins, now Treasurer of the Navy; and Hawkins believed with Drake that the best defense against the Armada was to rip it apart in its home ports. So, somehow, the ship bearing the countermanding order never caught up with Drake.

"To distress the ships within the havens themselves," Drake explained to the captains gathered in his big cabin under the poop deck of the *Elizabeth Bonaventure*, that was their business that day in Cadiz. The light of the dawn sun which streamed through the high stern windows behind Drake moved with the roll of his flagship across the faces of the officers before him. Uncertain faces, some of them; faces of men anxious to argue. Especially the face of his vice-admiral, William Borough, an officer of the old school, bred to tradition. The traditional thing, Borough pointed out haughtily, was to call a council of captains such as this before an attack and discuss what to do in detail—*if* the majority of them agreed to the attack.

Drake's answer was harsh and firm: He had called this council neither to quibble about details nor to ask anyone's opinion. The antiquated tradition of majority rule did not apply here. He was in sole command. The men before him were here to receive his orders.

Sir Francis Drake was much like the youth who had first sailed to the Caribbean to avenge himself personally against the power of Spain: still short, powerful, rust-haired, tough-faced. His clothes had changed; they were now gorgeous and costly as befitted a man grown to wealth and fame. And his young cockiness had hardened into complete confidence in his own decisions and absolute faith that God was on his side in all things.

His orders, he told them, were these: The harbor of Cadiz was packed with vessels being readied and equipped to join the Armada —and guarded only by galleys. He was going into that harbor to tear those vessels apart. He expected his captains to follow him and do the same. The details would work themselves out. If anything unexpected occurred, he would run up signals.

Vice-Admiral Borough protested again: The reason only a fleet of galleys guarded the harbor was that only galleys were needed. Everyone knew that. In calm harbor waters, sheltered from the winds, rowed galleys could easily outmaneuver sailing ships.

Drake's answer to this was to repeat his orders sharply and dismiss his officers. Borough left in a fury. Drake, watching him go, grinned at his back. When they were down in their boats being rowed back to their ships, Drake strode with his quick, short steps from his great cabin to the open quarter-deck, where his flag captain stood by the helmsman. He gave the order to take the *Elizabeth Bonaventure* into Cadiz with all sails set, and climbed the steep steps to the little poop deck.

Braced wide-legged, fists planted on his hips, he gazed past the

swinging bowsprit toward the arm of land that sheltered the harbor
of Cadiz. He recalled the layout of the harbor as it had been
pictured on his maps. The harbor was divided into two parts, an
outer and inner harbor, linked by a narrow stretch of water where
the land pinched together. The entrance to the outer harbor was
wide, but shoals would force his ships to sail close to land in order
to get inside. That would put him in range of the high fortress on
shore; but he doubted that its guns—if it had any—would be ready
to fire. The Spaniards could not expect him. No enemy had ever
dared sail into the harbor of Cadiz before. They probably relied
entirely on their galleys to defend the place against the unlikely
possibility of attack.

The *Elizabeth Bonaventure* rumbled throughout its length as the
cannons were rolled in on their carriages, shotted, and rolled out
to poke their snouts through the gunports along its sides. Drake
glanced back at the other three galleons as they churned through
the flagship's wake, the foam cleaved aside by their heaving bows.
Each showed its teeth in a long row down either side. Drake thought
of the galleys inside the harbor and grinned in tense anticipation.
He knew that men like Borough considered him an arrogant brag-
gart. But as Drake saw it, his was merely a confidence based on
past success. If he overrode the objections of others, he felt, it was
just that he was right and they were wrong. Take the question of
the galleys in Cadiz harbor: Borough and tradition be hanged.
Many nights Drake and Hawkins had spent working out the future
of their navy. They had come to put their full reliance on heavy,
long-range guns that would sink ships—rather than short-range
small shot aimed at cutting down men on an enemy deck prepara-
tory to boarding. He and Hawkins had argued the ancient idea of
galley superiority in calm water for hours. Drake intended to show
just how outmoded that idea was.

Beyond the bowsprit the high cliffs siding the harbor entrance
loomed nearer; atop them the red tile roofs of the old city of
Cadiz glowed in the sunlight. The *Elizabeth Bonaventure* swung
in close to the shore, avoiding the shoals to port, and slipped into
the outer harbor. Drake gripped the rail. He had thought Plymouth
crawling with ships—but never in his life had he seen a harbor
so jammed as that which was opened before him. More than seventy
vessels of all descriptions lay before him, packed into a dense
tangle.

Drake leaned over and called an order to the helmsman. The

Elizabeth Bonaventure swung to port and ploughed across the harbor toward the helpless mass of shipping. Many of the Spanish vessels were yet without masts or sails, and would be able to do nothing but stay where they were and await destruction. Those that could, cut their cables as soon as the first shock of surprise wore off, and tried to get away from their fellows to safety. Smaller vessels pushed inshore where shallow water would prevent Drake from following; larger ships desperately tried to sail around the oncoming English ships, to slip past them to the entrance. But there they found their path blocked as one after another of Drake's twenty-three ships drove into the harbor. The calm water began to rock with the thunder of heavy English guns.

The English ships worked their way through the maze of shipping, smashing apart hoys, galliots, carracks, and galleons on every side. The *Elizabeth Bonaventure* sped after the largest of the fleeing vessels, a thousand-tonner carrying forty guns—guns it had not had time to load. Drake waited till they were side by side. Then, as they passed at musket-shot distance going in opposite directions, his yell rang down to his gunners. The deck under his feet leaped with the concussion of all the big port guns letting go at the same time. Drake's flagship heeled over, then righted. The big Spanish vessel staggered as the broadside caved in its waterline. Drake looked back and saw it roll over on its injured side, then point its bow at the sky and begin sliding stern-first beneath the surface.

A cry from the foretop brought Drake spinning around. Ten long, sleek war galleys were slipping out from shore, their pointed bow rams knifing the water toward him, the huge oars sweeping back and forth to the rhythm of the steadily pounding slave drivers' gongs. The ten galleys came on at top speed, side-by-side in line abreast.

Drake shouted down to his flag captain, watched his signal flags go fluttering up to the tops. The *Elizabeth Bonaventure* came around in a half-circle and sped under full sail to cross the paths of the oncoming galleys. Behind him came three other navy galleons, in a single-file line. The flagship's sweating gunners heaved in their heavy weapons, readied and loaded them with their iron balls, shoved them out again as the ten Spanish galleys and the four English galleons closed in on each other.

The galleys continued to race forward intent on ramming. The soldiers packed on their decks were ready to board and subdue the English crews with their superior numbers. This was the centuries-old method of galley fighting. Drake gripped the rail and watched his flagship maneuver, trying to slip past the galleys' deadly pointed rams. It seemed like folly; this was what the galleys wanted—a chance to smash ram-first into the side of the enemy. But this was Drake's moment. He intended to finish the myth of galley superiority once and for all.

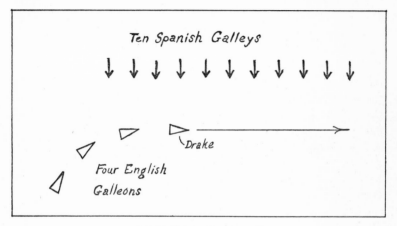

DRAKE "CROSSES THE T"

As the bow of his flagship crossed the path of the first onsurging galley, Drake shouted his last order to the gunners below. A moment later began—for the first time in naval history—the deadly maneuver of "crossing the T." As he sailed past the enemy's bow, each of his heavy guns sent its shot along the entire length of the enemy vessel.

Atop his poop deck, Drake watched triumphantly as his first gun pounded a hole in the galley's bow, his second smashed the sharp ram, the third sheared off a whole bank of oars. The screams of the slave-rowers within the galley were obliterated by the roar of the next cannon as its heavy iron ball spun down the length of the galley's deck. One after another the big guns thundered as the *Elizabeth Bonaventure* moved forward. Before half of them had taken their turn, the galley had been reduced to a splintered hulk drifting aimlessly away toward the shore with its dead and dying. Drake's flagship sailed on to rake the bow of the next galley.

The idea behind "crossing the T" was simple. It allowed the whole long row of guns along the side of the ship facing the enemy to bear, each in turn, on the enemy's bow—while that enemy could reply only with the few guns on its bow. It was simple, but no one had consciously used it before Drake.

Drake's forward guns were being reloaded swiftly as they passed the second galley. The galley fired its two bow chasers, but at that range their small shot bounced off the *Elizabeth Bonaventure's* side. Then the flagship was halfway past the galley's bows—and the big guns that had missed their chance at the first galley began to fire upon it. Drake felt the shock and recoil of each in turn through the trembling deck. One iron ball drove a hole through a mass of Spanish soldiers on the galley's forecastle, and whirled on to do the same through those packed on the aftercastle. Another shredded a dozen oars. The next two opened the galley's bow at the waterline. By the time the *Elizabeth Bonaventure's* stern rolled past its ripped-out bow, the second galley was drifting away in flames.

With the guns reloading, Drake was forced to pass the next few galleys without firing, taking two ineffectual blows from the little bow chasers on each. But the other three galleons trailing Drake crossed the enemy's Ts one by one behind him. They finished the destruction of the first two galleys and then struck at the ones Drake had passed by. Each gun fired in its turn, steadily, the repetitive pound-pound-pound of a giant drum of doom.

The galleys, stunned by the remorseless precision with which the English maneuver was devouring them, suddenly turned and fled in panic through the bobbing debris of their own shorn-off timbers and shattered oars. One went aground and burned to the water. The others managed to reach the safety of the inshore shallows. There they remained, watching Drake get on with his business of destroying the Armada supply and transport vessels.

Drake did a thorough job. At nightfall, he anchored his ships and waited for dawn. When it came, he fell to work again.

Late that next day, the breeze in the harbor fell to a whisper, then died altogether. The Spaniards, seeing Drake's ships becalmed in the middle of the harbor, decided that fate had turned in their favor. Without a wind, the sailing ships could not execute that deadly "crossing of the T," could not move at all, in fact. The galleys, on the other hand, would be at their most manageable. Those galleys that had not been seriously harmed in the first

encounter rowed out against the English ships. But one broadside
sent them reeling back to safety. Moving or stationary, sailing
warships were too formidably armed for the galleys to be able to
get near.

The Spanish next set fire to several small ships and sent them
drifting, crewless, toward the becalmed English vessels. Drake
quickly lowered ships' boats. His men rowed to the ondrifting
fireships, caught them with grappling hooks, and towed them away
from their fleet. Then they cast them loose, still burning, to drift
against the mass of small Spanish craft huddled close to shore.

By dawn of the following day, the English fleet had regained the
open sea, their work behind them. Drake tasted complete satisfaction as he stood in his great cabin and gazed through the open
stern windows at the receding shore. Smoke rolled out of the
harbor entrance and rose along the sheer cliffs until it obscured the
red tile roofs of Cadiz.

He had taken, sunk, demolished or burned thirty-seven Spanish
vessels for which the Armada assembling in Lisbon was waiting.
Some were badly needed new warships, almost completed. Most
were merchant vessels carrying what was needed even more: food,
guns, rope, sails, and other supplies. All would have to be replaced
before the Armada could sail.

The attack on Cadiz came as a jolting blow to King Philip's plans.
But what he had seen in Cadiz prevented Drake from indulging
overlong the satisfaction he naturally felt in his success. Cadiz was
only one of many ports—from Portugal all the way around to Italy
—from which warships, merchant vessels and troop transports were
no doubt being dispatched to the Armada gathering in Lisbon.

When land vanished below the rim of choppy ocean, Drake
turned away from the open stern windows. He sat at his ornate
table, feeling the cold wind that filled his sails blow in against the
back of his head, and began a message to be sent back to Walsingham by his swiftest small vessel: "I assure your honour, the like
preparation was never heard of or known, as the King of Spain
hath and daily maketh to invade England. . . . Prepare in England
strongly, and most by sea."

The message would go to England. As for himself, his business
was here—disrupting the Armada preparations.

He began to cruise the waters off Cape St. Vincent. No matter
whether the troops and supplies bound for Lisbon came from the

Mediterranean or America, if they came by ship they would have to pass this way. And to do so they must get through his fleet. Few managed it. Before long, few even tried it. For two months, Lisbon was virtually blockaded.

King Philip fumed. Santa Cruz, his admiral, sat with his whole navy in Lisbon, fuming too—but he did not sail out to get rid of his adversary. Drake had become the most famous name in Spain. The ravaging of Cadiz had reinforced the fear of him generated by his raids on both coasts of America. That fear had mounted to hysterical, superstitious awe. Drake, the Spanish whispered, had a devil's mirror in his cabin. When he looked into it, he could see exactly where all the ships on all the oceans were, and what each was up to. Who could outwit or outfight a demon?

With each move, Drake confirmed their opinion of him. He swept back and forth along the Spanish shores, seizing coasters carrying goods to the Armada. He pounced on the fishing fleet of Lagos, where it was employed in netting the salt fish that were to have fed the Armada, and sank fifty of its craft. He intercepted a pack of vessels carrying a year's supply of seasoned barrel staves from which were to have been made the casks for the Armada's water supply.

When he needed an anchorage to refresh his men and take water on board his ships, he sailed into the Bay of Belixe, and seized the landing place from the strong Spanish garrison in the castle of Sagres. Here he personally led eight hundred of his men inland against the castle. The walls were heavily manned, the main gates strong—and Drake was in too much of a hurry to haul big guns off his ships to destroy them. Entrenching his musketeers and bowmen where they could pick off the defenders on the walls, he set to work burning down the castle gates. Working side by side with his men, he carried armfuls of wood to the gates, started the fire himself while the defenders' shots rained down and his men fell about him. Sweating, yelling encouragement to his men, cursing wildly, he kept bringing more fuel for the flames. Until, finally, as the gates burned through, the castle surrendered.

Then he went back to searching the sea for Lisbon-bound shipping. Before long, the preparations of the Armada ground to a standstill. Supplies and troops, shunning a water route that would only bring them into Drake's grasp, had to make the trip to Lisbon overland—a slow method, in many cases taking months. But it would take even longer to replace the guns, food, and supplies already captured or destroyed by Drake.

His campaign lasted for two months. Then, with his food virtually used up and sickness running through his fleet, Drake was forced to point his ships homeward. But not without one last blow at Spanish pride and prestige. . . .

He paused off Lisbon—which was too strongly fortified for him to attack—and sent Admiral Santa Cruz a challenge to come out with his navy and fight. Santa Cruz declined the invitation.

Drake sailed home, capturing on the way a fully loaded Spanish treasure carrack worth many times the cost of his entire campaign —a campaign that left Spain dazed and shaken, left the Invincible Armada desperately short of everything it needed, and postponed its scheduled sailing for a full year.

The Armada would never have sailed at all, if Drake had had his way. He begged for another chance to strike at Spain on its own coasts, with a larger fleet: "I humbly beseech your good Lordships . . . with fifty sail we shall do more good upon their own coast than a great many more will do here at home."

But he could not make Elizabeth and her ministers understand. They feared the coming Armada, and wanted all available fighting ships and men kept close to home to protect England. He could not make them see what was so obvious to him: that England could best be defended by attacking, by destroying the Spanish warships before they left Spain.

For a year, England waited and prepared. Ships were built as fast as possible. And they were built the way Hawkins, as Treasurer of the Navy, and Drake wanted them: low, swift sailors, constructed to stand heavy weather, to be handled easily by a small crew, and to carry rows of the heaviest guns.

Drake and Hawkins spent a great deal of time together during that year, trying to evaluate what Drake had learned against the galleys in Cadiz of the role of heavy, long-range guns. The Armada would carry the largest, best-trained army in the world. Once on English soil, the English would be hard put to drive them out again. But Drake and Hawkins did not intend to let the Spanish army land. That army would be met and bested at sea.

Accurate gunnery, that was the answer. Aboard the ships under Drake's command, gunners found themselves hard at the most unusual task of daily practice. When Drake used up all the ammunition that had been supplied to him, and asked for more, the Queen's ministers were horrified. Powder and shot were in short supply and cost money. And here was Drake, using up his regular allotment for target practice! It was outrageous.

The time for the sailing of the Invincible Armada drew nearer.

The Invincible Armada came slowly, sailing north into the English Channel on the 20th of July, 1588—an enormous horde of almost two hundred vessels of ill-assorted sizes, types, and speeds. Its progress was so slow that the English had time to group their fleet, and Drake, in his new flagship, the *Revenge*, sailed out to intercept the Spanish. The titular head of the English fleet was the Lord High Admiral, Lord Howard of Effingham, but Drake, who had been appointed his Vice-Admiral, really commanded the fleet in action.

The dawn of Sunday, July 21, revealed the two opposing fleets to each other. This was the day of the first battle. The inner mass of the rigidly controlled Armada formation was composed of merchantmen and transports overflowing with troops that were to be landed for the invasion of England. The only ships that would do any real fighting were the sixty-four huge war galleons that guarded the outer edges of the fleet. These were impressive floating fortresses with castles fore and aft towering high above the low English decks. In close action, their higher guns could fire down on the English ships; if they managed to grapple, the troops crowding them would swarm aboard the English and crush them.

The English had about the same number of war galleons, but they were smaller vessels, faster, lower, more maneuverable, and they carried heavier guns. Manned by better seamen, with gunners trained and experienced at their jobs, they were commanded by the pick of the Sea Dogs—men like Drake, Hawkins, Seymour, Frobisher, Wynter, Crosse, the Fenners.

The English ships, cutting through the choppy waters in single file, sailed in a line past the Armada—each slamming a broadside into the Spaniards. Then they turned and came back on the opposite tack, firing the heavy cannons and culverins on their other sides.

The Spanish galleons, hard hit, fired back. But though the English bombardment went where it was aimed, most of the Spanish balls whistled harmlessly overhead in the first exchange. Drake's gunnery practice was proving its value. When the Spaniards at last began to find the range, the English ships slipped away to reload in safety.

Some of the Spanish galleons tried to close with the English, to grapple and board in the classic galley manner. But the English refused to fight on their terms. They wanted a gunnery duel only, and after about two hours the engagement was broken off. It was then that the superior sailing qualities so carefully built into the English ships by Hawkins and Drake told. The English vessels were able to get and keep the weather gauge at all times. That is, they were able to get to windward and keep the enemy to leeward. In such a position with wind blowing from behind the English toward the Spanish, the English could maintain complete control of the situation. For with the wind against them, the Spanish were unable to sail straight at the English. The English, on the other hand, *could* head straight into the Spanish—any time they chose. Or, when they wished, they could keep the distance between them, no matter how hard the Spanish tried to fight into the wind. The English had the offensive; the Spanish were forced to purely defensive fighting.

The Armada's commander, the Duke of Medina Sidonia (the original admiral, Santa Cruz, was dead as the result of his exertions in repairing the damage done to the Armada by Drake the year before), was forced to endure the harrying forays of the English. Stoically, he continued to sail his close, perfectly formed fleet up the Channel through a long week during which he was hit and hit again by the English. His orders from Philip II were exact: He was to sail up the Channel to Flanders with his fleet, manned by eight thousand sailors and carrying nineteen thousand troops. There, the Duke of Parma was to add to this force seventeen thousand Spanish soldiers seasoned in the long, losing struggle to regain the Netherlands for Spain. Then Medina was to take the Armada across the Channel and land the nearly forty thousand Spanish troops on English soil. The English would not have a hope of standing against this army—especially since they would also have to cope with their own Catholics, who would certainly rise up to aid Spain in overthrowing the Protestants.

But these orders of King Philip, based on a number of misconceptions, collapsed at the first touch. The Armada could not land on either Flemish or English soil without first winning a victory at sea. Unless Spain controlled the Channel, the English Sea Dogs would not permit the Armada to pause at Flanders to take on troops. The Dutch Sea Beggars could (and would) easily prevent the Duke of Parma from carrying his troops out in barges to the

Spanish fleet. And to land on English soil, the Armada would first have to fight its way through a solid wall of English ships. Lastly, those English Catholics on whom Philip was counting for support never materialized. With the threat of foreign invasion, the religious struggle was temporarily forgotten. England was their home; not Spain. English Catholics rushed to the coastal defenses and out to sea to swell the force aboard the ships to ten thousand.

On the 23rd of July, a battle was fought off Portland, and on the 25th another engagement took place off the Isle of Wight—still with no decisive result. So it went on and during all this time both fleets were sailing slowly up the Channel. The English, growing short of ammunition, bided their time, waiting for a favorable opportunity to deal a telling blow. It was slow work, but effective. As the Lord High Admiral commented: "Their force is wonderful great and strong; and yet we pluck their feathers by little and little."

On the 27th, the Armada reached Calais and anchored offshore. Admiral Medina watched the English fleet sail up and anchor a mile to windward of him—still carefully keeping the weather gauge. For over a week the English ships had sailed round and round him, hitting him as they pleased with that astonishingly accurate gunnery. Though all but three of his galleons were still afloat, many had been badly mauled, the troops aboard them thinned by English cannon balls. And though he had certainly tried, he had been able to do very little damage to the English in return. His own flagship, the *San Martin*, attested to the unevenness of the battle. He looked at the crewmen working on torn rigging, snapped spars; listened to the cries of the wounded below, the clank of pumps battling the water that poured in through holes in the hull, the hammering of carpenters repairing weakened bulkheads. In one engagement, he had gone against the English admiral in the classic galley manner, head on against the enemy's side. Met by Howard's crushing broadsides of more than thirty guns, he had been unable to get close enough to board, no matter how hard he tried. And then Howard's side slipped away—to be replaced by Drake's *Revenge* erupting another broadside at him. The *San Martin* had limped away from the encounter with 110 dead and wounded, its guns out of action, leaking badly.

But despite the reverses suffered by the Armada, Medina now had no alternative but to obey Philip's orders. He sent a message by land for the Duke of Parma to join him for the invasion of England.

Then he settled down to await a reply, unhappily watching the English fleet a mile away.

Before long, unusual activity became apparent in the English fleet. It involved eight closely huddled merchant vessels and went on all through Sunday. By nightfall, each vessel was filled with barrels of tar, its guns loaded, shotted and primed, its boats in the water astern, fastened by tow lines, ready to quickly take off the tiny crews left aboard.

At midnight, with the tide and wind strong toward the Armada, the eight merchant vessels cut their cables and sped through the darkness under full sail toward the anchored Armada. Their little crews waited till they saw the huge shapes of the Spanish ships dead ahead. Then they lit their torches, set fire to the spilled tar and loose powder on the decks, and scurried into the waiting boats. Flames leaped up the masts and consumed sails and rigging almost before they could cast loose and row back to the English fleet. The blazing fireships raced with the tide toward the close-packed Armada. The Spaniards looked up to see eight tremendous bonfires suddenly bearing down on them out of the darkness. The flames reached the priming of the guns on the fireships just as they drove into the Armada. The explosions of the guns, the whistling of unaimed iron balls, and the roaring heat of the fireships in their midst, broke the nerve of all but a few. Cables were cut; sails set. Ships collided and tangled in their rush to avoid the fire, to get away in the night. Aghast, Medina fired a gun as signal for his ships to regroup once the fireships were past. But only two obeyed him; the rest continued to flee.

A mile away, on the poop deck of the *Revenge,* Drake watched the debacle by the light of the fireships. Excitement ran hot through his veins. The days of slow tag-and-run skirmishing had worn his nerves thin. He had not dared do more against the bulk of the tight, perfectly formed Armada. But now the Armada was no longer in one piece. . . .

Dawn revealed the Armada strung out in disorganized, widely separated groups north along the Flanders coast. The Lord High Admiral sent pinnaces in against a tremendous galleass gone aground at Calais. Drake led the rest of the English fleet against the Spanish galleons. The great battle of Gravelines followed.

The *Revenge,* with its squadron of four other ships, was followed closely by the squadrons of Hawkins, Wynter, Frobisher and

Seymour. The light skirmishing was over. This was what they had been saving their ammunition for.

Ahead Drake saw three Spanish galleons come around to face him: Admiral Medina's *San Martin*, supported by the *San Marcos* and *San Juan,* determined to hold Drake off until the rest of the Armada behind them could re-form. But Drake this day was more interested in wrecking the Armada as a whole than in a personal fight with the Spanish admiral. He drove straight toward the *San Martin*—until they were so close that the shadow of its towering forecastle fell across his own low forecastle. Then, abruptly, Drake luffed and fired every gun of the *Revenge's* port battery simultaneously into the Spanish commander's hull. The *San Martin* staggered from the impact of the blow. Before Medina could recover, the *Revenge* slipped past him and sped toward the rest of the Armada.

The Spanish galleons had managed to draw together in a loose group. They were trying to tighten the grouping when Drake's squadron hit them. Their crashing guns sliced away Spanish rigging, battered down Spanish masts, stove in Spanish hulls. The Spaniards tried to trap them, grapple and board; but the English ships were too fast and agile for them. Drake raced through them, around them, and back in again—firing as fast as his gunners could reload, feeling the whole *Revenge* recoil with each broadside, feeling her tremble under the punishment she took in return. Forty holes were punched into her hull. When Drake went down to his cabin, hours after the battle had begun, he found it a mass of wreckage, the stern windows smashed away and two new windows opened on either side by shot that had passed through. Still the *Revenge* sailed, taking its toll of the enemy at every turn.

Through the heavy haze of gunsmoke that drifted through the interlocked fleets, Drake saw two Spanish galleons, trapped by a group of English ships, battered until blood ran out of their gunports and down into the water. Another Spanish ship, riddled like a sieve, suddenly disappeared beneath the waves. Three more Armada galleons, their yards, rigging and sails shorn away, drifted aground on the shoals.

The Spaniards could not cope with the English tactics. Instead of picking an enemy and fighting him to the end, each English vessel kept contantly on the move. It would hit a Spaniard with a broadside, dodge away quickly from the answering fire, and speed on to another Spaniard—using the time between to reload.

There wasn't a Spanish galleon that hadn't been hit by at least half a dozen English ships before the battle was done.

After many hours of fighting the English ran out of ammunition. At almost the same time a sudden storm forced them to leave off fighting, turn into the wind, and tend to sailing. The remaining Spaniards saw their chance to slip out from between them and the shore with the shifted wind.

Drake watched them go with regret. He wanted to fight on. For though this day's fighting had brought the Armada's war-galleon losses in the Channel to eleven, it didn't seem enough.

But it was enough. For over eight thousand men were dead aboard the Armada vessels. And the Spanish ships still afloat were little better than floating wrecks. Their superstructures were falling apart. Their gaping-holed, caved-in sides were taking in water as fast as their exhausted crews could pump it out. Their sprung masts and ruined rigging could barely handle the slightest breeze. The real damage done to the Armada by this day's accurate English gunnery was revealed in the weeks that followed. Dozens of Armada vessels sank, too broken to withstand the ordinary storms that hit them; dozens were wrecked against rocky shores, too weak to claw off against the strong winds that pushed them aground.

The Spanish commander, Medina Sidonia, knew before the battle was over that the plan to invade England was dead. He had only one purpose left: to get back to Spain. He could not return the way he had come; that would mean turning around and sailing back into the English fleet—and he didn't know the English were out of ammunition. So he sailed north, out of the Channel, around the northern coast of Scotland, and south past Ireland, to Spain— leaving shattered pieces of his fleet behind him on each coast he passed. Of the two hundred ships and twenty-seven thousand men that had sailed from Spain to invade England, only about half the ships and less than half the men returned.

By then, of course, the Spanish knew that Howard of Effingham was Lord High Admiral of the English fleet. But that meant nothing to them. So far as they were concerned, it was Drake, and the spirit of Drake, that had beaten Spain again—this time so badly that she never fully recovered. Before the destruction of the Invincible Armada, Spain had been regarded as the most powerful nation in the world. She was never to be regarded as such again.

6

Fifty-three Against One

It happened that three years after Drake's *Revenge* spearheaded the onslaught against the Armada in the English Channel, fifty-three Spanish warships cornered the same *Revenge* alone off the Azores. They closed around her for what they were certain would be quick victory over the ship they hated most in all the world. What followed, however, was the most fantastic last-ditch fight ever put up in the history of naval warfare: the incredible "last fight of the *Revenge*."

Lord Thomas Howard's squadron of six English warships had been six months at sea and was in a bad way when it put into the Azores while searching for Spanish treasure vessels. A third of his crews were down with scurvy. His ships' bottoms needed scraping. He anchored close to one of the islands, sent the sick men ashore to recover, and then removed the ballast from his vessels so they rode high and light, and could be scraped and careened. On August 31, 1591, the squadron was in this vulnerable situation—with men and ballast on the beach—when a fighting fleet of fifty-three Spanish ships suddenly appeared, headed straight for the English anchorage.

The sick men were rushed back from the beach, but there was no time to get the ballast back aboard. The English ships cut and ran—each pulling out as soon as it could and devil take the hindmost. All but one of Howard's squadron managed to get away in time to squeeze past the bows of the oncoming Spanish fleet, take the full force of the wind in their sails, and escape to open sea.

The last ship was Drake's old flagship, the *Revenge*—now commanded by the crusty old Sea Dog, Sir Richard Grenville. Ninety of its hundred and ninety men were ashore sick. By the time Grenville got those ninety invalids off the beach and below deck, his escape was cut off. The *Revenge* pulled away from the shore to find itself hemmed in by all fifty-three Spanish warships.

High on the little poop deck where Drake had directed the destruction of the Armada, Grenville looked through the forest of Spanish masts and rigging to the rest of the English squadron: five distant specks rolling on a gray-black sea under dark sky. There would be no help.

Grenville had no intention of allowing the *Revenge* to become the first English warship to strike its colors in this war. A man of gentle birth, and a cousin of Sir Walter Raleigh, Grenville had sought adventure all his life, in keeping with the illustrious traditions of his family. His grandfather, Henry the Eighth's Marshal of Calais, had written:

> *Who seeks the way to win renown,*
> *Or flies with wings to high desire,*
> *Who seeks to wear the laurel crown,*
> *Or hath the mind that would aspire—*
> *Let him his native soil eschew,*
> *Let him go range and seek a new.*

Grenville lived by this. It was he who carried the first English colonizers to Virginia, landing them on Roanoke under Governor Ralph Lane. Roving and fighting—that was all he knew or wanted to know. Once, as a younger man, he had come upon a Spanish treasure ship after a storm had carried away his ship's boats. He had quickly lashed together some chests to form a raft. It held together under him and his men just long enough to get them to the Spaniard; they boarded it as the raft sank. Now, against staggering odds, he directed the *Revenge's* sailing master to sail straight into the teeth of the fifty-three Spanish galleons. He intended to fight his way through the thick Spanish ring to the open sea beyond. With audacity, luck, and a good strong wind filling his sails, he just might do it. If he didn't . . .

High above him men clung to the yards, unfurling all sail. Across the deck men hauled at ropes; in the waist others clutched pikes and a few muskets. Below, the sick joined the able in shotting and running out the heavy guns that had taken their toll of the Armada.

Close-hauled, the *Revenge* plunged straight at the nearest Spanish galleon, forcing it to fall away to leeward to avoid collision. Grenville charged the next galleon behind it in the same way, steering for a crash that might sink them both. At the last moment the Spaniard retreated from Grenville's path to escape and fell to leeward. As the *Revenge* went through the gap, puffs of smoke mushroomed at the sides of the two outbluffed Spaniards, followed by the boom of their guns. The aim was too high. The shots whistled over the *Revenge's* masts and fell to sea far beyond, sending up harmless spouts of white froth.

Just as Grenville was picking out the next weak link in the chain of ships ahead of him, however, his sails began to luff and droop. Flashing a look in the direction the wind was coming from, he saw the huge galleon *San Felipe*—1,500 tons to the *Revenge's* 500 tons—rushing up to him. Its sides were so high that they accommodated three decks of guns. Above them towered its castles and the great sails. This mammoth was blocking the wind from the *Revenge*. The *Revenge* began to lose steerageway as the *San Felipe* loomed nearer. When it drew alongside, the sails of the *Revenge* hung slack from the yardarms.

The *Revenge* lay becalmed under the lee of the overhanging Spanish galleon. There could be no escape now. All that was left for Grenville and the *Revenge* was a fight. Grenville stared fiercely up at the banks of guns high above his head—and shouted the order to fire to his own gunners. The end of his yell was torn from his lips by the thunder of the *San Felipe's* downtrained guns erupting smoke and flame. Metal crashed down on the *Revenge* through the smoke. The mizzenmast broke in half and fell backwards, burying Grenville under the mizzen lateen sail and bonnet. Screams reached him as he fought free from the canvas. Then, as he rose again, the *Revenge* righted itself and jerked sideways with the recoil of its own broadside slamming into the *San Felipe's* side low at the waterline.

Grenville yelled for his gunners to fire as fast as they could. His deck was a chaos of broken, splintered planking, torn shrouds and dying men. The guns above were hauled back inside their ports for reloading. Then the *Revenge's* guns spoke heavily again, by threes and twos and singly, punching holes into the *San Felipe's* immense side. Splintered gaps appeared where gunports had been, and the ring of shot that had reached inside to overturn guns came down through the racket of gunfire.

All the English guns had had their second go at the Spaniard before the *San Felipe's* guns poked out of their ports for another broadside. But that broadside did not come. The *San Felipe,* close to foundering from the row of jagged holes at its waterline, pulled away to safety.

Still the *Revenge* could not get free. The two galleons that had swerved aside from Grenville's first charge had luffed up to his leeward side, and two more galleons were now revealed to windward. Through the volcanic roaring of broadsides from all four Spanish galleons, through the clouds of smoke and hail of metal flying across his decks, Grenville saw his main shrouds burn away, leaving the mainmast swaying loosely, saw the forecourse and spritsail evaporate. The *Revenge* shuddered and rolled under the blows that hammered at its sides. The great mainmast toppled forward and crashed down on the deck, flattening the shot-torn boat and crushing men at the waist and forecastle. But still the deck under Grenville's feet throbbed to the pounding of his guns below, sending their answering shots into the two Spanish ships on either side. These were the same guns that had begun the downfall of the Invincible Armada, manned by the same spirit.

One of the Spaniards to windward began to list. Its main and foremasts crashed down and hung there, increasing the list. Grenville, his own decks torn up all around him and his foremast going over the side, was able to enjoy the sight of the listing Spaniard drifting away, sinking fast.

Two more took its place. And there was a Spanish galleon off his stern now—and two off his bow. Their heavy iron shot ripped into the *Revenge* from every angle, caving in its sides, killing more of its men, knocking apart its upper decks. But still the guns of the *Revenge* fired back. Another Spanish vessel foundered and sank.

The ring of Spanish ships pulled back after that, giving the

Revenge a brief respite while the Spanish commanders discussed what to do next. The battle had been going on since three in the afternoon and it would soon be dusk. Yet there the *Revenge* remained, within their ring, mastless and unable to navigate, but unsurrendered.

When the Spanish ring closed in again, they did not stop within gunnery range, but kept coming on toward the *Revenge*, closing in for the kind of fight the Spanish knew best—a hand-to-hand boarders' fight on the enemy's deck.

Aboard the *Revenge*, the English were waiting for them with pikes, swords and knives clutched in their hands. There were more than enough weapons to go around; less than half of the one-hundred-and-ninety-man crew were still alive.

The first Spanish ship scraped along the side of the *Revenge*. Grappling hooks swung over. Spanish soldiers came leaping down from their higher deck, pouring out through the upper tier of gun-ports across the *Revenge's* bulwarks.

"Repel boarders!" Grenville screamed. Sword swinging, he rushed forward with his men against the invaders of his deck through a rain of musket balls from the Spanish masts. Almost at the same time, a second Spanish ship ground against his other side. Grenville's puny force divided itself to defend both sides of the deck. They were hopelessly, overwhelmingly outnumbered, but they fought like madmen. And all the while, the big guns below roared and recoiled, breaking into the underbellies of the two Spanish ships grappled to the *Revenge*.

Time and again, Grenville's men drove back the Spanish soldiers, fighting over the bodies of the fallen. At last, the two Spanish vessels having had enough of the guns pounding into their waterlines, the boarders scrambled back to their own ships and cut their grapples. A little knot of Spaniards left behind as their ship pulled away was cut down within minutes.

One of the vanquished boarding ships went to the bottom minutes later, the third victim of *Revenge* gunnery. But a fresh Spanish ship had already laid aboard the *Revenge's* port side. Another moved against its starboard. A third grappled its stern. Again the guns of the *Revenge* pounded while English and Spanish fought on deck.

And then, suddenly, the guns of the *Revenge* were still.

They had run out of ammunition.

Now there was only the boom of the Spanish guns, and the noise of clashing metal and screaming men on the *Revenge's* deck. Yet dusk fell with the *Revenge* still fighting. And on through the night, boarders were hurled back to their own vessels and into the sea. Spanish ships that had had enough made way for fresh ships—with fresh boarders to hurl against Grenville's dwindling pack of fighting madmen.

Around midnight one of the musket balls fired blindly through the darkness from the Spanish tops plunged into Grenville's side. He lay huddled in pain on his smashed quarter-deck until his surgeon rushed up to tend to him. The surgeon's fingers worked at his wound, stemmed the flowing blood as best he could, began bandaging. Then his hands fell away. Grenville looked down at the surgeon, saw that he was dead. As he started to rise, his brain seemed to explode. A musket ball had struck him in the head, knocking him back to the deck.

He lay there until the hideous turmoil of the battle filtered through the agony and assumed meaning for him. Barely half-conscious, bleeding from his head and body, he grasped the jagged stump of the mizzenmast and dragged himself to his feet. He no longer had the strength to fight beside his men. The most he could do was stand there, bracing himself against the remains of the mast, and let the few remaining warriors of the *Revenge* see him by the flashes of Spanish gunfire: the symbol of their vain heroism.

It was enough. Grenville served his ship that way through the rest of the night, inspiring his men. Drunk with exhaustion, dwindling steadily in numbers, not one among them unhurt, they fought off mass after mass of fresh boarders. By dawn, they had beaten back the boarding attacks of fifteen enemy ships.

But the dawn that spread across the Atlantic revealed the pitiful state to which the proud *Revenge* had been battered. The half-fainting Grenville saw that he commanded only a jungle of smashed wood, overturned guns and mangled corpses. There was hardly anything left of the *Revenge* above the waterline. Everything high enough for the Spanish guns to hit had been knocked into the sea, or battered down through the splinters of what had once been the main deck. What was left below the waterline reeked of death. Grenville could count the men still standing after fifteen hours of fighting on the fingers of his two hands.

With the dawn, the Spanish ceased their attempts at boarding. The remains of the *Revenge* floated only because of the buoyancy of the thick wood of its lower hull. Yet it remained unsurrendered and retained a bite at close quarters.

Now, with the light to show them where they were aiming, the Spanish ships moved off a bit and began sniping with cannon, musket and arrow. Even Grenville saw that the end had come. There was no way left to fight back. What was left of the *Revenge* was taking in water fast, and would soon sink. A last slow look through pain-blurred eyes at the surrounding enemy showed him that not one of the remaining fifty Spanish ships had been spared the wounds he had dealt them. One thousand of their men had been killed or put out of action.

Grenville surrendered. But the Spanish got little from the surrender. All that was left was a handful of English survivors. The *Revenge* was too shattered to save; it sank to the bottom in a storm, and Grenville's wound was mortal.

They treated him gently, almost reverently, filled with awe and admiration for his proud, stubborn courage. And they sat beside his deathbed three days after the battle to record his final words: "Here die I, Richard Grenville, with a joyful and a quiet mind, for I have ended my life as a good soldier ought to do."

PART THREE

Generals-at-Sea and Sailors

By the end of the sixteenth century, Spain's awesome reputa-
tion had been destroyed, her fighting fleets weakened and de-
moralized by the repeated victories of the Dutch and the English.
She maintained a state of war with the young Dutch Republic for
a time during the beginning of the seventeenth century, but her
ability to inflict damage on her enemies steadily diminished. Now,
although the Spanish fleets had still to be reckoned with because
of their size, and the sea power of France was increasing, it was
the Dutch and the English who had become masters of the seas.

The outstanding reason for the defeat of Spanish sea power was
that her commanders had tried to apply the ancient tactics of the
oar-driven war galley to the sailing warship, whereas the tough
new Dutch and English navies had developed methods of sea fight-
ing based on the special capacities of their sailing ships.

The Dutch assumed control of the oceans in the first part of the
1600s. Their warships and trading vessels seized trade routes,
hampered English merchants in Africa, the East Indies and India,
and finally eliminated them from the Spice Islands trade entirely.
They were to a great extent able to do all this because in England,
after the death of Queen Elizabeth, the ruling house of Stuart
neglected the British navy and allowed it to decay. Toward the
middle of the seventeenth century, however, Oliver Cromwell and
the Parliamentary forces rose against Charles I and drove his fol-

lowers into exile. When Cromwell gained power, one of his first concerns was to regain control of the seas around Britain. Within a few short years he doubled the size of the English navy. Special care was given to making the new warships seaworthy, stout, and heavily armed. As soon as an adequate fleet had been built up, England set out to wrest control of the sea from the Dutch.

The result was three great wars between England and the Netherlands. All three were fought, won, and lost entirely upon the sea— in a struggle between the descendants of the Sea Beggars and those of the Sea Dogs. Never were two navies more equally matched both in the courage and experience of their seamen and in the nerve and sharp-witted tactics of their commanders.

Four of these commanders, battering each other fiercely through these wars, held the fates of their two nations firmly in their fists: England's Blake and Monck; Holland's Tromp and Ruyter. Like a ball in a furious four-man game of catch, victory flew back and forth between them throughout the third quarter of the seventeenth century.

7

"... dreadful sights though glorious"

THE PERFECT CIVIL SERVANT GOES TO SEA

The short, incredible naval career of Robert Blake began when he was already fifty years old. He had no previous sea experience at all, and when he did go to sea, he had only eight years left to live. Yet in those eight years he exhibited a brilliance and originality that would cause Nelson, more than a century later, to admit he could not hope to equal Blake in sea-fighting strategy.

There was little in Robert Blake's first fifty years to suggest—even in retrospect—what he was to accomplish in those final eight years. He was born of a well-to-do Somerset family in 1599. Serious and scholarly, he attended Oxford for ten years, hoping to become a professor. But his father died when he was twenty-six, and Blake had to leave Oxford to manage the family estate and raise and educate a dozen young brothers and sisters.

A rigid Puritan, Blake sided with Parliament when it opposed Charles I's inept leadership and asserted its right to say how England was governed. Although not a man to proclaim his views, as a leading wealthy citizen of Bridgwater, he was elected to Parliament when he was forty-one.

When anger at the king's attempts to do away with the Parliament erupted into armed rebellion, Blake raised a troop of militia in his home county to fight against the Royalists. He managed himself well enough as a militia officer in the Civil War to be promoted to colonel. But when the war ended with victory for Cromwell, execution for Charles I, and exile for the Royalists, Blake returned to his seat in Parliament.

The Royalists might be beaten in England, but a group of them remained out at sea in navy ships commanded by Prince Rupert where they harassed Cromwell's newly set up Commonwealth. Their privateering raids on British shipping became more and more annoying. Yet it would be no easy job to put them down. In England, sea commanders whose loyalty to the new government could be trusted were scarce. Most had been drawn from the aristocracy and their sympathies lay with the Royalists. To fill their place, Cromwell turned to men like Blake. "I had rather," he declared, "have a plain, russet-coated captain that knows what he fights for and loves what he knows, than what you call a gentleman and is nothing else."

So, at the age of fifty, Robert Blake suddenly found himself appointed to command a squadron of fighting ships, sent out to stop the Royalist privateers. He still held the title of colonel. Blake hated life upon the ocean from the start, and he never got over hating it. He knew nothing of ships, sailing, or the sea. But he had a methodical mind and was quick to learn. Keeping his squadron at sea for a full year—a considerable feat for those days—he persistently badgered the smaller Royalist fleet until he had brought most of it to heel. Next he spent a year guarding the waters around Britain against possible attack by foreign nations supporting the Royalist cause—or, as he put it, "to keep foreigners from fooling us." At the end of that time the somber landsman found himself in command of a fleet.

It was a fleet being rapidly rebuilt. The new government was busy bringing the navy out of the state of decay in which the Stuarts had left it. Much of the new construction was supervised by Blake, who saw to it that ships were properly built and armed at breakneck speed. For the Dutch, having become steadily more arrogant, had begun to deny trading privileges to English merchants in far ports and to scorn English authority even in the English Channel itself. By 1652, relations between the two nations were rapidly deteriorating. But the new English fleet under Blake was in fighting shape.

Blake and Martin Tromp, the leading Dutch admiral, could hardly have been more unlike. Blake had just three years as a sea commander behind him; whereas Tromp, two years his senior, had spent an entire lifetime as a sailor and sea-fighter. Where Blake was solid and taciturn, Tromp gave free vent to his outbursts of humor and hate. Where Blake was still groping ahead with his lessons in sailing and sea fighting, Tromp had the assurance of a lifetime's experience.

Tromp had been born in Briel, the first town torn by the Sea Beggars from the grasp of Spain. And he was well aware of his heritage. When he was eight, his sea-captain father had begun taking him along on voyages. His first taste of sea fighting had come in 1607 when he was only ten. He had served as an apprentice seaman aboard his father's vessel when Heemskerck's fleet entered Gibraltar harbor and wiped out the Spanish galleons anchored there.

Just two years later, Martin and his father were sailing past the coast of Guinea on a Dutch West Indiaman when their vessel was attacked and boarded by an English pirate. Twelve-year-old Martin saw his father fight the pirate captain and die from a sword thrust. When the Dutch sailors surrendered, the boy screamed at them: "Will no one avenge the death of my father?" The pirate captain, amused by the boy's spirit, took him as a slave. Martin spent two years as the pirate's cabin boy before he managed to escape and make his way back to his homeland.

He was at sea again within the year, this time as an officer aboard a little navy ship hunting down pirates. Captured again by an Algerian pirate, Tromp this time was freed quickly by ransom. He went back to pirate fighting with a vengeance. By the time he was thirty, he was captain of his own navy warship. Once he became a captain, Tromp's rise to admiral of the Dutch navy was swift. In fight after fight he proved himself to be the best ocean battler the Dutch had.

The northern Netherlands had achieved their independence—and a twelve-year truce with Spain—by 1609. But by the time the truce was over, the Dutch had not only to face the Spanish navy but a huge pirate fleet operating out of Dunkirk, which at that time was controlled by Spain. Tromp's repeated victories over the Spanish navy and this pirate fleet earned him his title of lieutenant-admiral, leader of the Dutch navy.

In 1639 Tromp reached the pinnacle of his fame by leading

thirty warships to victory over sixty-seven Spanish galleons that had sailed up with the intention of wiping out the Dutch navy. Unwilling to cease battle when night closed in, Tromp continued to pursue the sorely pressed Spaniards with the cry, "They seem to be asleep. Let's wake them up!"—and harried the fleeing, dodging enemy fleet until what remained of it—eighteen leaking hulks—finally crawled back into Spanish ports.

This victory established Holland as the most potent naval power in the world. Even England, her navy by this time seriously weakened by the neglect of the Stuarts, deferred before the Dutch navy. When Oliver Cromwell came into power, however, he determined to restore the British navy to the position it had held under the Elizabethan Sea Dogs. He needed ships and he needed men to command them—men who would one day have to face the mighty Tromp himself. Cromwell could not have picked anyone seemingly less qualified to face Tromp than Robert Blake.

The Dutch and the English were not yet at war. But the thread of concord between the two nations was so frayed that only the slightest extra strain was needed to break it. On May 19, 1652, testy Martin Tromp and iron-willed Robert Blake spotted each other in the English Channel off Dover, misread each other's intentions (or so both claimed later)—and severed the final strand of peace.

Ten miles south of Dover late that morning, Blake's flagship, the *James,* lurched northward up the Channel through boiling seas at the head of thirteen warships. Blake's stare was directed at the northern horizon where he was beginning to see the mast-tops of the forty Dutch warships he had heard were anchored off Dover. Far above his heavy round head, sail trimmers raced aloft to coax a bit more speed out of the *James* against the contrary winds.

In almost three years at sea, Blake had never set foot on those rope ladders that led the way up from the deck to the tops of the swinging masts. As a "general-at-sea" he had never climbed higher than the poop deck on which he now stood. The sea did not agree with him. Although he looked robust, his health, used to the milder climate of the land, was beginning to break under the harsh extremes of the open sea. It was not yet precarious—but it was to grow worse. Still, he did not complain. He was always what some have termed him: the perfect civil servant, doing his job.

Three years had taught him something about this job—and he would continue to learn as long as he continued to sail. He already knew a great deal about the potentialities of a ship and a fleet. Although he did not understand the mechanics of sailing—and never would—most of the officers on his flagship, and the others trailing his wake, were seamen; they knew how to put his ideas into practice. Blake decided what should be done; the others figured out how to do it.

At the moment, Blake wanted to get to that Dutch fleet off Dover Roads as quickly as possible. His officers were doing their best against unfavorable winds to get him there. The night before he had received a hurried message from his rear-admiral, Bourne, who was stationed with nine ships in the Downs. According to Bourne, Tromp's fleet of forty ships, hit by bad weather in the Channel, had been forced to enter English waters and anchor off Dover. Tromp had given assurance that his presence was friendly and temporary—but he had refused to lower his flag to Dover Castle.

The dipping of foreign flags to acknowledge English authority on its side of the Channel was an established practice, long demanded by England and long observed by the ships of other nations. But the Dutch had neglected this customary courtesy salute ever since Tromp's great victory over Spain in 1639. And England's navy had grown too weak for her government to insist on the traditional right. Cromwell, anxious to reaffirm the strength of the new English navy, was no longer willing to tolerate any insult to England's authority. Blake's orders were to see to it that the Dutch struck their flag in salute—or got out of English waters. Tromp would dip his flag to him, or else.

Tromp, aboard his anchored flagship, the *Brederode,* watched the English ships laboring up the Channel toward him and fought with his own stubborn spirit. He knew quite well that Blake would demand that he lower his flag. But Tromp was determined to refuse. The Dutch were masters of the sea—and he had helped win this mastery. He recognized no other nation's authority over the Dutch —in *any* waters. Yet he knew he must not allow pride to carry him too far this day. Complete defiance might provoke a war which his country did not want. There seemed only one way out of his dilemma.

At two in the afternoon, with a northeasterly wind blowing and the English fleet drawing near, Tromp's *Brederode* upped anchor and made sail toward the French side of the Channel. The rest of his ships, obeying his signals, followed.

Blake saw, understood, and relaxed a bit. Once the Dutch fleet was out of English waters, there would be no need to demand what Tromp would refuse. Blake was willing to let it go at that. For though England wanted to reassert her rights on the ocean, she did not want to do so through war. Just to make sure Tromp kept going, Blake told his flag captain to lead their ships eastward also, following the Dutch fleet on a parallel course, but keeping the distance between them.

The English fleet had been trailing Tromp this way for two hours when Blake saw a swift little Dutch vessel slip over the horizon from the south and speed toward the Dutch fleet. He watched the newcomer haul up with the Dutch warships and send a boat over to Tromp's *Brederode*. Moments later, the boat pulled away from Tromp's flagship—and the Dutch fleet abruptly altered its course, coming about on the starboard tack and bearing straight for the English, with Tromp's ship in the lead. Blake, watching Tromp lead his fleet back with the wind full behind him, could think of only one reason for the Dutch ships' return: that little vessel must have brought word from Holland for Tromp to begin hostilities.

Moving quickly, Blake sent orders for Bourne's squadron to join him as soon as possible. He ran out his lower tier of guns, ordered the gunners to stand ready, and led his fleet of thirteen toward the approaching formation of forty Dutch ships.

From the *Brederode,* Tromp saw the smaller English fleet coming up to meet his, wondered at it, and barked his own orders: clear ships for action and shorten sails for battle. The news he had just received had been that a group of Dutch merchant vessels, heading up the Channel for Holland from the south, had run into a lone British warship several days before. The warship had demanded that the Dutch haul down their flags in salute. When the armed Dutch merchantmen refused, the warship had fired, beginning a hot contest. It was not known if the Dutch vessels had been captured, or had fled to some haven close to shore to await an opportunity to get away.

Tromp had checked his pride before. But not now. Instantly coming about, he had headed back toward the English shore. He intended to find those Dutch merchant vessels. If they were still free, he would take them under his protection. If they had been captured, he would free them. Either way, he intended to convoy them past the English fleet and safely back to Holland. And as for that English admiral approaching out there across the water— let him try to interfere!

The two flagships neared each other. Their fleets were roughly forming up into ragged lines behind them. Blake's *James* and Tromp's *Brederode* were similar in type: longer, lower and more maneuverable than the old towering Spanish monsters. Each carried two decks of guns: the *Brederode* 54 guns; the *James* 48. But the fact that the guns of the *James* were bigger, and its sides thicker, more than made up the difference in number.

The two ships got within range of each other at four in the afternoon. Blake, his eyes on Tromp's flag, had waited until now for it to be lowered from the masthead in recognition of English authority in these waters. It continued to flutter aloft.

Blake abruptly ordered his master gunner to fire a shot at Tromp's flag. A moment later the roar and recoil rumble of a single cannon broke the silence between the two fleets. It was the shot that began the war between England and Holland.

On the deck of the *Brederode*, Tromp watched the cannon ball arc high over his masts. When it was past, plunging downward into the sea, his eyes lowered to the poop of the *James*. The two flagships were close enough now for him to see the short, heavy figure of the English admiral who, his hands tightly gripping the rail, was in turn looking back across the water at him. The Dutchman, his fingers locked behind him, swayed to the roll of the *Brederode*. His face was graven with anger. Beside him, his gunnery officer waited. Tromp continued to stare across the water at Blake, saying nothing. He did not haul down his flag.

The gun aboard the *James* boomed again. This time the shot was lower, whistling between the main and mizzen tops.

Tromp turned, spoke quickly to his gunnery officer and, when he hurried off to carry out the order, returned his frozen gaze to the English flagship. He did not for a moment consider striking his flag.

Aboard the *James,* Blake ordered a third warning shot that Tromp must dip his flag. The iron ball crashed into the hull of the *Brederode*.

Instantly, the side of Tromp's flagship vanished behind clouds of erupting smoke through which twenty-seven iron balls in a high broadside hurtled over the water and across the *James'* deck.

Among the sudden havoc of breaking timbers, ripping sails, and the shocking thud of heavy iron balls striking home, Blake stood as solid as a deep-rooted tree. But his reaction was automatic and swift. The echoing thunder of that first broadside still hung in the air when the *James* leaped in recoil from her answering broadside. Blake aimed lower than Tromp. His shots tore into the *Brederode's* hull, starting great leaks and wrecking guns and crews inside the gun decks.

The two flagships stood in close to each other. Their gun crews began to fire as fast as they could reload their weapons. The two fleets toiled up to join the battle. But the Dutch ships, kept in close order by Tromp, had surrounded the *James* and were slamming their cannon fire into its hull while the English ships were still straggling up from behind.

For almost four hours, the *James* stood alone under the pounding of the ever-increasing enemy force. Blake's sails and rigging were torn away. His mizzenmast, shattered under continuous blows, crashed overboard. His decks became a patchwork of gaping holes, fallen spars, and uprooted planking. But he held on, firing constantly at his tormentors.

Unlike sea battles of the past, neither side made any attempt to board. From start to finish it was guns against guns. The *James* suffered terribly under the relentless pounding she received during the hours before her supporting fleet reached her. That she was able to remain in action at all was due to the fact that her hull, like the hulls of the rest of Blake's ships, was thicker and stronger than those of the Dutch warships. Her sides did not cave in under the heavy blows as did the Dutch sides. The comparatively fragile construction of Dutch ships had never hampered them before when dealing with the far from accurate gunnery of the Spanish and the pirates. But the accuracy of English gunnery, plus the fact that English shot was heavier than Dutch, soon began to tell on the Dutch ships.

The smaller English fleet held its own until nightfall, at which time the engagement was ended. By next day, both fleets were sailing away from each other, the commander of each having become quite worried about the probable reaction of this clash back home.

Blake's *James* was wrecked, but all his ships were still afloat. And he had with him a captured Dutch vessel, which had been seized by Bourne's squadron as it reached the battle toward dusk.

Tromp sailed on to find the Dutch merchant ships. Later he convoyed them past the British fleet, and sent them safely home.

Both commanders waited nervously for government reaction to the flareup in the Channel. Tromp, his anger cooling off, tried to minimize what had happened so that both nations could let the matter pass without either suffering a loss of face. But Blake, with his rigid conception of right and wrong, was not inclined to let the matter pass. He read the letter he received with righteous indignation:

May 23rd, 1652. Lieutenant-Admiral Tromp to General Blake:
Sir,
On the 19th . . . we met one another at sea. My intention was to greet you. But, seeing that I was attacked, and not knowing what was your intention . . . I was forced as a man of honor to defend myself. It has however been reported to me, lying at anchor at Calais, that one of our ships . . . has been brought into your road in Downs. It is the only one of ours missing, and I beg you for friendship's sake to be pleased to restore this ship and to place it in the hands of the bearer of this letter in the same state as it was taken. I assure myself that the good alliance and union between the government of your State and that of our Republic, our common religion and particular friendship will prevent you from refusing my request, for which I shall be under obligation to remain as I am now,
Your most humble servant,
Martin Harpertsz Tromp
From our ship the Brederode, in Calais roads

Blake sat down immediately and penned his reply:

May 30, 1652. General Blake to Lieutenant-Admiral Tromp.
Sir,
It is not without great astonishment that I have read yours of the 23rd May . . . wherein, though representing yourself as a person of honour, you introduce many gross misstatements. And this, just after having fought with the fleet of the Parliament of the English Republic . . . having thought fit to commit an act of hostility without receiving the slightest provocation. . . . But God (in whom we trust) having frustrated your purposes, to your own destruction, and seeing that we have taken some of your ships, you have thought well to demand the same of us again . . . to which the only meet answer that I can return is that I presume Parliament will keenly resent this great insult and the spilling of the blood of their un-

offending subjects, and that you will moreover find, in the under-
signed, one ever ready to carry out their commands.

Your humble servant,

Robert Blake

In the Downs, May 30th, 1652

England believed Blake's version of the encounter. The Dutch
believed Tromp's. And the two nations rushed into what was to be
the first of the three English-Dutch Wars.

The English struck first—at one of the softest and most vital
points of the Dutch economy. Blake sailed north with a squadron
of warships and smashed the Dutch herring fleet off the upper tip
of Scotland, wiping out the investment of hundreds of Dutch
families.

Tromp raced out to sea with one hundred ships to avenge the
loss. He had Blake's ships in sight when a howling gale struck.
Blake, forewarned by his officers, ordered his ships into the lee of
the Shetland Islands. Thus partially protected from the full force
of the gale, the English rode out the storm in safety.

But Tromp, superb seaman though he was, had been too eager
for a fight to seek a haven in time. His fleet, in the open near a lee
shore, was exposed to the fury of the wind. Clinging to the shrouds
to keep himself from being flung overboard, Tromp stayed top-
side while the *Brederode* was flung about by the mountainous
waves. Through the turmoil, his salt-blinded eyes caught heartbreak-
ing momentary glimpses of his fleet. One of his ships was foundering under tons of water. The masts of another crumbled under the
battering-ram blows of the waves. The seams of another's hull
opened like gaping mouths to gulp in the ocean. Another fought
desperately to drag itself away from the rocks.

By the time the storm blew itself out, three of Tromp's ships
had foundered and gone under. Two more had broken their backs
on the rocky shores. Exhausted crews worked the battered remains
of his fleet back to port. Tromp, called to account by an angry
government, could only explain: "Finding ourselves so extraordi-
narily punished by the mighty hand of God, we resolved for the
best to make for home with the ships at present with us."

Tromp's failure to protect the herring fleet, plus his failure to
catch Blake or avoid the storm disaster, put him under so much
criticism from his own people and government that he had to resign
his command under pressure. Bitterly, he swore that he would not
return to sea until his country begged him.

In his place, command of the Dutch navy was handed to two men: Admiral De Witt and Admiral Michael de Ruyter.

Michael de Ruyter, a merchant skipper who had been hastily grabbed up by the navy at the outbreak of war, set out to convoy a fleet of merchant ships south through the English Channel. The English fleet, under Admiral Sir George Ayscue, sailed out to intercept him. Ruyter beat Ayscue aside with ease and sailed on past him with his convoy.

Angered, England replaced Ayscue, and Blake was made commander-in-chief of its entire navy. His second in command, a great seaman, was thirty-one-year-old William Penn.

When Ruyter sailed back up the Channel with another convoy, Blake and Penn were waiting for him. But they too were unable to stop Ruyter. The Dutchman gave them the slip and got his whole convoy back home safely, leaving behind a grimly frustrated Blake.

Of this Michael de Ruyter, more will be said later. Now the Dutch made the mistake of putting him *under* Admiral De Witt. De Witt, a fiery, impetuous young commander, felt it was up to him to prove that his government had known what it was doing when it replaced Tromp with himself. He set sail with sixty-four fighting ships to find Blake and fight him in English waters. Trouble started for De Witt even before the battle began. Although his commission stated that he commanded the Dutch fleet, he discovered that he could not command the respect or obedience of the men who sailed it—men whose hearts still belonged to Tromp, men who resented the man presuming to take Tromp's place.

De Witt had intended to shift to Tromp's old flagship, *Brederode,* for the battle. But, as he wrote in his log, "I myself went on board the ship *Prins Willem,* the worst sailer we have, because the crew of Lt. Admiral Tromp's ship refused to have me over them (although I had written orders to the effect in abundance)."

A man who failed to command the respect of a ship's crew and officers could hardly exact discipline from the very independent commanders of his squadrons, either. De Witt had divided his fleet into four squadrons: the center squadron under himself, the van under Ruyter, the rear under De Wilde, a reserve squadron under Evertsen. He never succeeded in welding these separate squadrons into a single fleet.

It was under these conditions that De Witt led his sixty-four ships south along the coast of England in search of Blake.

Blake, on a new flagship, the sixty-gun *Resolution,* sailed from
his anchorage in the Downs on that crisp morning of September 28,
1652, at the head of fifty-eight ships. At three in the afternoon, as
he was sailing north past the Thames, he spotted the long line of
sixty-four Dutch ships ahead. The Dutch line was strung out close
to Kentish Knock, one of the huge, shifting underwater sandbars
north of the mouth of the Thames. As soon as he took in the size
and position of the Dutch fleet, Blake hove to and signaled for
the rest of his own ships to close up behind him. It took them a full
hour, during which time it became apparent to Blake that Admiral
De Witt was making no effort to interfere. The Dutch maintained
their position, waiting for Blake to form up and attack.

The wind was strong from the northwest, blowing off Kentish
Knock, which the Dutch fleet closely hugged. De Witt reasoned
that Blake would not try to get between the Dutch and Kentish
Knock for fear of grounding on the hidden sandbanks. If this were
so, Blake must attack from the other—the leeward—side. There
the wind would be blowing from the Dutch line against the English
ships. It would be slow work for the English to beat up to the
Dutch against the wind. And all the while, the Dutch broadsides
could pound into their oncoming bows, from which only a few guns
could reply. De Witt's position would also allow him to send fireships drifting with the wind into the onplodding English fleet.

Blake, aware of the advantages of the Dutch position, together
with Penn and his other sea-wise officers, worked out his own
countermoves. At four o'clock, he attacked—in typical, bullish
Blake fashion: into the teeth of the odds. According to his careful
assessment, however, those odds were less impressive than De Witt
had assumed.

Blake's *Resolution* led the way—but *between* De Witt's line and
Kentish Knock. As he bore in, Blake sent a broadside tearing
low through the hull of the first Dutch ship he passed, and sailed
on up the windward side of their line. The Dutch were completely
taken by surprise.

After a moment, answering Dutch salvos ripped across the
Resolution's decks and slashed through its sails. But Blake, hanging
on to the rail, ignored the shuddering crashes, the screams around
him. For once he was looking, not ahead, but back in the direction
from which he had come, toward the ships following him into the
invisible watery gap between the sandbank and the Dutch fleet.

His heart sank when Penn's ship, coming along on a slightly different course, suddenly ground to a halt. Moments later, he saw one of his best vessels, the *Sovereign,* go aground beside Penn on the underwater sandbar.

For a moment, the English cause seemed to tip with the masts of those two ships heeling over on the sand. Then it rose again: The following English ships now had perfect markers to sail by. Each in turn drove in through the gap between the pair of stranded

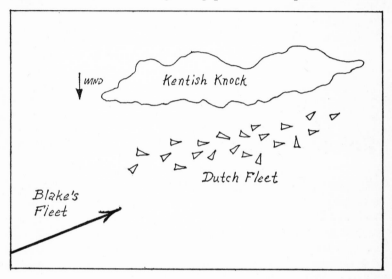

BATTLE OF KENTISH KNOCK

ships and the Dutch line. Each in turn glided up behind Blake, and delivered those hull-tearing broadsides into the Dutch vessels now caught on the English lee.

De Witt's fleet, stunned by the sudden reversal of positions, reeled away in disorder from the devastating blows that, at this point-blank range, caved in their timbers as though they were eggshells. But they could not escape. For in running from Blake's main attack, they fell against the rest of the English ships coming up along their other side. Caught thus between two fires, as Blake had planned it, De Witt was forced to fight it out with an enemy that was now all around him.

"We found," reported De Witt, "that the guns on their smallest frigates carry further than our heaviest cannon, and the English fired smarter and quicker than did many of ours."

That sums it up. The Dutch fleet disintegrated into a hodge-podge of vessels scrambling to get free. Yet through the confusion, Blake kept his iron hold on the English fleet. He had and kept his enemy hemmed in. The few Dutch ships that broke free of the tangle ran smack into Penn's ship and the *Sovereign,* both of which had worked off the sandbar at last and were sweeping up to join the fight.

Blake—his flagship slipping past a Dutch warship to deliver a starboard broadside, then coming about to thunder its port broadside—saw one of the Hollanders come apart and spread out upon the ocean as floating wreckage. Another, overloaded with water pouring in through its broken sides, sank from sight. Here one, its masts torn out and guns dismantled, struck its flag. There another with its hull ripped open surrendered.

So it went, until under the cover of night De Witt managed to escape. If he had only been able to start the battle earlier in the day, Blake decided, De Witt's entire fleet might have been demolished. Even so, it was a stunning defeat for the Dutch. Blake had lost two hundred men and no ships. De Witt staggered home with over a thousand casualties and minus four of his ships. "We are put to shame before the world," De Witt admitted.

When the Dutch saw boatload after boatload of wounded coming ashore from their mangled warships, they set up a howl. It did not cease until Tromp, grumbling about the way he had been treated, was taken from retirement and put back into command of the Dutch fleet.

The sun rode high above the English Channel on the afternoon of November 29, 1652, but Robert Blake felt no warmth. He was bitterly cold. The offshore wind bit through his uniform. The sight of almost ninety Dutch warships approaching—and the knowledge that he had only forty-two ships with which to oppose them—chilled him even more.

England, flushed with the Kentish Knock victory, had decided there would be no more sea battles this winter, and had divided its fleet into separate squadrons. Blake realized now how short-sighted it had been to do so. Winter did not stop a sea-fighter like Tromp, not when there was a big Dutch merchant fleet to be convoyed safely through the dangers of the Channel.

Tromp came sailing south with his war fleet under two orders.

The first: to act as a protective screen for over three hundred merchant vessels headed for the Mediterranean and Indian Ocean trade. The second: to attack Blake's fleet "with all force and might, and if possible destroy it." Now he had Blake outnumbered two-to-one.

Besides his bigger guns and stouter ships Blake saw that he had one slim advantage over Tromp: the weather gauge. The wind blew from shore toward the Dutch men-of-war, bearing Blake's fleet with it. Blake meant to cling to this advantage, and use it in every way he could.

Blake's flagships always took a beating. For he always spear-headed the battle, deliberately enduring the first enemy blows to set his fleet an example for close action and to drive a wedge deep into the enemy. On this day off Dungeness, his flagship of the Kentish Knock battle was still in the dock awaiting mast replacements. His new flagship was the 62-gun *Triumph*.

Again Blake began the battle. The *Triumph* drove the opening wedge into Tromp's fleet. It was like diving into a furnace. The Dutch force opened to allow the entrance of the *Triumph*—followed closely by the *Vanguard* and *Victory*—and then closed tightly around the three ships. Blake, his brain ringing from the concussion of never-ending gunfire, scorched by the flames and smoke, saw that his three ships were completely surrounded by twenty Dutch warships. They would be pounded to pieces.

He bellowed for his flag captain to drive straight ahead and force the *Triumph* out of this circle of destruction. The order was hardly out of his mouth when, with a tearing shock, the fore-topmast and mainstay were ripped away. Without them the *Triumph* was slow and awkward, but she pushed ahead anyway, the *Victory* and *Vanguard* hugging close to her stern. It was like battering head on through a wall. The *Triumph's* bows, having taken barrage after barrage, began to break open and let the sea in. The clank of the pumps below rose in tempo through the noise of gunnery. Yet the ship moved on, slowly, stubbornly, taking point-blank hull-fire to squeeze through the tight-packed ring and at last shake itself free. As he emerged into the open, Blake quickly assured himself that the other two ships had managed to force their way out behind him. Then he turned to see how the rest of his fleet fared.

The sight before him raised his blood pressure to a dangerous degree. He had never felt such pure anger in his life. Only twenty of his ships were engaged with the enemy! The rest were hanging back, off in the distance near the shore there, out of range! Blake's rage was mixed with anguish and contempt. The ships shunning the battle were overawed by the odds; but their cowardice increased those odds, insuring Blake's defeat. The twenty ships that *had* followed him into battle were being terribly torn by the enemy. Blake realized that he must wrench these ships free of Tromp's and get them to safety. Already it was too late for some of his fleet. Several, separately trapped by clusters of the enemy, as he himself had been a short time ago, were being beaten to splinters.

As he looked about him to try to determine where he might still be of some use, off in the distance he saw two of his ships, the *Garland* and the *Anthony Bonaventure,* attempting to capture Tromp himself. They had driven in against both sides of the *Brederode,* grappled the Dutch admiral's flagship and boarded her. For a short time, a hand-to-hand struggle had seesawed across Tromp's deck as his men held off boarding parties from both ships. Other Dutch commanders, seeing that their leader was in trouble, had closed in, grappled hold of the two English vessels, and boarded them. Captain Batten of the *Garland* and Captain Hoxton of the *Anthony Bonaventure* had been forced to rush back with their boarders from the Dutch flagship to defend their own decks. Now more and more Dutch ships were closing in to add their boarders to the jam-packed cluster of grappled ships.

As soon as he saw what was happening, Blake ordered his *Triumph* to join the fight. But a dozen Dutch warships slashed in ahead of him, blocking his way. Blake tried to cut his way through with his guns. But this time superior English gunnery failed against the enemy's greater number of guns. Blake could not break through the barricade.

Helplessly, he was forced to watch the men of the *Garland* and the *Anthony Bonaventure* defend their decks until Captain Hoxton and Captain Batten were dead and there were hardly enough Englishmen left to surrender the two ships.

Night had frustrated Blake at Kentish Knock. This time it came upon him as a divine mercy. By dusk, he had lost five ships; had the day lasted longer he would certainly have lost more. In the darkness, he disengaged the remains of his fleet and fled toward the shore.

With the coming of dawn, Tromp followed, and forced the

English to flee still further, into the Thames River. For a while thereafter, left free to do as he pleased, Tromp swept back and forth past the mouth of the Thames, seizing coastal shipping and capturing another stray English warship. Before many days went by, no English vessel dared venture out of its port.

Satisfied at last, Tromp triumphantly sailed back to his merchant ships. When he convoyed them on down through the Channel, the legend goes, he hoisted a broom to his masthead as a symbol of the fact that he had swept the English from the Channel. The legend may not be true, but the fact is: from shore to shore, from top to bottom, the Channel belonged to Tromp.

Blake, stunned and humiliated, wrote to Cromwell: "I hope it will not be unseasonable for me to desire . . . a discharge from this employment, so far too great for me . . . so that I may be freed from that trouble of spirit which lies upon me, arising from the sense of my own insufficiency and the usual effects thereof, reproach and contempt of men."

The English government refused Blake's resignation. The government was well aware that the blame for his defeat lay elsewhere, and the disaster off Dungeness had alarmed England to the point of doing something about it. Blake agreed to stay on—but demanded a cohesive sizable fleet and some means of assuring himself that none of his officers would fail in their duty again. At his suggestion, government investigators looked into the matter of the ships that had failed to follow him into battle. Five captains—one of whom was a younger brother of Blake's—were deprived of their commands as a result of the investigation. More important, the investigation also led to the drawing up of thirty-nine Articles of sea war which became the backbone of all future regulations governing the actions of the navy. These Articles signaled the end of the haphazard days of merchant-masters turned fighting-captains, the days when each captain acted for himself as he saw fit. There would be no more individual decisions to hold back from a fight ordered by a fleet commander:

. . . all who shall in time of any fight or engagement withdraw, or keep back, or not come into the fight and engage . . . shall for such cowardice or disaffection be tried, and suffer pain of death or other punishment. . . . Every Captain and Officer shall in his own person, and according to his place, hearten and encourage the sea-

men and common men to fight courageously, and not to behave
themselves faintly, nor yield to the enemy, or to cry for quarter,
upon pain of death or such other punishment as the offences shall
deserve.

Thus the proper rules for the way an officer should conduct himself in action were at last put down in black and white, as was
the penalty for failure to adhere to them: death.

While these Articles were being drawn up, the ships damaged off
Dungeness—and others still awaiting repairs from previous battles
—were swiftly refitted. Battleships would no longer lie in dock for
months waiting for work to be done on them. The defeat off Dungeness had awakened England to the folly of trying to operate the
fleet at less than full strength.

When Blake sailed again, for the first time he did not have
to shift to a new flagship. The *Triumph*—completely sound, seaworthy, fighting-fit—showed not a mark of the beating she had
taken from Tromp.

In mid-February, 1653, the English fleet sailed out formed into
three groups: the Red, White and Blue Squadrons, each with its
own admiral, vice-admiral and rear admiral. Blake and Richard
Deane, in joint command of the entire fleet, also led the Red
Squadron together in the *Triumph*. William Penn, on the 64-gun
Speaker, was admiral of the Blue Squadron. And General Monck
—the best soldier in England—had been appointed admiral of the
White Squadron, sailing in the 56-gun *Vanguard*. Their mission:
to stop Tromp, who with his fleet of about eighty warships was
convoying 150 merchant vessels back up the English Channel.

Blake rose in darkness on Friday morning, February 18. Before
the first gray light of dawn, he was on the quarter-deck near the
Triumph's helmsman. The freezing sea wind bit through his greatcoat. Stars hung as sharp as icicles in the darkness under which the
Triumph pitched in the rough, racing Channel tide.

Blake was anxious lest Tromp manage to slip past in the darkness and rob him of his chance to avenge the debacle off Dungeness.
He had spread his three squadrons out in three separate stations
across these waters: Penn's Blue Squadron was off to the west;
Monck's White Squadron far to the east. Although such separation
meant that whichever squadron first made contact with Tromp

would be outnumbered until the other two could close up, it was
a calculated risk which Blake felt obliged to take. Tromp must
not pass. The morale of England—and his own tender self-respect
—depended upon a victory here and now.

As dawn approached, Blake was joined on deck by Richard
Deane; Andrew Ball, the *Triumph's* captain; Blake's secretary,
Sparrow; and Broadridge, the sailing master. The rising sun revealed to them a horde of Dutch ships sailing up the choppy seas
past Portland. They were already close enough to make out the
Dutch sailing plan: Tromp's eighty warships were in the lead,
spread out to form a shield for the 150 merchant vessels sailing
close behind them in tight formation. Blake had to admire Tromp's
ability to keep the ranks of a vast gathering of ships closed up in
dirty weather.

Within minutes of the two fleets' sighting each other, Blake saw
Tromp's fighting fleet begin to draw together into three separate
tight squadrons—Tromp leading the center squadron, Michael de
Ruyter the squadron off his portside, Evertsen the starboard squad-
ron. With all sails set, they swooped up on the wind toward Blake's
Triumph.

With Blake were only thirty ships, most of which had straggled
far behind in the night. Off to the west, Penn's Blue Squadron
had the wind, and was approaching at top speed. But to the east,
Monck's White Squadron, with the wind against it, would be a long
time in reaching Blake.

Blake's decision—to which Deane agreed—was instant and inevitable: He would stay and hold Tromp until the rest of the
English fleet joined him. Captain Ball and sailing-master Broadridge rushed off to carry out his orders; secretary Sparrow jotted
them down for Blake's records. Signal flags raced aloft, the command for his thirty ships to beat their way up to support him without delay. The *Triumph* rumbled to the roll of her sixty-two guns
being run out as drums rattled and bugles shrilled. Sail trimmers
raced up the rigging to shorten the flagship to fighting canvas: main-
sail, foresail and fore-topsail.

Blake and Deane stood ready. Watching the Dutch warships
surge across the swells toward the *Triumph,* Blake recognized the
lead ship: it was his old opponent, the *Brederode,* flying Tromp's
flag.

Only ten English men-of-war had managed to reach Blake's

side when the Dutch struck. The first range-feeling salvos from the Dutch bow guns tore canvas at 8 A.M. Tromp, in the lead of his fleet, drove in against the *Triumph*. But several other English ships got in his way and bombarded him as he slipped past; and by the time he reached Blake, the *Brederode's* lower gun deck was aflame and a gang of crewmen were rushing below to fight the fire.

Tromp had saved his first gun loads for this moment, as had Blake. The *Triumph* and the *Brederode* swung port-to-port and simultaneously hurled their roaring broadsides into each other. A huge cloudbank of sulphurous smoke blossomed on the water between the two flagships. Through it, beyond the passing *Brederode,* Blake made out another Dutch ship driving in toward him. Then another, and still another—firing and taking broadsides in a rising crescendo of noise that finally merged into what seemed to be one continual, never-ending, ear-shattering explosion. Within half an hour, the *Triumph* and its ten supporting ships were being engaged by more than three times that number of enemy vessels.

The *Triumph,* principal target of the enemy, found itself cut off from its fellows, battling alone simultaneously against the *Brederode* and six other Dutch ships. Standing together in a tremendous din, Blake and Deane watched their wood-and-canvas world being smashed into a chaos of wreckage around them. Rigging shredded; sails came down; masts broke and tottered; guns overturned and crushed their handlers beneath them.

Blake, aware that neither the *Triumph* nor his ten other ships could hold out much longer against such overwhelming odds, strained to see through the drifts of throat-rasping smoke. Out there, beyond the locked battlers, the Dutch squadron under Evertsen was curving out in a line to block Penn's Blue Squadron from reaching the English flagship and its ten supporters. The third Dutch squadron, under Ruyter, was sailing to fence off the bulk of Blake's own Red Squadron from the fight. But Penn was sailing magnificently, tacking to cut right through Evertsen's squadron. And Lawson, Blake's vice-admiral, was swinging all the way around the head of Ruyter's line with the rest of Blake's squadron, attempting to get into Penn's wake and follow him into the fight. Monck's White Squadron, beating up slowly against the wind, was still too far away to reach him in time to save the day. The outcome of the struggle, and Blake's own fate, depended on whether or not

Penn's squadron, and the rest of his own, could reach the point of battle soon.

Blake, his attention fastened on the desperately maneuvering ships of Penn and Lawson, did not move when his secretary, Sparrow, was smashed apart by a cannon ball at his side. Nor when sailing master Broadridge was killed at his post. Nor when Captain Ball crumpled and died in a pool of his blood on his deck.

It took almost two hours for Penn's *Speaker* to move up and break through Evertsen's squadron. Then he saved both broadsides until he drove in against the seven enemies surrounding Blake's *Triumph* for a simultaneous explosion that knocked aside two Dutch ships. And there came the rest of the Blue Squadron, gliding in after Penn through the break and pouring broadsides into Tromp's close-packed ships.

A spinning iron ball ploughed up long showers of splinters across the *Triumph's* poop deck. Blake and Deane saw it coming too late to dodge. The ball was past and the air filled with deadly wooden hail when Blake felt a terrible burning pain in his thigh. Blood poured down his leg. Then the splinters were gone.

Deane, stunned but unhurt, stared down at where the side of his breeches had been torn away. Then he looked at Blake. When he saw his bleeding wound, he yelled for the surgeon. But Blake stubbornly refused to let his wound be tended yet. Turning his attention back toward the break in Evertsen's squadron, he was in time to see Lawson bring the rest of his own ships through in the wake of Penn's.

With the fresh weight Penn was leaning against the main body of the enemy, the intense fire that had been directed so long against the *Triumph* dwindled. The surrounding Dutch ships began to sheer away to meet the new menace. The *Triumph* was sorely battered, but it had been worth it. Blake had pinned Tromp's fleet in place long enough to swing the tide of battle.

Satisfied that the worst was over, Blake let the surgeon lead him below. But once out of sight of the battle, he became so impatient that he scarcely gave the surgeon time to stop his bleeding and bandage the wound crudely before he limped back out on deck. There he saw that the tide had already begun to turn. For now every ship in both fleets was engaged. Around his smashed *Triumph,* the English Red and Blue Squadrons were locked with the ships of Tromp and Ruyter. About a mile away, Monck's White Squadron was battling it out with Evertsen's ships.

The English had been able to outsail the Dutch because Tromp's ships were in poor condition from months at sea, while Blake's were all freshly repaired and refitted. Now the heavy English guns, firing low into the Dutch hulls, began to take their toll. The Dutch, aware that their guns could do little against the stouter sides of the English ships, were firing high, aiming to dismast and disable. But English hull-fire soon proved what it was to continue to prove in the coming days of sailing-ship battles: the key to victory. Dutch ships began to come apart and founder under the sledge-hammer blows.

By late afternoon, it became apparent that the Dutch ships had another disadvantage. The flat bottoms of Dutch vessels were excellently suited to getting through the shallow coastal waters of their homeland. But in deep sea, with rough weather, the Dutch ships rolled heavily and did not handle nearly so well as did the deep-keeled English ships.

The tight, swift-shifting battle continued until nightfall; then the guns fell silent. Blake, his wounded leg throbbing, sat in his wrecked cabin and tallied the results of the long, mind-numbing day. Both fleets had been badly hurt. A number of English ships were crawling home as shattered wrecks. The *Triumph* itself sailed only by virtue of hastily fashioned makeshift masts and rigging. Its pumps clanked steadily in a struggle to get water out as fast as it came in through hull rips now being patched. A hundred of Blake's 350-man crew were dead. But Tromp had lost six of his best men-of-war. Many more were close to sinking.

The English were in control. Tromp, now sailing away across the Channel through the darkness, knew he had been beaten this day. Blake, following closely all night, had every reason to feel triumphant—and to eagerly await the next day's dawn.

But the dawn—which revealed Tromp's fighting ships and merchant fleet scurrying up the coast of France—broke with a wind so faint that the English squadrons had to work all morning to inch within gunnery range. Blake limped impatiently up and down his small poop deck, until two in the afternoon. Then the fleets clashed again—Blake pressing home the attack, Tromp waging a running-defensive fight. The turnabout was complete. Several of the Dutch warships, their captains' nerve breaking under the bombardment of those terrible English guns, set all sail and fled for home. Tromp furiously fired shots after them, to bring them back to their job of protecting the merchant convoy. But in vain.

The great majority of Tromp's fighting ships, however, stayed with him, fighting their losing battle to the bitter end. An English account printed in the newspapers two days later reported: "All the men-of-war who are taken are much dyed with blood, their masts and tackle being moiled with brains, hair, pieces of skulls; dreadful sights though glorious. . . ."

Those that stayed with Tromp beat back six attempts by Blake to break through to the merchantmen. By nightfall five more Dutch warships were sunk or surrendered. And when Blake struck again the following morning, it was with overwhelmingly superior numbers.

Although Blake did not realize it at first, by the third day half of Tromp's fighters—so long away from home—were out of ammunition. The rest had not enough powder and balls left to last out the day.

Tromp had his fighting ships strung out in a crescent, acting as a shield between the English fleet and the merchantmen. When Blake struck at the shield, aiming to break through it and get to the helpless merchant vessels, he encountered less resistance than he had expected. The English squadrons were able to hit the Dutch at will, delivering broadsides at point-blank range. They received only scattered shots in return. Slowly a gap began to appear in the crescent of Dutch warships—as one by one Tromp's fighters sank or were reduced to drifting, dismasted hulks. By late in the day, eight Dutch warships had been knocked out of Tromp's line.

Before Tromp could close up the gap, Penn rammed through it with his squadron. Moments later, his ships were in amongst the unresisting merchant vessels, cutting them out in groups of dozens while Blake and Monck kept the Dutch fighting fleet engaged.

Night fell with fifty-six Dutch merchantmen in Blake's possession. By then, he knew that Tromp had exhausted his ammunition. Eagerly, he awaited the next day, knowing it would see the final, complete destruction of Tromp's fleet.

But there was to be no battle on the fourth day. During the night Tromp had managed to get his flat-bottomed vessels into the shallows where the deep-keeled English vessels could not follow. All day Blake stalked the Dutch ships as they sailed north, but he waited in vain for another chance to attack. Tromp stuck to the shallows all the way back to Holland.

The frustrated English fleet turned away at last and sailed home to a wildly jubilant country. For if Blake had not finished Tromp off, he had come very near to doing so. As the *Triumph* crawled into port, Blake—wracked with a fever brought on by his scarcely tended wound—sat in his cabin tallying the results of the three-day battle: Sunk or captured: 19 Dutch warships, 56 Dutch merchant ships.

The heavy, melancholy landlubber had achieved a tremendous victory over the best seaman the Dutch could boast. It was the victory that proved to be the turning point of the first English-Dutch War.

8

The Heaviest Man in the World

GENERAL MONCK ATTACKS

"It is believed," a London newspaper reported, "Blake will never be able to go to sea again; for one of his hamstrings is broken, and he has a continual rheum that falls into his eyes which almost blinds him."

Blake's health, never robust, had been seriously weakened by his wound. Sickness now seized him and would not let go. A full month after the Three Days' Battle, his doctor had to record the discouraging news that "General Blake mends but slowly."

Despite the newspaper's ominous prediction, Blake's greatest achievements lay still in the future. But for the time he kept to his bed, an invalid. When Tromp came back with his repaired fleet, seeking revenge, it was George Monck who led the English fleet out to battle.

Monck was, like Blake, a landlubber. But he was unlike Blake in every other way. His command at sea was not the peak, but merely one passing phase, of his many-faceted career. If Blake was the perfect civil servant, Monck was the perfect soldier of fortune.

He was handsome, hard, rough-mannered—a fighting man pure and simple. Born of good family, bred to rule, he had been schooled by the savagery of battle. He was rigidly loyal to his command, devoted to his fighters, and contemptuous of all who could not fight or who fought poorly. Monck seemed a throwback to the Elizabethan swashbucklers—a reincarnation of his distant kinsman Grenville, the man who had stood off fifty-three Spanish ships with the lone *Revenge*. His prescription for avoiding internal strife in England was typical of him: "The principal and able remedy against civil war is to entertain a foreign war. This chaseth away idleness, setteth all on work, and particularly giveth satisfaction to ambitious and stirring spirits."

George Monck looked on war as an art, to be cultivated in detail and constantly practiced. Fighting was all he knew, or cared to know. The basis of all his strategy—on land or sea—was the fierce attack pressed firmly home. He believed one should attack against odds, attack when in doubt, attack when all seemed lost. To hold back meant to lose. Attack brought victory. He was not a brilliant man, certainly; he was too single-minded to be brilliant. But for brilliance, he substituted raw nerve and death-grip tenacity. Had he lived in peacetime he might have been considered no more than a pugnacious bore. But Monck was lucky enough to live in a time of constant wars, and they provided him with an ideal métier. Before Monck died, Pepys was forced to say: "The blockhead hath strange luck to be loved, though he be (and every man must know it) the heaviest man in the world; but stout and honest to his country."

George Monck's first recorded fight took place when he was sixteen. His father, Sir Thomas Monck, was so deeply in debt at the time that to keep out of the clutches of angry creditors he was forced to remain locked within the walls of the family estate, Potheridge, in North Devon. When one fall day in 1625 Charles I rode by on his way toward Plymouth, however, Sir Thomas Monck's position demanded that he be on hand to greet the passing king. He sent his sixteen-year-old son, George, to bribe the under-sheriff of Devonshire not to arrest him for his debts; but as soon as the creditors learned that their quarry was out of Potheridge, they offered a larger bribe and Sir Thomas was arrested.

George, when he learned of the under-sheriff's treachery, stormed into the man's office, yanked him from behind his desk, and began mercilessly beating him. At sixteen, he had already achieved his full height and possessed more strength than many grown men. He might have killed the under-sheriff if people outside, hearing the thuds and screams, had not rushed in and dragged him off his victim.

In any case, thrashing a law official was a serious matter, and young George Monck, realizing that he faced jail at home, hurried to Plymouth and joined the king's army, which was embarking for an expedition against Cadiz.

George Monck, fighting on the losing side at Cadiz, on the Isle of Ré, and at Rochelle, found a home in the army and a profession in soldiering. He loved the excitement, the danger, the challenge. From the first, his superiors began to mark him as a youth to watch. No matter what the odds, the boy would charge into the enemy, brandishing the weapon that would always be his favorite, the deadly-pointed pike, and yelling his head off. Many were afraid to follow where he led; those who, stirred by his example, did follow performed as they never had before. He was only eighteen when, after carrying an important dispatch through an entire alerted enemy army, he was commissioned an ensign.

George Monck craved fighting as other men crave drink. When England found herself briefly at peace, he joined the volunteer English brigade fighting in the Thirty Years' War for the Netherlands against the renewed assaults of Spain. The command of the whole regiment falling temporarily on his shoulders after his colonel was killed, he handled his troops so expertly that he was promoted to captain at twenty-three. During six years of fighting with the English brigade, Monck became known as the man to lead any assault. He was the first man to storm through the breach in the walls of Breda on the day the city was finally entered after its desperate siege. He returned to England with a reputation and without a scratch. But he soon craved action again, and got it as a lieutenant-colonel in the king's army. First in the war to put down the Scottish revolt, and then in the fight against the Irish uprising, his daring exploits built him into a living legend.

When the battle lines were drawn between the Parliamentary forces and the Royalists, George Monck sided with the Royalists, though with no great enthusiasm. Like most professional soldiers, he cared little about politics. His loyalty was to England—and the king, as he saw it, was the leader of England. In 1644 he was taken prisoner.

From the first, he was a very special prisoner. Other officers were exchanged as the civil war went on, but not Monck. Cromwell and the other Parliamentary leaders considered him too dangerous a weapon to be handed back to the Royalists in exchange for any officer of their own. Instead, they tried to persuade Monck to switch to the Parliamentary side. He replied with ripe curses. He might not hold any real political convictions either way, but he did hold a commission as the king's officer. The offer to switch sides in mid-war he considered a vile insult to his honor. And so he remained throughout the rest of the civil war, a lonely prisoner in his room in the Tower of London.

He was not as lonely as he might have been, however. A young woman named Ann Ratsford, the wife of a local perfumer, came to the Tower from time to time to earn much-needed extra money by mending the clothes of well-to-do prisoners. Ann's husband was dull, and Monck was dashing. Monck was bored, and Mrs. Ratsford diverting. The two consoled each other so well that in time Ann was estranged from her husband. And when Monck was finally released in 1647, she went with him.

When Monck left the Tower, Cromwell again urged him to accept a commission in the Parliamentary army. This time, Monck saw no reason to refuse. The civil war was over; the king he'd served was dead. Monck's loyalty was to England, and the new government of England was still fighting the old war against the Irish rebels. He expected a colonel's commission, but instead found himself appointed Lieutenant-General.

Monck so well justified Cromwell's appraisal of his worth—in Ireland and later fighting the still-rebellious Scots—that by the time Blake and Tromp fired the cannons that opened the war between England and Holland, he was the most famous soldier in the country. Since this war was fought entirely on the ocean, and loyal sea commanders were scarce, Monck soon found himself commanding from the deck of a ship as one of Cromwell's three top "generals-at-sea." The fact that he knew little of the sea didn't worry him. As far as he was concerned, a battle was a battle, on land or sea. Now, with just one sea fight under his belt— the Three Days' Battle led by Blake—and Blake invalided, he found himself in command of one hundred ships, sailing out to take on Tromp.

The first article of Monck's faith was always that to attack was to win, but this time Tromp was determined to play a defensive game. The Three Days' Battle had taught him a lesson: Ship-for-ship, the Dutch delivered less fire power than the English, and did not stand up as well under steady pounding.

So, early on the second morning of June, 1653, when Tromp sighted Monck's hundred warships rushing toward him pell-mell

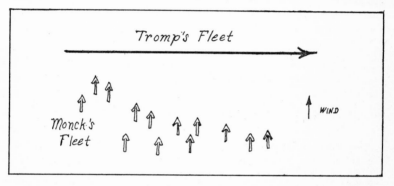

with the driving wind in their sails, he made no attempt to gain the weather gauge. Instead, he strung his ships out in a line-ahead— that is, following one another in a single file—beyond the mouth of the Thames, and awaited the Englishmen's coming. For by taking this position, he achieved an initial superiority of fire power. Until the attacking English actually reached Tromp's line, and could then swing side-by-side with them, they would be able to hit at the Dutch with only their few bow guns. All the while, every ship in Tromp's line could fire broadsides into the oncoming English.

Monck intended to fight now as he always had on land: charging straight in without considering the cost. The end result of coming to grips with the enemy at close quarters and slugging it out, he felt, justified a costly means. Together with Richard Deane, Monck exulted in the powerful forward thrust of his flagship, the *Resolution*, as it drew nearer the long line of Dutch warships. He was in too much of a hurry to take the time to group his fleet in any kind of formation. Close off the starboard rode Vice-Admiral Penn's flagship. Up ahead, Lawson's flagship and two others were outdistancing the *Resolution*. But the bulk of Monck's fleet straggled behind him.

From their poop deck, Monck and Deane watched Lawson's three ships close on Tromp's silent line. Lawson drove in, his bow guns trying a few ranging shots that tore Dutch canvas. A moment later, the sides of a dozen Dutch ships directly ahead of Lawson suddenly belched flame and smoke. The broadsides crashed into the bows of Lawson's three ships, staggering them.

Monck bellowed for his flag captain to crowd on more sail. The *Resolution* leaped ahead and ploughed into Lawson's wake. Monck, hunched forward as though attacking on foot with his favorite pike in hand, scanned the nearing Dutch walls, the gaping mouths of tier after tier of Dutch guns. Abruptly, more than a hundred of those guns exploded in deafening, blinding unison. A storm of lethal chain shot—two iron balls linked by a length of chain—swept across the *Resolution's* decks.

In the midst of the crashing carnage, Monck felt a rush of wind pass his side, heard distinctly a tearing of flesh, a thud. He whirled to see Richard Deane's blood-drenched body lying on the deck, torn in two by a chain shot that had caught him just above the hips. As others crowded round to stare, Monck straightened and roared at them: "Get back to your business!"

Pulling off his cloak, he draped it over Deane's remains. Then he returned his attention to the battle.

The *Resolution,* hurt by the first onslaught but not crippled, plunged into the Dutch line. The instant there were Dutch hulls to port and starboard, every gun aboard the *Resolution* joined in two salvos that opened the bow to one side, demolished the stern on the other. But Monck, Lawson and the other English ships that led the way were caught in a juggernaut of pounding, ripping metal from Tromp's superior number of ships. They took a terrible mauling.

Each fresh English ship brought down the odds, but the rest of Monck's fleet joined with straggling slowness. For hours, the total fire power of Tromp's fleet remained superior to that of Monck's slowly growing force. It was not till midafternoon that all the English ships finally were engaged, and Monck began to reap the advantage of his heavier ship-for-ship gunnery.

Tromp, however, had no intention of submitting his fleet to the full force of the English guns. He had planned the battle carefully.

So long as Monck's ships remained fewer than his own he would fight. But as soon as the entire English fleet engaged—and tipped the scales—Tromp neatly disengaged. Slipping his line expertly out of Monck's bearish grasp, he fled out of gun range.

Monck saw his attack close around empty water. Furious at what he considered Tromp's cowardly refusal to stand still and do battle, he pursued the Dutch under all sail.

Despite what the English general might think of his tactics, Tromp had come to fight, and he intended to stay and win. But nothing Monck could do would prevent him from fighting in the manner he thought best for his own fleet. He had put the English fleet at a disadvantage at the beginning and he would keep them there. As Monck closed in again, Tromp's line slanted away in perfect order, again hurling broadsides into the oncoming British bows and dodging off before the entire English force could come to grips with them. Tromp kept this edge as long as daylight lasted.

Night settled on a sorely frustrated Monck, but one grown a bit wiser too. When it came to fighting, Monck was willing to learn something new. Now he had learned that there was some difference between a sea fight and a battle on land. He still held to the all-out attack as the key to victory. But there were others in his fleet who knew more than he about exactly how to press home that attack on the water.

He summoned Penn, Lawson, and the other experienced seamen among his officers to his ripped and patched flagship. Facing them in his great cabin under the poop, he bluntly told them what he wanted to do, and asked them how to do it, adding for emphasis, "Your advice shall be as binding on me as an Act of Parliament."

They told him.

The next day dawned on an absolute calm. The two enemy fleets lay frozen by the lack of wind, just out of range of each other off Ostend.

Monck waited.

At noon, the slack sails began to fill with a wind that increased steadily through the rest of the day. The English attacked immediately.

As on the previous day, Tromp had strung his fleet out in a tight line-ahead, broadsides to the oncoming enemy bows. But this time everything else was different.

The English fleet drove into the teeth of Tromp's broadsides in three tightly formed lines, side by side. Monck led one line, Penn another, Lawson the third. Keeping pace with each other, they arrowed into Tromp's ships at three separate points, the three English squadrons immediately on the heels of their leaders. The whole English fleet engaged so swiftly that Tromp had little time to take advantage of his brief superiority of fire power.

This time there was no deft withdrawal of Tromp's line: he had no time to withdraw. Monck's attack had broken his fleet into three separate segments, two of which no longer responded to the

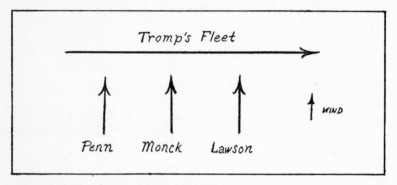

will of their leader. And each segment was caught in the grip of an adhesively clinging English squadron.

Now the battle belonged to the gunners. Below deck, the hot English gun decks resounded like the insides of pounding drums. The crews worked their big weapons with steady ferocity—hauling, swabbing, loading, shoving, aiming, firing. Blinded by the acid smoke and searing flashes of flame, deafened by the steady booming concussions, their hands burned by the scorching metal of their guns, they poured their massive shots into the half-seen enemy hulls.

But if the English gun decks were hot, the Dutch gun decks were infernos. Inside them the chances of survival steadily lessened as the heavy English iron shot burst in through gunports, dismantling cannons and crushing gun crews. It was like being locked inside a box through which sword after sword was being thrust.

Since the lighter Dutch shot mostly bounced off the thick English hulls, the Dutch gunners aimed high. They might tear English sails and rigging, smash English spars and masts, and dash men off the English decks, but they left the English gunners relatively untouched. And as the Dutch gun decks were rapidly reduced to slaughterhouse shambles Dutch fire steadily lessened.

The Dutch captains, watching others of their fleet founder, and feeling their own ships being torn apart under them, found it hard to control the impulse to break away from the battle and run for safety. Then, late in the day, the panicky ones saw something that gave them the final push. Over the horizon sailed eighteen fresh English warships, ploughing straight toward the roaring battle center. When the Dutch saw the flag of the new squadron's admiral, panic became rout.

It was Blake, out of his sickbed.

From the coast, he had listened to the continuing sound of the guns beyond the ocean horizon. Finally, unable to stand it any longer, he had rushed to his ship, gathered this squadron, and raced out to join the battle.

Blake's added weight, hurled against Tromp's already inferior numbers, tipped the scales. The bulk of Tromp's fleet turned and fled home. Tromp, unable to bring them back to order, was forced to follow them.

Monck and Blake stuck with them, keeping up a close running cannonade that ripped and clawed the Dutch fleet to shreds. Not until dark did the smashed remains of Tromp's flat-bottomed ships gain the haven of their shallow coastal waters. Twenty of them never made it.

The English fleet returned home with its prizes and its victory. The Dutch government sued for peace but found Cromwell's peace terms too harsh to accept. There was no choice but for Tromp and his countrymen to gird themselves for a last desperate fight.

For two months, Monck had been blockading the Dutch coast with Penn, Lawson, and almost a hundred ships. He knew that a fleet of eighty warships was being fitted for sea under Tromp in Flushing; that another of thirty ships was being readied under De Witt in Texel. But he couldn't take his heavy, deep-keeled two-deckers across the shallows to get at them. And he was unwilling to risk sending his lighter frigates—with their single decks of guns—in by themselves. There was nothing for him to do but wait until the Dutch considered their fleet strong enough to sail out and take him on. In fair weather and foul, Monck maintained his station, carefully guarding against one thing in particular; he meant to be certain that the two Dutch fleets were given no chance to get at each other and join.

Tromp was just as determined that Monck would not prevent his and De Witt's fleet units from joining. When his fleet was ready, he sat down and worked out a game of moves and counter-moves. If it had been simply a matter of force against force, Monck could have stopped the Dutch commander. But there was only one man who could outguess the wily, agile Tromp, and Blake was suffering a relapse so severe that he could hardly stand. Tromp bided his time until the coast was slashed by summer storms. Then, one blustery morning late in July, he sailed out across the shallows—and Monck's eight weeks of careful blockading might just as well have never taken place.

Under the whine of the rigging, Monck braced himself on the deck of the *Resolution* against the driving offshore wind and watched Tromp come on toward him with his eighty frigates and two-deckers, plus five fireships. Surprised but delighted that Tromp was willing to fight with his smaller fleet, Monck ordered his own ships to stand ready. That Tromp had the weather gauge bothered him very little; he could count on his superiority in ships and gunnery to offset that.

The two fleets were almost in range of each other when the wind suddenly shifted, began driving from the English towards the Dutch. This was even better, as far as Monck was concerned. He ran up the signal for attack, and raced toward the enemy.

Tromp, however, instead of waiting for the attack, turned tail and ran before the wind. Tromp crowded on all sail, but Monck surged after him, sticking tenaciously, following wherever he led. Tromp headed south—into a heavy rainstorm through which Monck could barely see the fleeing Dutch ships. Night fell, and Monck lost sight of them entirely.

Morning found Tromp—not ahead of Monck to the south, but far behind him on the northern horizon. He had doubled back through the darkness, as he had planned to do from the start, and was beating his way up toward Texel.

Cursing, Monck came about with his whole fleet and raced north in pursuit. But it was too late. By the time he caught Tromp, the Dutchman was standing off the coast and waiting for him, his fleet reinforced by De Witt's thirty ships. Now the combined Dutch fleet outnumbered the English. Now Tromp was ready to fight.

Monck knew he had been outwitted but he wasted no time in berating himself. His fighter's face was dangerously taut as he gave his orders for the battle: Give no quarter, take no quarter. This was going to be a fight to the finish.

That was the way Tromp wanted it, too. The Dutch would win this day or never. His country's resources had been squeezed dry to fashion this fleet.

The two fleets—each ranged out in a long line-ahead—sailed parallel to each other, gradually closing the distance between them. Here and there, single guns boomed, testing the range, then testing it again. Finally, the two enemy lines were close enough for their shots to strike home. The ocean rocked with the convulsion of over two hundred broadsides letting go at each other.

The thunder of it rolled across the water and beat against the dunes of the Dutch coast, which were lined with people come out to watch the battle. By the time the muffled explosions reached them, the two fleets had vanished in a cloudbank of gray-black smoke shot through with sheets of flame.

Within that obscuring mass of drifting smoke, the two enemy lines edged closer to each other, their guns continuing the smashing slaughter. Tromp, having kept the weather gauge, now lighted his fireships and set them adrift before the wind. As Monck saw them rolling his way, he ordered his line to open, then close after they passed. But this was easier said than done. One of his ships became entangled with a floating torch and went up in flames; then another, and another.

Suddenly, Monck tacked, in an attempt to pierce Tromp's line and break it apart. Tromp tacked to prevent it, succeeded, and then tacked again with the idea of himself cutting through the English line. Monck dodged back in time. Each line tried again, was frustrated, then tried once more. Mile after mile, the two fleets zigzagged their way across the water, closer and closer to each other, pounding at each other all the while with unremitting fury. The din was tremendous. Thousands of heavy cast-iron balls did their terrible work against wood, canvas, rope and flesh. "The very heavens were obscured with smoke," one of the ship's officers recorded; "the air rent with the thundering noise; the sea all in a breach with the shot that fell; the ships even trembling, and we hearing everywhere the messengers of death flying about."

The Dutch and English lines had zigzagged their way across forty miles of ocean when a shift in wind suddenly gave Monck the extra push he needed. Instantly, he tacked his line again— and this time arrowed through the rear of Tromp's line, smashing away several of the last Dutch ships and sinking them within minutes.

Now the two fleets were locked side by side at point-blank distance—less than three hundred paces apart. Most of Monck's ships carried demicannons that hurled shot weighing 32 pounds. A few of his largest ships mounted 42-pounders on the lower gun deck. Against these, the heaviest guns at Tromp's command were 24-pounders. But at this close range, even 24-pounders could punch through the stout English walls. If they could not disable and sink, as the heavier English shot did, they could at least break into wooden armor, and kill. The death rate in the gun decks down inside the hulls was fantastic. Little powder-monkey boys, who raced back and forth between the powder stores and the guns carrying bags of powder charges in their leather passing boxes, had to twist their way through a maze of stove-in timbers, over-turned cannons, dead gunners.

The guns of both fleets were being fired as quickly as they could be loaded. Once the guns became overheated they were supposed to be allowed to cool off. But now there was no time. They went on firing until they were too hot to touch. Some began recoiling wildly against their breechings, breaking the cap squares that secured their trunnions to the brackets of their carriages. Others overturned, trucks and all. Others blew up as linstocks touched vents, killing all their handlers.

Still the cannonading went on. And as it happened, it was not the great guns below decks that determined which side should have victory, but a single musket ball.

The two fleets were so closely engaged now that marksmen in the rigging began firing down at enemy decks through the billowing smoke—aiming for officers on deck.

On the poop of the quaking *Brederode* stood old Tromp, deftly directing the movements of the Dutch fleet. An English two-decker came through the smoke haze and bore in close. Tromp's guns raked its decks, knocked over a mast, drove it off. A frigate swept in, slipping by so close that it almost brushed the *Brederode's* stern as it passed. The patter of metal hail rained down on the planks around Tromp. He raised his haggard face to stare upward at the marksmen in the English masts. A musket ball struck his chest, drove in through his heart. Tromp collapsed on his deck with a deep moan. He was unconscious within seconds, dead within minutes.

The command of the fleet now fell on Vice-Admiral Evertsen, who took it up as soon as the news reached his ship. But at either end of the long Dutch line, far away and obscured by the drifting smoke, were squadron leaders unaware that Tromp was dead. When Monck tacked his fleet for another try at a break-through, the Dutch squadron leaders looked to the *Brederode* for signals. Seeing none, they became confused. They began to maneuver on their own, commanding their separate battles instead of straining to hold the temporarily masterless line intact. Evertsen signaled for a defensive tack; but Ruyter, not seeing the signal, kept his squadron on its old course; De Witt took his squadron off in another direction.

The full weight of Monck's furious onslaught hurtled into Evertsen's unsupported squadron. Within a half hour the Dutch fleet was again without a commander. Evertsen's crumpled flagship, heeled over until the waves licked the ends of its yardarms, was sinking under him. The Dutch command now automatically settled upon De Witt. But De Witt, off fighting his separate squadron battle, did not know it.

The masterless Dutch fleet came apart completely. Monck hurled his fleet at the separate pieces, destroyed them, swept on. Soon the Dutch were outnumbered. Yet they fought on through the long terrible afternoon, fought valiantly. Ship after ship of the Dutch fleet was blown out of the water by the big English guns, or reduced to dismasted pieces of junk drifting out of the battle. Some exploded into flame and burned to the waterline.

Desperately, the Dutch tried to cut out Monck's flagship. Several of them managed to close in for a boarding attempt. But Monck let them get just so close—and then his *Resolution's* guns sent them reeling back, wrecked and dripping blood from the scuppers.

At last, unable to take more, the remaining ships of the Dutch fleet dragged themselves into the safety of their coastal shallows. Tromp was dead. Twenty of their ships were gone. They were beaten.

But the English had gotten off anything but lightly. Monck's crews had been decimated by over one thousand casualties. Eight of his captains were dead. His ships were so shattered that his fleet was unable to continue the desired blockade of Dutch shipping and had to creep back to England.

The eighteen months of war and the blockade had already ruined the merchant trade and fisheries upon which the Dutch economy rested. This battle was the final blow. The Dutch people —exhausted, impoverished—had nothing left to fight with, and were forced at last to surrender to Cromwell's hard peace terms.

Monck, the hero of the day in England, rode home through cheering crowds—home to his mistress, Ann Ratsford, and her tearful welcome: she was going to bear his baby. Quickly and ungrudgingly, George Monck married her.

Then, having done his duty as he saw it, he left his bride and home to return to the world stage. But not, for the moment, to the sea.

9

"... for the honour of the fleet"

A MIRACLE AT SANTA CRUZ

Robert Blake entered the Mediterranean in 1655 with a small, strongly armed fleet, a determined spirit, and a troubled mind.

The dark gray Atlantic slipped away behind the high stern of his flagship, the *George*. His heeling ships, wafted eastward by the gentle wind, left trailing wakes of white foam across water of incredible blue. But Blake saw no beauty in this ocean. To him it presented a jumble of problems, the combined weight of which was enough to stagger the strongest of men. And Blake was far from strong. The rigors of the sea and the spartan life aboard a man-of-war had already begun to undermine his health again. He was in no condition to withstand the anxiety that plucked at his nerves.

Together with Monck, Blake had established England's domination over her coastal waters and the narrow seas between her and the shores of northern Europe. Now Oliver Cromwell, Lord Protector of England, had sent him to establish respect for the English flag in the Mediterranean. But beyond this, all was vague. Exactly how he was to accomplish his mission here had been left up to him. He had complete freedom of action. England simply wanted him "to do something." Yet he had no guarantee that England would back up whatever he did do.

Take the problem of Spain: Cromwell had told the Spanish ambassador that Philip IV, king of Spain, must stop subjecting English citizens to the Inquisition, and must allow English merchants to trade in America. To which the ambassador had replied: "My master has but two eyes, and you ask him for both." Blake was in the Mediterranean to help bend Spain to Cromwell's will. But how—without starting an open war?

Take the problem of the Italian State of Tuscany, whose port of Leghorn had sheltered the Royalist privateers under Prince Rupert. Italy was to be taught a lesson, and be made to pay for the captured English ships and goods bought from Rupert. But how?

Take the problem of the Barbary pirate nations of North Africa. They seized English merchant ships, made slaves of captured English men and women. There were Englishmen now chained in the slave-prisons of Tunis and Algiers who must be freed. The Barbary States—and all the other nations lining the Mediterranean —must be taught to respect the flag of the smallest English vessel, the person of the meanest English citizen. But how?

Another man might have been content with a mere show of power—a sail around the Mediterranean with his war fleet. But it was not in Blake to use his lack of instructions as an excuse for protecting himself by an avoidance of direct action. He knew, as the *George* carried him across the vivid blue sea toward Italy, that he would have to do whatever seemed right when the time came, and take his chances with England's reaction.

Italy first. Blake drew up his fleet of warships before the port of Leghorn, ran out his guns, and sent his ultimatum ashore: The Duke of Tuscany must pay for all English prizes captured by Rupert while his Royalist fleet had operated from that port.

The sight of those guns—and the knowledge of what they had done to the famous Dutch navy—decided the Duke of Tuscany in a hurry. He paid as much as he could. As for the rest of the huge sum Blake demanded, the Duke pointed out that the Royalist privateers had sold many of their prizes to the Papal States.

Blake made sure he had squeezed Tuscany dry, then sailed his fleet to Civitavecchia. He informed Rome that unless paid promptly, he would bring his ships up the Tiber and bombard the Eternal City itself. His stern face and flat words left no doubt that he meant it. Rome paid: sixty thousand ducats.

So far, so good. His first mission was accomplished and without a shot having been fired. Now, if strong words and the sight of fighting ships would only suffice with the Barbary rulers. . . . Blake sailed south to North Africa.

But words were not enough with the Dey of Algiers. Blake demanded that the Algerian ruler release all English captives. The Dey refused. Blake tried threats. The Dey was unmoved. Fuming, Blake offered to pay ransom money for the prisoners. The Dey shook his head; the sum Blake was willing to pay was not enough. Bluff had worked with Italy, but not here. The Dey of Algiers had called the English bluff.

Frustrated but unwilling to risk war unless it became absolutely necessary, Blake left Algiers and sailed his fleet to Tunis. But bluff failed there, too. When Blake threatened violence unless the English captives were released, the contemptuous Pasha of Tunis anchored nine mighty warships before the mole inside his "impregnable" fortress-harbor of Porto Farina—and dared Blake to come in and fight.

Blake had reached the point of no return. He had come to these waters to establish respect for the English flag. He had made a specific threat. If he backed down now, he might as well slink out of the Mediterranean and admit he had failed in his mission. Aboard his flagship, Blake studied the plan of Porto Farina. The inner shores of the harbor were lined with thick-walled fortifications from which poked the snouts of heavy guns. It was universally believed impossible, in those days, for wooden-hulled ships to wage a duel with solid shore batteries. But Blake was not so sure. He thought he saw a way. . . .

The Pasha of Tunis had every reason to smile contemptuously as he watched Blake's fifteen ships sail away over the blue horizon. Six days later, however, dawn revealed that English fleet coming back fast under fighting sails, all guns run out.

The defenders of Porto Farina rushed to the shore batteries, the guns of which, they were confident, would soon reduce the foolhardy English ships to wreckage. All they noticed about the gale-force wind that churned the surface of the Bay of Tunis was that it was blowing Blake's fleet straight toward the forts and waiting warships anchored before the mole. But Blake foresaw that the gale would blow more than his ships against Porto Farina. It was the very thing he had been waiting for.

As the *George* surged into the bay, Blake seemed to be sailing straight into the open, sharp-fanged jaws of destruction. But his face was composed, impassive; his orders delivered in an even tone.

His fleet pulled apart into two squadrons as it sailed through the entrance of the bay. The eight frigates, with their single main gun decks and shallow keels, drove toward the nine anchored Tunisian cruisers. Blake's flagship, with his six other heavier two-deckers, swung in against the shore forts.

In the past, Blake had saved his fire until he was close to an enemy. But this time his ships fired every single gun the moment they entered the bay, and fired again and again, as rapidly as his gun crews could reload—even before they were in range of anything. The Tunisian reply was instantaneous. Every ship and fort in Porto Farina opened up as Blake's roaring fleet charged in through the entrance.

For a moment, a dense pall of gunsmoke shrouded the bay. Then Blake watched what he had pictured in his imagination: the wind, driving in from the sea, hurled all that smoke against the shore batteries and anchored ships of the enemy. Hidden by this smoke screen, Blake's fleet pushed deep into the bay—his frigates anchoring within musket shot of the Tunisian cruisers, his two-deckers close to the forts.

The steady gale kept blowing all the smoke of battle back against the Tunisian gunners. They were firing completely blind. Most of their shots were wasted ploughing up the waters of the bay; the few that struck Blake's ships did so only by chance.

The English warships, on the other hand, with the smoke constantly blown away from them, were able to sight their targets. Blake watched with heavy satisfaction as his gunners aimed carefully and drilled their shots in with unerring accuracy.

Through a long hour of this steady, one-sided bombardment, then through another, and a third, the heavy guns of his barely touched two-deckers pulverized the fort walls to rubble, demolished the shore batteries, and began scoring direct hits on the exposed Tunisian cannons. His frigates hacked away at the enemy cruisers, knocking over their masts, sweeping their decks, hammering their hulls. Blake waited until barely a score of enemy guns were left firing; then signals were run up to the *George's* tops. Boarding parties pushed away from his frigates, rowed to the wrecked Tunisian warships, scrambled up the splintered sides with pike, sword and pistol.

The English boarders charged the few remaining defenders and drove them overboard, set fire to the abandoned wrecks, and rowed back to the frigates. By the time Blake took his fleet out of the bay, the harbor of Porto Farina was a ruin and the Pasha's nine cruisers—his entire navy—burned to ashes.

The Pasha, proving himself a reasonable man, hastily came to terms on the English prisoners and promised to be careful about English shipping in the future.

Blake sailed back to Algiers. The news of Porto Farina had raced ahead of him and he found the Dey of Algiers' attitude now completely changed—as sweetly ready to talk terms as the ruler of Tunis.

But Blake was deeply worried about England's reaction to his unauthorized attack on a foreign ruler. He sat for hours at his desk in his stern cabin, formulating a carefully worded report to Cromwell. "Their barbarous provocations," he explained, "did so work upon our spirits that we judged it necessary for the honour of the fleet, our nation and religion, seeing that they would not deal with us as friends, to make them feel us as enemies. . . ."

The Barbary States had indeed "felt" Blake. All the Mediterranean now felt him—and the might of the English navy.

Blake was in the Spanish port of Malaga loading food and water when some of his crew who had been granted shore leave came staggering back to their ship, bloody and battered. A monk leading a Catholic procession, they said, had incited a crowd of Spaniards to attack "the heretics." When Blake's demand that the Malaga authorities turn the offending monk over to him for hanging was refused, he ran out his guns and threatened to bombard the harbor.

The Malaga authorities, with the news of Porto Farina fresh in their ears, quickly sent the offending monk to the English flagship. Blake was waiting for him on the quarter-deck, prepared for the hanging. But the monk's explanation of what had really happened changed his mind. The sailors, the monk told Blake, had jeered and hooted insults at the religious procession.

Agreeing that his beaten men had provoked the assault upon

them—and feeling he had already upheld the honor of his flag by making the Spaniards deliver up the monk—he sent him back ashore unharmed; but with a stern warning that the next time an Englishman did something wrong in a Spanish port hands were to be kept off and the offense reported to the British authorities. No one must touch an Englishman but another Englishman.

When word of this incident—together with the news of Porto Farina—reached England, Cromwell, vastly pleased, boasted: "I will make the name of Englishman to be as much dreaded as ever was the name of Roman Citizen!"

Relieved that his actions had been approved at home, Blake went on to his next task. This was not to be like the flashing thrust at Porto Farina; it was the dreary, unending work of a 27-month-long blockade.

By the spring of 1655, Cromwell, eager to get his hands on some of those treasure ships that still arrived in Spain from America, was pushing toward a state of war with Spain. To intercept these ships, and blockade all shipping in and out of Spanish ports, was Blake's next assignment.

In those days, it was extremely difficult to keep a fleet at sea far from home for any long stretch of time. With few foreign ports open for repairs and supplies, hulls became rotted, food ran out, men died of scurvy. But for two years—with only a few short returns to England—Blake kept his ships off the coasts of Spain, capturing one rich treasure fleet and sending it back to England. Extended cruising in bad weather was especially arduous for the vessels of that time. But Blake at one point blockaded Cadiz through an entire fall and winter of stormy weather without once touching shore. If his fleet suffered under such punishment, Blake suffered as much. The old sickness, begun by his wound in the Three Days' Battle with Tromp, was back with him. He became subject to burning fevers, agonizing cramps. His dispatches to Cromwell contained pitiful pleas for release from this duty. But he was doing too good a job to be released as yet.

By the time the long blockade drew to an end, Blake was so weak he could barely stand. But he still had strength to perform one final "impossible" task: the fabulous assault on Santa Cruz de Tenerife.

The Spanish treasure fleet of sixteen ships for which Blake had waited all winter dodged into the protection of Santa Cruz.

It seemed to be the safest place in the world for it—the one place where Blake wouldn't dare follow. But Blake did follow. "The whole action," an old historian said in describing his attack on Santa Cruz, "was so miraculous, that all men who knew the place wondered that any sober man would ever have undertaken it."

This was to be Blake's crowning achievement. His chess player's mind tackled—one by one—the factors that made an attack on Santa Cruz impossible. And, one by one, he nullified them all.

Blake arrived off the bay of Santa Cruz in the middle of April, 1657, and cruised back and forth past the entrance, taking a hard, calculating look for himself. He counted the warships inside the bay, giving them time to study his fleet in turn. The Spanish warships made no effort to come out after him, but they did form up inside—just in case. The governor of Santa Cruz, Don Diego Diagues, was certain that Blake would not attack—and even more certain that if he did, the whole English fleet would be obliterated. For if Porto Farina had been considered impregnable, Santa Cruz bay was twenty times more so.

To sail into it would be like diving into a vast wine bottle. The entrance of the bay, the neck of the bottle, was long and narrow. The bay itself was deep. The harbor where the treasure ships were moored was at the end of this bay, at the bottom of the bottle. To get at the treasure fleet. Blake would not only have to fight past the Spanish warships, he would also have to contend with the heavily gunned forts on either side of the entrance and on the shores of the inner bay itself.

But the most formidable defenses of Santa Cruz were neither its ships nor forts but the high hills that surrounded the bay and kept any steady wind from blowing into it from the shore. Once inside the bay, Blake might not be able to get out. And if his ships once got stuck in the middle of the bay, the shore guns must eventually—even if it required days—pound them apart.

The most heavily armed forts of Santa Cruz were at the entrance of the bay. Blake's first problem was to get his fleet past these forts and inside the bay, where their guns could not be aimed at him. Now, as at Porto Farina, he waited for the right wind at the right time. On the dawn of the twentieth of April, conditions were perfect.

Blake ran up his signal. With all sails set, his ships swept into the long, narrow entrance. A strong shoreward breeze combined with the inrushing morning tide to hurl them through at top speed—so fast that the guns of the entrance forts got only a few tries at the English fleet before it was through the entrance and into the bay, out of their range. The English ships were hit hard in that short time, but they all survived. The first obstacle was behind them.

Now they must face the Spanish ships, divided into two groups. Six big war galleons were anchored in a line so that they could hurl their broadsides against the oncoming enemy. Between this first battle line and the harbor at the bottom of the bay were ten smaller ships, also anchored with their broadsides to the entrance. All sixteen ships were thus prepared to join the shore batteries in pounding the English fleet.

Blake instantly saw that what the Spaniards had actually done was to diminish their *effective* fire power by more than half. For those six anchored galleons were between him and the harbor; by pressing his attack closely against the galleons, he could turn them into a shield for himself. The ten Spanish ships on the other side of them—and the forts beyond those ten—could not strike at Blake without endangering their own ships.

Dividing his fleet into two squadrons, Blake sent the larger one in to trade broadsides with the six anchored galleons. His second squadron he led against the fortifications of the bay shore. The shore here was high, but though the forts smashed their shots down on Blake's decks, he staggered through the barrage and sailed right up to the shore under the forts. By the time he anchored he was so close that half the fort guns above him could not be depressed far enough to bear on his ships, and were thus rendered useless. Then Blake's gunners began to let go, giving the shore batteries a foretaste of the kind of pounding that had reduced the fortress walls of Porto Farina to rubble.

Again, as at Porto Farina, the offshore wind blew the battle smoke against the enemy, partially blinding them, while the English gunners had a clear view of their victims.

All day long, Blake battered the forts, caving in their walls and overturning their big guns. During that time, he watched his other squadron smash each of the six big Spanish galleons into surrender and then push on, still using the six captured vessels as a shield, against the ten smaller treasure ships. All ten surrendered in short order.

But with all the ships in the bay in English hands, Blake lost the great advantage he had held up until now. The big batteries of the harbor suddenly came alive with a rumbling crash. The first salvos tore into the shield of surrendered vessels, and before long they were sinking. Once they slipped below the water, Blake knew, his fleet would be starkly exposed. It was time to get out of Santa Cruz bay.

There was no hope of towing out the smashed treasure ships against a breeze that still blew into the bay. But if they could not be taken with him, they could be destroyed—and in such a way as to protect his retreat. Dusk was approaching as Blake gave the order for every one of the sixteen Spanish ships to be put to the torch. When the English sailed away from the harbor, the flames and rolling smoke of the sixteen burning wrecks completely obliterated them from the view of the shore batteries, which could only shoot blindly in their general direction, scoring few hits.

Then, when the English ships were almost to the entrance of the bay, the sea breeze, against which Blake was slowly working his way out of the bay, stopped entirely. His whole fleet was becalmed.

Before long those harbor batteries would be able to see him again. But, as Blake had foreseen, with dusk came the ebbtide. As it began rushing out of the bay, it carried Blake's fleet with it to the open sea.

The news of Santa Cruz electrified the military world. Blake's achievement was considered a miracle by English navy men, witchcraft by the Spanish. But Blake had no time left to hear the acclaim. Permission to come home arrived at last, too late. The *George* carried back toward England a Blake unable to rise from his bed. Trembling with weakness, consumed by fever, and still a landsman at heart, he longed only to live long enough to die on the solid soil of his native land. He almost made it. The *George* was entering Plymouth harbor when Robert Blake died—on the sea he hated and had made his own.

10

"You must now fight with the fist"

The son of a poor beer hauler, Michael de Ruyter grew up along the Flushing docks, a fast, cocky and undisciplined boy. He was ten when his exuberance drove him to the top of the tallest church steeple in town. Workmen repairing the roof had gone to lunch, leaving their ladders in place. The Ruyter boy, chancing that way and unable to pass up such an excellent opportunity for mischief, scrambled up the ladders—all the way to the dizzy height of the cross. Balancing dangerously, he flapped his arms and chortled like a rooster, until a crowd began to gather below. One of the workmen decided to teach the boy a lesson, and pulled down the ladders, leaving Michael stranded on his lofty perch.

As Michael stood there, staring down at the raised faces of the tiny people below, knowing that they were waiting for him to cry for help, his impudent expression hardened into something else. Deliberately, he rammed the hobnail heel of his boot down on one of the steeple shingles, knocking it out of place. It slithered down and crashed to the street below. The boy rested one foot on the wooden frame joist that had held the missing shingle and dislodged

134

the next shingle below it. One after another, he kicked out shingles, descending the steeple on the wooden crosspieces underneath as easily as if they were a ladder.

His parents punished him for it, severely. But they knew it would take more than punishment to tame Michael. They apprenticed him to a ropemaker, but it was no use. Then, when he was eleven, they sent him to sea as a master mate's boy.

There was no more mischief. Sailing the oceans as a merchant sailor satisfied the young Michael de Ruyter's craving for excitement at last. He was a ship's officer by the time he was sixteen, a merchant skipper by twenty-seven. The whole world was his for roaming. He sailed to the Pacific, the Mediterranean; to South America, Africa, the East Indies, Greenland.

Unlike George Monck of England, he did not require the extra thrill of battle. But when a fight was forced on him he fought with a fierce spirit and cool nerve that drew the respect of Spaniards and Barbary pirates alike. He became a favorite all along the North African coast; and once, when his ship was wrecked in a storm, Barbary pirate-sailors even helped him retrieve the wreck and reload the cargo!

When the first English-Dutch war began, Ruyter was forty-five. Men aged fast in those days, but Ruyter was quick and agile. There was not an ounce of fat on his short, square, hard-muscled body. His face, dominated by hard brown eyes under a massive wide forehead, was burned to a permanent redness by wind and sun and deeply creased by laughter. He loved to sing at the top of his lungs—up in the rigging of his ship at sea, on the docks of Oriental seaports, before the fireplace in his home with his children gathered around him. He was a man who fully enjoyed all life's pleasures.

Perhaps he had learned to value life more than other men because of the tragic deaths that stalked his life. He married for the first time when he was a twenty-four-year-old ship's mate. Marie Velters was her name; a pretty girl of eighteen. They had only a brief honeymoon together before he sailed to South America. Ten months later he returned to find that she had died of fever. At twenty-nine he married again: Cornelie Engels, a girl of his native Flushing. As the years went by, and she bore him children, he began to desire his home more than adventure, and at last he quit the sea and settled down as a shore merchant. A year later, Cornelie was dead. Inconsolable, the forty-three-year-old Ruyter shipped out again, to seek at sea a release for his grief.

Several encounters with French pirates during the next two years enhanced Ruyter's reputation as a battler. But, with time, his bitter grief gave way to longing for his home and children. He was soon ashore again, and soon remarried. His third wife, Anne van Gelder, was the widow of a merchant skipper by whom she had had children. Like Ruyter, she had learned through sorrow how to cherish happiness. Their home quickly became a refuge of love and warmth for their children and themselves. Then, within months after their marriage, came the first war with England, and Ruyter was called to defend his country.

During his years on the sea, he had gotten to know many of the English captains he was later to fight. Men like Lawson and Penn, who had known him as a friend, were aware of his danger as an enemy. But many English commanders—men like George Monck —could not believe that a man who enjoyed himself as much as Michael de Ruyter, a man who burst into song for no reason and cherished domesticity and the "softer" side of life, was made of the stuff of a true fighter.

They learned. Three sea wars with the Dutch were to teach the English quite a lot about Ruyter. Just as they were to teach Ruyter much about war.

Although Ruyter saw his country badly beaten in the first war, he emerged with a reputation that towered over the other captains who fought under Martin Tromp. As a squadron commander, he absorbed quickly and thoroughly the lessons of sea fighting. From his admiral, Tromp, and from his chief enemy, Blake, Ruyter learned the principles of sea-war strategy and learned to temper his fighting spirit with planned skill.

The war ended, but Ruyter's duties at sea continued. His country was on the brink of economic disaster and only trade could revive it. Ruyter's naval squadron roamed the oceans, making sure that Dutch merchant vessels could sail without fear. The Straits of Gibraltar must be kept clear of pirates, Dutch trading posts in Africa defended against English forays. His country began to recover—slowly at first, then with enormous strides. Ruyter began to think he might soon be able to return to his wife and home. He was cruising the Atlantic coasts of North America when he received news that made him rush back to Holland—but not to the warmth of his home. England had declared war on the Dutch again.

"What matters this or that reason?" demanded George Monck, summing up England's eagerness for its second war against the Dutch in 1665: "What we want is more of the trade which the Dutch now have!"

Cromwell had died, leaving Monck the most powerful man in England. Without Cromwell's strength and purpose, the English republican experiment lacked the vigor to survive. And when Monck, always a Royalist at heart, brought the son of the executed Charles I back from exile and set him solidly on the throne as King Charles II, England found itself once more a monarchy.

Dashing Prince Rupert, cousin to the new king, forced to a life of privateering during Cromwell's rule, was brought back and appointed admiral of a squadron in the Royal Navy. The elegant Duke of York—younger brother of King Charles II, and one day to become King James II—was made Lord High Admiral of the English navy. And tough George Monck, raised to the peerage, became Duke of Albemarle, Earl of Torrington, Baron Monck of Potheridge, Beauchamp and Tees.

There were those who laughed at the awkward, heavy-footed figure he cut among the dandies at court, those who sneered at the vulgarity of his mistress turned Duchess-wife. But they did so in private or in whispers. For Monck had been elevated to more than a resounding title. The king took his advice, never gave him orders, would not make a move without his consent and support.

King Charles II had his own reasons for making war on the Dutch. He hated them for their republican form of government. He hated them for having complied with Cromwell's peace term after the first Anglo-Dutch War which had closed Holland to the exiled Royalists. But his private grievances would not have allowed him sufficient excuse to declare war on the Dutch Republic; what did was England's hunger—summed up by Monck—for a bigger bite of world trade.

Monck was supremely confident that England would win the war. Even though it would be fought, as had been the first, on the water, it did not bother him that the Dutch commanders were better sailors. He had nothing but contempt for their fighting quality. English superiority in heavy gunnery and military discipline would, he was certain, again "sweep the Dutch from the sea by sheer hard-hitting."

It had worked against Martin Tromp. But Tromp was dead. In the next two wars with the Dutch, the English would have to deal with Michael de Ruyter. And Ruyter was quite a different Dutchman. In fact, once he took over his country's sea forces, Ruyter began to develop into the greatest naval figure of the century.

Terrible news greeted Ruyter's homecoming. The Dutch fleet had already met the English navy at sea, and had been disastrously beaten—with the loss of eighteen ships, four admirals (including its commander-in-chief), and seven thousand men. The blame— as Ruyter guessed even before he learned the details—lay in that chronic disease of the Dutch navy: lack of discipline.

Urgently summoned from his home by the government, Ruyter was surprised to find himself snubbed by a younger admiral whom he knew quite well: Cornelis van Tromp, son of Ruyter's old chief, Martin Tromp. He learned the reason from the navy commissioners. After the defeat of the Dutch navy in the war's first battle, Cornelis van Tromp had been made commander-in-chief of the fleet. But now that Ruyter was back, the country wanted Ruyter in command. Van Tromp, deprived of the position to which he felt his fighting spirit and illustrious name entitled him, was furious. Indeed, it had taken a great deal of arguing to persuade him to sail under Ruyter at all.

Ruyter was distressed to hear of this, but he was sure he could win young Van Tromp's full cooperation once they were actually at sea together. He was doomed to find out—under the worst possible circumstances—that he was wrong.

Having placed Ruyter formally in charge of the fleet, the chiefs of the government gave him the details of the first, disastrous battle. The Dutch fleet of about 100 ships, under Admiral Opdam, had met an equal number of English ships under the Duke of York early in June off Lowestoft. The Duke of York's "Fighting Instructions" to his fleet called for a close-hauled single-file "line-ahead" order of battle. Opdam strung the Dutch fleet out in a similar line and the two enemy fleets coming together side by side, began to pound each other with broadsides. Then the English, having the weather gauge, sent fireships drifting against the Dutch line, setting seven Dutch warships aflame. A number of captains in the center of the Dutch line, horrified by the threat of those floating torches, and by the destruction wrought by the heavy English guns, broke and ran to save their ships.

The English fleet sliced through the gap they left and, by concentrating their superior fire on the separate parts of the Dutch line, began to send ship after ship to the bottom. Finally, when the Dutch flagship blew up, killing Admiral Opdam and all but five of the 500 men aboard, those Dutch ships that were still afloat fled toward their own coast.

There was such disorder that the English, following the deserters closely, would have all but wiped them out—had it not been for one Dutch squadron. This squadron, the last to flee, retreated in perfect order and fought a hard delaying action all the way. It was commanded by Cornelis van Tromp.

Ruyter's face grew livid with shame and anger as he listened. But the sight of those wrecked ships, when he went down to the docks to look at the fleet, was worse. A wild resolve claimed his heart. He would take this fleet back to settle matters with the English; he would make them suffer as his men must have suffered!

But before he could sail against the English he knew that he must somehow make the Dutch officers understand the meaning of military discipline in war. There was no trace of the "soft" Ruyter of peacetime now. The captains who had brought about the disaster by pulling their ships out of the center of the Dutch line were stripped of their commands; he ordered four of them shot for cowardice. Next came the back-breaking job of repairing the smashed ships.

Exactly one year after the disaster off Lowestoft, Ruyter took his fleet down into the Channel to meet the English navy—now commanded by Monck himself—in the staggering "Four Days' Battle."

The two enemy commanders summoned their captains to them as their fleets neared each other in mid-Channel through a warm June night in 1666. The surface similarity of these two men was remarkable. Both were short, square, hard, brave. Yet in reality they were strikingly different. Monck fought for the love of fighting. Ruyter fought to protect what he loved: his home, his family, his country.

Monck, discussing plans with his captains on this night, spoke as a man absolutely sure of victory. The Dutch had over ninety ships, the English only eighty. Both fleets carried about 21,000 men and 4,500 guns. But the English guns were bigger and would throw a heavier total weight of shot. And the Dutch had nothing to match the big three-deckers which were being introduced into the English navy. These carried about one hundred guns in all: four 3-pounders on the forecastle and four more on the poop; ten 6-pounder sakers on the quarter-deck; twenty-eight 18-pounders in the upper gun deck; twenty-eight 32-pounders in the middle gun deck; twenty-six 42-pounders in the lower gun deck. Against such juggernauts the Dutch would have to pit two-deckers with 24-pounders as their heaviest guns.

Monck was so sure of what this strength could do that when false word reached him that a French fleet might be sailing out to side with the Dutch, he allowed Prince Rupert to go off with twenty ships to meet the possible new threat. Even with only sixty ships left, Monck assured the officers assembled in his cabin—some of whom did not share his disdain for the Dutch—the heavier guns, bigger ships, and stronger military discipline of the English would break the enemy apart.

As the officers of the Dutch ships gathered in Ruyter's cabin that night before the battle, he pondered the next day's clash with a harsh realism unsweetened by the knowledge that he had more ships than Monck. It was not only those heavy English guns and bigger ships, he knew, that evened the odds. It was more the *disciplined* battle-courage of the English fighters. Of his own men and officers he was not so sure.

Ruyter chose his words with care: "The time has nearly arrived when we shall meet the enemy," he told the captains standing before him under the swinging lanterns. "We have here a chance to wipe out the dishonor of last year—by bravery. We have no need to fear our enemies. Nor to despise them. They are sailors and soldiers too."

It was not that his own officers lacked courage; each had proved his spirit many times—as an individual. It was disciplined military feeling they lacked. In battle they remained individuals, saved their ships instead of holding to the common good of the whole fleet, broke and ran—which the English never did—once they decided that the battle was lost; or that their admiral wasn't handling it wisely. The execution of the four Lowestoft deserters had made some impression on his officers, but he was well aware that these individuals were still far from being welded into a single battle unit.

"Be resolved to conquer," he told them, "or die." He made each captain meet his iron stare in turn as he placed harsh emphasis on his words: "Courage will be rewarded. The coward shall be punished by death."

That, he noted with satisfaction, made their faces red. It didn't matter whether they flushed with anger or shame: the result was the same. "Let each of you remember his honor and his oath, and follow my example. Each of you knows what instructions I have given. Let each do his duty."

Almost in chorus, they swore to fight and obey to the death. But Ruyter did not soften his expression or his tone: "I thank you for your good *intentions*. I hope you will indeed show courage." With that, he let them go back to their ships to wait out the night.

For himself, there was no sleep. He paced his ship, checking the readiness of the guns and their crews, waiting. At the first streaks of dawn, he hurriedly fed the chickens he kept in his cabin to supply him with eggs, buckled sword and pistol around his thick, hard waist, and climbed up to the poop deck to lead his fleet into battle.

The glow of dawn, spreading over that great bowl of turbulent water, revealed that his fleet was already in danger. The English had had the luck to draw very close in the darkness, and the strong wind of morning had given them the weather gauge. With the wind behind them, the English line was knifing under all sail toward Ruyter's own anchored and disordered fleet.

Whirling toward the officers of his flagship, the *Delfland,* Ruyter bellowed his orders. Signal flags raced to the *Delfland's* tops. There was no time to weigh anchor; the English would be upon them too soon for that. The Dutch ships must cut their cables and try to attain some semblance of order.

Ruyter saw that he would not be able to win back the weather gauge from Monck. The Dutch ships barely had time to assemble in three widely separated squadrons before the English, arrowing toward them in a long single-file line that stretched back for miles, struck at the nearest Dutch squadron: Van Tromp's. Monck hoped to reverse the numerical odds by sweeping his whole line past Van

Tromp and letting each of his vessels in turn broadside the lone
Dutch squadron. If all went well he might destroy Van Tromp's
squadron before the other two Dutch groups could reach the point
of battle.

But Van Tromp refused to let Monck rake him with all his
sixty ships. Instead, when he saw the head of the English line close
in, hurl broadsides at him and then sheer off on the starboard tack,
Van Tromp made sail on the same tack. Moving in a parallel
formation, he kept his squadron side by side with the first thirty-
five ships of the English line, slamming back at them with his own
guns at point-blank range.

The thunder of this massed running duel rolled back over Ruyter,
whose squadron was now the center one, and beyond him to
Admiral Evertsen, who now brought up the rear. Ruyter fought to
get his own and Evertsen's ships into the battle, but it was hard,
slow work. They must beat against the wind every inch of the way.

Although the number of enemy ships actually engaged was about
equal, Ruyter saw that the heavier guns of the English were hitting
Van Tromp's squadron with devastating effect. As the morning
wore into afternoon, Ruyter, choked with frustration at still not
having reached the enemy, watched Van Tromp's distant ships
steadily losing sails and masts. He could see the English, with the
weather gauge, drifting little fireships before the wind against Van
Tromp. One Dutch warship, unable to free itself from one of those
fireships, was devoured by towering flames. Some of its men managed to get away in boats; the rest flung themselves into the churn-
ing water. The heavy cannonading went on. At last Van Tromp and
his rear-admiral, Van Ness, their ships near sinking, were forced
to cut away and limp toward shore for repairs.

It would have been the end of Van Tromp's squadron—and the
battle—had not the engaged ships of both fleets been fast approaching the coast of France. To avoid driving aground, Monck was
forced to about-face the entire English line and sail back in the
opposite direction. Now the rear of his line became its head. And
at this moment, the two leeward Dutch squadrons finally closed in.

Ruyter, in a release of pent-up fury, hurtled his two fresh
squadrons into the van of the reversed English line. He smashed
his way through it, surrounded part of it. Dusk was now settling
in, but Ruyter would not let go of the advantage he had waited
all day to grasp. He hemmed in little groups of the broken English

line and chopped them down with ear-stopping broadsides, hurled blazing fireships against them; closed in, grappled their sides, and boarded them.

The English fought back with all the disciplined courage Ruyter had expected of them. One English ship, under Admiral Sir John Harman, was grappled on the starboard quarter by a Dutch fireship. His lieutenant dashed into the flames and hacked away the grappling irons just as another fireship struck against the larboard side, igniting the sails. The crew started to panic and jump overboard, but Sir John Harman raged among them with his sword

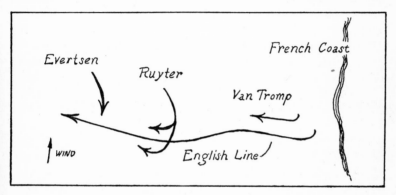

TURNING POINT IN FIRST DAY'S BATTLE

drawn, screaming that he would kill the next man who left off fighting the Dutch or the flames. Getting them back under control, he beat out the flames and cast loose the second fireship. He broadsided a third fireship into the water before a falling topsail yard crashed down and broke his leg. Stretched out on the deck, he went right on directing the fighting of his ship. The flagship of Dutch Admiral Evertsen swung alongside out of the smoke and offered quarter. Harman roared: "No! No! It's not come to that yet!" and loosed a full broadside that swept the Dutch deck and killed Evertsen. Then Harman worked his wreck out of the battle. He managed to keep it afloat until he and the forty men left of his 300-man crew reached the English shore.

By ten that night, when pitch-blackness finally forced an end to the battle, it was evident that the tide of the day's long fight had gone against Monck. For the single Dutch ship burned earlier in the battle, the English had lost three in the closing hours.

Ruyter knew that the day had been only a prelude; the next would be the important one. All night he worked feverishly, directing the repair of his maimed vessels. Shortly before dawn, Van Tromp and Van Ness, their ships hastily patched, returned to their squadron. Ruyter appointed Van Ness to command the dead Evertsen's squadron, and had a serious talk with his officers.

He took little satisfaction in the first day's action. He had saved the day by breaking the English line, but the victory was a small one. The reason it had not been larger lay in the perfect battle order of the English: They stuck to the line; even when the line broke, each separate part held together rigidly. His own Dutch officers, on the other hand, kept fighting separate battles with their ships or squadrons, ignoring the action of the rest of their fleet. Their ranks often became so disorganized that half their ships would be out of action, blocked by the other half when it got between them and the enemy. Explaining again the need for discipline, he gave his officers the plan for the next day, and hoped they would do better. They didn't.

The English came on in their perfect battle line with the first light of dawn, maneuvering again for the weather gauge. And again—because the deeper-keeled English ships handled better— they succeeded. They struck at six in the morning, with the wind blowing them toward the Dutch.

Ruyter strung his three squadrons out in a line and swung to meet Monck's fleet, which was sailing in the opposite direction. It was only by this method, he saw, that each of his ships could have its chance at the enemy—and that he could make his greater number of ships and guns weigh against the enemy's bigger ships and heavier guns.

The lead ships of the two lines sailed past each other on opposite tacks, and the lines—miles in length—followed, close and parallel to each other, belching broadsides as they came into action.

Ruyter, with his squadron in the center of the Dutch line, watched anxiously as Van Ness, leading the van squadron, sailed past the first English ships up ahead, firing all guns as they bore on the enemy. Then his own flagship swept past the first English ship and sailed on along the English line, quaking to the roar of its guns, staggering from the battering-ram blows of English 32- and 42-pounders. It was hard to take a smashing from that heavy shot and not flinch. But Ruyter took it, and prayed that the rest of his officers would take it too. If they could hold to this close action until every one of his ships had passed down the shorter English line, the sheer weight of Dutch numbers would decide the issue.

It was too much to hope for. Van Ness, up ahead, broke first. His lead squadron, forced to bear the brunt of the English powerhouse broadsides, began to jumble up. From one perfect line, it dissolved into two helter-skelter lines, then three. Then the whole squadron suddenly turned their high, ornamented sterns to the English and fled for a more comfortable range.

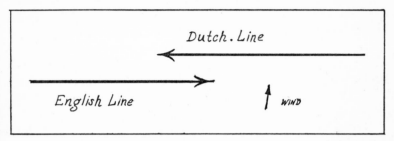

START OF SECOND DAY

Ruyter, aghast, had no choice but to follow if he hoped to keep his fleet together. Burning with humiliation, he pulled out his center squadron and raced after Van Ness—expecting Van Tromp to follow him.

But Van Tromp had ideas of his own. His rear squadron, far back in the Dutch line, had not yet reached the point of the English line. Now he saw what he thought was a chance to win the battle by himself, and show his country that it was he—and *not* Ruyter—who should be commander-in-chief. He pulled his squadron off to port, swinging to cut past the point of the English line and gain the weather gauge against it.

Ruyter, seeing what was happening, was stunned. Monck hadn't had to do a thing; his own admirals had done it for him: torn the Dutch fleet apart into three separate groups!

Monck was delighted. Ignoring Ruyter and Van Ness, he drove his line straight ahead against Van Tromp's squadron, intending to crush it with the weight of his entire fleet.

He would succeed, Ruyter saw. Van Tromp couldn't last long against all of Monck's ships—weather gauge or no weather gauge. Almost as if he were a sheep dog bullying an unruly herd, Ruyter caught up with Van Ness, drew their two squadrons into a single mass. Then he raced back in the opposite direction to hurl this mass against the English line.

Monck, seeing that if he let himself be delayed by Van Tromp he would be hit by the rest of Ruyter's ships on his free side, and thus caught between two fires, sheered off past Van Tromp and let the three Dutch squadrons join together again. But he retained the windward position.

When Ruyter and Van Tromp reached each other, the men aboard Ruyter's flagship began to cheer Van Tromp for his bravery

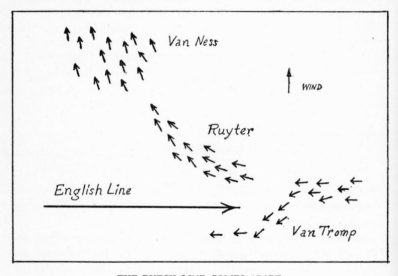

THE DUTCH LINE COMES APART

in attempting to take on the English line by himself. Furious, Ruyter turned on them: "This is no time for rejoicing, but for tears!"

He was right. His three squadrons were milling about in complete disorder. Monck sailed his perfect line past this jumble, firing every single gun along his port sides into it. The Dutch could reply with only a few scattered shots for fear of hitting their own ships.

When the English line was past, and its rearmost ship had had its taste of mauling the close-packed Dutch mob, Monck turned his line around and swept back on the opposite tack to have another go at it.

But this time in the midst of the cannonade, Ruyter—with

another fantastic demonstration of skill and power—pulled apart the tangle of his fleet and rearranged it as an ordered line again—did it while being raked and hammered by the starboard sides of Monck's line. The next time Monck swept back, he found a Dutch line almost as neat as his own sailing to meet him.

It was the beginning of the battle all over again: the two fleets, strung out in long lines, sailing past each other on parallel courses, going in opposite directions. Only this time, none of the Dutch ships ran. Ruyter had threatened to kill the next officer who pulled away. And this time he sailed his flagship at the very rear of his line, where he could watch the performance of every ship in his fleet.

The heavy English guns did their damage as before. Ruyter experienced the suffering of his fleet as his own ship butted through the iron wall thrown out by the guns of the lead English ship, then the second, the third, the fourth . . . and so on, down the line. He crashed through broadside after broadside until the *Delfland* finally limped past the last ship of the English line. Its planks came apart under Ruyter's feet. Water poured into the lower deck through gaping shot holes. The main yard was torn away; the main-topmast came splintering down. Men died all around Ruyter. But by the time his flagship got past the last English ship, his entire line had taken its toll of the shorter English line.

Monck was slower to re-engage this time; there were gaps in his line to be closed up first. The two enemy lines came back on opposite tacks and swept thunderingly past each other. And again none of Ruyter's ships faltered—and each had its turn at the enemy.

This time it was the English who turned away. But they did it with their usual military precision, not singly or as squadrons, but as a whole, well-ordered unit.

Now that Ruyter had his whole fleet in hand Monck saw reason at last. Against his fighting instinct, he retreated and went in search of those twenty ships he had allowed to go off with Prince Rupert.

Ruyter followed—all through the night, and all the third day. The Dutch were too badly damaged themselves to catch Monck, but Ruyter, his blood up, was determined to keep after his enemy and bring the battle to a conclusive end. He caught one of the English ships—the three-decker *Royal Prince*—when it went aground near the English coast. But he didn't let it delay his pursuit. At dusk, he was rewarded by the sight of twenty fresh warships under Prince Rupert coming up over the horizon ahead, to join Monck. Each of those fresh ships was worth two or three of Ruyter's battle-cripples. But Ruyter was content. Now Monck would stand and finish the fight.

Shortly before dawn, Ruyter assembled his captains on the quarter-deck of the *Delfland*. With some sleep and breakfast under his belt, he felt oddly confident. For he had gotten his captains in hand at last, and if he could only manage to keep them in hand. . . . He was ready for this day, ready even for those twenty fresh ships that would bolster Monck.

"The last few days have shown all that the English can do against us," he told his men. "This one day's fight you still have to go through with me. It is the same enemy you saw fly yesterday. Show yourselves to be soldiers."

His lieutenant hurried up to whisper in his ear. Ruyter turned and saw in the light of the rising sun, which flooded sky and water with reddish-gold light, a distant fleet of ships gliding out toward them from the coast of England. He turned back to the officers on whom he must depend. "You see the enemy coming. Nothing more can be done with the tongue. You must now fight with the fist."

This time the Dutch fleet caught the wind, strong from the southwest, and got the weather gauge. Monck, shunning the passing fight that had gone against him two days before, brought his line up to windward alongside the Dutch. Sailing in the same direction, the two enemy lines drew within effective gunnery range around nine in the morning, and the artillery duel began again between the two parallel forces.

A third force entered the fight, and grew stronger all through it: the wind. Ruyter's flat-bottomed ships had not been constructed to keep their course in such wind and rough water. They rolled badly and lost their positions. After two hours of it, a number of ships ahead of Ruyter, and Van Tromp's whole squadron behind him, had been pushed well to leeward—so far, in fact, that both ends of the Dutch fleet were now on the other side of the English. To make matters worse, Van Ness, ignoring his orders as usual, had taken fourteen ships off to chase three English ships that had separated from their line. Ruyter, with only thirty-five ships remaining with his squadron, found himself being pressed hard by Monck's entire fleet.

The English ships, better able to handle in this weather, kept pushing against the wind toward Ruyter, who himself beat to windward to prevent them from breaking his group apart. After hours of this, Monck's line—trying to surround Ruyter's squadron and failing because of Ruyter's agility—had degenerated, like Ruyter's, into a sprawled cluster of ships. And still the two enemies pushed against the wind and pounded each other through hour after hour.

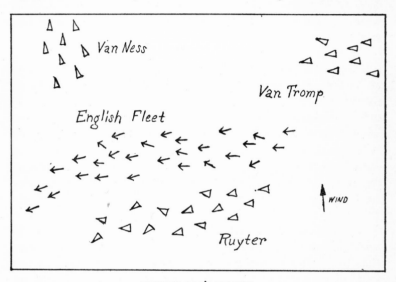

FOURTH DAY'S BATTLE

The battle that now raged on the stormy ocean became a wild, disorganized clash of ships fighting wherever they chanced to get close to each other. Ruyter had been—to his frequent sorrow in the past—used to fighting under such chaotic conditions. But to the English it meant the end of all planning. It was impossible for the English military discipline to function, and without it Monck's captains were at a loss. Ruyter held his thirty-five ships in as tight a grip as possible while he engaged Monck's disorganized fleet, and watched the fringes of the battle for some sign of relief by his other squadrons. At last he saw it: Van Ness, with his truant ships, was making his way back toward the fight. So was Van Tromp's wind-scattered squadron.

Up raced the signal flags on Ruyter's flagship. Van Ness and Van Tromp responded, closing in on the leeward side of the English fleet. Monck prepared to seize the advantage of his windward position and throw his whole fleet against the much smaller numbers of Van Ness and Van Tromp.

But before he could, Ruyter acted. For hours he had been beating against the wind to keep the English ships from pressing him too close. Now he turned with his thirty-five ships, the wind full behind him, and plunged straight in amongst Monck's ships—driving through them toward Van Ness and Van Tromp.

The English fleet, hemmed in on both sides and quickly infiltrated by Ruyter's gale-pushed squadron, came completely apart. Ruyter roamed through the confusion, ruthlessly grinding Monck down with his guns as he approached Van Tromp. Then, with his whole fleet joined together once more, he shoved back in amongst Monck's ships. In the jam-up of fleets, the English fought now only to get free.

By seven in the evening, most of those English ships that were still able to maneuver did get free, in a final convulsion of effort, and retreated hastily toward the English coast. Ruyter watched them go, knowing they would not be back. The English ships were too disabled, their crews too thinned, to fight any more.

Ruyter had lost four ships and two thousand men. Monck had lost seventeen ships and eight thousand men. A Dutch fleet had at last beaten an English one. The great admiral who had accomplished this wearily turned his ships back toward Holland, went to his cabin, swept it clean with a broom, fed his chickens, and went to sleep.

Monck refused to admit he had been beaten. He swore he had inflicted more damage on Ruyter than he had received, and that it was only the cowardice of many of his captains that had forced him to retreat in the end. But the nation soon learned the truth. His seamen came ashore calling the fight "The Four Days' Bloody Blunder."

Ruyter returned to set up a blockade of the Channel. Humiliated, England rushed the rebuilding of its shattered fleet, added to it, and in less than two months Monck sailed out to meet Ruyter off North Foreland with an equal number of ships, determined to taste his full measure of revenge.

It was a black day for Michael de Ruyter. He was ready to fight, eager to test the new discipline of the Dutch navy. He had with him another Evertsen, brother of the one who had died in the last battle—a man whose father, three other brothers and one son had given their lives to the wars with England; a man as dependable as a rock. He had Vice-Admiral Bankert, a Zeelander from whose family came two admirals and seven captains during these wars; a new type of Dutch commander who followed his orders with nerveless and undeviating fervor. But he also still had the brave, unruly, jealous Cornelis van Tromp.

The Dutch fleet—with Evertsen commanding the lead squadron, Ruyter the center, and Van Tromp the rear—met the perfect English line on the morning of August 4, 1666. The fight was lost for Ruyter from the moment it began. For Van Tromp hung back, and never did close with the main body of Monck's fleet.

Van Tromp thought he saw his opportunity to win the fight alone when a small number of ships under Admiral Smith detached itself from the English line and swung down toward his squadron. Van Tromp attacked. Smith promptly fled. Van Tromp sailed after him, away from the main battle, leaving Ruyter and Evertsen to face Monck's superior force, which had the wind behind it. Led on a wild-goose chase for the rest of the day, Van Tromp never did realize that Smith had been sent by Monck for the express purpose of luring his squadron away from the battle proper.

Ruyter watched him go in frustrated rage. He knew the day was lost, but it was too late to pull away and run for it. Evertsen's squadron was already getting a terrible smashing from Monck's entire line. One of his ships was a mass of flames and billowing smoke. Others were losing masts, being pounded into the water. Vice-Admiral Bankert, his ship foundering under him, took to a boat and had himself rowed through the carnage to another.

Ruyter hurled his center squadron against the English line in a desperate effort to break up its concentration of force against Evertsen. But without the support of Van Tromp's squadron, the struggle was hopelessly uneven. Trembling with rage and despair, he watched the destruction of his outnumbered fleet.

Then, through the destruction, he saw the larger English flagship, the *Royal Charles*, carrying both Monck and Prince Rupert, come toward him. From the depths of his misery, a flame of pure savagery rose to engulf Ruyter. He swung his own ship around and plunged in to meet the *Royal Charles.*

Monck impassivley watched Ruyter's swift approach. "Now," he sneered to the officers with him, "this fellow will come and give me two broadsides. And then he shall run."

Ruyter closed to point-blank range. He took a broadside that heeled his ship over, and then smashed his own broadside into the *Royal Charles.* Both ships went around at the same time, drove their other broadsides into each other. They passed, reeling from the crushing blows and their own recoils, reloaded, and swung back on each other again. And again. And again.

It went on and on, an unending nightmare of splintering timbers, screaming men, booming guns. After two hours of it, both ships were almost shorn of canvas and rigging. Their decks were a jumble of wreckage and corpses, their sides were riddled with jagged holes. But their guns still roared.

A junior officer on the *Royal Charles* glanced quizzically at Monck and summoned up his courage. "Methinks, sir, that this Ruyter has given us more than two broadsides."

Glaring at Ruyter's smoking guns across the narrow expanse of wreckage-littered water, Monck answered, "You shall find him run, by and by."

After another hour of Ruyter's toe-to-toe slugging, the *Royal Charles* was helplessly adrift, unable to maneuver at all. Monck brought in another of his warships to keep Ruyter engaged and had the *Royal Charles* towed out of range to be repaired and rerigged. Ruyter drove his crew to bend new tackle, set up jury rigging and patch the holes in his sides—while he fought uninterruptedly with the new enemy.

In half an hour, the *Royal Charles* was back. Ruyter met it with unabated violence, hacking and hammering at it. In another hour he had reduced it again to a drifting hulk. Monck had the *Royal Charles* towed away once more, shifted to the *Royal James,* and came back.

By then, the reports reaching Ruyter of the state of the rest of his fleet had smothered his fighting anger under a blanket of dark despair. Twenty Dutch ships were sunk. Evertsen was dead. So were Admiral Vries, Captain Hogenhoek, Captain Poel, Captain Nyhof, Captain Maximillian . . . and God knew how many more.

"Oh God!" he muttered aloud as he fought Monck's new flagship. "Must I be so unhappy? Out of so many thousands of shots, is there not one to kill me?"

But when one of the officers beside him, catching his mood, cried out that they would all fight on to the end and die for Dutch glory, Ruyter snapped back to his common sense. He was not here for glory. He was here to save his country. This battle was lost. Now his country's future depended on his saving himself—and as many of his ships as possible—to fight another day.

Pulling out of his personal duel with Monck, Ruyter wove through the embattled fleets, gathering up his ships and leading them out of the fight. It was another example of his amazing knack of reuniting a fleet that seemed hopelessly dispersed. Monck tried to stop him, but failed. By nightfall, Ruyter had his remaining ships gathered about him and was heading for the Dutch coast.

Monck followed close all night, hoping to finish Ruyter off the next day. But the next day the wind fell to a whisper. It barely moved the big, heavy English ships—while Ruyter's light, flat-bottomed ships glided away on that breath of a breeze and reached the protective shoals of home.

It was a terrible defeat for the Dutch; a great victory for England. With the Dutch navy destroyed, the English decided they no longer need bear the expense of keeping a mighty war fleet on the sea. The Dutch economy, after all, depended on commerce, and the war could be carried on merely by raids aimed at destroying that commerce.

The English warships were brought into port and their crews let go. Privateering fleets began to prey on Dutch merchant shipping—in one raid alone destroying over 160 merchant ships on the Dutch coast.

But all this time, Ruyter was busy, preparing. His first act was to strip Van Tromp of his command and force him to retire. There were howls of protest from those who admired Van Tromp's bravery and respected his illustrious name. But Ruyter insisted. It was either him or Van Tromp. Bravery was a quality that should be taken for granted in a naval officer; it was discipline that counted at the height of a battle.

Then with Van Tromp out of his way, Ruyter concentrated on the task of reconditioning and bolstering the Dutch fleet.

One year after his defeat, Ruyter sailed his fleet right into the

Thames, sending all England into panic. Monck worked like a madman, day and night, to get batteries in place along the shores to oppose the Dutch fleet working its way up the river. He also tried to ready some of the warships that had been laid up. But there was not time. Ruyter bombarded the puny shore defenses, easily beat aside weak attempts to stop him, broke through a chain that had been drawn across the Thames, and kept right on feeling his way up the river—all the way to Chatham. For two weeks he stayed in the Thames, destroying all merchant shipping and burning England's seven greatest warships, including Monck's flagship, the *Royal Charles*. Then he sailed out and shut down the entire Channel coast of England under a tight blockade for six straight weeks, forcing England to call off the war.

The English had learned, the hard way, that they couldn't beat the Dutch in one battle and call it a won war. George Monck went home to a sickbed, hurried to his death by the exhaustion and humiliation of his fruitless attempt to halt Ruyter.

Ruyter went home to the pleasures of his family and friends; to the fireplace and Bible-reading and singing loudly to himself while he tended his garden; to the pride of watching a son and a stepson emulate him and become captains in the Dutch navy. For himself, he was more than content to put his naval career behind him.

But it was not behind him. Another war was on the way—a war in which he was to be always outnumbered, never outfought.

11

The Good Father

RUYTER WINS A WAR

The Dutch, worn out by the two wars with England, wanted nothing but peace in which to devote themselves to rebuilding their ruined fisheries and trade. But two powerful kings—Louis XIV of France and Charles II of England—wanted it otherwise. Louis, with plans for bringing all of Europe under the domination of France, had already conquered most of Belgium. Holland was next on his list. Charles, smarting at the outcome of the last war, wanted revenge. More than that, he wanted the Dutch ports for himself. Within five years, England and France united for the sole purpose of conquering the Dutch. The land invasion was to be undertaken by France; the sea attack by the combined navies of England and France, under an English admiral. In return for helping France absorb Holland, England was to get much of the spoils —plus some of the best Dutch ports.

The Dutch didn't want to fight. They were even willing to accept humiliating conditions to placate their powerful enemies. But they refused to be subjugated. Opening their dikes, they flooded their land to halt the advance of the massive French armies; and sent Ruyter out with every available fighting ship to cope with the French and English navies.

155

Fastened to the poop deck of the rolling Dutch flagship, the *Seven Provinces,* was an immense chair covered with a velvet tapestry on which were embroidered in gold the arms of the Dutch nation. Slouched in this chair was the aging and sickly commissioner of the Dutch navy: Cornelis de Witt, here to exercise the authority of his government in whatever was about to happen.

De Witt had no intention of exercising that authority. He had complete confidence in his friend, Michael de Ruyter, who stood beside him swaying so easily to the ocean-surged movements of the ship. Ruyter was watching the enemy fleets approaching them up the coast of England. De Witt was watching Ruyter.

It was startling to De Witt how much younger than himself Ruyter looked, despite his sixty-five years. His body seemed as tough and resilient as those of the young seamen now racing up the rigging. His weather-carved face was hard as a ruddy nut. His clear brown eyes reflected sky and sea—and the direct, alert quality of the mind behind them.

Quietly, Ruyter totaled the odds for De Witt: The approaching fleet of France and England numbered over one hundred ships, many of them massive three-deckers. Ruyter had ninety-one ships; the largest were only two-deckers, and many more were frigates, with single gun decks, plus a good number of tiny fireships. The combined fleets of France and England carried at least 12,000 more men and over a thousand more guns than the Dutch.

That enemy fleet was preparing for an attack on the Dutch coast in conjunction with a French land assault. Ruyter knew that, despite the odds, he must fight and win a victory over it sufficient to stop its planned attack. His ninety-one ships constituted his country's main defense. If they were beaten, the Dutch nation was beaten.

After studying the approaching enemy for some time, Ruyter turned his fleet around and retreated, back toward the coast of Holland. De Witt sat very still, drumming his fingers on the arm of his velvet-covered chair, and did not question Ruyter.

The commander-in-chief of the English and French fleet, the Duke of York, did not question Ruyter's decision to withdraw beyond the horizon either. To him and his admirals—the courtly Earl of Sandwich, who commanded the Blue Squadron; and D'Estrées, commander of the French division—it seemed natural that Ruyter, completely outnumbered, outgunned and outmanned, should refuse battle and flee. They anchored along the English coast at Solebay, to await the time for their descent on the Dutch coast. Now that Ruyter realized the futility of trying to stop them with a sea battle, nothing seemed to stand in the way of an easy success.

At two o'clock on Tuesday morning, May 28, 1672, John Narbrough, lieutenant of the *Prince,* the Duke of York's flagship, came out on the quarter-deck and looked about him. Under thousands of glistening stars, the air was warm and still, the water smooth, dark glass. The only sounds were the splashes of oars from boats bringing supplies from the shore. Having every reason to feel serene and secure, Lieutenant Narbrough followed the instructions given him earlier by his captain, Sir John Cox, and ordered the *Prince* careened so that her underbelly might be washed down.

By the time the ship was heeled over, Narbrough felt a wind begin to fan his face. It was from the east, blowing toward shore. He saw no reason why such a wind should worry him and ordered the men to proceed with the washing of the *Prince's* hull.

He was taking a pleasant stroll around the deck when he heard a cannon. It was a faint sound, from the east, carried by the freshening wind. Puzzled, he hurried to the starboard bulwarks, stared out into the star-filled darkness. The cannon sounded again. And again. Nearer now. It took a long time before he saw it: one of the French scout frigates, standing toward the anchored allied fleet with its topgallant sails flying and its signal gun booming.

Lieutenant Narbrough rushed to wake Sir John Cox and the Duke of York. Cox was on the deck first. By the time the Duke of York got out there, the first dirty graying of predawn was tingeing the horizon. By its faint light, they could see, astern of the oncoming scout frigate—just a length behind—the Dutch fleet plunging toward them under all sail, the wind directly behind it.

The Duke of York spoke sharply to Cox and Narbrough, who began bellowing orders for the heeled-over flagship to be righted and cleared for action, for the seamen to come off the yards, for the sleeping crew to be snapped to action, for the sails to be loosed, for the guns to be run out and loaded, for a gun to signal the other ships to get under sail and draw into a line of battle.

Ruyter, standing beside the chair in which De Witt sat (erect now, and quivering with excitement), saw that the enemy was

completely surprised. Lulled by his retreat, they were utterly unprepared for his reappearance. The number of boats scurrying to
bring back crewmen from shore proved that. As he had anticipated,
the English and French admirals had made no plans to counter such
an attack. Ruyter didn't intend to give them time to make any
plans now. That was why he had waited until the wind began to
blow against the English coast during the night: so that he could
get quite close in the darkness before he was spotted. That was
why he had his ships lined up side by side in a line-abreast—
instead of in a single-file line-ahead: so that he could strike the
enemy with his whole force at the same time.

It worked. The English and French admirals, trying to get out
of the wind trap that caught them between the on-plunging Dutch
warships and the coast, didn't have time to consult one another
about details. Heaving up their anchors and opening sails, their
ships moved to get out of the trap—and their fleet came apart in
two separated divisions, the English running north along the coast,
the French heading south.

The instant Ruyter saw the French and English fleets part, he
made a very rapid adjustment in his strategy. According to intelligence reports, Louis XIV secretly felt that since he was carrying
the entire cost of the land war, England should be made to pay its
way by bearing the brunt of the sea fighting. If this were true,
Ruyter calculated, the French ships, now separated from the English, might be kept separated with little effort. Ruyter had a healthy
respect for the courage of the French. But he decided that if he
handled the present situation with care, the French admiral,
D'Estrées, might be inclined to sit by and let the English fight
the Dutch pretty much by themselves.

Acting on this calculation, Ruyter sent Vice-Admiral Bankert
off, with a small number of ships, to get between the French and
English. Bankert was given strict orders to fire at the French
at long distance and make no attempt to close with them as long as
they stayed where they were. If they did try to rejoin the English,
he was to hold them in check as best he could, and as long as he
could.

Despite the odds in numbers, Ruyter saw that the French would
have a hard time getting past Bankert to unite with the English
again; for Bankert had the weather gauge. D'Estrées, thinking of
Louis XIV's instructions, saw it that way too. Bankert sat with

his small squadron, firing his salvos from long range at the French, making no attempt to close in. D'Estrées sat with his large squadron, firing back and making no attempt to close, and watched Ruyter fall upon the two English squadrons with almost his entire fleet.

It was a stunning piece of planning. By it, Ruyter turned the odds down to even. He had with him almost exactly the same number of ships as those two English squadrons. If they had more and bigger guns on their side, he had the wind on his. And his fleet was

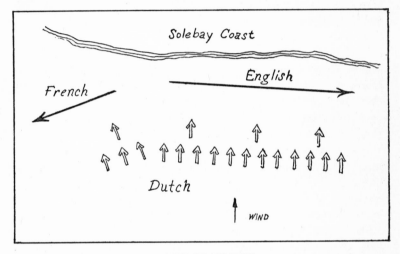

BATTLE OF SOLEBAY

in perfect formation, while the enemy was still trying to straighten out their ranks.

Ruyter set his fireships ablaze and threw them against the English. Fire was the most terrifying thing that could happen to a warship constructed entirely of wood, rope and canvas, and carrying a huge quantity of gunpowder. The English order was further disarranged by the floating furnaces—dangling grappling hooks from bowsprit and yardarms—that blindly sailed into their midst, infesting everything they touched with the same blazing disease that consumed themselves.

Close behind the fireships came Ruyter and the rest of his fleet, clamping the Duke of York and the Earl of Sandwich between himself and the coast. Spotting the flagship of the English commander-in-chief, the Duke of York's *Prince,* he drove the *Seven*

Provinces alongside it, yardarm to yardarm, and unleased a storm of metal across its decks.

All along the line, other Dutch fighters were following his example. Van Ness' ship pushed in after Ruyter's and joined the *Seven Provinces* in pounding away at the *Prince*. Ruyter clung close to the Duke of York's side, taking his punishment and counterpunching at masts, decks and gunports. De Witt, holding fast to the arms of his chair, his sunken eyes aglow, refused to go below to a place less exposed. This was too exciting to miss. His feverish eyes darted back and forth, from the smoke-vomiting mouths of the enemy cannons to the savage, fire-flecked concentration of Ruyter directing the battle.

Several of the Dutch soldiers stationed around De Witt's chair to protect him were suddenly flung against him by a flashing iron ball, fell broken and dead at his feet. De Witt brusquely ordered their bodies tossed over the side, stayed where he was.

On the poop deck of the English flagship, the Duke of York and Sir John Cox stood watching the heavy iron shot raging steadily in both directions between the *Prince* and the *Seven Provinces*. It was nine in the morning when one of those heavy iron balls smashed Cox into eternity. The Duke of York called for Lieutenant Narbrough, informed him that he was now captain of the *Prince*. By noon, Narbrough was captain of a ship that had become useless to the fleet and his commander.

Ruyter watched with satisfaction as the *Prince's* main-topmast crashed down, bringing rigging, spars and sails with it, smothering the deck. The English flagship heeled over. Ruyter's guns hacked at the exposed underbelly of the ship. On the other side of the *Prince,* a boat was hastily lowered, rowed away. It was the Duke of York, going off to find a ship that could still maneuver.

He found it in the *St. Michael.* Four hours later the *St. Michael's* rigging was withered away and the sea was pouring in through its riddled sides. The Duke of York had to transfer again, this time to Admiral Spragge's *London.*

The whole English line was in trouble by now: ships spouting flame and billowing black smoke; other ships, mastless, drifting against the shoals.

Far down the line, the lead ship of the English Blue Squadron, the three-decker *Royal James,* was fighting for its life. On its quarter-deck stood the famous cavalier, the Earl of Sandwich, his gorgeous medals gleaming on his chest, his long wavy hair fanned by iron balls whirling past, his elegant features blackened by smoke, smeared with streaks of tar. Sword in one hand, his black-plumed hat in the other, he coolly directed his eight-hundred-man crew, his hundred mighty guns. The Dutch were loosing fireships at him. His guns blew one out of the water; they disabled another. And all the time Dutch warships continued to swing in close, raking him with heavy shot. He fought them off, but they kept coming, cutting down his strength. Most of his upper-deck guns were out of action, and three hundred of his men were down, when Dutch Captain Braakel pushed his 60-gun two-decker in through Sandwich's barrage and grappled the bows of the *Royal James*. Sandwich drove across Braakel's bulwarks, smothered his 300-man crew with overwhelming numbers, and cut the Dutch ship loose. But the diversion had done its work. While Sandwich was busy with Braakel, a fourth fireship crashed against his side, flinging its burning masts into the *Royal James'* sails, down on its decks. The flames spread, shot up the masts and rigging, probed down deep—all the way to the powder stores. The *Royal James* blew sky-high, taking the Earl of Sandwich with it.

Ruyter was satisfied. His ships had taken a brutal beating from English guns. One, the *Josua,* was sunk. Another, the *Stavoren,* had been captured. But his fleet had given much worse than it had gotten. He had extracted everything he could from his surprise attack. He gathered up his fleet and sailed it back to Holland.

It was over that abruptly. Ruyter's fleet was his country's last hope, and he did not intend to damage it any more than necessary. It had accomplished what it had come for: The allied enemy fleet was no longer in any condition to attack the Dutch coast.

France and England understood fully now that before any assault on the Dutch coast could be attempted, Ruyter and his fleet must be destroyed. Having delivered his surprise lesson at Solebay, he cruised his coastal waters, waiting, his fleet a long floating wall, a shield. There was no getting past him to land troops; he was too skillful, and he would not run. Ruyter would have to be blasted out of the way.

It was a full year before the combined English and French fleets were ready to try it. While thousands of soldiers waited on the English shore for word to board their assault transports, eighty-one warships crossed the Narrow Seas to chop a path for them through Ruyter's wooden walls.

Ruyter, who had his fleet spread out along the coast to watch for such an attempt, had only fifty-five warships with him when he saw the enemy fleet approaching off Schoneveldt. But although seriously outnumbered, he didn't wait for their attack. He crossed the shoals and slammed into them, before they were ready for him. For Ruyter had complete confidence in his fleet now. By force, by example and by shame, he had at last welded his officers into a single, disciplined battle unit. He ordered; they obeyed.

His most satisfying experience had been with young, rebellious Van Tromp. Mutual friends had begged Ruyter to have a talk with the officer who had caused him so much trouble and whom he had forced out of the navy. They said that Van Tromp, once so jealous of Ruyter, was now open in his admiration of Ruyter's Solebay victory—and would give anything for a chance to get back into action. After all, he was brave, and the son of Martin Tromp. . . . Ruyter agreed to see Van Tromp. The two rivals had a drink together, then a long talk. The younger man admitted the error of his ways. Whatever Ruyter did, he did all the way. When he forgave Van Tromp, he also let him resume his rank, and gave him back command of one of his three squadrons. He would never have reason to be sorry for his decision.

This was a disciplined fighting unit that came across the shoals with the offshore wind and ploughed into the allied fleet. Before the English and French could organize their line, Ruyter cut through them and began his barrage. In the midst of that vast tangle of fleets, he was constantly aware of the situation of each of his ships. When Bankert's ship lost a mast and could no longer lead his squadron, Ruyter swung over, re-established order among the leaderless ships, and led them back into the fight. When Van Tromp's ship was cut off and surrounded, Ruyter drove in to get him out. Van Tromp, looking around, saw the commander of whom he had so long been jealous breaking through his ring of enemies. "There is our good father, coming to help us," he said softly to the men around him. "As long as I live, I'll never abandon him."

Ruyter didn't try for a decisive victory this time. With his limited number of ships, he couldn't. He had only one objective: to inflict as much damage on the French and English ships as he could—as long as they were disorganized. As soon as their battered ranks managed to attain a semblance of order, he pulled off, slipping back across the protective coastal shallows.

The French and English sailed away with their eighty-one ships to repair the damage and tend to the wounded. Their new commander-in-chief, Prince Rupert, wrote unhappily to King Charles: "I hope your Majesty will be satisfied that there was as much done as could be expected," and pointed out that the Dutch were, after all, "rather better seamen than we."

His vice-admiral, Spragge, more frankly declared that the battle was "in truth as ill fought of our side as ever yet I saw." He blamed it on "our ill conduct and most notorious cowardice."

No one was willing to admit the real reason: Ruyter. Two weeks later they came back—and Ruyter again sailed out, struck, pounded them savagely up to the moment when their superior numbers began to tell, and then quickly drew back across the shallows. The English and French ships were filled with dead and wounded, and too damaged to repair at sea. They limped away to their ports not to come back for two months.

This time the combined English and French fleet numbered almost one hundred ships. Ruyter had seventy. Enough, in his opinion, to wage an all-out battle to match Solebay.

There was no disorganization in the allied fleet this time. Ruyter, gazing out across the ocean from the quarter-deck of the *Seven Provinces*, admired the enemy's long, perfect line. It was a beautiful sight: each ship with its cannon-quilled side, its tall masts pointing skyward, bowing under the weight of the wind that ballooned its immense sails, its bowsprit turning slowly over the foaming wake of the ship ahead of it. A stately, deadly line of ships, sailing parallel to the coast off Texel, gradually moving in closer against the steady offshore wind.

Ruyter watched the nearing line and waited, his own fleet huddled close around him against the coast. Visibility was poor. Overhead, the sky was completely blanketed by heavy, dark clouds. Although it was August, the wet air was cold. Ruyter had waited this way all the previous day, keeping his flat-bottomed ships in the shallows where the big enemy ships could not get at them; for the wind had been blowing against the shore. Now, seeing that the thirty ships of the French division were leading the enemy line, Ruyter gave his orders.

The Dutch sails billowed out as they caught the wind. The masts creaked, strained at the shrouds. The ships surged out through the choppy water toward the enemy line, pulling up parallel to it in the same direction. As it moved from the shallows, the Dutch fleet stretched itself out in a long line. Ruyter kept his squadron in the center of this line, where he could watch what happened to Van Tromp's squadron behind him, to Bankert's squadron up ahead. Bankert had only twelve ships with him; enough, Ruyter had decided, for the part he was to play in this battle.

The two lines drew closer. Guns began to boom, puffs of smoke blossomed from ships' sides. First only a few guns, feeling out the range—then, as the gap between the enemy lines narrowed, more, rising in an ocean-rocking crescendo until every gun along the two facing lines was belching smoke, flame and iron.

For months, Ruyter had concentrated on his gun crews, drilling them to the limits of human speed. If his guns could not hurl shots as heavy as those of the enemy, Ruyter had decided that they would have to make up for it by hurling *more* shots, by firing faster. Now his Dutch guns roared, recoiled, were reloaded, rolled out, and roared again—twice as fast as the English guns, three times faster than the French. The enemy was amazed at the speed of the Dutch gunnery, even more amazed at its uncanny accuracy.

Water-clinging clouds of gun smoke began to make it difficult for Ruyter to see what was happening at either end of the two lines. He squinted through the smoke at Bankert's little squadron up ahead. It was performing on schedule, cutting in against the rear ships of the French division that led the enemy line.

Drops of water splashed against Ruyter's face; it had begun to rain. Swaying to the roll and recoil of his thundering flagship, Ruyter shielded his eyes from the rain with both hands, continued to watch Bankert's twelve ships closing in against the last of the thirty French ships. Bankert's withering, incredibly fast salvos smashed into the sterns of the rearmost French ships again and again. D'Estrées, the French admiral, found himself in a position not to his taste and decided to get out of it. His squadron suddenly increased its sail-speed, began pulling away from the English ships behind.

The moment Ruyter saw this happening, he threw the whole weight of his center squadron against the lead English squadron, which was under Prince Rupert, commander-in-chief of the whole enemy fleet. Rupert began to haul off to starboard, reeling from the suddenly increased force of Ruyter's attack. And the gap between the first English ships and the rearmost French ships up ahead widened.

Into this gap plunged Bankert with his twelve-ship squadron. Now, if D'Estrées wanted to bring his French squadron back to rejoin his allies, he would first have to fight his way through Bankert. D'Estrées, remembering Louis XIV's orders to preserve his ships insofar as possible, was not anxious to try it.

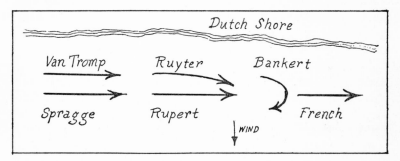

BATTLE OF TEXEL

Bankert's squadron, still acting as a wall between the French and the English, deliberately sagged back against the point of Prince Rupert's squadron. The rain was slashing down harder now, bringing with it banks of fog. The fog combined with the gun smoke to smother the French division from sight up ahead—making it even more difficult for D'Estrées to find his way back safely to the English. Rupert found his port and front hemmed in by the superior combined forces of Ruyter's and Bankert's ships. Once more, Ruyter had succeeded in cutting apparently impossible odds down to manageable size.

Ruyter drove in through the tumultuous squadrons, searching through the rain, fog and smoke until he found Prince Rupert's flagship. It bulked longer and higher than his own, but Ruyter drew the *Seven Provinces* up alongside Rupert's three-decker and took it on. In his excitement he raced up and down the decks, driving his gun crews to strength-draining bursts of speed.

Rupert fought back with all he had; his big guns staggered the *Seven Provinces*, smashing in its timbers, riddling its sails. But Ruyter's lighter guns were firing faster—much faster. Rupert found out what Monck and the Duke of York had learned before him; that no one could stand up to Ruyter for long in a toe-to-toe brawl. Ruyter swept Rupert's decks with wave after wave of massed iron balls and chains, slashed his rigging apart, tore down his sails, hammered over his masts. Rupert was forced to take to a boat, carry his flag to another ship.

Ruyter turned his attention anxiously toward the rear. There Sir Edward Spragge's rear English squadron had fallen behind and been set upon by Van Tromp's ships. It was impossible any longer to see Van Tromp's or Spragge's squadrons through the haze of smoke-filled fog. But the thundering of hundreds of cannons told of a desperate battle being waged back there.

Beyond the wall of smoke and mist, Van Tromp was locked in the most stubborn fight of his life with Sir Edward Spragge. Spragge, who had chosen Van Tromp as a personal enemy, had sworn to King Charles that if he did not bring Van Tromp back— dead or alive—it would be because he himself was dead.

Hour after hour their squadrons fought it out. Spragge and Van Tromp found each other early in the battle, kept chopping away from then on in a ship-to-ship duel. Spragge's ship was dismasted. He had himself rowed through the wreckage-and-corpse-strewn waves to another ship, and came back for Van Tromp. His guns crushed Van Tromp's sides. Van Tromp transferred to another ship and returned for more. Spragge's second ship became unmanageable. He lowered a boat and headed for a third ship. But the sides of the ship he was leaving were like a sieve by then. One of Van Tromp's cannon balls rammed through a hole on one side, flew through the hull and out the other side, smashing down into Spragge's boat and annihilating it. In the turbulent, storm-slashed ocean, Spragge grabbed a piece of floating wreckage and fought to keep his head above the surging waves. But by the time his men got to him in another boat and pulled him out, he had drowned. He had such a tight grip on his piece of wreckage in death that it was almost impossible to pry his cold, stiff fingers loose from it.

The fog lifted and revealed the milling shambles of the squadron Spragge had left behind him. Prince Rupert immediately began to tack his own battered squadron, heading back to join the dead Spragge's. Ruyter and Bankert followed, mauling Rupert all the way, and rejoined the triumphant Van Tromp.

But with the lifting of the fog, D'Estrées' French ships reappeared, coming back at last to join the English. Ruyter took in the changing situation quickly: He had come into the battle with only seventy ships against an enemy of over ninety. He had managed to temporarily wage an even struggle against the English by fencing off the French from the fight. But once the French were reunited with the English, his advantage would disappear.

Deciding that he had milked the last ounce of gain to be had from his tactics, Ruyter pulled out his fleet and sailed back to the coastal shallows. From there he watched the enemy fleet—all the fight knocked out of it—turn away and limp slowly back toward England.

The sight of their wrecked fleet was the last straw for the disgusted English people. Four times Ruyter had beaten them where they considered themselves strongest: on the sea. The pressure became too strong for Charles II to resist. England withdrew from the war.

And more: The battle Ruyter fought off Texel emboldened other countries who feared the growing strength of France. Nine days after the battle, Germany, Lorraine and Spain allied themselves with the Dutch against the French. This, plus the fact that Louis XIV knew his navy didn't stand a chance alone against Ruyter, caused the king to transfer his fleet from the Dutch coast to the Mediterranean. And pull his troops out of Holland.

The Dutch were saved. Ruyter, and Ruyter alone, had saved them.

Ruyter was against the project from the start. Spain had asked for help against the French navy in the Mediterranean. The Dutch, too impoverished by their wars to maintain a large war fleet during the two years since the Battle of Texel, could supply only eighteen warships in answer to the plea but these would be commanded by Ruyter. The Spanish would add twenty of their own when Ruyter arrived. Ruyter pointed out that the French navy had grown stronger and more experienced during the past two years—and that the Spanish navy was about as useful as a shadow in the kind of sea battles now being fought. He would rather do without the Spanish navy. He begged, instead, for more than eighteen Dutch warships.

One of the navy officials pointed out that Ruyter was now sixty-seven; perhaps age was undercutting his famous bravery.

"I have not begun to lose courage!" Ruyter thundered back.

"But I am surprised—and regret—that you should so expose the flag!"

The navy commissioners were sorry about it, but they just couldn't afford to send more than eighteen ships. Would not Ruyter please lead them?

"The Ministers of the State must not beseech me, but bid me," Ruyter wearily told them at last. "If I am ordered to go with a *single* ship, I will not refuse. Wherever the State wishes to risk its banner, I am ready to risk my life."

He became sick shortly before sailing time. A friend pointed out that it was a good excuse for not going. But to this suggestion he replied angrily: "I shall make this campaign even if I have to be carried on board."

He recovered enough to climb aboard himself. But his heart was heavy with gloom. "I say adieu to you," he told his wife as he left. "Not only adieu, but adieu forever. I don't expect to come back. I feel it."

He sailed from Holland with his eighteen ships on August 11, 1675. And he never returned.

Duquesne was, in Ruyter's opinion, the best fighting admiral the French had. And it was Duquesne who commanded the twenty big warships Ruyter met off the Sicilian island of Stromboli. Ruyter had managed to shake loose most of the Spanish ships that had accompanied him into the Mediterranean. Only one remained with him, bringing his strength to nineteen battleships. None was as big as any of the twenty French ships, and he had far fewer guns. To counter these disadvantages, Ruyter stretched his ships out in a line-ahead to leeward, letting the French have the weather gauge!

The reason for this unusual tactic became apparent as soon as the two enemy lines drew close enough to begin bombarding each other. The French ships, with a strong wind blowing from behind them, were heeled over toward Ruyter's line. This pushed the lower tier of gunports on each ship—on the side facing Ruyter—under water half the time. These ports had to remain closed, and the guns behind them were rendered useless. Ruyter's ships, on the other hand, were heeled over by the same wind—*away* from the French. Thus the lower tiers of Dutch guns on the side facing the enemy were raised high above the water and could remain open and in use. It was a trick Ruyter had learned from old Martin Tromp, dead so long ago of a musket ball in the heart.

There were futher advantages to a leeward position—if the superior enemy attacked. And Ruyter, knowing Duquesne, was sure that the French *would* attack. To make even surer, he had drawn his line between Duquesne and the port of Messina, where French ships were awaiting Duquesne's arrival. Duquesne, having to break past Ruyter to get to Messina, attacked.

It was what Ruyter had been waiting for. As the French line curved toward his, Ruyter was able to open with all his broadsides, to which the French could reply with only their few bow guns until they got in close. And, until the whole French line finally was closed in, their lead ships had to take a terrible mauling from Ruyter's entire line.

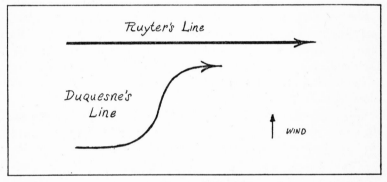

BATTLE OF STROMBOLI

But Duquesne kept coming on, as Ruyter knew he would, until the whole French line was engaged at close quarters with the Dutch. As soon as that happened, Ruyter pulled his line away to leeward, and Duquesne had to go through it all over again, taking Ruyter's bow-shattering broadsides to get in close. And yet again, Ruyter pulled his line to leeward, and Duquesne had to brave his temporarily superior fire power to get in close.

When night ended it, Ruyter had lost one ship; he had sixty men dead, including his rear admiral, and about thirty wounded. The French, also minus one ship, sailed away with Duquesne wounded, and two captains and four hundred others dead.

Three months later, Ruyter and Duquesne met again, off Palermo. Duquesne this time had twenty-nine ships. Ruyter had his seventeen Dutch warships—plus ten Spaniards.

The Spanish navy fully met Ruyter's gloomy expectations. As the two fleets swung in against each other with guns crashing, the ten Spanish ships hung back. And they stayed back—barely within long-distance gunnery range—for the rest of the fight.

Ruyter, his seventeen ships engulfed by Duquesne's twenty-nine, fought back the only way he could. He drove his ships in against the enemy's sides at pistol-shot range—where the rapid firing he had drilled into his men could make his lighter, out-numbered guns count. With enemy ships all around him, he drove in again and again, keeping his seventeen ships in his grip, fighting with that savagery that had always seemed so strange in a man who preferred the "softer" side of life.

There he fell at last. One moment he was on his feet, shouting encouragement to his seamen and gunners, his deep-lined face, still strong and tough, blackened by smoke and washed by the glare of flames. The next moment he was sprawled on the deck, a terrible pain shooting up his leg. A splinter of metal had torn away most of his ankle and foot; from the wound his blood pumped out onto the quarter-deck.

He was dazed when they carried him below. As though drifting in a fog, he lay still while the surgeon worked on him, listened to the engulfing thunder of his guns and the crashing of enemy shot against his ship. "Courage," he muttered. "Courage, my children."

He could command no longer.

But the Dutch fought on with everything he had drilled into them through the years of desperate wars. Outnumbered 29 to 17, they held their own hour after hour. Seven big French warships in turn closed in to try to board Ruyter's flagship. One after another, they were driven off by the tearing shot flung at them from Dutch guns firing with unbelievable rapidity. Until at last Duquesne, for all his superior numbers, was forced to call it a draw and sail away.

Ruyter lived out the week. "Lord," he prayed aloud toward the end, "take care of our country's fleet. Spare mercifully our officers, sailors and soldiers, who for a little money have to bear so much."

Then: "Gracious God, I thank Thee with all my heart for having kept me through so many dangers with such kindness . . . and now for visiting me in this fatherly fashion. . . ."

And then Michael de Ruyter was dead.

PART FOUR

Three Fires in the Dark

Ruyter saved his country from subjugation. But the three exhausting wars had used up the strength and resources of the Dutch. Though they held onto their freedom, they were forced to relinquish their position among the most powerful nations of the world.

By the end of the seventeenth century, England and Louis XIV's France were the world's leading powers. And, inevitably they clashed—each striving to be the power. Thus, in 1688, began a series of wars between them that ranged over the next 125 years.

The first century of this conflict was notable for the lackluster of its sea fighting. The British navy was clamped in the vise of the "Fighting Instructions," which insisted—whatever the circumstances of a particular battle—on strict adherence to the line-ahead. No commander dared break this line; it was the method of fighting with warships. This strategy-less order of battle stifled captains' initiative and made for dull, inconclusive encounters.

The French navy, for its part, held to the theory that since a fleet was a powerful force in world affairs, the best thing that any commander could do was to see that it was kept at its largest and most powerful-looking; to take no chances, that is, on getting any part of it sunk. Following the tactics of Ruyter at Stromboli, they made a policy of letting the enemy have the weather gauge in battle. From their defensive position, they would damage him as much as possible when he attacked, and pull away as soon as he got too close for comfort. Defense dictated the entire French naval strategy.

With the English sticking to the "Line" even if it meant allowing the bulk of the enemy's force to escape—and with the French escaping whenever possible—the battles of the early part of this conflict were dim skirmishes.

But through this dimness three bright fires flash: three men who believed that the purpose of having a ship under them was not just to keep that ship under them—but to reach enemy ships and destroy them. These three were an Englishman named Hawke, an adopted American named John Paul, and a Frenchman named Suffren.

12

The Old Way of Fighting

B ack in London on that miserably cold, stormy November 20 of 1759, the mob was heating itself on fear and anger. They surged through the rain-slashed streets carrying an effigy of Admiral Sir Edward Hawke, a lumpish figure dangling by its neck from a rope. For the news had reached England that Hawke had let the French battle fleet get out of Brest.

It was England's most frightening moment in this phase of the conflict with France—the Seven Years' War. Only a month before, there had been glorious news from across the Atlantic (where they called it the French and Indian War) that the English army had ripped Canada from the grasp of France. But the Atlantic was wide, the English Channel narrow. Fear of invasion gripped the Channel coast of England. On the shores of France an enormous army waited to cross. Admiral Hawke had been sent to Brest to prevent Marshal Conflans' French war fleet from getting out and convoying troop-laden transports across the Channel for the invasion. But the storms that continued day after day had forced Hawke to abandon his Brest blockade and seek safety in the port of Torbay. According to the news, Hawke had put to sea again now—but so had Conflans' French fleet. No one knew where

Conflans was. If he reached the French troop transports, however —if he gave Hawke the slip and brought them across to England. . . . Terror of invasion became hatred toward Hawke. If England was invaded, it would be Hawke's fault!

It was hard to get a fire started in that rain. The flames sputtered wetly, took hold at last, and blazed up to consume the effigy of Admiral Sir Edward Hawke.

Out on the storm-torn Channel on that same morning, Hawke drove his fleet through screaming wind under low black clouds in search of Conflans' warships.

His ship climbed a mountainous wave, rolled across its crest, and caromed down the off slope into the trough. It struck the solid mass of the next wave with a jolt that stopped it dead in its tracks. Then the bows shuddered up, running rivers of foam. The *Royal George* shook itself free, and fought its way over the next wave.

Drenched with rain and spray, Edward Hawke strained for some sight of the French fleet. Conflans couldn't have gotten far from Brest in this weather. But where was he? Lightning stabbed across the wild water, but revealed nothing to his desperately anxious scrutiny. The sea was deserted, except for his own 23 two-deckers and three-deckers—ships-of-the-line, as they'd come to be called—battling the storm.

He had sent two of his frigates—*Coventry* and *Maidstone*—to scout out the enemy, but though he had been watching for their return since dawn, there was still no sign of them—and it was now 8 A.M. Once he found Conflans' fleet, Hawke had told the officers of his ships, he had no intention of indulging in one of those stately line-against-line long-distance gunnery maneuvers. He was "for the old way of fighting"—get in close to the enemy ships "to make downright work of them." But first he had to find Conflans.

Hawke was a big man, with big features. The strong, calm, weather-roughened face under his unkempt white hair bore a remarkable resemblance to that of an American who was at that moment working with the British army in the French and Indian War: George Washington. The sea had been his home since he had joined the Royal Navy at the age of twelve. He was now fifty-four, a solid, do-your-duty professional sea officer; a bulldog who fastened his teeth in an enemy's leg and didn't let go till he had torn it off. But first he had to find his enemy. If he didn't, if he let

Conflans evade him, he knew he was ruined. Even if England hurled back the invading troops, he would be blamed. And no one would accept this storm as an excuse.

At half-past eight, Hawke thought he saw the tiny shape of a sail show itself momentarily over the crest of a wave beyond his bow. Then he saw it again—coming toward him. Soon it was near enough to make out that it was a frigate. One of his own, the *Maidstone*. Excitement raced through him. The *Maidstone*, tossed from wave to wave like a chip, was nevertheless flying her topgallants—the signal that she had spotted another fleet!

The fact that the *Maidstone* was coming from the general direction of land meant that, with this gale blowing against the coast of Brittany, he had the enemy fleet caught between his ships and the shore. If it was the enemy. Hawke ran up signals for his twenty-two other battleships to pull up close to the *Royal George* as quickly as possible in this storm. He took his flagship toward the *Maidstone*.

Within an hour word was passed down from the masthead to Hawke on the quarter-deck that twenty-one ships of the line and three frigates were just over the lee horizon. Fifteen minutes later one of the ships he had sent ahead ran up a signal. Hawke wiped the water from his eyes and squinted hard at it, made it out even before the masthead report reached him. The war fleet just beginning to show its upper sails over the distant wave tops was French. It was Conflans at last. Hawke's smile widened his big features.

The sails of the enemy rose above the horizon; their hulls came into view. But the ships were no sooner in sight than they turned away. Conflans obviously had taken one look at Hawke's force, and decided to turn tail and run for it.

Hawke sought a firmer balance on his lurching deck and yelled orders. Signals ran up the mast. The English ships shook out the reefs in their sails and surged ahead after the fleeing French fleet. Crowding on every inch of canvas he dared, Hawke got the wind directly behind him. The *Royal George* plunged ahead madly, staggering through the huge waves. At times the ship was in danger of foundering. The wind rammed into the great expanses of sail, straining the rigging and topmasts ominously. One of Hawke's junior officers pointed out the danger that the rigging might snap, the sails tear, the masts split.

"We are under the necessity," Hawke said calmly, "of running all risks to break this strong force of the enemy."

He had no intention of taking in an inch of sail. He ran up signals for the other ships to follow his example, to do their utmost to catch the fleeing French ships. They were to form up in as much of a line-ahead as they could—but not at the expense of speed. The order of each ship was to be dictated entirely by its speed. His swiftest ships began to draw far ahead of his slower ones.

It worked out well. For in a wind this strong his big three-deckers, able to crowd on more canvas, were faster than the smaller two-deckers. The biggest, most heavily-gunned ships would thus be the first to catch up with the rear of the fleeing French fleet.

By noon the coast was in sight through the downpour. Hawke—who, with his heaviest ships, was now close on the heels of the rearmost French ships—saw that Conflans intended to escape him by running his fleet into the safety of Quiberon Bay, up ahead.

Quiberon Bay was one of the most dangerous in the world, choked with hidden shoals and sharp-toothed reefs. With this howling gale driving straight into the bay, each ship would be hurled inside at breakneck speed. Furthermore, the mountainous, turbulent waves would make the ships hard to handle.

To Conflans, Quiberon Bay must have represented escape and safety. He had aboard every one of his ships a pilot who knew the bay blindfolded. Even at this speed the pilots would be able to thread the French ships safely through those reefs and shoals. But Hawke had not a single man in his fleet who knew the position of the under-surface shoals. And a ship that rushed blindly into Quiberon Bay in a storm like this stood an excellent chance of ripping out its bottom before it was through the entrance.

Conflans sailed into Quiberon Bay certain that no English commander would dare follow him and run the risk of sinking most of a fleet on the hidden rocks. And indeed, it was a risk no other commander of the time *would* have dared to take. But Hawke was a bulldog. As Conflans led the way into Quiberon Bay, Hawke's foremost ships began to engage the rearmost French. Hawke refused to let go.

"Where there is a passage for the enemy," he reasoned aloud to his officers as he watched Conflans' flagship curve around a wave-smashed reef far up ahead, "there is a passage for me."

He watched the few English ships ahead of him overhauling the last French ships. The muffled roar of cannons drifted back to him through the shriek of the wind, the pound of the ocean against the reefs and the lee shore. And he made his decision to drive into Quiberon Bay, with every ship carrying as much canvas as it could bear without pulling out the masts. "We are so close up to them," he shouted through the wind at his officers as he pointed ahead to the French, "that their pilots shall be ours. If they go to pieces on the shoals, they'll serve as beacons. If they have the advantage of knowing the way, we have that of a superior seamanship and gunnery when we overtake them."

It was almost three in the afternoon when the English surged into Quiberon Bay on the heels of the French. The storm clouds and the downpour made it seem more like dusk. It became increasingly difficult for Hawke to make out what was happening at the fringes of the fleets as his ships pulled up alongside the French and engaged. But there was no longer any order to this battle, anyway. There couldn't be, with two large fleets clashing inside a tight, shoal-strewn bay in the midst of driving wind and high seas. It was each ship for itself.

Hawke, confident that his captains knew what he expected of them in this ship-to-ship melee, concentrated on the fighting and sailing of his flagship. The ports of the two upper gun tiers of the *Royal George* had been opened, their guns forced out along with the guns on the forecastle and quarter-deck. The ports of the lowest gun deck of the three-decker, being only four or five feet above water in the calmest weather, were closed—in this turbulent storm it would be suicide to open them. As it was, while the *Royal George* lurched into the bay toward the nearest French ships, huge waves crashed against its sides and hurled up torrents of ocean through the open ports of the middle and upper gun decks. Water sprayed over the guns and their crews, poured across the decks inside. The men sloshed around in the water, hanging onto the gun breechings and relieving tackle, battling to hold the heavy guns in position against the wild rolling of the ship. Hawke rationed out the crews from the unused lower guns among the guns that were in use, to help to keep them from breaking loose in the battle.

Foaming wavetops creamed over the bows of the *Royal George* and across the forecastle deck. Hawke drove in amongst the embattled fleets and began to pound cannon fire into the French ships as he overhauled them. Without pausing to duel with them, he rushed deeper into the heart of the battle. He was searching for Conflans' flagship, the *Soleil Royal*.

As the close-hauled *Royal George* heaved itself on through the storm, Hawke had a shocking glimpse that proved the wisdom of doing without his lower-deck guns. As he pulled up to a French seventy-four, the enemy ship suddenly opened its lower gunports to take him on. The ocean rushed in, and the French ship sank from Hawke's sight.

The *Royal George* pushed on, her topmasts bending, straining— her taut, shivering shrouds wrestling the gale for control of her sails. Up ahead, Hawke saw one of his ships, the *Resolution*, exchanging point-blank broadsides with the French rear admiral's flagship, the *Formidable*. He swung the *Royal George* over against the *Formidable's* other side and raked it with every one of his usable guns. Caught between two English ships, the *Formidable* struck its colors.

Leaving the captured prize in the possession of the *Resolution*, Hawke drove on, deeper into the battle, and passed the English *Torbay,* which had just ripped the French *Thésée* into a sinking wreck. As he continued his search, he came upon the huge French *Héros* and the English *Magnanime*, which had managed to rake the Frenchman again and again. The *Héros* surrendered as Hawke passed by, but by then the sea was so savage no boat could be sent to take possession of it.

At last Hawke saw what he sought, Conflans' *Soleil Royal*. He turned quickly to his flag captain and ordered him to catch the enemy flagship. The flag captain peered at the foam-churned reefs close to Conflans and shook his head darkly, arguing that they would be running the danger of putting the *Royal George* on a shoal.

Hawke nodded tightly. "You have done your duty, sir, in showing me the danger. Now comply with my order. Lay me alongside Conflans."

Having said his say, Hawke's flag captain obeyed without another word. The *Royal George* surged forward. Hawke saw, with pleasure, that Conflans was bringing the *Soleil Royal* around to meet him. He watched the distance between them narrow. His gun crews, working on decks now as slippery as wet soap, struggled with extra in-tackles to keep their guns run out against the pitch and wallow of the ship.

The *Royal George* and *Soleil Royal* swung broadside-to-broadside. The guns roared. Heavy iron shot crashed into their sides and dug across their decks. Both commanders tried to come about, but Hawke beat Conflans and raked him with every usable gun in his other broadside. Then he swept past, reloaded, and lurched back.

Conflans' broadside missed almost entirely as a huge wave lifted the *Soleil Royal* and hurled it to one side, throwing the French shots wild. The *Royal George*, rolling badly as it fired its answering broadside, went wide of the mark too.

Hawke swung around and came in close for his next broadside, saw it rip its way through Conflans' sails and rigging. Conflans' shots thudded into Hawke's hull. The *Royal George* came around again, fired. The shots crashed into the *Soleil Royal's* side, many of them breaking in through the open gunports. Hawke pulled away for reloading, came back with yet another broadside.

Conflans moved off, obviously having had more than enough. Hawke, triumphant, plunged after him. But the French 74-gun *Superbe* drove in between Hawke and Conflans, ready to take on the *Royal George*. As soon as Hawke saw the *Superbe* slipping in across his bows, he ordered the *Royal George* swung from its course, bringing it suddenly side-by-side with the *Superbe* at musket-shot distance. The *Royal George* leaped as its guns fired together, with a sound like one long roll of thunder. Hawke's broadside rammed low against the hull of the *Superbe*, caving it in. Hawke came about. The *Superbe*, with the ocean pouring in through its maimed side, was listing so badly she could not maneuver at all—could only wallow, and wait. Hawke pushed in close and smashed his broadside into the maimed hull, opening it completely. The *Superbe* foundered, sank beneath the waves with almost every man on board.

Conflans' *Soleil Royal* had taken advantage of the respite to put distance between itself and the *Royal George*. And when Hawke took up the pursuit again, he was beset by other French ships now coming to Conflans' assistance. Interposing themselves between the *Soleil Royal* and its pursuer, these began to swarm all around the *Royal George*. Hawke, his guns firing continuously, found himself engaged with seven enemy ships at the same time.

Hundreds of French shots hammered his sides, swept his decks, slashed his rigging and sails. Hawke fought back fiercely, but for a time he seemed doomed. Then the French ships surrounding him began to fall away. Hawke's other ships had seen his danger and were streaming in from all sides to get him out of it. Hawke saw the *Union* rolling up; then the *Hero* and the *Mars*. English ships were approaching from all directions.

The seven French ships let go of the *Royal George* and beat a hasty retreat at the heels of Conflans' *Soleil Royal*.

Hawke took up the pursuit again. But it was too late to press it home. Somewhere behind the dense curtain of black storm clouds, the sun went down. Within minutes, the bay was engulfed in the shrieking night. Here and there, ships still found enemies to fire at, but the storm-filled darkness put an end to effective battling. Hawke, with no way of finding out the results of the battle until there was light, anxiously waited out the night.

In the morning, he counted the casualties—and realized his job was done. The broken French fleet was scattered to the winds. Completely disunited in their mad flight out of Quiberon Bay, some of the French ships had made it; others had not.

Conflans' *Soleil Royal* had gone aground, and been abandoned. So had the *Héros*. Hawke ordered both ships burned. Four other French ships had been sunk, and one captured. Seven French battleships and three frigates had managed to escape into the shallow Vilaine River, throwing their guns and supplies overboard so they would be light enough to get over the bar at its mouth. But many of them broke their backs on the bottom of the shallow little river; the rest were not able to work their way back across the bar, out of the river, for over a year. Only about seven of the French ships-of-the-line had managed to get out of Quiberon Bay and safely out of Hawke's reach.

Hawke, in turn, had lost two ships—both to the hidden shoals. The *Resolution* and the *Essex* had broken themselves on the same underwater rocks.

Hawke had shown that he had more fight in him than anyone on the sea since Ruyter. His forthright courage had stopped cold the French plan of invading England.

The news sped home to England. And the same crowds that had burned Sir Edward Hawke in effigy just two days before rushed down the streets again, cheering his name this time until they were hoarse.

13

The Officer of Fine Feelings

CAPTAIN JONES AND THE SEA RAPER

It was in 1775 that young John Paul Jones first fell deeply in love. The girl was nineteen-year-old Dorothea Spottswood Dandridge, the sparkling belle of Hanover County, Virginia. He longed to marry her—but dared not even ask. For Dorothea belonged to one of the best families in the colonies. Her grandfather had been Virginia's governor; her father's lawyer was Patrick Henry; her cousin was Martha Washington. Such a family would want to know something about his past: who he was, what he was—whether it was true that Jones was not his real last name; and if so, why he had assumed it. And he didn't dare tell them. If he did, whatever hope he had of marrying Dorothea Dandridge would be smashed.

Who was he? What was he? The answers are almost as cloudy today as they were while he lived. "The first duty of a gentleman," he said, "is to respect his own character." But an effort to find the true character of John Paul Jones leads into a maze of contradictions. He was, in turn, a Scottish merchant seaman, an English navy midshipman, mate of a slaver, an actor, skipper of a merchant ship, and America's most famous naval hero.

181

His name was actually John Paul. He took the last name of "Jones" for the usual reason: to conceal his past. Two charges of murder hung over him—and a strong suspicion of piracy. Some of the troubles that plagued him undoubtedly were of his own making. He was vain, highly ambitious and had an ungovernable temper. But much of the blight on his name was certainly placed there by men—like those who late in his life brought forward the ridiculous charge that he had raped a ten-year-old girl— whose jealousy was enflamed by his brilliance. "It may be said that I have been unfortunate," John Paul Jones said. "But it cannot be made to appear that I have ever, even in the weakest Moment of my Life, been capable of a Base or mean Action. Nature has given me a heart that is highly susceptible to the finer feelings."

What *was* he like? John Adams, who was a commissioner to France when he met the captain soon to gain his highest fame in the service of the American Revolution, described him this way: "Jones has art and secrecy, and aspires very high. Eccentricities and irregularities are to be expected from him. They are in his character, they are visible in his eye. His voice is soft and still and small; his eye has keenness and wildness and softness in it."

And Adams' wife, Abigail, gave another impression of John Paul Jones in writing to Elizabeth Cranch: "From the intrepid character he justly supported in the American Navy, I expected to have seen a rough, stout, warlike Roman—instead of that I should sooner think of wrapping him up in cotton-wool, and putting him into my pocket, than sending him to contend with cannon balls. He is small of stature, well proportioned, soft in his speech, easy in his address, polite in his manners, vastly civil, understands all the etiquette of a lady's toilette as perfectly as he does the mast, sails and rigging of his ship. Under all this appearance of softness he is bold, enterprising, ambitious and active . . . he is said to be a man of gallantry and a favorite amongst the French ladies. . . ."

A man of contradictions, difficult to understand. The mystery begins with his birth in a cottage on the coast of Scotland. His father, John Paul, Sr., was gardener for Robert Craik's Arbigland estate. But there were rumors that the elder John Paul was not his real father—that he was actually the illegitimate son of the Earl of Selkirk. The gossip was apparently unfounded. But there are indications that John Paul Jones may himself have half-believed it to be true. Most of his childhood was spent on the Earl of Selkirk's nearby estate, on Saint Mary's Isle, where his Uncle George was a gardener. There he may have daydreamed that he was the secret son of the nobleman around whose castle he played. It is the sort of notion that might get into the head of a child of overactive imagination. But though most people would leave such romantic imaginings behind with their childhood, John Paul did not.

He was twelve when he went to sea, an ambitious boy determined to make his mark in the world. Focusing his considerable energy on the job of learning his trade, he became so proficient during many voyages to Virginia (where his brother William had settled as a tailor) and the West Indies, that he was made a first mate by the time he was nineteen. He was on his way to solid success. It was a success, however, lacking in romance; and so he left merchant shipping for a try at the Royal Navy as a midshipman.

Soon after he realized that he lacked sufficient influence in high places to rise in officer rank, his restless seeking drove him from the navy to the slave trade. But two years of this traffic sickened him beyond continuing. He quit just as he was on his way to making a fortune as a slaver—and turned to acting.

Although he had had little formal education before the age of twelve—and none after that—John Paul was well-read at the age of twenty-one. Books—especially poetry and plays—were his constant companions aboard ship. When he auditioned for John Moody's theatrical company, then playing on Jamaica, his ability to read lines so impressed Moody that he was taken into the company despite his total lack of experience. As he worked at this new profession, his poise and ability to handle words (and people with them) swiftly grew. But though the life of an actor might be romantic, it was sadly lacking in physical action. After a short spell with Moody's company, John Paul took his wages and bought a passage back to Scotland on a vessel named the *John*. He sailed as a passenger, but when the master and chief mate died early in the voyage he was the only man aboard able to take over. Upon getting the *John* safely back to Scotland, he was rewarded by being made its official master. And it was later on the *John* that the first of what he referred to later as "my great misfortunes" occurred—in the person of Mungo Maxwell.

Mungo Maxwell was a sailor aboard the *John* when it was

anchored at Tobago. Seamen are notoriously not up to their best work when within sight and smell of land, but young skipper John Paul could not allow for that. He warned Maxwell about his laziness. Instead of heeding the warning, Maxwell became even more negligent. John Paul's growing anger finally erupted in blind rage. Grabbing up a cat-o'-nine-tails, he tried to beat Maxwell into obedience. When Maxwell went ashore, he showed his wounds to the Court of Vice-Admiralty, and lodged a complaint. Summoned by the court, John Paul explained about Maxwell's laziness and admitted he was ashamed to have lost control of himself. The complaint was dismissed, and Maxwell, still grumbling about John Paul's treatment of him, shipped out on another vessel.

It would have ended there had not Mungo Maxwell come from the same section of Scotland as John Paul—and had he not died aboard his new ship.

John Paul did not learn of Maxwell's death until his return to Scotland. There he found old friends turning their backs on him. Maxwell's father charged formally that he had "unmercifully . . . beat, bled and bruised" his son, and thus caused his subsequent death. John Paul was arrested, and put in prison.

He finally managed to get out on bail for the purpose of proving that he hadn't killed Mungo Maxwell and sailed back to Tobago to try to ward off a trial for murder. There, as proofs of his innocence, he obtained a written statement by the Judge Advocate of the Tobago Vice-Admiralty that the charge was "without justification"—and a declaration by the master of the ship on which Maxwell had died that Maxwell seemed "in perfect health for some days after he came aboard . . . his death was occasioned by a fever or lowness of spirits."

The trial never materialized, but it would have been better if John Paul *had* been tried. For his name was never officially cleared and the stories about his murderous viciousness remained in circulation in Tobago and Scotland, magnified with time, and were there to condemn him in his second "great misfortune."

This occurred when his new ship, the *Betsy,* sailed into Tobago in the last month of 1772. His crew wanted some of their wages to spend on the island. But John Paul, having spent every cent of what he had made on his cargo to buy more cargo to take back to Britain, intended to pay his crew at the end of the voyage.

The men became surly. One of them, possessed of a temper equal to John Paul's, got into a vicious argument with him. At its height, John Paul's fury boiled over and he snatched up his sword. The sailor grabbed a bludgeon, lunged with it. John Paul drove his sword through the sailor and killed him.

Sobering instantly, John Paul stared down at the dead man, shocked at what he had done. In killing the sailor, he had destroyed the future he had worked for through most of his twenty-six years. He could plead self-defense; but he knew that this time he had no hope of being exonerated in a trial for murder—not with the memory of Mungo Maxwell in people's minds; not when most of the witnesses hated him.

The dazed John Paul went ashore and on the advice of friends mounted a fast horse, raced across the island to another harbor, and shipped out on the first vessel he found ready to sail. He sailed into two years of almost complete obscurity.

What sort of ship did he sail during those two years? We have one report, told by Thomas Chase of Martha's Vineyard:

In September 1773, the people living near Holme's Hole, Martha's Vineyard, were astonished to see a rather singular craft put into their port. The vessel was a sharp, rakish, clipper built craft, painted entirely black, with no name whatever marked upon her. She carried three long nine-pounders, which could be moved to any part of her deck; one "long-tom" on a pivot and apparently a full supply of small arms of every description. She was a very fast sailer. The crew seemed to consist of about forty men, mostly Spaniards with a few Portuguese among them. The captain announced himself as Paul Jones.

The ship had been in a fight with another ship somewhere off Long Island. Several of the crew had been wounded, and an officer killed. Captain "Paul Jones" had put into the port to bury the officer. Thomas Chase got the job of making the coffin and became friendly with the strange captain, who told him "in private, that his men were 'a set of Spanish and Portuguese desperadoes.' They were under excellent control however."

It had, in short, the look of a pirate ship—and "Paul Jones" was her captain. There can be no question that Paul Jones and John Paul were the same man. For Thomas Chase joined the navy during the Revolution and ended up on one of John Paul Jones' ships, where the two men recognized each other and renewed their friendliness. Chase describes John Paul as he was when he brought his mysterious black vessel into Martha's Vineyard:

He stood about five feet six inches high; he was stoutly built but not corpulent, and had a very broad chest and shoulders, and arms unusually long for a man of his height. He was remarkably muscular, and seemed able to use almost all of his great strength in his sword arm. The muscles of his face were firm, giving great severity to his expression. Among his peculiarities was that of an uncommonly deep, strong, resonant and powerful voice, of that peculiar carrying quality which made it distinctly audible, even in the greatest noise and confusion.

John Paul, forced to the life of a fugitive from justice, seems to have fled aboard a pirate ship and ended up as its captain. But piracy could hardly be any more in keeping with his own image of himself than a career in the slave trade had been. There was no sign of him until he appeared in the beginning of 1775, alone in Virginia—determined to leave the sea behind him and try for a change of fortune as a landsman in the New World. He called himself, variously: Paul Jones, J. Paul Jones, and sometimes just J. P. Jones. And his fortunes did begin to change. He made influential friends, became well-liked around Hanover County, and met and fell in love with the beautiful Dorothea Dandridge.

It was love that brought him torment. Between him and his love stood his past. If he could not ask for Dorothea's hand without revealing it, he could even less hope to win that hand once it was revealed. He thought he saw a way out of his dilemma in the American War of Independence from England, which broke out that year. Here was a chance to make up for everything that had gone before in his life. John Paul Jones resolved to so distinguish himself that his fame would overshadow anything that might creep from his past to haunt him. Once redeemed, he could ask the girl he loved to marry him, and settle down to a solid future of Virginian respectability. But first he must persuade his influential friends to obtain a commission for him in the infant American navy.

The "Continental Navy" of the rebel colonies was a farce as far as England was concerned. For the most part, its record throughout the Revolution was shameful. Many of the officers and crewmen who might have accomplished something with naval vessels preferred the profits of privateering. Those officers who did join the new navy, from Commander-in-Chief Ezek Hopkins on down, were apt to be appointed solely through family influence. In their timidity and unsureness, they accomplished almost nothing. Their pallid records made the work of the few naval officers who deserved the name shine more brilliantly by comparison. And John Paul Jones—originally appointed first lieutenant of the *Alfred* under Captain Dudley Saltonstall—swiftly proved himself the most brilliant and energetic of all.

He accepted his appointment as a first lieutenant without disappointment, determined to learn the fine points of naval warfare from his superiors. But he soon realized that they had nothing to teach him—that there wasn't a captain in the new navy, with the exception of Nicholas Biddle, who wouldn't profit from working *under him.* Commander-in-Chief Hopkins so thoroughly botched his first mission—a raid on the British powder stores in the Bahamas—that only John Paul's initiative prevented a complete fiasco. When one of the captains was dismissed for cowardice on this cruise, John Paul got his reward: The command of the fast little 12-gun *Providence.*

As captain of the *Providence,* he sailed out alone to raid English shipping along the American coast. Outsailing every large English navy ship that tried to stop him, in just seven weeks he had captured or sunk sixteen enemy merchant vessels. Hopkins became so jealous of his subordinate's achievements that when John Paul was appointed to the command of a squadron, Hopkins refused to recognize the appointment. Although Hopkins' stupidity and incompetence finally got him removed from his position as commander-in-chief, John Paul's opportunity had by then slipped out of his grasp. Bitterly, he transferred his command to the *Alfred* alone and with her continued to ravage English shipping in American waters. His bitterness increased as men of far inferior ability continued to rise above him. It seemed that the more he accomplished the lower his fortunes ebbed. And then, his fortunes turned again.

On June 14, 1777, the Continental Congress passed a number of resolutions—two of which make that day most memorable:

Resolved: That the flag of the thirteen United States be thirteen stripes, alternate red and white, that the Union be thirteen stars, white on a blue field, representing a new constellation.

Resolved: That Captain Paul Jones be appointed to command the ship *Ranger*.

On October 31 of that year, John Paul Jones pointed the *Ranger*—a fast, 18-gun war sloop—across the Atlantic toward friendly France, from whose shores he intended to carry the war to mighty England itself. His orders from the Marine Committee read: "We shall not limit you to any particular cruising station, but leave you at large to search for yourself where the greatest chance of success presents."

Benjamin Franklin, America's chief representative in France, liked John Paul Jones from the moment he met him. "When face to face with him," Franklin said, "neither man, nor, so far as I can learn, woman, can resist the strange magnetism of his presence, the indescribable charm of his manner."

John Paul was at his best, brimming over with excitement, energy and plans. This was his opportunity to win the fame that would eclipse his past. The *Ranger* slashed through English shipping all around the British coasts. English insurance rates sky-rocketed as he snatched his prizes from under the nose of the powerful British navy. England's faith in its own invulnerability was badly shaken when he sailed into the harbor of Whitehaven, surprised its fort and spiked its guns, set fire to ships in the harbor, and sailed away without a single casualty.

The American Revolution had seemed far away, hardly real, to the English until John Paul Jones brought it into their laps. Now they demanded that the famous British navy catch "the pirate." One English warship, the 20-gun *Drake,* did catch him. The *Ranger* and the *Drake* fought for one hour and four minutes. And every minute of that time, John Paul Jones outmaneuvered and outfought Burden, the English captain. By the time the *Drake* surrendered—the first English warship ever to strike to an American flag—its rigging was in shreds, its sides broken, its captain and first lieutenant killed, and forty others dead or wounded. John Paul had lost three men killed and had five others injured.

The effect of this fight was fantastic. Wealthy people living on the English coast retired inland. Militia camps, filled with volunteers prepared to repel any invasion attempt by John Paul Jones, sprang up all over the country. Shipping insurance rates tripled overnight.

It was the evening before his victory over the *Drake* that John

Paul Jones pulled his puzzling raid on Saint Mary's Isle, with the intention of kidnapping the Earl of Selkirk. There is a strong suspicion that he did it merely for the purpose of facing the man he thought to be his real father. But he said afterwards that he intended to use the Earl as a hostage to persuade the King of England to allow an exchange of American prisoners of war. Whatever he really wanted, he learned on landing that the Earl of Selkirk was not at home. This made the raid completely purposeless, and his officers and men began to grumble that they should gain something for the danger they had run in making the landing. To placate them, Jones sent two of his officers into the Earl's home to demand all the silver plate in the place. He himself did not enter the house, but waited outside, strolling around the gardens in which he had played as a child, keeping an eye on the rest of his men to make sure they remained quiet and did no damage.

Lady Selkirk, with perfect composure, saw to it that all the silver plate was delivered up as demanded. Then, when they had gone, she sat down and wrote to her husband in some astonishment that they had just taken the plate and themselves off to the *Ranger* and sailed away without harming a soul. "This Paul Jones," she added at the end of her note, "is one John Paul, born at Arbigland . . . a great villain as ever was born, guilty of many crimes and several murders by ill usage, was tried and condemned for one, escaped, and followed a piratical life, till he engaged with the Americans. He seems to delight in that still, as robbing a house is below the dignity of the States of America."

Imagine her amazement, then, when not long afterwards she found herself receiving a letter from the villainous John Paul Jones:

Ranger, Brest, 8th May, 1778.

MADAM:

It cannot be too much lamented that in the profession of arms, the Officer of fine feelings, and of real sensibility, should be under the necessity of winking at any action of persons under his command, which his heart cannot approve. . . . This hard case was mine when on the 23rd. of April last I landed on St. Mary's Isle. Knowing Lord Selkirk's interest with his King, and esteeming as I do his private Character . . . it was my intention to have taken him on board the *Ranger,* and to have detained him till thro' his means, a general and fair exchange of Prisoners as well in Europe as in America had been effected. When I was informed that his Lordship was absent, I walked back to my boat determining to leave the Island; by the way, however, some officers who were with me could not forbear expressing their discontent, observing that in America no delicacy was shown by the English, who took away all sorts of movable property. . . . I had but a moment to think how I might gratify them, and at the same time do your Ladyship the least injury. . . . I have gratified my men, and when the plate is sold, I shall become the purchaser, and I will *gratify my own feelings* by restoring it to you. . . .

I have the Honour to be with much Esteem and with profound Respect,

Madam,

Your most obedient and most humble servant,

Paul Jones

It was the Earl of Selkirk who undertook to answer this strange letter from the enemy, explaining to Lord Despenser, the Postmaster-General who must pass his answer: "He is such an odd fellow by what I hear of him, (for we were perfectly unacquainted with him till his landing at my house) that it is not easy to know how to write him. You would see by his strange ridiculous bombast letter, that he is altogether an exotick character. . . . He is said to be a most cruel fellow, to have committed no less than three murders. . . . I have made my letter to him intolerably long, but I could not well help it, unless I had given him a very short answer, which might have made him burn my house at his next trip to these coasts. . . ."

And to John Paul Jones he wrote, in part: "The letter you wrote to Lady Selkirk . . . was matter of surprise both to my wife and me, as no apology was expected. . . . I own I do not understand how a man of *Sensibility to fine feelings* could reconcile [the raid] to what his heart approved, especially as the carrying me off could have no possible effect for the purpose you mention. . . . It was certainly fortunate both for Lady Selkirk and me, that I was from home, and it was also fortunate for you, Sir, that your officers and men behaved well, for had any of my family suffered outrage, murder or violence, no quarter of the Globe should have secured you nor even some of those under whose commission you act, from my vengeance. But, Sir, I am happy that their welfare enables me to inform you . . . your two Officers and Men . . . in every respect behaved as well as could be expected on such an occasion. . . . You, Sir, are entitled to the Praise of having your men under good discipline, which on all occasions I take care to make known."

After the war was over, a large package arrived at Saint Mary's Isle. The Earl of Selkirk, opening it, found that it was from John Paul Jones—and that it contained all the silver plate which had been taken from his home. The Earl proudly put the silver on exhibition, for by then John Paul Jones was a world-famous name. One year after the raid on Saint Mary's Isle, he had come out in a new ship called the *Bon Homme Richard,* and fought the *Serapis.* . . .

John Paul Jones had it at last: a really big ship under him. She bore the name *Bon Homme Richard,* and she mounted forty guns.

He turned from watching the British merchant convoy coming over the horizon toward him down the coast of England at six o'clock on that evening of September 23, 1779, and looked around at the squadron trailing behind him: the 30-gun *Alliance,* the 32-gun *Pallas,* the little 12-gun *Vengeance.* The enemy merchant fleet was convoyed by only two English warships, which should have given him a big advantage in numbers—but it didn't. Because his other three ships were commanded by Frenchmen, who considered themselves under no real obligation to obey him. Whatever he had achieved so far on this voyage had been in spite of them. Captain Ricot of the *Vengeance* and Captain Cottineau of the *Pallas* might or might not do their duty. But he could absolutely depend on Captain Landais of the *Alliance* to do the wrong thing. Landais was the latest of John Paul's "great misfortunes." The politicians back in America had given a commission to Landais as a gesture of good will toward France. But John Paul knew the French navy had thrown Landais out for insubordination. On this voyage, Landais had shown all the qualities that had wrecked his career in the French navy—refusing to obey John Paul's orders at every turn, disappearing repeatedly with his ship, running away at every sniff of danger. John Paul treated Landais with the thin edge of his contempt, and Landais in turn loathed John Paul with hatred bordering on insanity.

Under these conditions, it was miraculous that John Paul had accomplished so much on this voyage. The combined fleets of France and America had not achieved a fraction of the effect produced among the English people by this lone captain. It was he who made them take the American war seriously and begin creating a movement to call the war off. "For God's sake get to sea instantly," were the orders the British Admiralty gave one of its commanders. "If you can take Paul Jones you will be as high in the estimation of the public as if you had beat the combined fleets."

And now he saw ahead of him his supreme opportunity: a large merchant fleet and two enemy warships. Always before, sailing on small vessels, he had been forced to flee those big English men-of-war. This time he had a big ship of his own—though it was old and lumbering and cranky—and forty guns of his own—though they were secondhand and unpredictable.

John Paul signaled for the rest of his squadron to draw up in line-of-battle behind him, and began pushing the *Bon Homme Richard* across the smooth water toward the merchant convoy. Glancing back, he saw that the *Pallas* and *Vengeance* were coming along with him. The *Alliance* was not; Landais had instead sailed her away to wait and watch from a safe distance. John Paul shrugged and returned his attention to the enemy ahead. He was not surprised by Landais' action—would not be surprised if Ricot and Cottineau also pulled away at the last moment. He was counting only on himself this evening—and on the *Bon Homme Richard*.

The *Richard* was actually not much to count on, as he knew only too well. He had begged for a bigger ship than the *Ranger*, and this was what they had given him: a twenty-three-year-old merchant tub, slow, hard to handle at sea; a sluggish sailer with rotting timbers. She had been named the *Duc de Duras* when he had gotten her. He had wanted to rename her after Ben Franklin, who had helped him so much in France. But Franklin had powerful political enemies, and John Paul got along badly enough with politicians as it was. He compromised by calling her *Bon Homme Richard* in honor of Franklin's *Poor Richard's Almanack*.

Naming the ship was easier than converting it into a man-of-war. He spent weeks trying to find guns for it. Those he managed to collect were pretty old, some so old as to be downright dangerous to the men handling them. The worst were the biggest ones: six 18-pounders. He put these in the lower gun deck, where there were just six gunports on either side. In the main gun deck he positioned twenty-eight 12-pounders. Eight 9-pounders he distributed among the quarter-deck, forecastle and gangways.

A sluggish ship, a motley collection of guns, and an even more motley crew: French sailors and marines, exchanged American prisoners of war, some Spaniards, Portuguese and Malay seamen —and even some English deserters. They filled out a crew whose core consisted of twenty-eight men, like Midshipman Nathaniel Fanning and the Narragansett Indian gunner Red Cherry, who had been with him on the *Ranger*. With this ship, battery and crew he would take on this evening the trained gunners and sailors of a larger, faster, more heavily gunned English warship.

The enemy merchant fleet had spotted him now, John Paul saw. They were tacking, to dash in to the safety of Scarborough harbor. John Paul, following as fast as the *Bon Homme Richard* could go, saw the two English men-of-war come up around the merchant ships and slip in between them and their pursuers.

Captains Ricot and Cottineau saw them too. The *Pallas* and *Vengeance* began to fall away to leeward. Knowing the futility of trying to bring them back to order, John Paul picked up his spyglass and concentrated on the enemy.

It was almost dusk now, but a full moon was rising over the smooth sea to help him make out the nature of his foe. The smaller of the two warships was a converted yacht carrying twenty guns: the *Countess of Scarborough*. John Paul moved his glass till he got the much larger warship in focus. It was a brand-new, copper-sheathed vessel carrying fifty guns—all good guns; twenty of them 18-pounders. It took a while for John Paul and his officers to make out its name: *Serapis*. The name passed swiftly among the crew of the *Bon Homme Richard,* who had difficulty pronouncing it. One of the gunners solved this problem by yelling at the top of his lungs: "Look out boys! Here comes the Sea Raper!"

The howl of laughter that swept through the ship after that was music to John Paul's ears. He closed his spyglass with a snap and gave his orders. The *Bon Homme Richard* rolled in to get between the two English warships and the coast—to make sure they didn't try to escape after the merchant ships. His moment for full glory was on hand and he knew it. He didn't intend to be cheated of it.

A look back now revealed that none of his squadron was with him any more. Landais' *Alliance* was still far off there in the distance, motionless. The other two were fleeing out of range. Fury at this desertion added to his determination to tackle the two

nearing Englishmen. Quickly, he assigned his officers: Pierre
Girard to stick by him wherever he went and interpret his orders
to the French crewmen; master-at-arms John Burbank to keep
watch on the two hundred prisoners from captured English ships
who were locked up in the hold; Colonel Chamillard to station his
French marines on the top of the poop deck; Lieutenant Stack and
Midshipman Fanning to direct the marksmen up in the masts;
First Lieutenant Richard Dale and Colonel Weibert to direct the
American and French gunners on the main gun deck; Acting Lieutenant Mayrant to direct the six 18-pounders in the lower deck;
purser Matthew Mease to take charge of the quarter-deck guns.

Officers and men rushed away to man their stations. John Paul
Jones remained where he was, Pierre Girard by his side, watching
the nearing enemy ships. In the gathering darkness, the *Bon
Homme Richard* and the larger of the two Englishmen, the *Serapis,*
drifted slowly closer to each other on the same tack.

Aboard the *Serapis,* Captain Pearson was studying the black-
painted ship intently through his spyglass, unable to make out
what it was since it flew no colors. "It is probably Paul Jones," he
said to his officers. "If so, there's work to be done."

He lowered his spyglass and sent the crews to their guns. But
still, he wasn't sure. He held fire as the *Serapis* and the strange
black ship moved slowly closer, within hailing distance.

"What ship is that?" he shouted at the *Bon Homme Richard.*

"I can't hear what you say!" yelled back John Paul, stalling for
time, trying to let his ship fall back so that he could maneuver
to rake the stern of the *Serapis.* But Captain Pearson was too
canny for that, and the *Serapis* was so much the better sailer
that he was easily able to prevent the maneuver.

He hailed for identification again: "Answer immediately! Or
I shall be under the necessity of firing upon you!"

The two ships were side by side now at close range. John Paul's
shout rang through the ship: Fire all starboard guns! The *Bon
Homme Richard's* first broadside thundered out through the
moonlit dusk and tore its way across the decks of the *Serapis.*

On its heels came two tremendous shocks that ripped through
the vitals of the ship under his feet: the answering broadside from
the *Serapis* crashing low against its hull above the waterline, and a
violent explosion from the lower steerage gun deck.

John Paul raced down to see what had happened, met Lieutenant

Mayrant coming up, his face blackened and his clothes smoking, blood running down the side of his head. Leaning against the bulkhead for support, Mayrant reported that two of the ancient 18-pounders in the lower gun deck had exploded, killing their crews, wounding every other man on that station, blowing a large hole in the hull, and wrecking the deck so thoroughly that the other 18-pounders could hardly be used even if they wanted to risk it.

Livid with rage, John Paul cursed with a vivid fluency that excited the admiration of Pierre Girard—who later claimed that John Paul Jones kept it up throughout the rest of the fight without once repeating himself. He ordered the lower-deck ports closed, sent Mayrant and the other survivors to help on the main gun deck, and rushed back up onto his quarter-deck. As his own lower-deck ports closed, he saw those of the *Serapis* opening for the first time. Out through those lower ports came the mouths of Pearson's own 18-pounders—ten of them. The *Bon Homme Richard* staggered under their impact, let loose its reply—and then staggered again as an unexpected salvo from another direction raked its port side.

John Paul whirled toward the new danger. He'd almost forgotten the other British ship, the 20-gun *Countess of Scarborough*. There she was, slipping past after having emptied her battery at him, swinging around for another try.

Suddenly, out of the dimness behind the *Countess of Scarborough,* another ship appeared: the 30-gun *Pallas.* Captain Cottineau had left the *Vengeance* and *Alliance* and sped back across the smooth, moonlit water to throw his weight into the fight.

The *Countess of Scarborough,* finding herself attacked by the bigger warship, swung away from the *Bon Homme Richard* and ran for her life, the *Pallas* in close pursuit. Captain John Paul Jones and Captain Pearson were left to fight it out between them.

The *Bon Homme Richard* was taking an awful smashing. From the wreckage of his quarter-deck, John Paul watched his guns overturned and demolished, called to his men to help him as he began to drag guns from his unengaged port-side battery to replace them. But there was no way to go on replacing the men who manned the guns. They were dying all about him.

Purser Mease collapsed with blood streaming from his scalp

and was carried below to the surgeon. John Paul took his place directing the quarter-deck battery, and ended by joining the decimated gun crew at one of the 9-pounders until Mease returned, his head swathed in a bloody bandage. Then he hurried down the ladder to see what was happening on his main gun deck, where the salvos were becoming more and more scattered. The gaping holes in the hull, the caved-in ports, the dismantled guns, the corpses—all told their story. He had to scream at Lieutenant Dale to make himself heard through the roaring of guns in the smoke-filled deck: "His metal is too heavy for us, Dick! He's hammering us to pieces! We must close with him!"

It was his last hope. If he could only get close enough to the enemy so that the French marines on his high poop and the marksmen in the tops could bring their muskets to bear on the *Serapis'* decks. . . . He sprang back up to the quarter-deck beside the helmsman to try for it.

But the *Serapis,* moving twice as fast as the *Bon Homme Richard* and maneuvering more cleanly, dodged his every attempt to close. Captain Pearson, in turn, was able to take the *Serapis* past *Bon Homme Richard's* stern repeatedly, raking it each time from stern to bow.

John Paul realized that if Pearson continued to outmaneuver him, he was doomed. He raged through his ship screaming at the gunners to aim higher—for the *Serapis'* sails and rigging—to cut the *Serapis* down to the speed of the *Bon Homme Richard.* Girard panted after him, breathlessly translating to the French gunners. His shots began to do their work. The *Serapis'* sails were riddled with holes. Pearson's rigging began to dissolve. His hard-hammered mainmast showed a dangerous shakiness. The *Serapis* had become as sluggish a sailer as the *Bon Homme Richard*—which loomed closer with very minute. Around Pearson, officers and men exposed on the decks started to drop under a hail of musket balls from John Paul's marksmen.

But at this musket-shot distance, the big guns of the *Serapis* became even more devastating. Their smashing blows put one of John Paul's guns after another out of action. Fires sprang up through his ship. He had fewer and fewer men left to fight either the fires or the enemy.

The French marines up on the exposed poop deck were suffering most at this point, being cut down like wheat in a threshing machine. When their colonel, Chamillard, dropped unconscious to the deck, they finally broke and started pushing off the poop to find shelter.

Into their midst sprang John Paul, his face smudged, his legs spattered with blood. "Frenchmen!" he yelled. "Will you give way before the eyes of the Americans and English?"

The sight and sound of him stopped their panicked rush momentarily. And while they hesitated, he turned his face toward the bulk of the *Serapis* across the water, and, in a voice that carried all the way up to Midshipman Fanning in the tops, screamed "such imprecations upon the enemy as I never before or since heard in French or any other language." Then he grabbed six muskets in succession from them and fired each in turn at the *Serapis* as fast as he could pull the triggers.

The French marines, inspirited by the American's example, surged back to their station. Their shots—plus those of the marksmen in the masts, whose ranks were constantly increased by gunners whose guns had been put out of action—made the open decks of the *Serapis* almost impossible to live on. Eleven English helmsmen in turn had their try at handling the wheel of the *Serapis;* each died under the fusillade as had the man before him.

But from the protected lower gun deck of the *Serapis* the 18-pounders continued to slam their heavy metal into the hull of the *Bon Homme Richard,* enlarging the hole in its side caused by the explosion of the two cannons at the beginning of the fight. In time, the entire main gun deck was laid open, and still the heavy shots continued to pour in—until not a single gun was left in action out of John Paul's entire battery of twenty-eight 12-pounders. The only guns he had left were three 9-pounders on the quarter-deck, one of which he himself was aiming at the *Serapis'* mainmast. Half his crew was gone. His ship was beginning to settle. The first wave or heavy swell that disturbed the glass-smooth sea would pour into that gaping hole in his hull and sink the *Bon Homme Richard* like a shot.

He should have known he was beaten. But he didn't. He was in the grip of an overpowering rage—and out of that rage flashed an idea: It was not enough to close with the *Serapis.* He must grapple it, so tightly that the *Serapis* would become his sinking ship's life buoy, keeping it afloat. Then he could fight on—somehow.

The ships were side by side now. John Paul suddenly swung over for a crash. For an instant, they touched. John Paul's men hurled their grappling hooks. Then there was water between the ships, and the grappling irons struck the enemy's bulwarks and fell away. Seething, John Paul pulled up again, waiting tensely for another chance. He must hurry. At any moment the *Bon Homme Richard* might abruptly go under. Casting about in his mind desperately for some way to outwit Captain Pearson—who instantly countered every move he made—John Paul suddenly ordered his seamen to take in canvas—and then wait, not securing it. He watched the *Serapis,* his nerves singing with excitement. With its sail shortened, the *Bon Homme Richard* dropped back toward the *Serapis'* stern. Captain Pearson, believing that John Paul was attempting to rake his stern or ram it, laid his own topsails aback. The *Serapis* slowed and began to fall back to get even with the *Bon Homme Richard* again.

Instantly, John Paul's shout rang up to his sail trimmers. Every sail on his ship that could still be handled was laid on in a flash. The *Bon Homme Richard* shot forward. Pearson, seeing his enemy drawing ahead of him, quickly reset his own shortened sails. The *Serapis* shot forward.

It was what John Paul had anticipated. As the *Serapis* drew up to come alongside him again, he put his helm hard a-weather. The *Bon Homme Richard* swung across the path of the *Serapis.* Pearson saw the danger and tried to swing away—too late. The jibboom of the *Serapis* drove over John Paul's deck between the starboard mizzen shrouds and became entangled.

"I've got him!" John Paul screamed, as he leaped with his waiting seamen upon the *Serapis'* bowsprit and began lashing it to his own mizzenmast.

Captain Pearson quickly ordered men forward to cut away the lashings. Each of his men in turn was knocked over by the musket fire of John Paul's French marines. Pearson then let go his port anchor, on the chance that its pull would break his ship away from John Paul's grip. The opposite happened. The two ships were wrenched together starboard side to starboard side, bow to stern. And when Pearson's starboard anchor hooked the *Bon Homme Richard's* quarter, the interlocking of the two ships was complete. Above, their yards now overhung each other's decks. Below, their sides were so close that Pearson could not open the ports of his lower starboard battery, unused till now. He got them open finally only by shooting them open with his own cannons.

With the mouths of those English 18-pounders almost touching the hull of the *Bon Homme Richard,* the American ship's under-belly was literally torn to shreds. The only thing holding the *Bon Homme Richard* up now was the *Serapis* itself.

Up on deck, where the marksmen were fighting it out with their muskets, John Paul had his three remaining 9-pounders pulled into position to sweep the enemy's deck. Directing their fire himself, amidst a holocaust of musket balls, he had one loaded with double-shot to concentrate on the *Serapis'* mainmast. He loaded the other two 9-pounders with grapeshot and canister shot, which scattered across the decks of the *Serapis* mowing down officers and men who exposed themselves. The enemy decks were soon clear of any except dead men.

Up in the tops, John Paul's marksmen under Midshipman Fanning and Lieutenant Stack were shooting it out with the English marksmen, and hurling hand grenades down on the enemy's decks. But the clearing of the *Serapis'* decks, and the mob on his own, suddenly, unexpectedly, became a hazard for John Paul.

It was a little after eight now, and the two locked ships were clearly outlined in the silver glow of the full moon. Across the shimmering sea there suddenly appeared Landais' *Alliance,* sailing toward the battlers. John Paul turned to see the *Alliance* coming on, and thrilled to the certainty that the fight was now as good as won. All Landais had to do was grapple the *Alliance* to the other side of the *Serapis,* add his fresh men and guns to the battle, and Captain Pearson must surrender. The *Alliance* crept up to nearly musket-shot distance, swung to cross the locked bow of the *Bon Homme Richard* and stern of the *Serapis,* paused and roared a broadside of crossbar and chain shot across the decks of *both* ships!

Stunned, John Paul saw the flying death sweep his forecastle, killing every man caught on it. Recovering, he sprang to the side of his ship and screamed across the water at Landais, who was within earshot. To no avail. The *Alliance* drew away a bit, then came back. John Paul quickly ran up three signal lanterns to identify himself. But the *Alliance* sailed in, fired another broadside full against the *Bon Homme Richard*, and dodged away again.

Now John Paul was certain that Landais, his hatred swollen

to insanity, was deliberately trying to sink him. He watched with helpless fury as the *Alliance* once more slipped past, firing at both locked ships indiscriminately, and then sailed away into the surrounding darkness.

By now the situation of the *Bon Homme Richard* was ghastly. Her starboard side gaped open from rail to waterline. Pearson's 18-pounders fired into emptiness, their shots passing clear through what had once been John Paul's main gun deck. The ship was taking in water so fast that the pumps were next to useless. There was increasing danger that the weight of water would finally break the grip of the two ships and sink the *Bon Homme Richard*.

John Paul rushed back and forth through his ship, bolstering the nerve of his men. He led the groups that beat back the fires that kept breaking out and threatening to reach the powder stores. He spearheaded a charge that threw back a sudden attempt by Pearson to board his ship. He directed the shots of his marksmen and the crews of the three 9-pounders.

Weary to the core, streaked with sweat and smoke and blood, he stumbled and sat down for a moment's rest on an overturned cannon. One of his exhausted men trudged over to him through the wreckage.

"For God's sake, Captain," he pleaded, "strike!"

Dazed, John Paul stared up at him. It was a man whose courage he respected. He understood the sense of the man's plea: Their ship, smashed to splinters by the English guns below, was ravaged by flames, filling with water. . . .

Abruptly, John Paul jumped to his feet, snapping out of it. "No!" he cried. "I will sink, but I'll never strike!"

Suddenly, his deck was aswarm with men rushing up from below in panic—Englishmen. Master-at-arms Burbank, sure the ship was about to sink, had unlocked the two hundred prisoners. Burbank ran over now to explain. Choked with fury, John Paul snatched one of the pistols from his belt, aimed it at Burbank and pulled the trigger. The pistol misfired. Cursing, John Paul slammed its barrel across Burbank's head. The master-at-arms crumpled to the deck.

A pistol cracked sharply behind John Paul. He whirled to find that his interpreter, Pierre Girard, had shot one of the prisoners just as he was about to leap on the American captain. The shot stopped the others for a moment. While they hesitated, unsure whether to rush the captain or make good their escape, John Paul yelled at them that it was the *Serapis* that was sinking—that their only hope of staying alive lay in helping him keep the *Bon Homme Richard* afloat. That stopped them long enough for a dozen of John Paul's men to hurry up beside him armed for trouble. The prisoners' uprising was over as abruptly as it had begun; they were forced below to man the pumps.

But all the while the guns of the *Serapis*—every one of them still in action below, though there was hardly a man left on the open deck—continued to demolish the *Bon Homme Richard*. The mainmast was wrapped in flames which blazed up higher despite all efforts to quench them. Dead and wounded lay everywhere; the surgeon was unconscious from a wound of his own and could not tend them. A heavy iron ball broke into the hold and smashed one of the pumps. The water rose faster inside the hull.

The carpenter, wounded in the head, rushed up on deck and screamed to one of the gunners that the ship was about to go under. The gunner, completely unnerved, turned back toward the *Serapis* and began to shout for quarter. The carpenter took up the call.

Suddenly they were aware of their captain sprinting toward them, pistol in hand, his face livid. Both men ran from him in terror. John Paul hurled his empty pistol, which caught the gunner in the head and stretched him out near the gangway.

Across the bulwarks, Captain Pearson had heard their shouts. Now he stilled his guns and hailed John Paul:

"Have you struck?"

John Paul whirled and shouted back at the top of his lungs: "Struck? I have not yet begun to fight!"

Pearson's guns, stilled for a moment, answered for him: a crashing broadside that shook the *Bon Homme Richard* from stem to stern. And on its heels came Pearson and a large body of men who threw themselves at the bulwarks in a boarding attempt.

John Paul's men met them at the bulwarks, and drove them back. His marksmen up in the tops, having completely cleared the *Serapis'* tops of musketeers, sent down a hail of musket balls and grenades on the enemy's deck. The surviving boarders crowded below to safety.

John Paul went back to aiming one of the 9-pounders at the enemy's mainmast. At the same time, he directed Lieutenant Mayrant to assemble a large party of boarders under the break of the quarter-deck, and arm them with cutlasses, pikes and pistols.

At this moment, high above John Paul Jones and without his knowledge, a Scots seaman named Willie Hamilton gathered himself up a basketful of grenades and a lighted slow match, and started to walk out along the mainyard. He kept walking till he was directly above the decks of the *Serapis*. Then he began lighting his grenades and tossing them down at little clusters of men who were hidden behind the protection of the *Serapis'* wreckage on the far side of the deck.

When they had all vanished below, he looked around for other targets and spotted an open hatchway almost under his balancing feet, far below. Taking careful aim, he dropped several of his grenades through the open hatchway.

One of the grenades bounced down into the gun deck, landed among a bunch of cannon cartridges. The entire gun deck suddenly exploded in one horrible upheaval. Twenty men were killed instantly; almost every other man on that deck was burned; the main battery of the *Serapis* was demolished.

Before Captain Pearson could comprehend the disaster, one of John Paul's 9-pound shots struck his mainmast the final blow, and it came crashing down on the *Serapis'* deck. Seconds later, Mayrant led a yelling, leaping boarders' charge against the dazed English.

Captain Pearson sadly hauled down his flag with his own hands, climbed across the bulwarks, and surrendered his sword to Captain John Paul Jones. It was 10:35 P.M.

John Paul boarded the *Serapis* in triumph with his men, made it his ship. The *Bon Homme Richard*, cut away from the *Serapis*, sank.

He sailed back to France to find that he had achieved the full measure of glory for which he had thirsted. But that glory could no longer have much importance for the girl back in Virginia whom he had loved. There was a letter, sent to him in France by a friend in Virginia, Doctor Read:

You tell me you are under some expectation of purchasing a Virginia estate, but some more agreeable idea will I fear call you off and deprive us of you. Miss Dandridge is no more, that is, she a few months ago gave herself into the arms of Patrick Henry.

Once the American Revolution was won, the new nation could find little peacetime use for a warrior like John Paul Jones. In fact, America could not even find its way clear to give him his back pay—and never did. John Paul, casting around for some means of employment, finally found someone who could use a man like himself: Catherine the Great, Empress of Russia.

Catherine, at war with the Turks, invited him to come and be admiral of her Black Sea fleet. Dazzled by the opportunity, "Admiral Jones" went to Russia—and eventually found himself more warred upon by Catherine's courtiers than by the Turks. A direct, rather naïve man, John Paul was helpless against men jealous of his power and position. Their intrigues whittled down his power, hacked away at his professional and personal reputation, and finally ended in an accusation that he had raped a ten-year-old girl.

The charge was transparently false. But by this time the intrigues had weakened Empress Catherine's belief in "Admiral Jones." She left him to his fate, and might even have let him be found guilty of the charge—and suffer the consequences—if important French friends of John Paul's had not intervened and persuaded her to let him leave Russia with a small pension.

John Paul returned to France a bewildered and broken man. He died alone in his little room in Paris in 1792. He was standing up when he died, and he was found fallen against his bed, his feet still on the floor. They buried him on French soil.

He knew he died forgotten by the new nation he had helped create. And for one hundred years, he *was* forgotten—until finally the United States of America, embarking on a big naval-building project, remembered him again and demanded one last great service of him: to become the symbol of its naval spirit.

In 1905, America decided that the man who said "I have not yet begun to fight" from the deck of a beaten, broken, sinking ship—though dead for so long—still had a great deal to tell the future officers of its navy.

They found his body and dug it up. He was carried back across the Atlantic with an honor escort of French and American warships, and taken to the Naval Academy at Annapolis. His body rests there now, in a marble sarcophagus in the Chapel. In the marble floor around him are inlaid in bronze the names of his ships—and this: HE GAVE OUR NAVY ITS EARLIEST TRADITIONS OF HEROISM AND VICTORY.

14

A Commander Without Captains

At fifty-two—after thirty-eight years in the French navy—nobleman Pierre-André de Suffren held only the rank of captain. Frustration had settled on his proud spirit as fat had collected on his once-elegant figure. Frustration not only at his rank—but at being part of a navy in which he could take no pride.

How it had galled Suffren to have to abide by the French navy's elaborate tactical maneuvers designed for the purpose of remaining on the defensive in any fight! The only reason the English hadn't destroyed the French fleet through all the battles Suffren could remember was that the English commanders were also addicted to elaborate maneuvers. Tactics, Suffren said with scorn, "are the veil of timidity." Tactics, he felt, were an excuse used by both sides to avoid getting caught in a fight to the finish. For thirty-eight years, Suffren's outspoken contempt for the rules of naval warfare had only succeeded in making his superiors uncomfortable.

But on the 29th of March, 1781, Suffren's galled spirit gave a bound and broke free. He was alone on the sea at last—with a squadron of five ships-of-the-line under him, and with no one over him to tell him what not to do. It was what he had dreamed of ever since he had entered the navy as a raw cadet at the age of fourteen. It was what he had gone on dreaming through all his years of snail's-pace career climbing, all those wars and battles in which he had served under men he didn't respect, those two separate terms as an English prisoner of war.

Now, at last, he was on his own. Of course, this independent command, handed him so late in his career, was to be only temporary—until he reached the Indian Ocean and placed his squadron under Commodore Count d'Orves. But for the moment he was free, his own master.

Suffren sailed south along the coast of Africa in command of the *Héros,* trailed by four other line-of-battle ships and a number of troop transports. His orders were clear: On his way to the Indian Ocean he was to land the troops at the Cape of Good Hope, whose job would be to help defend this possession of France's ally Holland, against an English attack. Intelligence reports received just before he sailed from Brest had warned that an English war squadron and troop convoy were sailing at the same time—to attack the Cape before the reinforcements were landed. Captain Suffren's job was to get there first.

But as they sailed down the coast of Africa, one of Suffren's battleships, the 64-gun *Artésien,* sent word that it was low on water. Suffren decided to pull over to the Cape Verde Islands, on the way south, and let the *Artésien* sail into Porto Praya to take water aboard.

The *Artésien* went on ahead as they reached the islands. Suffren watched her reach the jut of shore that hid the bay of Porto Praya, hesitate, and suddenly turn and dash back toward him. The English war squadron and troop transports Suffren had been warned of were anchored in Porto Praya! The fighting squadron numbered four line ships and three frigates—under Commodore George Johnstone—and all the transports carried guns.

Suffren knew that any other French captain would have obeyed the letter of his orders, and made all sail straight for the Cape on the even chance of beating Johnstone there. But the purpose of his orders was to make sure that he landed troops at the Cape, and that Johnstone did not. Could that not be best accomplished by attacking the English right here—while they were anchored and unprepared for a fight—and smashing the convoy so badly that it *never* could reach the Cape?

Laying on sail, Suffren took the *Héros* swiftly into Porto Praya, signaling his other four line ships to follow. There was no time to discuss plans with his captains, or to form up a line of battle. He had to hit Johnstone before the English could up anchor and maneuver for defense. He relied on surprise and the enemy's anchored disorder to win the day.

The surprise was complete for Johnstone. He had not been aware that there were any French warships in the vicinity when he sailed into Porto Praya for water. He had no idea the French squadron headed for the Cape would do the same. His ships were anchored in disorder, strung out in bunches. When he looked out and saw Suffren's flagship standing in to attack him, his ships erupted into action, the necessity for clearing for action allowing no time even to up-anchor.

Moving through his ship with a nimble energy startling in a man of his corpulence, Suffren had the *Héros'* seventy-four guns loaded and run out as he hauled into the bay. The moment he spotted Johnstone's flagship among the tangle of anchored vessels, he drove in toward it, noting with surprise as it loomed closer that it bore the same name as his own: *Hero.* He noted also that he had been right to attack without taking time to make the customary preparations. The English ships were anchored in such disorder that they masked each other's batteries. Only a few of them had a clear field to fire on his ship as he sailed the *Héros* in.

Suffren had to maintain a strong control over his impatient gunnery officers, to keep them from firing back. Traditional long-range gunnery duels were for the timid; it was short-range fighting that Suffren's thwarted spirit craved. He waited till the *Héros* was within five hundred feet of Johnstone's starboard beam. Then he dropped his anchor and let go both broadsides simultaneously— one into the *Hero,* the other into another English warship off his starboard. Through the smoke and thunder of his own guns came the whirling heavy shot of the English ships on both sides of him, slashing away his shrouds and hammering his masts. Suffren yelled himself hoarse exhorting his gunners to speed up their reloading, running-out and firing. When it came to gunnery, the French knew their business. If the rest of Suffren's squadron could maintain the initial drive of his surprise attack, he was confident he could crush the whole English squadron.

Another ship loomed up alongside the stern of the *Héros.* It was one of Suffren's seventy-fours, Captain Trémigon's *Annibal*, coming in close on Suffren's heels. If Suffren was pleased with Captain Trémigon's promptness, he was less pleased with his good sense. The *Annibal* swept past the *Héros'* starboard, cut in across its bows, and dropped anchor beside Johnstone's flagship. This placed the *Annibal's* stern so close to the *Héros'* bows that there was danger of their swinging against each other. Suffren was forced to veer anchor and let his ship drift back farther behind the sterns of both ships.

He thought even less of Captain Trémigon's good sense later when he learned that Trémigon had not managed to clear his decks for action as he sailed into Porto Praya, that he drew up alongside Johnstone's flagship with his guns still unloaded and secured inside the gun decks.

Suffren, slugging it out with ships on both sides of him, watched in amazement as the *Annibal* up ahead took devastating fire from the *Hero* and another English warship without replying. He turned quickly and looked back for the other three ships of his squadron which should be coming in by now to support him. They were not.

The *Artésien,* which had closely followed the *Annibal* into the bay, was now drifting back out of it! (Later he learned that her captain had been killed by the fire of the first English ship he passed, and before his lieutenant was able to take hold in his place the tide had caught the ship and shoved it out of range.) The other two ships in his squadron had been so laggard in following him into Porto Praya—and so inexpert in their handling—that the offshore wind and tide had pushed them to leeward, preventing them from entering the bay at all.

With only two ships in action, what had started out as a daring thrust into the vitals of the enemy's squadron became a dangerous trap of his own making. Up ahead, the *Annibal* had her guns out and firing at last. But it was too late. Her foremast came crashing down under the pounding broadsides of the English ships on both sides of her.

Helpless in his anger, Suffren choked down his pride and signaled the *Annibal* to pull out. He cut the cable of the *Héros,* turned until his sails billowed with the offshore wind, and fought his ship out of the bay to the open sea.

Behind him, the *Annibal* almost didn't make it. Her mainmast fell over as she turned away from the shore, and as she drifted aimlessly on the tide, English ships all around her poured in a deluge of heavy shot that killed Captain Trémigon and seventy of his crew, wounded one hundred and thirty others. Lieutenant Galles seized command and managed to rig some jury sails that dragged the *Annibal* out of the bay. One of the other French ships, the *Sphinx,* took her in tow.

Suffren was limp, dazed. What should have been a glorious victory had been changed by the inefficiency of his captains into a near-disaster. The truth was that in his zeal, Suffren had not taken the quality of his subordinates into consideration. Gripped by the lethargy and overcaution induced by the French sea tradition of defensive fighting, they had been stunned by Suffren's sudden decision to attack Porto Praya. And they were far from being the best officers in the French navy. The pick of the crop were off in American waters.

Now there was only one thing Suffren could do. Picking up his troop transports, he sailed south, hoping to reach the Cape of Good Hope before Johnstone.

Johnstone, once he recovered from the surprise of the sudden attack and withdrawal, patched up his own damaged warships and sailed out after Suffren. Suffren was slowed by the dismasted *Annibal,* and Johnstone's war squadron caught up with him. But once Johnstone spotted the French ships ahead of him, he turned his squadron around and sailed back to Porto Praya to pick up his transports. English commanders weren't used to the idea of Frenchmen driving in so swiftly and attacking so fiercely.

In Johnstone's indecision before the unexpected attack he let Suffren get a lead on him. And by the time the English convoy finally reached the Cape of Good Hope, the French had already landed their troops. His mission a failure, Johnstone sailed back to England.

Rounding the Cape, Suffren sailed his squadron north toward India. On the way, he met Count d'Orves' squadron as ordered, and placed himself under d'Orves' command. After repairing the damages done to the *Annibal* and *Héros* in Porto Praya, the combined squadrons, now numbering twelve ships, sailed on.

Suffren shuffled about his ship in a black mood, once more under a superior officer. He felt that he had had his one chance for glory at Porto Praya; having missed it, he would not have another. But he was wrong. In mid-February, 1782, just a few days before they sighted the Madras coast of India, Count d'Orves died aboard his ship. At fifty-two—and in the absence of orders from France—Suffren's long years in the service automatically gave him seniority over the captains of the other eleven ships. He found himself unexpectedly once more in command.

Suffren determined to make the most of it. His vision of what could be done soared beyond the flat orders that now passed down to him. On the mainland of India and on Ceylon, French troops, in shaky alliance with native forces, were engaged in a struggle with the English army. The mission of the French warships now under Suffren's command was to harry British merchant shipping, and give the French army commander whatever help he demanded. But Suffren wanted to wrest control of the Indian Ocean from the British navy. As he saw it, only the nation that won complete control of this sea could hold the mainland for long.

He knew what he was up against. The one thing on his side was numbers: The English fleet in the Indian Ocean, under Vice-Admiral Sir Edward Hughes, consisted of only nine warships. Captain Suffren had twelve. But everything else was on Hughes' side. All ports were in English hands. Hughes had bases from which to operate, sources of supplies. Suffren had neither. And there was the record of the past, to give the English captains complete confidence and the French captains none. Though the material results of most of the battles over the previous hundred years had been indecisive, the English had always acted as aggressors, the French as defenders. Now, typically, France expected little of Suffren's squadron. But Suffren expected much of himself. He was here, as he saw it, to fight the English ships under Vice-Admiral Hughes, and do his best to destroy them.

The five battles between Suffren and Hughes were among the oddest in character ever fought between the sea forces of France and England. First of all, they reversed the usual role of French and English ships: Suffren was always the aggressor, Hughes on the defensive. For if Suffren was the most spirited captain in his navy, Hughes was one of the most cautious in *his*.

As Hughes saw it, the only thing worth fighting Suffren for was control of a port. Since all the ports were already in English hands, he had little reason to fight. Without a harbor in which to repair, without a port from which to draw supplies, Suffren could sail this ocean until he ran out of stores. Then he would be forced to sail away to get them. It was only when Suffren made a thrust at seizing a port on the coast of India or Ceylon, that Hughes felt he had to sail out and thwart the French squadron.

Suffren was brilliant. Hughes was not, though he was a good seaman. But the English captains under Hughes—trained, experienced, brave and proud—were far and away superior to the French captains under Suffren. This fact gave the oddity of the five battles their final twist. Each was a battle between a superb commander dragging dull captains in with him, on the one hand, and a dull commander magnificently supported by excellent captains, on the other.

When Suffren first spotted the English squadron, Hughes was anchored inside the port of Madras. Suffren eyed the fortifications of the harbor, and decided they were too heavy for him to challenge. So he hauled up outside Madras and waited for Hughes to come out and fight. But Hughes surprised Suffren—who had a great respect for the traditional aggressiveness of English sea-fighters—by staying where he was, in the safety of Madras.

Finally, Suffren pulled away and sailed south, a move which forced Hughes to come out and chase him. For south lay the excellent Ceylon port of Trincomalee. And Hughes would be in disgrace if he allowed Suffren to grab such a prefect base of operations.

At dawn on the 17th of February, Suffren saw the English ships drawn up in line of battle between him and the coast. It was another surprise for Suffren. For the wind was blowing lightly toward the coast, which gave the French the weather gauge—the chance to attack with the wind behind them. Hughes was accepting the defensive position usually taken by the French in the past!

Drawing his own squadron up in two parallel lines-ahead, Suffren swung around to hit the rear of Hughes' single line. Suffren led one column of six ships; his second-in-command, Tromelin, led the other six. Tromelin was to take his ships around the rear of Hughes' line, and sail up close to the starboard side of the last six ships, while Suffren threw his column against their port side. With twelve French ships thus concentrating point-blank fire on only six of the English ships, they should smash Hughes' squadron apart. Suffren himself, instead of closing in to pistol-shot distance

with the rest of his squadron, would keep off a bit to hinder any
attempt on the part of the first three ships of Hughes' line to
double back and join the fight.

It was a perfect plan. But again, as at Porto Praya, Suffren had
to watch with helpless rage his officers fail him and his attack
crumble in his hands. Only two of his ships managed to double the
English rear and sail up the lee side of Hughes' line. Tromelin
himself failed to, and so did the others who were following
Tromelin instead of Suffren's orders. This follow-the-leader mentality also spoiled the second part of Suffren's plan. Instead of

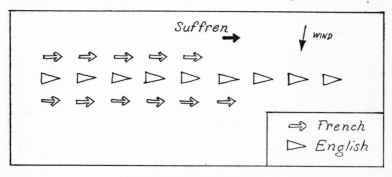

WHAT SUFFREN INTENDED

driving in to point-blank range of the English line, as ordered, the
captains following Suffren—who was keeping his distance for a
specific reason—kept exactly the same distance between themselves
and the English. Their shots, consequently, had much less effect
on Hughes' ships than Suffren had expected.

In contrast, the English officers fought back with hot courage
and determination. Commodore King, commanding the last ship
in Hughes' line, the 64-gun *Exeter,* was shelled by every French
ship as it passed. Their broadsides were tearing the *Exeter* apart,
slaughtering the men aboard, reducing it to a floating hulk. The
Exeter drifted farther behind the rest of the English line, was cut
off, and pressed hard by two fresh French ships. The master rushed
up to King to ask what they could do now. At that moment, a
cannon ball smashed his senior officer, Captain Reynolds, apart,
spattering Commodore King with blood and brains. King wiped
the gore from his eyes and said coldly to the master: "There is
nothing to be done but fight her till she sinks." So they fought on,

so savagely that the two French ships—relatively unhurt—finally pulled away, and the *Exeter* remained in English hands.

The advantage Suffren had conceived evaporated before the timidity and inefficiency of his captains. Before he could drive in to close range himself, the wind suddenly shifted to the southeast, giving Hughes the weather gauge and stalling Suffren's squadron. The first three ships of the English line quickly tacked to join the fight and for a short time they came to grips. Then night ended the battle. By the next dawn, the two fleets had lost sight of each other.

WHAT DID HAPPEN

Hughes had been hurt, but far from crushed as Suffren had planned. The English had lost not a single ship. Suffren sailed away in gloom.

But if Suffren had not won the devastating material victory he had envisioned, he had—though he refused to be comforted by it —won an important psychological victory. This time it was the French who had attacked, while the English had remained on the defensive. If Suffren's own captains didn't appreciate the brilliance and audacity of what he had tried to do in the battle, the English captains under Hughes *did*. Their admiration for Suffren began to approach his admiration for them. As far as they were concerned, Suffren had won the day.

He had won more than a day, as far as the native rulers of Ceylon and India were concerned. When they heard that a French fleet had fought an English fleet *and had not been beaten,* their flimsy alliance with the French land forces abruptly became more solid. French prestige throughout the whole area took an upward bound.

When the two forces met again in battle on April 12, Hughes' squadron had been bolstered by the arrival from England of two more big seventy-fours. Now there were eleven English ships to meet the French twelve. But Hughes, like Johnstone before him, had been impressed by Suffren's boldness in the first battle—so impressed that he still didn't feel strong enough to risk an attack of his own. Instead, he drew his eleven ships up in what he considered the most advantageous position off the coast of Ceylon, and prepared to defend himself again. Actually, he wouldn't have come out to fight at all, had not Suffren again been threatening to sail into Trincomalee, which Hughes had orders to defend. So he waited, with his squadron stretched out in an excellent line of battle—and Suffren, coming upon him, attacked without hesitation.

Sailing along on a parallel line to Hughes, Suffren suddenly ordered all his ships to swing toward the English line together and drive in against it, head-first. They were to hold their fire until they got within pistol-shot range, then swing sharply around and let go their broadsides.

This time Suffren meant to be sure his captains had no excuse for not sailing in close. He led the way with the fastest ship in his squadron, the *Héros,* and set the example which the rest were to follow. As he plunged in at top speed against the waiting enemy, only four of his ships were able to keep up with him. They followed in a tight bunch, driving toward the center of the English line with him. The rest of the French ships were left lagging behind.

Suffren held his fire until his bows seemed about to crash into the side of Hughes' flagship, the *Superbe,* which was firing wildly at him as he came on. Then, a split second before the crash, Suffren swung his ship in the same direction as the *Superbe* and let go a booming broadside that shattered Hughes' rigging, sails and yards.

All these lagging French ships had to do now was to keep coming into the enemy before delivering their broadsides. Instead, all of them chose to obey the letter of Suffren's instructions to them. He had said they were all to follow his example, so they did. The second Suffren swung his flagship broadside-to-broadside with the English line, his lagging ships followed suit—although this prevented them from coming any closer for the rest of the fight!

They stayed out there, exchanging long-distance shots with the English, while Suffren and the four ships that had followed him closely fought it out almost yardarm to yardarm with Hughes' center.

But this time, if Suffren was again frustrated in his attempt at a decisive fight to the finish, *part* of his squadron *did* fight as directed. His *Héros,* and the four ships that had kept up with him, struck the center of Hughes' line with crushing impact.

The five French ships were bunched close together. The English line was strung out with a good amount of space between each ship. Hughes suddenly found his three center ships—his own *Superbe,* the *Monarca* behind him, and the *Monmouth* up ahead —caught by a pulverizing concentration of five French ships.

For nine minutes Suffren's *Héros* and Hughes' *Superbe* hacked at each other, with the French ship behind Suffren, the 74-gun *L'Orient,* slamming at Hughes' stern. By the time the *Héros,* its braces shredded, began to drift ahead of Hughes' flagship, the *Superbe's* decks were wreckage.

The *Héros* drifted until it came up alongside the next English ship, the *Monmouth.* A French sixty-four, which had been battling point-blank with the *Monmouth,* pulled up to make room for Suffren. Behind the *Héros,* the comparatively fresh *L'Orient* moved up to take its place alongside Hughes' *Superbe,* which could now be battered almost at will.

Suffren poured his broadsides over the *Monmouth's* decks until he sheered off its mizzenmast, then tore out its mainmast a few minutes later. The *Monmouth* began trying to pull away from him, out of its line. Suffren hugged it close, would not let it go.

At last, after three hours of it, Hughes could take no more. He signaled his line to slip ahead, out of Suffren's grip. It was a tricky job. Suffren and the wind had combined to pin Hughes tight against the coast. But the English captains succeeded.

Even at that late point in the battle, Suffren's laggard captains could have prevented Hughes' move by at last coming in close and helping Suffren and the other four French ships pin the English to the shore. But they didn't. The English got free with their two wrecks, and night came shortly after that to put an end to further fighting.

Suffren and Hughes met three more times after that, and on each occasion the fight went much the same way: Each time Suffren was the aggressor, Hughes fighting on the defensive. Each time Suffren's captains prevented him from achieving a real victory. Each time Hughes' captains saved him from defeat. Each time, both sides emerged hurt but without the loss of a ship. Yet after each battle, French prestige in the area rose, British naval prestige sank lower.

Even between the battles, Suffren accomplished things that added to the shine of his peculiar brand of lonely glory in the face of tormenting difficulties. After the second battle, for example, Suffren, with no port to go to, no base of supplies, had to find some way to replace masts lost in the battle and to replenish his almost-empty stores of food and gunpowder. He did it by raiding English shipping in the Indian Ocean for food and other supplies, taking masts off ships he seized and putting them on his warships. In a few weeks of driven effort he was able to announce that the English had been forced to refit his ships for battle and give him enough food and gunpowder to last him another half year. It took Hughes six weeks *in* port to refit his ships!

Again, after their next battle—in which both fleets were severely damaged—it took Hughes almost two months in port to put his squadron back in shape for fighting. Suffren accomplished the same tasks without a port, in just two weeks. And this time his speed enabled him finally to get the port he needed. While Hughes was still fussing with his broken ships, Suffren sailed freely into Trincomalee and seized it for the French. He fortified it so strongly that the English could not retake it—and gained a base to operate from for the last two battles.

Right up to the end, those battles kept their peculiar quality. Numbers of ships had nothing to do with it. Reinforcements arrived from home for both squadrons as time went on. In the third battle, they fought even. And by their fifth—and final—battle, Hughes outnumbered Suffren 18 to 15. But by then Hughes had stomached so many of Suffren's attacks that he flinched at the mere sight of the strange French captain.

It was extremely important, that last time they met, for Hughes *not* to flinch. On the mainland of India, the English army had the French troops in Cuddalore surrounded and cut off from all communication by land. It was Hughes' job to make sure that the Cuddalore garrison did not establish any communication with Suffren by sea. Hughes had his eighteen warships drawn up at the sea approach to Cuddalore when he sighted the fifteen French ships coming over the horizon toward him just before dusk one evening. After thinking about Suffren a bit, he decided his squadron was disadvantageously placed to receive what the Frenchman was undoubtedly going to hurl at him. So thinking, Hughes took his eighteen ships and headed out to open sea, away from Suffren, in search of an advantage.

Suffren sailed up to Cuddalore and made the desired contact with the French garrison there. He had been in poor condition to fight Hughes when he sailed into Cuddalore, as a matter of fact. Sickness —death-dealing fevers—had depleted his crews so badly that there weren't enough men to man his ships' guns. There were plenty when he sailed *away* from Cuddalore, however. Twelve hundred soldiers from the garrison had come aboard and swelled his gun crews to peak strength.

Suffren caught up with Hughes three days later. For two hours the eighteen English ships and fifteen French ships hammered each other. When Hughes had had as much of it as he could take, he pulled his squadron out of the battle and sailed away.

One thing Hughes could be thankful for: He never had to meet Suffren again. Soon after their fifth encounter, news reached them that one of the lulls that frequently interrupted this century and a quarter of hostilities between France and England had been formally declared. Captain Pierre-André de Suffren, his year and a half of glory at an end, sailed back to France.

To have achieved what he did, in the face of such terrific handi-caps, ranks him as one of the geniuses of naval history. But there would have been few limits to what he might have achieved if he had had under him the same English captains that he had fought, ten of whom had died fighting him.

Some of those captains who survived the battles with Suffren met him at the Cape of Good Hope as he journeyed homeward, and sought him out to tell him what they thought of him. As he spent his last years in honored retirement, he treasured the memories of the praise on their lips and the admiration in their eyes more than the acclaim and title of Vice-Admiral that awaited him when he set foot on the soil of France.

PART FIVE

The Great Captain

Horatio Nelson stands alone in the history of naval warfare. He is the greatest figure not only in the history of fighting with sailing ships—but in all naval history. He is one of those extremely rare occurrences: a colorful personality combined with a vivid mentality and forceful, daring character, who happened to step onto the stage of world events at exactly the moment when conditions were perfectly tuned to allow him to express his capabilities to the utmost.

Nelson is the great captain. His story speaks for itself.

15

"... to covet glory"

Strained as the wind-taut rigging above him, Nelson watched the oncoming enemy fleet revealed by the lifting of the icy morning mist. Bitterness and weariness and impatience drained out of him. A dazzling smile took possession of his weathered features. His mind was busy with the details of a dozen different methods of dealing with the dozen different ways the battle might go. There was no part of his brain left to wonder why he, who went hunting with friends with his gun unloaded because he couldn't stand to shoot anything, should look forward with such relish to the coming slaughter on the sea.

The 74-gun line-of-battle ship *Captain* carried Horatio Nelson out of obscurity and into the pages of history on that Saint Valentine's Day: February 14, 1797. He was a sensitive, self-willed man—slight, wiry, alive with energy enclosed in a narrow purpose. He was a man with a curving, humorous mouth, a long proud nose, and bright-blue, eager eyes—one of them blinded. Later, an artist was to explain the difficulty of painting his portrait with: "There is such a mixture of humility with ambition in Lord Nelson's countenance."

221

In times to come, Theodore Roosevelt was to refer to Nelson as "the greatest of all sea captains," and Admiral Mahan would call Nelson's "the most dazzling career the sea has ever seen." But as that cold Saint Valentine's Day dawned, Nelson was only one of many seasoned officers on the fifteen English warships sailing in two close, parallel lines toward a superior Spanish fleet. He was thirty-eight; he had been a captain since twenty. There were just two things he had to show for those eighteen intervening years of thwarted ambition: a blinded eye and a crumb of official recognition—his recent promotion to Commodore.

Nelson's two closest navy friends were among those fifteen ships: Captain Troubridge on the *Culloden*; Captain Collingwood on the *Excellent*. Like Nelson, they were skilled, courageous men, as were most of the other officers in that English fleet. But it was Nelson alone who disobeyed orders and went against the sacred Fighting Instructions—who broke the line *that day* and thus won the battle and his first fame. Why Nelson? Why not one of the others?

Nelson accomplished what he did in the battle that followed by risking court-martial and disgrace. The opportunity was there for any of the officers. But only Nelson seized it. The others were brave men. They were willing to risk losing their lives at any hour. But they were not willing to risk disgrace. It was a case of different kinds of ambition. The others wanted success in their careers. Nelson's ambition soared far beyond that. He hungered for immortality. And that hunger had been frustrated for so long that it was tearing him apart.

Nelson's favorite passage from Shakespeare was Henry V's:

> *By Jove, I am not covetous for gold . . .*
> *But if it be a sin to covet glory,*
> *I am the most offending soul alive.*

Actually, the correct phrase is, "to covet honour," but when Nelson wrote or spoke it, he made the significant mistake of substituting the word "glory."

Horatio's mother had liked to read Shakespeare's patriotic history plays to her children. His father was a minister, as had been most of his family before him. But his mother's forebears had been warriors since they fought the Norman conquerors. Great-uncle Galfridus Walpole, a sea officer, had given up his right arm fighting the French in 1711. And the greatest hero of all was still alive. He was Captain Maurice Suckling, Mrs. Nelson's brother, who in 1759 led three ships against a superior French force. It is not surprising that the Word of his father's Bible did not thrill the young Horatio as much as his mother's stories of service to Crown and country.

After his mother died, Horatio's father, saddled with eight children, did his best by them, but urged them out into the world as early as possible. It seemed strange that it was Horatio who chose the sea. His two older brothers were husky lads, fine solid sea-meat. Horatio was such a small sliver of a child, with such a fragile face, that the family had decided Horatio was too big a name for him; they called him Horace.

Horatio Nelson was twelve in 1770 when Spain gave England trouble in the Falkland Islands. Captain Maurice Suckling was commissioned into a new ship-of-war. When Horatio read of it, he persuaded his father to write his uncle, asking if he might come aboard as a midshipman. A navy captain had the privilege of signing aboard his ship young boys, thus giving children of relatives a start in an honorable career. Edmund Nelson wrote to his brother-in-law, and received this answer: "What has poor little Horace done that he, being so weak, should be sent to rough it at sea? But let him come, and if a cannon-ball takes off his head, he will at least be provided for."

It took the boy a long time to get used to his new home: the dark, low-ceilinged cockpit deep in the hold; the stench of bilge water, gunpowder, and the sweat of the packed-in midshipmen.

Each of the midshipmen had achieved his position of apprentice-officer by the exercise of influence on the navy by a relative or high-positioned friend. They were there to learn the handling of ships and crews, so that eventually they might take the examination for lieutenant. After that, the stupendously difficult climb to captain depended on luck, ability and—always the most important factor—influence. Once a captain, the rest of it was a matter of living long enough to become an admiral. It was strictly a matter of seniority. If the navy wanted to raise an able captain to admiral, all captains senior to him had to be made admirals too. Then these less able ones would be swiftly retired on half pay so that the ocean would not be cluttered with admirals. But an admiral's half pay was comfortable, his position in society secure.

Young Nelson found the training given midshipmen by no means easy. The schoolmaster spent the mornings instructing them in trigonometry, astronomy and navigation. At noon the midshipmen assembled on the quarter-deck to learn the use of the quadrant from the captain. Nelson had to struggle to hold his own in the ship's classroom. Studying came hard to him. But he quickly found he had a natural ability at practical seamanship. Slow as he was to grasp mathematics, he was swift to comprehend the duties of the ship, and to learn the name and purpose of every sail, line and stick aboard. And he felt most at home aloft. Once the master organized the boys into teams and began to race them up the masts, Nelson, moving with the ease of an aerialist, won most of the races. This gave him a position in the cockpit that excellence in navigation would never have earned him.

When the Spanish gave in to England in the matter of the Falklands, and war was averted, Captain Suckling, pleased and surprised with his fragile nephew's progress, sent him off to the West Indies on a merchant ship to gain more practical knowledge. During the long voyage, Nelson became one of the quickest Able Seamen aboard. A year later he was back, and his uncle was amazed at his robust health. The sea had obviously agreed with him. But merchant service as a common seaman had also taught the boy disrespect for navy discipline in general and for officers in particular.

Captain Suckling took instant pains to check his nephew's growing rebelliousness and from then on supervised his career with care. He gave Nelson the handling of one of the ship's boats, which the youth swiftly learned to sail in shallow river waters. At the same time, he learned to supervise crews composed of men much older than himself. This was not difficult for him. He was an easy boy to like, relaxed and friendly, and his ability earned respect.

Later, Nelson sailed on an arctic expedition, and still later he shipped to the East Indies on a 20-gun vessel. There, tropic fever seized on him, rendering his limbs useless for a month, his frame a skeleton. He recovered much of his health—though not much weight—on the voyage back to England. But he could not shake off a conviction that had seized him with the fever, that he had no chance of getting anywhere in the navy. He had become a midshipman at twelve; now eighteen, he was still a midshipman. There were hundreds of other midshipmen with captains for relatives. You needed more than that. By the time the ship docked he had worried himself into abject despair.

The first news that reached him on landing was that Captain Suckling had been named to the extremely influential position of Comptroller of the Navy. Two days later Nelson was made a lieutenant, and felt in the most exuberant health. His uncle died a short time later, and his influence passed with him. But by then Nelson had come in full possession of his ability at handling men under him, and charming men over him. He deftly achieved his captaincy at twenty, the youngest captain in the British navy.

Now the path to glory seemed open before him. Fame must surely follow such early success. But what followed, instead, were eighteen maddeningly long years of bitter frustration and rebuff. Strangely enough, Nelson's long disappointment resulted from an act which he committed out of the same stubborn independence that was finally to win him the fame he hungered for. And at the same time that he blighted his career, he took to himself a wife who was later to seem to him an almost equal blight.

Fanny Nesbit heard about the terrible Captain Nelson for months before she met him. Although only twenty-four, she was already a widow with a little son. When her husband died after a fit of madness, her uncle John Herbert invited her to come with her son and live in his great house. Mr. Herbert, a pompous but goodhearted man, was president of the Council of the Island of Nevis, one of the richest British islands in the West Indies. His house was always filled with visitors, and Fanny, cultured, well-educated and elegant, was admirably suited to become its hostess. It was from her uncle's guests that she first heard of the newly arrived Captain Nelson, a devil perversely intent on ruining them all.

The British Navigation Act strictly excluded the new United States from trading with the British colonies. But the merchants in these colonies—Mr. Herbert among them—had long grown fat through trade with American ships. Despite the Navigation Act, a flourishing black market spread through the West Indies, which British officials, including Admiral Sir Richard Hughes, most understandingly ignored. Until the arrival of Captain Nelson, who, professing to be shocked at the black market, immediately gathered other captains into a plot and began seizing American ships and cargoes that entered British ports illegally. The merchants protested to Admiral Hughes, and he promised to speak to his new captain.

But the admiral came away from his interview with Nelson quite embarrassed, and pointed out that, after all, the black market was against British law, and he could hardly force Nelson to stop enforcing the law.

Although the merchants of the islands were joined as one in hatred of Captain Nelson, he went on visiting the various islands and dealing with their officials as though he had every reason to expect their thanks. This much Fanny knew before she received a letter from a cousin on the island of St. Kitts:

We have at last seen the Captain of the *Boreas,* of whom so much has been said. It was impossible, during this visit, for any of us to make out his real character; there was such a reserve and sternness in his behavior with occasional sallies, though very transient, of a superior mind. Being placed by him, I endeavoured to rouse his attention by showing him all the civilities in my power; but I drew out little more than "Yes" and "No." If you, Fanny, had been there, we think you would have made something of him; for you have been in the habit of attending to these odd sort of people.

One morning, Fanny did finally meet the odd Captain Nelson, just after her uncle burst into her room, crying, "Good God! I just found that little man of whom everybody is afraid playing under the dining table with your child!"

She was surprised when she was presented to Nelson to find that, despite his prematurely white hair, he was a very young man. At twenty-seven, his wind-reddened cheeks, bright blue eyes, and softly curved mouth gave him almost pretty good looks. He was far from the taciturn captain she had been led to expect. Though set in his ideas of right and wrong, he was also a high-humored, graceful gallant. Altogether, she found him charming.

The merchants, however, did not share her good opinion of Captain Nelson. Pooling their influence and money, they took out a writ against him. Nelson, aware that he could not expect a fair prosecution of the case in any court in the islands, retreated to his ship. There he could not be served with the writ, and there he stayed for seven weeks. He wrote his case to the King, and waited. At the end of the seven weeks, notice arrived from the Admiralty in England, completely backing up Nelson's fight against the black market. As a result, all the captains around the islands joined Nelson in enforcing the Navigation Act. Before Nelson left for England, the black market was crippled. And before he left, he made Fanny his wife.

When the newly married couple arrived in England, their fortunes suffered an unexpected reverse. Nelson suddenly found himself on the beach, without a ship. They would have to live on his small inactive-service half pay, until he could get another ship. Unable to afford a home of their own, they moved in with his father.

Nelson had been forced into inactivity because of his actions in stamping out the West Indies black market. Although the Admiralty had had to back him up, it was not forgotten that he had embarrassed his superior officer. No admiral wanted a captain under him who was that independent. Right was right, but tact was a prime peacetime merit. If war came, of course, then there might be use for a captain willing to take chances. But England was at peace, and Nelson could wait.

Five long years dragged by before war finally came, probably just in time to save Nelson's sanity. Revolutionary France declared war on England, and within a week Nelson had a ship. This time he was determined to so distinguish himself that he would never again suffer such humiliation as the five inactive years had dealt him.

As France began to march across Europe under Bonaparte, Nelson found himself at last in sea actions in the Mediterranean. But though he fought small battles, he was given no official recognition, and little money or supplies for his ship and men. "All we get here is honour and salt beef," he wrote to Fanny. "My poor fellows have not had a morsel of fresh meat or vegetable for near nineteen weeks. . . . We are absolutely sick with fatigue. . . . They look up to their Captain as their friend and protector but . . ."

There was one respite for him. He wrote from Naples, where he'd been sent ashore on a short mission, that the English ambassador there, Sir William Hamilton, had treated him handsomely. This letter contained words which Fanny Nelson would one day remember with bitterness: "Lady Hamilton has been wonderfully kind and good. . . . She is a young woman of amiable manners, and who does honour to the station to which she is raised."

Later came a letter informing Fanny that her husband had distinguished himself by personally leading the land battle that seized Corsica from the French—but in doing so he had been hit in the right eye by sand thrown up by a cannon ball. He could now see out of his left eye only.

Still there was no official recognition: "Probably my services may be forgotten by the great by the time I get home." A succession of superior officers continued to thwart what Nelson conceived to be his abilities, until, at last, he was placed under the service of Sir John Jervis. Admiral Jervis knew how to find uses for an unruly but eager captain.

Then came a day in February—St. Valentine's Day—and news of the Battle of Cape St. Vincent.

The commander-in-chief of the English fleet on that Saint Valentine's Day, Admiral Sir John Jervis, was a taut, pugnacious martinet with shrewd eyes in a wide face. He squinted at the distant sails coming toward his flagship, *Victory,* estimated that they were about twenty-five miles west of Cape St. Vincent, on the coast of Portugal. The wind had come around during the night, was now blowing strong southwesterly.

"There are eight sail-of-the-line in sight, Sir!"

It was Captain Calder, reporting breathlessly.

"Very well," came Jervis' growling, snappish voice. "There'll be more in sight soon."

There would soon be many more if, as Jervis hoped, it was the main Spanish fleet they had found. His own fifteen ships were pointed south by west. Those ships in the distance were heading about east-southeast. Therefore . . .

Calder interrupted: "Twenty sail-of-the-line now!"

. . . Therefore their paths should cross about noon.

"Twenty-five sail," reported Calder. And then: "There are twenty-seven sail-of-the-line, Sir. Near double our own."

"Enough of that!" Jervis snapped. "If there are fifty sail, I'll go through them. England badly needs a victory."

Very badly. The spirit at home was sullen. Bonaparte's French troops had rolled down northern Italy and were lording it over all Europe. The Spanish had joined him against England, chasing English ships out of the Mediterranean.

The oncoming Spanish fleet was twice the size of his English one—with bigger and better ships and double the number of guns. But if the Spanish ships were superior, the Spaniards themselves were no match for Jervis' men. He thought of his seasoned captains and drilled crews and prepared to fight.

Aboard Nelson's *Captain,* over six hundred men stood at their battle stations: the lookouts on the mastheads; the sail trimmers out on the yards and down on the deck; marines in the tops with their rifles and down on the deck with their boarding pikes, cutlasses and pistols; gun crews clustered behind the seventy-four cannons that poked their deadly snouts through the bulkheads fore and aft on the main deck, and in long rows from the two gun decks below; dozens of wretched little slum boys ready to run cartridges to the guns from the powder magazine deep in the bowels of the two-decker; the surgeon and his helpers waiting in the dim cockpit below for the bleeding scraps of humanity that would soon be pouring down upon them.

All waiting. Each man waiting for a command from his officer, and each officer waiting tensely for a command from the small, spare man on the poop deck.

Nelson shifted his glance from the line of enemy sails to Jervis, awaiting signals from the commander-in-chief's ship. He did not need to worry, as other captains were doing, about the conduct of his crew under fire. Aboard some ships, officers prowled the decks cajoling or threatening their men to stiffen their spines, but Nelson stayed where he was, with his subordinate, Captain Miller, beside him. For he had won the trust of each of his men. Other captains exacted rigid obedience through iron discipline. Nelson exacted personal loyalty to himself by avoiding formulae, treating each man and officer as a separate challenge. It was distinctly against navy tradition, this playing to an audience aboard ship. He knew that even his friends, Troubridge and Collingwood, considered his compulsion to charm everyone somehow womanish. He offered no excuses; the method worked for him.

Nelson frowned at the signal flags going up on the *Victory.* His column was ordered to tack to form a single line of battle ahead with the column to starboard. Taking up his telescope, he left Captain Miller to handle the ship and leaped into the rigging, climbing with a swift, athletic ease surprising in so slight a figure. Hanging onto the swaying ropes, he put the telescope to his eye and examined the nearing Spanish ships.

The Spaniards had apparently not expected to meet an English fleet. At dawn their ships had been scattered over miles of ocean, but on spotting the English, they had rushed to join together in a single fighting group. By now most of them had succeeded: eighteen ships were formed in a ragged but substantially compact group.

Six miles away, however, was a lee division of nine more Spanish ships, desperately beating to windward in an effort to close the gap and join with the main body of their fleet.

The English line of fifteen ships, led by Troubridge in the *Culloden,* was also knifing for this same gap. If the English line got through the gap before it closed, the battle would be half-won. For with the English line between two Spanish divisions, Jervis would have a choice of easily swallowing the inferior nine-ship group, or of warding off the nine and throwing his 15 against the Spanish 18 in an almost even fight.

Clinging to the shrouds and watching the *Culloden* ahead, Nelson longed to be Troubridge. For the day would belong to him. With the *Captain* far back in thirteenth position in the English line, Nelson could only hope for the last dregs of a battle almost fought-out by the lead ships.

The three groups of ships, one English and two Spanish, flew under full sail toward the same spot in the choppy ocean, like three spokes of a wheel seeking to join themselves at a common center. The gap closed. Troubridge's *Culloden* and one of the Spanish ships approached the spot at the same time. From far back in the English line, Nelson watched the bows of the two ships dash the foaming waters apart as they raced toward each other, certain to collide unless one of them sheered off at the last minute. If Troubridge gave way, the two Spanish groups would join; if the Spaniard veered, they'd be kept apart. And then the Spaniard veered away from the crash. Troubridge led the English line south through the gap between the two Spanish divisions. The larger Spanish group of 18 ships hauled their wind and headed north, coming down the weather side of the English line toward Nelson.

Nelson saw smoke and flashes of flame as the lead Spanish and English ships began exchanging broadsides as they passed each other going in opposite directions. But they were too far apart for effective shooting.

He swung around on the rigging and squinted beyond the other side of the English line at the smaller Spanish division of nine ships. The line of fifteen British ships was sailing south, while on either side of it, too distant for effective cannon hits, Spanish ships were sailing past going north, hoping obviously to join their two units together after they passed the rear of the English line.

Nelson knew that if he were Jervis he would order all his ships to reverse their direction—so that the English ships would be sailing side-by-side with the Spanish, going in the same direction in a rousing broadside duel. Then the position of every ship in the line would be reversed: Collingwood's *Excellent,* now the last ship in the line going south, would be the first, and Nelson's *Captain,* now thirteenth in the line, would suddenly be third. He would have his bellyful of battle and honor within the hour.

Tucking his telescope under his arm, Nelson raced down the rigging and onto the quarter-deck beside Captain Miller. He gave the order for the guns to fire as they bore on the oncoming Spanish ships. The deck under his feet began to tremble with the roaring of the cannons as they fired. The air became murky with smoke. Nelson watched the rigging of Jervis' *Victory,* leaving the sailing to Captain Miller and the firing to the gunnery officers. The Spaniards were firing back at the *Captain.* But they were too far away, and passing too fast for really effective gunnery. Now every English ship was engaged with at least one passing Spaniard. Now, Nelson was certain, Jervis would give the order for the entire line to go about in the same direction as the Spaniards and close with them.

Signals were going up on the *Victory.* Nelson watched them unbelievingly. Jervis had hoisted the signal to tack in succession! The *Culloden,* lead ship of the English line, began slowly to tack to starboard in pursuit of the rear ships of the fleeing Spanish weather division. Jervis' order meant that though the Spanish were sailing past them going north, the ship directly behind the *Culloden* must continue to sail south, *away* from the enemy, until it reached the point where the *Culloden* had tacked. Then, and only then, could it, too, turn and follow the *Culloden* in pursuit of the fleeing Spanish. And the same tactic for every ship down the line: Each one must keep sailing in the wrong direction until it reached the spot where the *Culloden* had turned. They might *never* catch the Spaniards! And if they did, the separated enemy divisions would be joined together by then, presenting a powerful front of 27 ships against their 15.

Nelson understood: This was Jervis' method of preserving the line of battle. He was afraid that an about-face of all his ships might result in confusion and break up the line. Nelson had never agreed that the single line-of-battle-ahead was the correct method of handling every situation in sea war. Well-drilled English gun crews would remain steady where less-practiced enemy gun crews might get rattled. Confusion could actually be favorable to the English ships. But Nelson was not admiral of this fleet; Jervis was. And to Jervis the line was more than traditional; it was sacred.

Nelson watched the smoke-shrouded Spaniards slipping past. Only the two ships directly following the *Culloden* had so far reached the place where they could tack back. The English line was forming an irregular V, the smaller leg following the Spaniards, the larger sailing away from them.

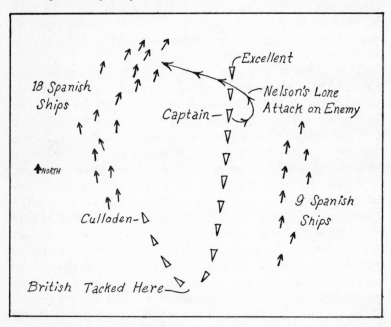

18 Spanish Ships

NORTH

Culloden-

British Tacked Here

Excellent

Nelson's Lone Attack on Enemy

Captain-

9 Spanish Ships

BATTLE OF CAPE ST. VINCENT

If only Jervis would signal for a few of his rear ships to detach from the line at once! They could attack the main body of the Spanish and, even if badly mauled, hold the Spaniards in place until the rest of the fleet could reach the fight. It was the only sensible tactic, now.

The bulk of the Spanish ships were now passing the *Captain*. Two more English ships to pass, and then they would be beyond the rear of the English line—able to unite their separated divisions and flee or fight together. There was no help for it now. Unless they were stopped.

Nelson turned to the officer beside him, forcing the words of command: "Wear ship, Captain Miller."

Miller was stunned. Nelson was telling him to break the line —against orders! Captain Miller recovered himself quickly and bawled out the orders that would take the ship out of the line; it was not his head that would be forfeit for this. But dishonorable dismissal was certain for Nelson; hanging quite possible.

Aboard the *Victory,* Jervis was watching Troubridge's *Culloden* with approval when Captain Calder rushed up to him with the news that the *Captain* had broken the line. Jervis whirled around and saw the two-decked *Captain* circle behind the *Diadem* and cross the line in front of the *Excellent,* in solitary pursuit of the monstrous bulks of the three- and four-decked Spanish warships—a lion attacking a herd of elephants. Then he looked at the weather and lee divisions of the enemy fleet, racing to join each other beyond the rear of his line.

Aboard the *Captain,* Commander Berry, recently promoted from Nelson's lieutenant, hurried aft to where Nelson and Captain Miller stood by the helmsman with news that Admiral Jervis was making signals—signals for the *Excellent,* commanded by Collingwood, to tack out of the line and follow the *Captain!*

Nelson looked gratefully at Berry's tough, handsome face. Jervis' signal could only mean that now Jervis, too, saw the need for Nelson's disobedience. But if the British fleet failed this day, Nelson realized, Jervis would have the perfect excuse: he would place the blame on Nelson's breaking of the British line of battle. On the other hand, Nelson knew that all would be forgiven in exchange for a victory.

Nelson pointed across the narrowing gap of water. "Captain Miller, take us across their bows, if you please."

Amid the deafening thunder of broadsides, cut through by the shocked screams of the maimed aboard his own ship, Nelson kept calm by counting the Spanish ships that loomed over the *Captain's* bow. There were seven of them, huge sea-mammoths that dwarfed his own two-decker. They were across the bow of the biggest enemy ship, sending broadsides to both sides of them. And then the *Captain* was abruptly swallowed into the midst of the 136-cannon *Santissima Trinidad,* the 112-cannon *San Josef,* the 112-cannon *Salvador del Mundo,* the 80-cannon *San Nicolas,* the 74-cannon

San Isidro, and two others. It was a descent into a flaming, crashing, smoking hell.

In the haze, Nelson lost sight of the full progress of the battle, caught instead quick glimpses through rents in the smoke: a network of rigging dissolving into nothing; a cannon ball gouging across the deck, sending up showers of jagged splinters that disappeared suddenly into the bodies of a group of men and dropped them screaming by their cannon; blood spread over the deck, absorbed by the waiting sand, streaming toward the scuppers; the foremast of a Spanish ship crashing down under the still-accurate fire of the *Captain's* guns.

And there came Troubridge's *Culloden* through the smoke, spouting flames and iron from both sides into Spanish hulls as it plunged forward. Three Spanish ships let go at the *Culloden* simultaneously, burning away its entire upper framework of masts, rigging and sails and leaving it to drift helplessly.

The steep wall of a huge Spanish ship suddenly hung high over Nelson's head. There was the roar of a volcano erupting. Even before his sight cleared, Nelson sensed that the *Captain* was now wallowing under him, out of control. He turned toward the helm as the ship quaked again. The helmsman was gone. So was most of the wheel, torn off by a giant hand.

Nelson looked almost as bad as his ship. His hat was half gone, shot away. His coat and shirt had been ripped to shreds by flying pieces of metal and wood splinters. His face was black with powder smoke. His stomach hurt badly where something had struck him a violent blow. But the *Captain's* cannons were still firing, recoiling, being cleaned and reloaded, firing again, their shouting, black-faced crews pouring shot after shot against the hull which towered over them. And near the hatch, Miller and Berry were dazed but still whole.

Nelson shouted for Miller to man the relieving tackles. With a crew down below heaving on the cables from the rudder, they might yet be able to steer through the holocaust.

Nelson looked to starboard and saw a British ship slip in through the haze. It began firing at the Spaniard hanging over the *Captain,* luring it away. That Spanish ship was instantly replaced by another, the 80-gun *San Nicolas.* From its superior height, it began pouring destruction down on the decks of the *Captain,* ripping up planks and slaughtering men. Almost hull-to-hull, the *Captain* and the *San Nicolas* poured broadsides into each other.

The sobs and screams of the hurt clashed with the whistling of heavy metal through the smoke around Nelson. His world was dissolving around him. The fore-topmast snapped and fell crashing onto the deck. Men plunged down as the rigging disappeared from under their feet. Canvas was shorn away. One great portion of sail cascaded down on top of the men Miller was rushing below to the relieving tackles.

Nelson took in the full sweep of his deck, a jungle of wreckage which the remnants of the boatswain's crew tried vainly to clear, a slaughterhouse with the dead men being hurled overboard and the wounded being rushed below decks to the surgeon. And yet, under Nelson's feet, the deck still bucked and heaved as his cannons fired at the *San Nicolas,* giving back all they got. In the smoky hell below, sweat-streaked, insanely yelling, bare-torsoed gun crews still sent shot after shot pounding into the hull of the enemy ship. They aimed at gunports and prayed their balls would kill the enemy gun crews.

Nelson spotted another danger, coming around the *San Nicolas.* One of the biggest of the Spanish ships, the 112-cannon *San Josef,* was circling to hem the *Captain* in on the other side. Nelson's ship had not a single sail left with which to maneuver. Trapped between the *San Nicolas* and the *San Josef,* unable to escape, the *Captain* would be ground to splinters.

But in the same instant that Nelson saw this danger, Collingwood's *Excellent* emerged from the smoke on his starboard. Clearing the *Captain,* it hauled in ten feet from the *San Nicolas* and let go its entire broadside into the Spaniard. Then it passed on.

The *San Nicolas,* smashed by this unexpected fire, luffed and crashed its other side into the *San Josef.* The masts of the two Spanish ships rocked toward each other. Their riggings became intertangled, and they found themselves suddenly locked together.

"Captain Miller!" Nelson's voice cracked with charged excitement. "Helm a-starboard!"

And as Miller shouted the order down to the men straining below at the relieving tackles, Nelson's next call rang high-pitched across his shattered ship: "Boarders! Boarders!"

The *Captain* swung her bow clumsily around toward the high port side of the *San Nicolas.* English marines rushed to the rail, were joined by dozens of yelling, blood-crazed sailors who snatched pistols and cutlasses from buckets waiting under the bulwarks. A dozen cannon muzzles still pointing from the *San Nicolas'* shattered side pounded their shot at the oncoming ship in a vain effort to stop her. But the crippled *Captain* staggered on. The *Captain* ground against the enemy ship with a groaning and cracking of timbers. Her spritsail yard snagged over the enemy's poop and caught fast into the Spaniard's mizzen rigging.

Sliding his sword from its scabbard, Nelson caught a glimpse of the pugnacious Berry leading a rush along the spritsail yard and onto the Spaniard's mizzen chains. A hefty marine jumped past Nelson and clubbed the butt of his musket against the *San Nicolas'* upper quarter gallery window that hung over the deck of the *Captain*. Nelson leaped up onto the fore chains and pulled himself through the smashed window.

He dropped into a large, dim, disordered cabin. Bullets fanned past his head, splattered the deck at his feet. Looking up quickly, he saw Spanish officers firing down at him through the skylights. He and the pack of marines and sailors who had followed him through the window fired back up at the skylight, clearing it in an instant. Then they threw themselves at the cabin's locked door. The door crashed open. Nelson stormed through it with his men.

A group of Spaniards attacked across the deck at him. Nelson's men fired their guns into them and then charged them, swinging their swords and jabbing with their pikes. The Spaniards broke and ran. Nelson led his shouting band up onto the poop.

Berry was there waiting for him, grinning, already tearing down the Spanish flag. Nelson halted, panting, his sword in one hand, his empty pistol in the other. Then he took in the length of the *San Nicolas,* swarming with his boarders. The ship was surrendered; the few final pockets of Spaniards were being subdued by Lieutenant Pierson's marines.

Suddenly, Nelson heard the splutter of small-arms fire from overhead. On all sides of him men began to drop. They were caught by the fire of Spaniards above them in the high stern gallery of the *San Josef,* which was still locked to the smaller *San Nicolas*. His marines began to kneel and fire back up at the stern gallery. Nelson's yell came again: "Boarders! Boarders!"

He raced Berry across the deck. They leaped together onto the main chains of the *San Josef,* began climbing up toward the huge three-decker's rail, marines and sailors crowding behind them. Nelson was reaching up to haul himself over the quarter-deck rail when the face of a Spanish officer appeared above him. Their eyes met. For an instant, Nelson hung there, looking up at the Spaniard. When the officer didn't shoot him, Nelson took advantage of the moment to yank himself up onto the deck, getting quickly to his feet. The Spaniard was the captain of the *San Josef,* and behind him stood his officers, making no effort to resist. They were offering him their swords!

It was impossible. A three-decker carried over a thousand men. Against a handful! Berry and Pierson and the band of boarders from the *Captain* came up the chains and climbed to the deck beside Nelson, as surprised as he at the sight of the proffered swords.

"On your honor, sir," Nelson asked the Spanish captain, "is this ship surrendered?"

The captain shrugged stiffly, unhappily. His admiral was dying below, he explained. His men would fight no more. His ship was surrendered.

Dazed, Nelson took the swords, handed them to the nearest of his men. It was Fearney, one of his bargemen, who grinned proudly at Nelson and stuck the swords under his arm, leaning sideways to spit a stream of tobacco juice over the rail.

From the quarter-deck of the *San Josef,* Nelson looked down at the deck of the lower *San Nicolas,* and down beyond that to the smashed deck of the still lower *Captain.* The three ships were caught together, his own and his two prizes.

From the distance, a sound of shouting swelled across the water. Nelson looked up sharply. Admiral Jervis' ship, the *Victory,* was passing. Every man and officer aboard her was cheering— cheering Nelson. And each of the English ships that slipped by following the *Victory* sent a cheer ringing across the water to Nelson.

The years of frustration and envy were over.

The Battle of Cape St. Vincent was won because Nelson broke the line, chancing personal and professional ruin. He got away with it because of what he accomplished. The Spanish fleet fled to Cadiz, leaving behind four of their ships to the British—including the two which had surrendered to Nelson. It was a victory, and a badly needed one. England was more than satisfied with him. From the King came news that he was now Sir Horatio Nelson, Knight of the Bath. From the navy came a promotion to Rear Admiral of the Blue. The First Lord of the Admiralty notified him that he was being given a pension of one thousand pounds a year. For the first time in his career he was able to feel a degree of financial security.

Sir John Jervis received his reward, too. As admiral of the victorious fleet, he was made Lord St. Vincent. Jervis knew quite well whom he could thank for his title; he expressed his gratitude by appointing Nelson to command of a squadron of ten battle-ships.

Then, in July of that year, the god of war who had smiled on Nelson at Cape St. Vincent struck him a terrible blow.

It was the end of July, but it was cold down on the water that night. The wind that had kept Nelson's ships off Santa Cruz for three days was still driving hard in the darkness. His boat plunged down into the wild sea, then shuddered its way up huge waves threatening to topple into it.

The army had refused to lend Nelson's squadron any support in his plan to seize the Spanish treasure at Santa Cruz, for though he might capture enough to keep England at war for an entire year, they thought the task of getting it impossible. Yet Blake had done it, once, and Nelson was determined that he could do it too.

In the stormy darkness of the Santa Cruz bay, Nelson huddled between his stepson, Josiah, and a seaman who was fighting the waves for possession of his oar. The boat was jammed with men shoulder-to-shoulder and knee-to-back, in a tangle of attack equipment: ladders, axes, sledge hammers, pikes, cutlasses, muskets and pistols.

In the darkness, Nelson could see none of his other boats. But they were there, all around him in the night: dozens of them carrying a thousand of his men, divided into six groups. They were all heading toward the mole between the bay and the town of Santa Cruz. The plan was to creep forward in the dark until discovered, then rush the mole, fight to the town and seize the treasure.

Night abruptly vanished as the blinding blue glare of three high-curving flares from the mole lit up an entire area of sea, surf and shore. Dozens of other flares followed. Cannon balls, grapeshot and canister shot smashed into the boats. The Spaniards had been expecting them.

Nelson leaped up and stood balanced in the bobbing boat, raising the sword handed down through his mother's family. "Cast off!" he yelled against the cannon thunder. "Take the batteries! Remember your orders!"

He fell forward on top of Josiah as his boat pitched into the surf and ground to a sudden stop on the beach, directly under the downpointed cannon muzzles.

Nelson pulled himself upright, jumped out of the boat onto the sharp-stoned beach, waving his sword for his men to follow. He was spun around and fell to his knees, facing back towards the sea, agony in his right arm wrenching him down further, grinding his face in the close-packed pebbles. He fell over on his side, clutched his right arm with his left hand. Where the hard structure of his elbow should have been, his left hand felt only a pulpy mass. Dizzily, he stared at his lifeblood pumping out of his smashed arm. He saw his sword lying beside him. His great-uncle Captain Galfridus Walpole had carried that sword when he lost his right arm eighty-six years before, but had stooped down and picked it up with his left hand.

Nelson reached out his left hand and took the hilt of the sword. He was seized by strong hands and turned over, lifted. It was his stepson, Josiah, winding a strip of cloth in a noose around Nelson's upper right arm, drawing it tight. Nelson was half-conscious when Josiah and a seaman carried him back into the boat, shouting for oarsmen.

He regained consciousness as the boat reached his ship. He refused to be lifted aboard in a lowered chair: "I have my legs left and one arm." He caught the end of a lowered rope in his left hand and managed to climb up the ladder to the deck of his ship.

"Tell the surgeon to make haste and get his instruments," he told the frightened midshipman who met him on deck. "I know I must lose my right arm. So the sooner it is off, the better."

Two days later, Nelson sat at his desk as his ship rolled its way north at the head of his squadron. He was preparing to write a letter to Jervis, the first letter he was to write with his left hand. The short stump at his right shoulder throbbed steadily, painfully. He could not get rid of the memory of the terrible coldness of the knife that had hacked his arm away. He had fainted during the operation. When he opened his eyes later, lying on his bunk, they had asked what they should do with his arm. He told them to throw it overboard.

What should he write to Jervis? Troubridge had been the only one of his captains to get his group to the town square. He had waited for the others till dawn, when he found himself surrounded by thousands of Spanish troops. Troubridge, trapped, had threatened to set fire to the town unless allowed to take his men back to the ships. The Spanish governor, having won the battle, was generous, even lending some boats to help carry the English out to the fleet.

As for the others: two hundred and fifty dead. As for Nelson himself: he was a one-eyed, one-armed cripple.

Nelson picked up the pen awkwardly in his left hand, began to write in big, straggling, barely readable letters: "I am become a burthen to my friends and useless to my Country. When I leave your command, I become dead to the world; I go hence and am no more seen. . . ."

16

"We will set our course east— for Alexandria"

Through the following months the agony in the stump of Nelson's right arm failed to abate. He could stand the pain only with the aid of large, steady doses of drugs. The doctors thought the artery had been tied improperly. They spoke of amputating higher to relieve him. He was willing to have it done: anything to get the pain out of him. But there was little left below the shoulder to amputate.

During those long months, Nelson was plagued not only by pain but by the fear that he would never go to sea again. For he had discovered that success had only whetted his ambitions. He brooded heavily and his wife's desire that he never go to sea again angered him.

On the morning that he awoke to find the pain finally gone, he was wild with joy. That very afternoon he got into his best dress uniform and went off to demand a ship. When he got back, he wrote to Captain Berry, who had been at his side in the charge across the Spanish ships at Cape St. Vincent and was in England now preparing to be married. He told him to hurry up with the nuptials, for he was to be Nelson's flag captain on his new ship.

England stood alone. Revolutionary France was in the hands of Napoleon Bonaparte, who had absorbed part of Europe, aligned most of the rest of it on his side, and frightened the few remaining countries into shaky neutrality. Bonaparte declared: "Either our government must destroy the English monarchy, or must expect itself to be destroyed by the corruption and intrigue of those active islanders."

One of those active islanders, though passionately disturbed by this threat, was, on the last day of April, 1798, more immediately annoyed by the ridiculous figure he imagined himself to appear as he went up the side of Jervis' flagship off Cadiz. The voyage from England in his new ship, the *Vanguard,* had been humiliating. The relationship between himself and his ship had changed. He was no longer an agile sailor, able to enjoy the freedom of his vessel. He was a one-armed admiral, a burden to himself and a care to others aboard. He could not escape up into the rigging; he was awkward even on a ladder or gangway. He was stuck on the deck, and even there he had to hold himself lopsided to balance his one-sided weight against the roll and pitch of the ship. The motto aboard a sailing vessel was "One hand for the ship and one for yourself." He now had only the hand for himself, to cling to a rope or rail.

But Jervis' smile, when Nelson lurched onto the deck of the flagship, was a rare one of genuine pleasure. He was happy to have Nelson back with him, and sorry they would have to part so soon. He explained why they were parting: France was equipping ships in Toulon, Genoa and Civita Vecchia. Twenty ships-of-the-line, four hundred troop carriers, thousands of soldiers aboard them. Bonaparte was getting a fleet and his army ready to sail somewhere in the Mediterranean—or out of it. There was no solid information on where he planned to go but there were plenty of rumors: an attack on Greece, or Sicily, or Naples; or he was going to come out of the Mediterranean and head for the West Indies, or Portugal, or England by way of Ireland. Bonaparte had the run of the Mediterranean, for there had not been a single English warship there since the evacuation of Elba. Now it was imperative that Bonaparte's fleet be watched. Jervis showed Nelson a letter from the Admiralty: "The appearance of a British Fleet in the Mediterranean is a condition on which the fate of Europe may be stated to depend." Jervis was operating a blockade against the Spanish off Cadiz, so he was sending Nelson to stalk Bonaparte and catch the French fleet if it ventured outside its ports.

In the middle of May, Nelson was driving his ships under full sail northward over the choppy Mediterranean toward Toulon. Besides his own *Vanguard,* he had two other ships-of-the-line (the *Orion,* under Captain Saumarez, and the *Alexander,* with Captain Ball) and four fast frigates. A few days earlier, he had caught a French corvette and, questioning its officers, learned that fifteen French ships-of-the-line and seven frigates were ready to sail from Toulon, ready to convoy two hundred transports loaded with French troops. More important: General Bonaparte had arrived in Toulon.

This, Nelson was certain, meant that wherever Bonaparte was headed, he was heading there sooner than anyone in England had expected. Nelson sent a sloop back to Jervis with the news—and a plea for more ships. Then he raced toward Toulon, praying fervently that he would reach there before the French fleet sailed.

What he intended to do if the French put to sea while he was watching them was another matter. His three battleships and four small frigates would not stand a chance against fifteen bigger French battleships and seven frigates. Nelson could only hope to follow the French and keep contact until more English ships arrived from Jervis. If worst came to worst, he was determined to drive his few ships in among the helpless French troop carriers and sink as many of them as possible before Bonaparte's battle line destroyed his own tiny fleet.

Alone in his cabin, Nelson worked out dozens of battle plans under the shifting light of an overhead lantern. As he drew his precise patterns, he mused upon the qualities of the men who would put them into action.

Captain Berry, with him on the *Vanguard,* was the sort of fighting tool Nelson liked: a keen, dependable cutting edge. The captains of his other two line ships were not of his choosing and not much to his liking. Captain Ball, on the *Alexander,* was a dandy. Nelson, who had come to make a virtue of plain dress and manner after his former near-poverty, resented him. Saumarez, commanding the

Orion, possessed a superior, reserved manner that in former days had repelled the friendly, exuberant young Nelson.

He was happier with Hope, the senior captain of his frigates. He was sure that he could count on him to use the fast, maneuverable frigates—the scouts for his squadron—to their best advantage.

Nelson was going over his battle plans the night before he expected to reach Toulon, when a vicious gale swept suddenly over the dark horizon and struck his small squadron. Within a half hour, Nelson's ships were scattered into the darkness of night, lost to each other's sight.

Making his way up to the quarter-deck, Nelson clung with his one hand to an iron ringbolt and helplessly watched Berry fight to save the *Vanguard* from the fury of the storm. The ship lurched as huge waves smashed down across its waist, heeled over as the gale tore at its masts and sails. Nelson watched in horror as, one by one, the masts came crashing down.

All through the night the ship wallowed helplessly between mountains of water, a dismasted hulk. Then, just before dawn, the storm relaxed into ordinary gale force. The *Vanguard* was no longer pointing toward Toulon, but was drifting away south, past the rocky coast of Corsica.

In the morning, two ships appeared over the gray horizon and bore toward the *Vanguard* under masses of fast-moving, low-hanging clouds: Ball's *Alexander* and Saumarez's *Orion,* neither much hurt by the storm. By noon, the *Alexander* had the *Vanguard* in tow, while the *Orion,* off the starboard, kept watch.

Nelson's aim now was to reach Sardinia, which was halfway neutral, and find some small, secluded bay where his ship could be refitted. But by evening a new danger presented itself. A strong gale, blowing from the west, was forcing the *Vanguard* and *Alexander* against the reefs which line the coast of Sardinia. Alone, the *Alexander* would have had no trouble clawing its way out from that threatening coast. But with the dead, unwieldy weight of the *Vanguard* dragging the hawser attached to its stern. . . .

Nelson snatched up his speaking trumpet and shouted for Captain Ball to cast off and save his own ship. But Ball, whom Nelson had thought a mincing dandy, refused to obey the order. Stubbornly determined to save Nelson and his flagship, Ball towed the *Vanguard* past the reefs all night, until a lessening of the gale finally allowed the two ships to veer away from the rocky coast.

Shortly after dawn of the next day, the three ships entered the sheltered bay of a tiny Sardinian island. Nelson, ashamed of how badly he had underestimated Ball and Saumarez, worked off his confusion by driving the crews of all three ships to an astounding feat of repair. In a regular dock back in England, it would probably have taken about a month to refit Nelson's dismasted *Vanguard*. But four days after entering that little bay, the *Vanguard,* fitted with jury masts, sailed out again under its own sail, leading the *Alexander* and the *Orion* north, back toward Toulon.

As they sailed, Nelson kept a sharp watch for his four frigates. He needed those fast vessels to act as lookouts beyond his horizon. On May 31, as he was nearing the French coast, a sail was sighted to the west, running rapidly toward his three-ship squadron. It turned out to be young Captain Hardy with his swift little sixteen-gun brig, *Mutine*.

Nelson knew that the twenty-eight-year-old Hardy, who had briefly served as his lieutenant before the Battle of Cape St. Vincent, worshipped him. But this time Hardy brought bad news. Captain Hope, senior captain of the frigates, had gone back to Gibraltar, and was still there. Hope had seen Nelson's ship dismasted, and had assumed Nelson would have to put back to Gibraltar for repairs.

Nelson was furious. Hope should have known him better than that! Nelson resolved never again to judge a man before he saw how he acted in trouble. Hope, whom he had trusted, had failed him. Ball, whom he had despised, had saved his life and his ship. Next he could expect the haughty Saumarez to dance a jig! Now, Hardy's little *Mutine* would have to do the work of those four missing frigates.

Nelson sent Hardy away to reconnoiter the harbor at Toulon and see how Bonaparte was coming along with his preparations to set sail. By noon, the next day, the *Mutine* reappeared, bearing the worst possible news. There was no fleet in Toulon. Bonaparte, with his hundreds of ships and thousands of troops, had already sailed. Where? Only Bonaparte knew.

Bonaparte had an army four times the size of anything England could muster aboard his transports. Wherever he intended to land his troops, no force would be able to stand against him. Only at sea was there a chance for him to be beaten—if he could only be found. . . .

Nelson sailed east, toward Italy. Wherever Bonaparte was headed, his fleet must first be joined by the ships gathered in Genoa and Civita Vecchia. The *Mutine* darted in for a look at Genoa. As at Toulon, the French warships and transports had already sailed. At Civita Vecchia it was the same: The French fleet was gone.

From the very beginning, Nelson's search was hamstrung by lack of frigates. He sailed with his three battleships spread out over as large an area of ocean as possible, hoping one of them would spot the enemy fleet over the horizon. But the battleships were big and slow. Hardy's *Mutine* was sent darting back and forth across the sea in search of the French fleet, but it could not do the work of the four missing frigates.

On the seventh of June, reinforcements sailed over the horizon: Tom Troubridge's *Culloden*, leading a squadron of nine other 74-gun battleships and a fifty. Jervis had sent Nelson the pick of his captains and ships.

Nelson received Troubridge aboard with affection and led his old friend below to his cabin. There he opened the dispatch Troubridge brought from Jervis. It contained explicit orders: Nelson was now in complete command of the Mediterranean fleet. He was to destroy the French fleet. But there was still no information on Bonaparte's intended destination.

The French held all the north of Italy, down to the Kingdom of the Two Sicilies. Naples, the capital of that kingdom, was the nearest and most convenient object of attack. Nelson decided to have a look at Naples.

Standing on his quarter-deck beside Berry, Nelson squinted through the shimmering heat-waves at the ships following in the *Vanguard's* wake. His own fleet at last! Thirteen seventy-fours, the fifty-gun *Leander*, and the little *Mutine*. Fifteen seasoned captains under his command: Berry on the *Vanguard*, Troubridge on the *Culloden*, Ball on the *Alexander*, Saumarez on the *Orion*, Hallowell on the *Swiftsure*, Miller on the *Theseus*, Westcott on the *Majestic*, Darby on the *Bellerophon*, Peyton on the *Defence*, Hood on the *Zealous*, Foley on the *Goliath*, Louis on the *Minotaur*, Gould on the *Audacious*, Thompson on the *Leander*, Hardy on the *Mutine*. His captains and his fleet. No matter how many ships-of-the-line Bonaparte managed to bring together, Nelson was sure this group could beat them. *If* he could find the French fleet.

A week passed. A week of sailing down the coast of Italy, sending the *Mutine* in close to shore every day to stop small boats and question their masters. But no one had seen Bonaparte's fleet. The English ships reached Naples. No French ships were to be seen. The word there was that Bonaparte's combined fleet now numbered twenty fighting ships-of-the-line, plus four hundred transports carrying forty-five thousand troops. But no one in Naples had any idea where this fleet was, nor where it was going.

Nelson sailed south. Then, at last, a month after Bonaparte sailed from Toulon, a captured boat had some news: Bonaparte's fleet had stopped at the island of Malta, seized it with no trouble, and sailed away six days before. Where had the fleet sailed? South.

Nelson hove to his fleet and summoned aboard the four captains whose intelligence he rated highest: Troubridge, Ball, Saumarez and Darby. He spread out a big map of the Mediterranean upon his desk.

Bonaparte might be headed for Corfu. Or, he might be tricking the English, sailing south and then doubling back to hit at Sicily. Or, he could turn west and head out of the Mediterranean past Gibraltar. Nelson drew his forefinger back and forth across the map. The tip of his finger touched Malta; then it moved slowly in a straight line to the southeast. To the coast of Egypt. To Alexandria.

Egypt was the crossroads of three continents. It was also the natural road to England's possessions in India. Outside of attacking England itself, Bonaparte could damage the English most by taking the most valuable part of England's Empire.

The four captains stared at the map and nodded, warily. It was very possible. On the other hand . . . Bonaparte might be headed *west*. And the prevailing winds were then from the west. If Nelson's fleet sailed east to Egypt, and then found Bonaparte had gone west, the English ships would have to sail against the wind to catch up. If that happened, they probably never would catch the French fleet. But the decision was not the captains'. It was up to Nelson.

"In the end," Nelson pointed out, "one must go one way or the other. We will set our course east—for Alexandria."

During the week that followed, Nelson turned his fleet into a floating classroom. On every ship, the men were drilled for hours at the guns. Then for more hours every man in the fleet practiced handling pistols and muskets for close-quarters work. Every afternoon, cannons and small arms were used in an hour of actual target practice. Each day Nelson went aboard several of his ships to inspect them for battle fitness, insisting that there be not a single frayed rope or sail tear, that each vessel be spotless. And each day he had his captains visit him on the *Vanguard* for several hours of reviewing battle plans. There was not a single possible situation in which the two enemy fleets might meet that Nelson did not discuss with them repeatedly, in detail. When they encountered the French, Nelson did not want time wasted in last-minute conferences. "Instant action is the key to most victories," he said. "Five minutes can mean the difference between winning or losing a battle."

They were off the crowded twin harbors of Alexandria at the end of June. The *Mutine* sailed in close, entered the harbor. Nelson, watching through his spyglass, seeing not a single French flag, felt a sickness grow in him.

The *Mutine* returned: The French fleet was not in Alexandria. No one along the coast of Egypt had seen Bonaparte's armada or heard news of it.

Nelson stared bitterly at the Egyptian coast. He had been so sure. If Bonaparte had sailed west to get past Gibraltar into the Atlantic, there was no help for it now. But there were other places Bonaparte might have taken his fleet in that vast sea. Nelson called his fleet together and sailed north—toward Syria. He searched along the Asiatic coast. No sign or word of Bonaparte's fleet. He turned around and sailed back west. Past Crete. No sign of Bonaparte. No word.

Two months had passed since Bonaparte's fleet left Toulon. Nelson doubled the hours of drilling and practice for the crews of his ships to keep them from going stale. To everyone in the fleet, he seemed, incredibly, to still be his old cheerful, certain, determined self. Only his servant knew how little he ate.

If only he had had those four missing frigates, Nelson was certain, he would have found the French long before. "If I die," he wrote home, "the word 'frigates' will be found carved on my heart."

Nine weeks after Bonaparte had left Toulon, Nelson and his fleet were back at Sicily, still searching. He picked up letters that had been left for him by Jervis' dispatch boat. From them he learned that all England was muttering against him. There was one letter from a navy friend back home: "People know my attachment to you, and how often have I been questioned: 'What is your favorite hero about? The French fleet has passed under his nose!'"

Nelson was wracked with frustration. "The devil's children," he growled, "have the devil's luck."

On July 28, Troubridge's *Culloden,* which had been off on the horizon, came sailing back to Nelson's ship with news. Troubridge had stopped a little wine boat an hour before; the men on the boat said they had seen the French fleet a number of weeks back, sailing southeast from the coast of Crete.

Nelson had been right all along. Bonaparte *had* gone to Egypt. Apparently Nelson had arrived in Egypt too early, left too soon. The French and English fleets had sailed right past each other, going in opposite directions—just out of sight of each other.

The last time Nelson had sailed from Sicily to Alexandria, it had taken him six days. This time, with Nelson constantly on deck signaling for more speed, it took just four days. They were off Alexandria on August 1, with no French ships in sight, when the *Mutine* came racing from the east. Hardy reported aboard Nelson's flagship in a sweat of excitement. The whole French line of battleships was anchored in Aboukir Bay. Hardy had counted twenty-two of them. Within minutes, fifteen English fighting ships were racing eastward along the Egyptian coast, scattered in order of their speed, headed for Aboukir Bay.

The odds seemed weighted in favor of the French fleet, under Admiral Brueys. Nelson had thirteen 74-gun battleships and one of fifty guns. French Admiral Brueys had thirteen battleships; nine of them seventy-fours comparable to Nelson's biggest ships. The others were bigger: three of 80 cannons, and the admiral's flagship, the *Orient,* with 120 guns. And besides these ships-of-the-line, Brueys had four frigates and five smaller vessels.

High on the poop deck of his three-decked *Orient,* Admiral Brueys watched the approaching English ships and prepared to fight. He was aware that he had a number of natural advantages over the English. Even apart from his superior number of cannons and men, he was fortunate in the protection afforded by the bay itself, situated at the headwaters of the Nile. It was small and tightly curved, the approach to it from the sea full of hidden shoals. The attacking fleet would have to pick its way slowly through those shoals, sounding continually as they came. And they could only get into the bay one at a time. The guns of his combined ships could pound each of them to bits as they came on toward the center of his line.

And that was the way they must come. For Brueys had his thirteen heavy battleships anchored close to shore in a long line following the inner curve of the bay. There was a gap of about 150 yards between the stern of one ship and the bow of the one behind it, so that the guns pointed from the seaward sides of all his ships commanded the entrance to the bay.

Unfortunately, many of Brueys' men were ashore for supplies at the time he sighted Nelson's fleet, but it would be dusk by the time the English ships reached the entrance to the bay. Nelson's fleet would have to wait till the next day's dawn before there was light enough for them to enter through the dangerous shoals of the bay entrance. And during the night, Brueys would be able to get the rest of his men back at their battle stations.

But Nelson had no intention of cooling his battle lust outside the bay all night. He realized that it would be completely dark by the time the entire battle inside the bay could be joined. It would then be impossible for him to signal to his other ships, or even to see clearly what they were doing. But it didn't matter. The two months of searching that had worn him down had also served to knit his captains into a single fighting unit. They did not need to see his signals to know his mind. Each captain could be counted on to do the job Nelson had drilled him for, without running instructions.

Nelson ran up signals for his fleet to attack the van and center of the French line according to prearranged plan, which called for the English ships to enter the bay, break into two separate lines, and attack one *end* of the French line of ships. One of the lines of English ships was to sail down one side of the French line; the other to go around the end of the French ships and strike down along the other side. Thus, at any actual point of fighting along the French line, the English would have a superiority: A pair of English ships could get a French ship between them, smash it, and move on down the line to the next French ship.

At first glance, it seemed that there was no room for a ship to sail between the French line and the shore. But Nelson saw that the wind was blowing the French ships away from the shore to the full length of their anchor chains. Where there was room for a French ship to swing on its anchor, there was room for an English ship to slip inside.

Nelson's captains read the signals and raced for the entrance to the bay, the fastest ships first. Aboard the *Culloden,* Troubridge was jubilant. His ship led the others.

Sounding only intermittently for shoals, Troubridge pushed his ship forward swiftly. The *Culloden* was slipping past a small island at the bay entrance when she abruptly went aground on a shoal. While his crew labored to get her off into deep water again, Troubridge looked on, heartbroken, at the other ships as one by one they curved past him into the bay, warned away from the shallows by his fate.

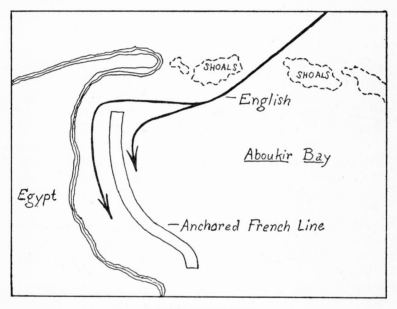

BATTLE OF THE NILE

Aboard the *Vanguard,* Nelson's sympathy for Troubridge gave way before his realization that the absence of one 74-cannon ship in the coming fight could be ruinous. He ran up signals for the 50-gun *Leander* to help get the *Culloden* off.

The entire seaward side of the French line opened fire on the bows of the first British ships as they cleared the shoals and entered the harbor. Nelson saw with satisfaction that none of his ships wasted time or ammunition in replying; the distance was still too great for accurate fire.

Nelson's eye was fixed on two of his ships, the *Zealous* and the

Goliath, which were racing each other for the honor of being first into the fight. Captain Foley's *Goliath* nosed ahead and pointed its bows at the lead ship of the French line, the *Guerrier.*

The sun set. The battle was joined.

The first two ships in the French line—*Guerrier* and *Conquérant* —fired all their seaward cannons at the *Goliath* as it came on toward them. The *Goliath* staggered as the French broadsides began to find their mark.

Coolly, Captain Foley issued a warning that no gun crew was to fire until he gave the order. He called directions to the hands aloft, furling the sails, and sent his lieutenant aft to stand by the stern anchor and await his word.

Foley recited orders to the quartermaster and bore for a rake across the bow of the *Guerrier.* The two lead French ships were now hitting the *Goliath* with every shot, drilling holes in her side, shaking her masts. But the discipline drilled into the English crews by Nelson bore fruit. Behind each cannon a gun crew stood stripped to the waist, eyeing the looming hull of the *Guerrier,* waiting. Men spun about and dropped as flying iron and splinters of wood swept the deck. The fallen, dragged below to the surgeon, were instantly replaced. The muzzles of the *Goliath's* cannons, each heavy with a double load of two iron balls, were trained on the enemy ship. But no gun fired.

The bow of the *Goliath* shot past that of the *Guerrier.* Captain Foley saw they were so close that the enemy's bowsprit would almost scrape along the rail of his ship.

"Fire as your guns bear!"

The command was hardly past Foley's teeth when the *Goliath* shook to the roar and recoil of its own portside cannons, each one smashing two heavy cannon balls into the bow of the *Guerrier* in passing. By the time the *Goliath's* stern passed the first French ship, thirty-seven cannons had spewed their double loads into the French bow and opened it up like a monstrous wooden flower.

Foley brought his ship around and passed along the shoreward side of the *Guerrier.* His gun crews, released at last from the strain of the long hunt, cleaned, reloaded and pointed their cannons with fantastic speed. As they drew alongside the French ship, not a French gun fired at the *Goliath:* The French, sure the English ships could not get between them and the shore, had not even readied their shoreward guns! Foley saw French crews working desperately to prepare those guns now—too late.

The *Goliath* rolled as its entire port battery let go a roaring broadside at pistol-shot distance. The *Goliath's* lower-deck guns sent a line of shots punching holes in the enemy's waterline. The upper guns sent a whirling swath of cannon balls raging across the *Guerrier's* decks, mowing down whole sections of the crew, slamming against the masts, dissolving lower rigging, overturning cannons.

Foley shouted to his lieutenant to let go the stern anchor. It rattled down and plunged into the water. But it dragged on the bay floor. The *Goliath* continued to move forward until it came alongside the second ship in the French line, the *Conquérant*. There it stopped. His guns spewed forth another torrent of iron. A few cannons on the *Conquérant* replied. The *Goliath's* broadsides thundered with deadly regularity. Foley saw the *Conquérant's* mainmast crack and go crashing down onto the deck.

Behind the *Goliath,* Captain Sam Hood brought his *Zealous* foaming along in Foley's wake, his cannons completing the destruction of the *Guerrier's* opened-out bow and bringing down its foremast. Hood swung the *Zealous* around the French line's end, came alongside the *Guerrier,* and dropped anchor. The deck under him quaked constantly as his port cannons sent broadside after broadside hammering against the *Guerrier*. After ten minutes of this steady bombardment, not a moving figure could be seen on the *Guerrier's* demolished decks.

The third British ship into action, Captain Saumarez's *Orion*, followed the example of the first two, doubling the enemy's van, and getting between the French line and the shore. The *Guerrier's* starboard batteries had not yet been harmed, and all its guns fired at the *Orion* as it came on. But they did little damage. For by then water was pouring in the *Guerrier's* port side, tipping the ship over so far that its starboard guns pointed skyward. Only a few of its shots hit the *Orion's* upper rigging or landed on its deck. Saumarez took his ship in a daring sweep around past the *Zealous*, which brought him in so close to shore that he could feel the keel scrape bottom. But the *Orion* sailed on.

Aboard the *Goliath*, Foley held his fire to let the *Orion* slip between him and the French *Conquérant,* then let go another broadside into the Frenchman. Saumarez folded his arms on his chest and murmured orders to the helmsman to take the ship farther down the French line. As he did so, a French 40-gun frigate dashed toward the *Orion* from inshore intending to rake his bow. But when the frigate was a hundred yards away, about to slip across his bow, the *Orion* suddenly wore to port and let go its entire starboard battery at the frigate. The result was devastating. Saumarez had ordered his gun crews to aim for masts. When the smoke of the broadside cleared, the frigate lay helpless without a single mast left. Two more broadsides utterly demolished the frigate, sent it drifting away toward shore, falling apart and sinking.

The *Orion's* bow came around again and Saumarez sailed his ship farther down the French line, bringing it to anchor between the port quarter of the fifth French ship and the port bow of the sixth. Then he began to hammer at both of them with all the guns he could bring to bear. The two French ships, having managed by then to get some of their shoreward cannons ready, replied. But under the steady, accurate pounding of the English gunners, the French cannons began to go silent, one by one.

The fourth English ship into the battle, Captain Gould's *Audacious,* drove between the stern of the first French ship and the bow of the second, dropping anchor just inside the latter's port bow. Seeing that the *Goliath* was already wreaking havoc with the *Conquérant's* waist, Gould trained his guns on its bow and began to disintegrate it.

The fifth English captain into action, Miller aboard the *Theseus,* saw that the *Guerrier's* starboard guns were canted too high to cause him any real damage, and closed in on its starboard until his rigging was six feet from its jibboom. He had his cannons double-shotted—some even triple-shotted. His first broadside took away the *Guerrier's* two remaining masts. Miller sailed on past, got inside the French line, found himself a position opposite the third French ship, the *Spartiate,* and settled down to the job of destroying it. But the *Spartiate* had by now readied most of its port guns. Within seconds, the *Theseus* and the *Spartiate* were engaged in a duel of broadsides.

This much Nelson had seen from the deck of his *Vanguard,* which was in sixth place. His plan was unfolding piece by piece, exactly as he had intended it to. Five of his ships were now inside the enemy line, between the French ships and the shore. Four more were coming up just behind his *Vanguard,* into the entrance of the bay. Beyond them, the *Leander* and the *Mutine* were struggling to get the *Culloden* off the shoal, a task which Nelson soon realized was hopeless. Beyond the *Culloden,* Nelson's two remaining ships, the *Swiftsure* and Ball's *Alexander,* were still out at sea, pushing toward the bay under full sail. But it would be dark before they arrived. And Nelson himself wanted to be in position by dark.

Deciding that the first five ships of his fleet were doing well enough inside the French line, he rapped out orders to Berry and the *Vanguard* swept into the bay, leading the rest of the English ships against the outside of the French van and center.

The seaward side of the French line proved to be tougher meat than the shoreward one had been. For the French starboard cannons were quite ready, some loaded with double helpings of iron balls, others crammed full of grapeshot, scrap iron and chains. And though the French sailors were inferior to the English, the French gunners were among the best in the world.

Nelson, seeing that the first two French ships had already been completely shattered, pointed the *Vanguard* at the third Frenchman, the *Spartiate.* He withheld the order to drop anchor until the sides of the two ships were almost touching. Then, at the same instant, both ships let go their broadsides.

Time and again the two ships drove their iron balls into each other. The smoke-hung air was filled with invisible, shrieking death. Aboard the *Vanguard,* a young midshipman came dashing aft, shaking like the ship itself: every single man at the first six cannons was dead. Nelson ordered them replaced with new gun crews and looked away, watching four of his ships slip past the *Vanguard's* port to engage farther down the line.

Within minutes, the *Minotaur* and the *Defence* were broadside-to-broadside with the fourth and fifth ships of the French line. Darkness closed in on the two embattled fleets, only to be split again and again by the flash of fire from smoking cannon muzzles. The stabs of this fitful lightning were now all that Egyptians on shore could see of the battle, but its tumult could be heard far inland.

Aboard the *Bellerophon* Captain Darby was trying to get his ship anchored next to the sixth French ship in the line. But it was tricky work in the dark. The ship dragged its anchor and kept moving ahead. All at once, Darby saw three long lines of cannon muzzles abruptly emerge from the darkness above the side of his ship: the towering, 120-gun *Orient,* Admiral Brueys' flagship. Darby shouted his order for the starboard guns to fire.

The blast of the *Bellerophon's* broadside was swallowed in that of the *Orient's*. More than seventy massive cannon balls crashed down on the deck of the English ship, slaughtering the crew, ripping out two masts and flinging them into the bay, caving the entire ship in upon itself. Captain Darby lay unconscious beside the splintered wheel. The *Bellerophon* drifted masterless across the dark bay, lost to the battle raging around it.

Meanwhile, Captain Westcott's *Majestic* had gotten its jibboom caught in the rigging of the ninth French ship. It was an awkward, dangerous position, for the French ship was able to discharge broadside after broadside against the *Majestic's* bows, while the English ship could only bring to bear its foremost guns against its opponent. Aware that his ship was in mortal danger, Captain Westcott drove his crew furiously, trying to cut the *Majestic* loose from the French ship.

The eighth ship in the French line now also trained its guns on the caught *Majestic*. Westcott, working desperately up in the bow under the merciless fire of two French battleships, watched his rigging wither away in a twisted tangle, saw an entire gun crew blown to bits . . . and then saw no more.

Lieutenant Cuthbert, hacking away at the caught rigging beside him, heard Westcott's strangled cry. He whirled in time to see Westcott fall dead across a cannon. Cuthbert, now in command of the *Majestic,* leaped ahead and slashed his ax at the rigging with doubled fury, yelling himself hoarse at the crew which worked behind him.

By sheer effort of rage, Cuthbert tore the *Majestic* free. Sprinting back along the gutted, splintered deck, he reached the wheel and rasped orders to the quartermaster, yelled others to the crew. The *Majestic's* few remaining sails caught the wind, pulled the ship away.

Cuthbert saw the tenth French ship, the *Mercure,* loom out of the darkness. He drove the *Majestic* in a slow rake across the *Mercure's* bow, dropped anchor close to her, and began to cannonade her systematically.

Back at the entrance of the bay, Captain Troubridge watched the *Leander* leave him. There was now no hope of getting his ship off the shoal. He went down to his cabin and stared for some time at his pistol. Finally, he put the pistol away, not sure if it was an act of cowardice or bravery to go on living.

On his return to the deck, he made the one contribution to the battle still possible to him. The sails of the two last English ships to reach the scene were spotted in the darkness, making toward the bay entrance. Troubridge lighted lanterns and had them swung aloft. At least he could warn them away from his position.

The *Alexander* and the *Swiftsure,* racing anxiously, were driving straight for the hidden shoal when they saw the lanterns of the *Culloden*. They sheered off just in time to avoid the same fate as Troubridge. Sailing past, they signaled their gratitude. Then they plunged into the thunder-and-lightning-filled darkness of the bay.

Inside, the first six ships of the French line were caught between the grip of eight English seventy-fours. The seventh ship, Admiral Brueys' colossal 120-gun *Orient,* had just sent Darby's ship reeling away a dismasted hulk, and was now unengaged. It was against this huge warship that the last three English ships, groping their way in the dark, combined.

Captain Hollowell, taking his *Swiftsure* past the engaged van of the French line in search of a victim, found it suddenly—in the sheer wall of the *Orient's* three decks of cannon muzzles. Hollowell tipped back his head, stared up at the guns. Then he dropped his stern anchor off the *Orient's* starboard bow and took on the monster.

Minutes later, Captain Ball's *Alexander* materialized out of the haze-drifted darkness. Ball saw at once that the *Swiftsure* was being badly mauled. Ball took his ship around the *Orient,* raking the French admiral's stern with a broadside. Then he dropped his bow anchor off the *Orient's* larboard quarter. Although the three-decker's top row of cannons sent broadsides smashing down on the *Alexander's* deck, Ball kept his head. He saw that a fire had broken out high on the *Orient's* poop and sent orders for his gun crews and the marines in his masts to concentrate on the *Orient's* blazing poop—to hamper the Frenchmen rushing to put out the fire.

Meanwhile, the 50-gun *Leander* had found a position athwart-hawse the French ship just ahead of the *Orient*. From there, it was able to fire broadsides at the bows of both French ships, while they in turn could only bring a few forward cannons to bear on the *Leander*.

The arrival of these last three English ships completed the first phase of Nelson's plan. The enemy's line had been doubled; its van and center engaged by a superior concentration of English ships. His captains had followed his orders perfectly. Now the outcome of the first phase lay in the hands of the frenzied, blood-and-sweat-streaked gun crews.

Nelson was straining forward, trying to see what was happening through the flame-lit darkness when a jagged piece of iron struck him in the forehead. The edge of it seemed to break through his skull and pierce his brain. He fell backward in a rush of agony. Arms caught him before he hit the deck. They were Berry's arms. And he could hear Berry's frantic voice. But he could not see Berry. He could see absolutely nothing. His hand sought for his good eye, touched where it should be—felt only gushing blood and pulpy flesh. He decided that he had lost his good eye, that he was now totally blind.

He was carried below, down a ladder, into the stifling-hot cockpit. The surgeon's fingers tugged at Nelson's forehead, burning. A palm wiped across his left eye. A yellow lantern, dancing to the shock of recoiling gun carriages, blurred into focus through wet, red fog. Nelson saw the surgeon's hovering, anxious face.

He was not blind. The piece of metal had ripped a flap of forehead flesh down over his good eye.

Nelson refused to let the surgeon sew him up until the other men who had been brought into the cockpit before him were tended. He watched the surgeon prepare to amputate a seaman's mangled leg and, remembering the coldness of the knife that had removed his torn arm at Teneriffe, he shouted: "Jefferson! Warm your instruments in hot water!" Then he fainted.

He regained consciousness under the prick of the surgeon's needles sewing through the flesh of his forehead. The next thing he became conscious of was that the *Vanguard's* guns were silent. Berry entered the cockpit with news: The *Spartiate* had surrendered to the *Vanguard*. Also surrendered were the first two ships of the French line. Berry could not see the rest of the ships in the darkness.

Nelson sent Berry back on deck with orders to report to him as soon as he found out what was happening to the rest of the battle. Then he sent for his secretary, Campbell, and began to dictate his report of the commencement of the battle which was to be sent to Jervis. He was too keyed up to just sit on his cot and do nothing. But his secretary could not help but stare at the frightening spectacle his admiral made: the one eye fixed, the other almost hidden under a bloody bandage; the facial bones showing sharply through taut, shrunken, parchmentlike flesh; the dried streak of blood against a gray cheek; the lips trembling with pain.

Campbell's hand shook so that what he wrote was an illegible scrawl. Impatiently, Nelson snatched the pen out of his secretary's hand and began to write the dispatch himself with his inexpert left hand, trying to ignore the throbbing agony in his head.

Berry reappeared: Two more French ships had struck to the English; the French admiral's flagship appeared to be on fire. Nelson could remain below no longer. He forced Berry to help him up the ladder onto the quarter-deck. There, exhausted, Nelson lowered his sore body onto a gun carriage and stared out at the flashing gunfire as though in a trance.

He spotted the big three-decked *Orient* down the line, its entire upper deck, poop, and lower rigging ablaze. He saw three of his own ships clustered around the French flagship, pouring a steady barrage of broadsides into her. And getting smashed back in return. For despite the fire, the *Orient's* lower-deck guns were still functioning. The blaze on the French flagship shot up suddenly to envelop the masts. The *Orient* became a veritable torch, illuminating the entire bay. Moments later, the sound of gunfire, the cries of the wounded, all were smothered by a volcanic detonation. The fire had licked into the *Orient's* powder magazine.

Nelson felt his own ship rock under him from the water-transmitted force of the explosion. Incredibly, the great French warship seemed to hurl itself up into the air and fall apart. The bulk of its shattered hull fell instantly in separate parts to the water and sank. But masts, spars, men, ropes and timbers continued to rise toward the sky as though pulled from above. For a moment, a deathlike silence hung across the bay. Not a gun was fired anywhere. Every man in both fleets stared as the hurled wreckage of the *Orient*—wooden, iron, and human—began to rain down on the water and the decks of other ships.

Neslon recovered from his shock sufficiently to send off the sole unsmashed boat of the *Vanguard* to pick up survivors. He leaned his weary, hurt frame against the bulwark. The moon had risen high above and its ghostly gray light revealed the ships still in combat. The English ships that had surrounded the *Orient* now moved on to close around the last ships of the French line. These had cut their anchors and were trying to escape from the bay.

Nelson watched, drugged with pain and weariness, as the night retreated from the advance of dawn. The guns began to go silent, ship by ship. The hot sun rose to reveal the carnage. The last gun ceased firing. The absence of sound rocked across the bay.

One by one, the English captains came aboard the *Vanguard* with their reports, took them to the figure which sagged on the cannon. Nelson seemed to have shrunk within his uniform. All around the deck the exhausted crew lay crumpled in sleep, by the masts, behind the cannons. The boatswain's mates managed to kick some of them awake and began the work of scrubbing the blood out of the decks with boiling vinegar.

Nelson read the reports, the results of the battle. The French had started with thirteen ships-of-the-line, four frigates and some smaller craft. Of these, only two ships-of-the-line and two frigates had escaped to sea. The rest were burned, sunk or surrendered. The French admiral was dead; over five thousand French officers and men had been killed or wounded. In contrast to these figures, all of the fourteen English ships-of-the-line in that battle were still afloat and in English hands, though some were in near-sinking condition. Nine hundred Englishmen were dead or wounded. Captain Darby was badly hurt. Captain Westcott was dead. Nelson, exhausted and wounded, sick in body and mind, had achieved the greatest, most one-sided naval victory in history.

17

The Best Negotiators in Europe

THE DEFEAT OF COPENHAGEN

A sickening weight of lethargy disabled Nelson after the Nile. At thirty-nine, he was weary of life, despairing of the future, sick in body and soul. It was the toll exacted in payment for months of tension during his search for the French fleet, months which had so drained him that the emotional release of the battle, capped by the blow to his head, emptied him of his life juices. "My head is splitting, splitting, splitting!" he wrote home.

And in this condition he spent interminable days in Egypt, tending to the mountain of tasks that victory brought upon him: dispatches, letter writing, provisioning and patching his ships, disposal of the captured vessels, mass burials at sea, visits to the maimed and wounded. He moved through the days mechanically, doing the correct things out of habit. He yearned to sleep forever, but could do so only in snatches. Even under drugs, he woke repeatedly to find himself seized by painful fits of coughing. A strap seemed buckled taut across his chest whenever he lay down. He spent most of his nights trying to force himself to breathe normally.

261

England officially showed its appreciation of his victory with a surprisingly small reward for those days and ways: Nelson was given a yearly pension of two thousand pounds and named Baron Nelson of the Nile. But the people of England took him to their hearts. The little one-armed, one-eyed admiral who gave all the credit for his victory to his captains—"my band of brothers"— caught their fancy. They toasted him, sang songs about him, and demanded pictures of him. A nation had fallen in love with a man.

Letters of praise came from all parts of the world. Between bouts of nausea, he read and reread each one, savoring the words of adulation, deriving from them the cranky comfort that a sick child might receive from the cool hand and soft, reassuring words of its mother.

The wildest praise came from Naples, from Emma Hamilton. Nelson had met her four years before, when he had gone on a mission to Naples. He was only an unknown captain then, untried in battle; but both the English ambassador, Sir William Hamilton, and his beautiful young wife had been more than kind to him. Although Nelson, under the press of urgent business, had been able to spend only a few days in Naples, he had not forgotten the beauty and knowing charm of Emma Hamilton. And apparently she had not forgotten him.

Now she wrote: "How shall I begin, what shall I say to you. I am delirious with joy. . . . I would not like to die till I see and embrace the victor of the Nile! . . . I walk and tread in the air with pride, feeling I was born in the same land with the victor Nelson and his gallant band. . . . For God's sake come to Naples soon. . . ." It was heady stuff for a man whose wife had never regarded him as a hero, but merely as a more-than-ordinarily trying, rather vain husband. ". . . My dress from head to foot is all Nelson; even my shawl is in Blue with gold anchors all over. My ear rings are Nelson's anchors . . . come soon to Naples."

Nelson sailed to Naples.

They fell in love. What Ambassador Hamilton thought about it no one knows, for he never spoke or wrote of it. Of course, he knew—before long all England knew of it. But he showed no resentment, indeed continued to the end of his life to regard Nelson as his greatest friend, and never interfered between the lovers.

When Nelson returned to England more than two years later,

bringing the Hamiltons with him, Emma was pregnant with Nelson's child. Wherever Nelson went, Emma was almost sure to be beside him. And her condition soon became quite obvious. Nelson's wife left him. But the crowds cheered their hero lustily wherever he appeared—despite the fact that they also made him the butt of their most vicious laughter.

When Nelson was assigned to the Baltic fleet, one of the most popular cartoons of the day—it was exhibited, framed, in print-shop windows all over London—showed an obviously pregnant woman bawling ludicrously as she watched a fleet of ships sail away. Behind her, an aged fool was fast asleep. The woman was meant to be Emma Hamilton, the fool her husband, and the lines below the cartoon read:

> *Ah; where, and oh! where is my gallant sailor gone?*
> *He's gone to fight the French for George upon the throne.*
> *He's gone to fight the French, t'lose t'other arm and eye,*
> *And left me with old Antiquity, to lay me down and cry.*

The government of England, understandably displeased with Nelson's romantic doings, found an incredible way to express its disapproval. Nelson, now the most famous sea-fighter in the world, could certainly expect to command any fleet to which he was attached; but when he was assigned to the Baltic fleet, he found himself *second* in command. Over him was placed a mediocre admiral named Sir Hyde Parker.

But there was a new First Lord of the Admiralty: John Jervis. And Jervis, knowing Nelson so well of old, had his own opinions of the man—and acted on them. He agreed that "the Almighty was in a glorious mood when he formed Lady Emma," but believed Nelson had acted the sentimental fool in making public his attachment to her. However, this did not alter his opinion of what Nelson could do with a fleet of ships. Therefore, although Nelson was officially only the second-in-command, it was to him, not to Sir Hyde Parker that Jervis most carefully explained the thorny problem facing the Baltic fleet.

Prussia, Denmark, Sweden and Russia had formed a Northern Armed Neutrality Alliance that threatened England in its continuing conflict with France by backing up the refusal of its member nations to allow England to stop them from trading vital supplies with Bonaparte. It was a formidable group and England was determined to break it up.

The English government was sending an envoy—Nicholas Vansittart—along with Sir Hyde Parker and the Baltic fleet, to try to persuade the Danes that they should get out of the Alliance. If they refused to negotiate, the Northern Alliance would have to be forced to come to terms. How this was to be done was left quite vague, but Jervis made it clear that any decision was to be Nelson's. As he put it to Nelson: "Send them to the Devil your own way."

Nelson paced the quarter-deck of the warship *St. George* with his short, swift steps, while behind him stalked his flag captain, Hardy. Big white flakes of snow slowly fell about them, as they had intermittently all during the long week the Baltic fleet had waited for action. Back in England, spring was beginning to breathe in the air, but up there off the northern tip of Denmark it was miserably cold. Were it not for his anxious waiting for something to happen, Nelson would have sought the comparative warmth of his cabin, there to gaze at the framed painting of Emma and think of the daughter who had been born to them and named Horatia.

Following Nelson's quick step, Hardy stared in wonder at his admiral's slim back. Hardy had expected to sail with the gloomiest of superiors. The official snubs Nelson had experienced in England had persisted through the voyage to Denmark. Sir Hyde Parker had avoided Nelson like a pariah. He had not had the courtesy to invite him to a single of the conferences held on his flagship, the *London*. Yet Nelson had been in a merry mood from the moment of sailing, exhibiting a jauntiness which Hardy hadn't seen in him since the old days, back before the Battle of Cape St. Vincent.

There was a hail from the masthead: a frigate was approaching from the direction of Copenhagen. Nelson slapped his gloved hand on the rail and smiled, relaxing from the tension that had gripped him. Aboard that frigate would be Mr. Vansittart. Nelson was certain he was returning from Copenhagen to tell Sir Hyde Parker that he had talked sense to the Danes and that the Danes would have none of it. For Nelson was sure that the only sense the Northern Alliance would listen to would be a show of force: "Twenty ships-of-the-line are the best negotiators in Europe."

And Nelson was also sure that Sir Hyde Parker would now seek him out. "While the prospect of fighting was a joke, they kept me in the background. Now we are sure of fighting, I'll be sent for."

He was right.

Gloom sat at the long table in the *London's* cabin with the sea officers who, having heard Vansittart's report of Denmark's sharp refusal to come to terms, now listened while the diplomat passed on what he had learned of the defenses of the Danish capital. The more Vansittart talked, the worse the idea of attacking Copenhagen seemed. The port lay to the south of the British fleet, down in the sound leading to the Baltic Sea. A huge shoal, Middle Ground Shoal, protected the entire waterfront length of the city. In order for the British ships to get close enough to Copenhagen to do it any damage, they would have to sail south, down through the narrow gap of water between the Middle Ground Shoal and the coast. But before the British ships could reach the city by this route, they would have to pass directly under the 700 guns of Three Crown Fort.

Any British ships that managed to get past the fort would face a further obstacle. The Danes, anticipating attack by the British fleet, had stretched a line of anchored ships and hulks along the entire waterfront. Before the British could get at the city itself, they would have to fight that line. And half the male population of Copenhagen manned the cannons on those ships and hulks.

The situation, as far as Sir Hyde Parker could tell, looked impossible. He was caught between two fires: Any attack he might launch stood a good chance of ending in disaster; but on the other hand, were he not to attack he would almost certainly face disgrace at home.

It was at this point that Nelson stepped in. He agreed that to sail south between the Shoal and the coast would be folly. But he had an alternative ready. The Danes had placed their most formidable ships at the head of their line, the northern end. Nelson's plan was simple: The British would sail south *around the outside* of the Middle Ground Shoal; then, once they got past it, they could double back inside the Shoal, approaching the city from the south rather than the north. That way, there would be no Three Crown Fort to slip past. And they would hit the anchored Danish line at its southern end, where it was weakest.

Hyde Parker pointed out that Nelson's plan was too risky. The gap between the southern end of Middle Ground Shoal and the coast was not only dangerously narrow but rock-infested. The fleet would go aground. But Nelson knew of a channel through those rocks at the southern end, a channel marked with buoys. He had found it on one of his charts.

The other admiral still vacillated. What if the Swedish and Russian navies showed up while the British fleet was bottled up inside the Shoal? Nelson suggested that he should be allowed to take just the lighter line ships and all the frigates in against Copenhagen. These would run less risk of going aground. Meanwhile, Hyde Parker could keep the heavier ships off the north of Middle Ground Shoal—away from the battle—ready to fend off the Russians or Swedes if they showed up.

With this suggestion resistance crumpled. Nelson's plan was adopted in its entirety. Nelson left the *London* and transferred his command to a lighter ship, the *Elephant*. Taking Hardy with him, he sailed south toward Copenhagen.

The night before the attack, Nelson's squadron lay inside the southern tip of Middle Ground Shoal, two miles below Copenhagen. With Nelson were twelve battleships and all the smaller vessels of the fleet. Before dusk, he had assessed the wall of eighteen battleships and twenty smaller craft with which the Danes intended to defend their capital. The anchored Danish ships, needing no sail power in the coming fight, had had their masts taken down, so that there would be no timbers and rigging to fall on their decks. The fact that half the men of Copenhagen manned the Danish cannons did not worry Nelson. On the contrary, he was sure that such a mass of untrained civilians would not be able to fire as fast and accurately as his own veteran gun crews.

The most difficult problem before the English would be to get to the Danish line to fight it. For the Danes had removed the buoys which usually marked the channel up which Nelson's squadron must sail. Nelson had spent the previous day personally supervising the small boats as their crews sounded out the channel and put down new buoys. But there was a dangerous stretch of water between the point where the buoys ended and the Danish line began.

After dark that night, Nelson discussed this problem with Hardy, who set out in a boat bearing muffled oars and equipped with a long pole, since a sounding line would have made noisy splashes.

In the chartroom of the *Elephant,* Nelson spent the next few hours working out details of the Order of Battle with the officers of his squadron. The disposition of the ships was complicated, but the strategy which dictated their positions was simple: His battleships initially would attack only the weak southern end of the Danish line, anchoring close alongside it and concentrating all fire there. When they had crushed this part of the line, they would cut their cables and move ahead to the northern group of Danish ships.

It was late that night when Hardy stomped into the chartroom to join Nelson and his officers. Huge drops of water fell from his soaked clothes. It had been foggy, down on the water, and under the cover provided by the fog Hardy had gotten closer to the Danish line than Nelson had expected or dared hope. Sounding the channel, he had actually gone as far as the end ship of the Danish line and circled it in the dark. Hardy marked the channel he had sounded on Nelson's charts. By following the line he drew, he assured Nelson, none of the ships would go aground.

At six in the morning the fog began to lift. Nelson, already on deck, saw that the wind was perfect to carry his squadron up through the channel to the Danish line. He signaled for all pilots and captains to come aboard the *Elephant* for a last conference.

But when he laid out the sailing plans for the pilots, all of whom had sailed those waters in merchant ships, he ran into unexpected opposition. The pilots refused to follow the channel Hardy had sounded during the night. They all swore that the British ships could not get in that close to the Danish line without going aground—the Danish ships and hulks must have their keels resting right on the gravel bottom. To get through, the British ships would have to hug the inside of the Shoal.

Hardy argued, but the pilots insisted that he was wrong. After all, it had been dark and foggy when he made his soundings; it would have been easy for him to make a mistake under these conditions. Before the pilots' certainty, Hardy at last grudgingly admitted that he *could* have been mistaken.

Nelson didn't like it, but he was in a bad spot. He needed the pilots to guide the ships to the Danish line; they were the only men who had sailed these waters before. He reasoned that they should know best—and decided to sail the route they demanded. It was one of his worst errors of military judgment.

By nine-thirty that morning, every one in Nelson's squadron was at his proper ship's station for the attack. It gave Nelson a feeling of added weight and strength to have among his squadron leaders men like Foley and Fremantle, veterans of the Battle of the Nile. He sent up the signal to weigh anchor in succession and sail for the anchored Danish line.

Still worried about the controversy between Hardy—who stood beside him—and the pilots, Nelson watched the *Edgar* catch the wind and lead the way toward the waiting Danish hulks. Hugging close to Middle Ground Shoal, as the pilots had insisted, the *Edgar* got through the shallows and took the booming fire of the first two Danish ships without replying. Then it veered to larboard and dropped anchor beside the third Dane. The opposing ships recoiled from each other as they slammed out their first broadsides.

It seemed the pilots had been right, and Hardy wrong. The *Edgar* was through and . . . Nelson lurched forward a step, staring. The second ship in his line, the *Agamemnon,* was aground!

Rooted to the deck, Nelson watched his third ship slip through safely. The next also went through. And then the *Bellona,* holding to the same general line, shuddered to an abrupt halt, swung part way around, hung motionless on a shoal with its masts quivering. The *Russell,* directly behind it—and in front of Nelson's ship— veered to starboard, taking a course between the grounded *Bellona* and Middle Ground Shoal, where the water deepened, according to the pilots. The *Russell* grounded.

Nelson swung toward Captain Foley, screamed at him to star- board the helm and take the ship through on Hardy's line. The *Elephant* swung around the port sides of the grounded ships, leaped forward into the shallows on the larboard side, away from Middle Ground Shoal. This route, Hardy's line, took the ship so close to the Danish line that shot began hitting its masts and hull before it was halfway through. But a moment later the *Elephant* was past the narrows, shuddering to its cannons as they pounded their iron weights into the Danish line beside it.

Hardy had been right. By trusting the pilots instead of his flag captain, Nelson had lost one-quarter of his battleships on the shoal before the battle started. Nelson assured himself that the ships behind him were following Hardy's course, then turned his attention to the fight.

The *Elephant* dropped anchor alongside a Danish battleship and a string of floating batteries. Every port cannon under Nelson let go with a full-throated explosion. Nelson's frigates and bomb vessels slipped ahead and closed in on the shore batteries. Behind the *Elephant,* the last ships of Nelson's squadron got through the channel and dropped anchor alongside the Danes. The first phase of the battle was joined.

Nelson looked up and down the Danish line. Each of the nine battleships left him was anchored and engaged with the enemy. It was the end of the maneuvering. From now on it would be brute slaughter. Nelson smoothed his white forelock down over his scarred forehead, began his quick, short-stepped pacing of the quarter-deck.

The sounds that jammed the cold, misty air—the roar of exploding gunpowder, the whine of shot through the air, the screams of the hurt—combined into one monstrous storm of noise that rolled in against the buildings of Copenhagen. There the people crowded the waterfront to stare in fury and awe at the two lines of ships locked together in impersonal murder, shrouded most of the time in great clouds of smoke that were held down by the mist. Even the men dripping sweat and blood down in the suffocating hells of the ships' gun decks could hardly see their targets. They loaded and fired blindly into the smoke outside their gunports.

An hour after the carnage had begun, a freshening wind blew the smoke away sufficiently for Nelson to see the long line of ships. Some of the Danish vessels were on fire. Some of his own were almost mastless, their decks shrouded with fallen rigging. But not a single ship on either side had struck its colors.

An hour later, it was the same. There was havoc aplenty, but still not a ship had surrendered. Boatloads of men streamed out from the city constantly to take the places of the Danish gun crews that Nelson's cannons had wiped out. The crews behind some of the Danish guns were completely replaced five times. Nelson had never had to deal with such an impossibly stubborn foe.

But while the Danes had a limitless supply of men, they did not have a limitless supply of ships. The Danish ship opposite to Nelson's was an example of what was happening. The *Elephant's* guns had opened up its side so completely that Nelson could see the men inside laboring at the guns; loading, firing, being flung backwards with their overturned cannons as shots from the *Elephant* hit them. But the Danes were giving as well as taking. Half the *Elephant's* crew was down in the cockpit under the surgeon's knife.

At this moment, the signal lieutenant hurried up to Nelson, saluted smartly, and informed him that Sir Hyde Parker's ship was flying signal 39: Leave Off Action.

Nelson, looking up and down the locked lines, realized that the battle must look like a stalemate from where Hyde Parker was watching through his spyglass. Coolly, he resumed pacing the short space of starboard quarter-deck still navigable. The signal lieutenant uncomfortably asked if he should repeat the signal to Nelson's ships.

Leave off action? "Now damn me if I do," said Nelson. He asked if his own signal for Close Action was still hoisted. It was. Nelson told his signal lieutenant to make sure it stayed hoisted, to nail it to the mast if necessary. He noticed that Captain Foley was staring anxiously toward the distant squadron of Sir Hyde Parker's ships. Grinning, Nelson strolled over to him. "Foley," he said, "I understand Sir Hyde Parker is flying some signal or other."

"Yes sir."

Nelson picked up Foley's spyglass.

"You know, Foley, I have only one eye. I have a right to be blind sometimes."

He put the glass to his blind eye theatrically, then announced to the quarter-deck in general: "I really do not see the signal."

Then Nelson put down the glass and stepped away to watch the Danish flagship, which had begun to burn like a box of matches.

The Danish commander-in-chief's pendant fluttered down from its mast. Men began to leap from the burning vessel into the cold water. At the same time, a boat full of officers shoved off from it and made for another Danish ship. A few minutes later, the Danish commander's pendant rose to the top of the mast of the new ship.

Within half an hour the Danish commander's new ship, its cable cut by a shot, was drifting helplessly toward the beach, beginning to burn. The Danish commander's pendant was shifted again— this time to the Three Crown Fort.

By half past two in the afternoon, many of the Danish floating batteries were helplessly adrift; some of the Danish battleships were on fire; others seemed to have only a few guns still working. One by one, the Danish vessels at the southern end of the line ceased fire and lowered their colors. Boats with prize crews set out from the British ships to take possession of the surrendered Danes.

But then it developed that these Danish ships had not really surrendered. As a boat from the *Elephant* neared one Dane, its colors suddenly shot up to the top of the mast again. A fresh supply of men from shore resumed the firing of its cannons—this time at the prize boat, smashing it to kindling and drowning its men.

Enraged, Nelson watched this happen again and again, up and down the line. Danish vessels that no longer showed their colors would fire on the English boats that came to accept their surrenders. Even allowing for the fact that most of the men manning those ships were civilians, such actions were criminal murder. In retaliation, the English ships began a heavy bombardment of every vessel within range, surrendered or not. Between the two enemy lines, four unresisting, helplessly drifting Danish vessels were hammered apart between shots from English ships and their own Danish shore batteries. The situation was impossible. Surrendered ships that could not be taken; a beaten fleet that would not stop fighting.

Nelson decided the time had come for diplomacy. Not Vansittart's kind of diplomacy, but Nelson's—backed by a naked threat. He strode into the stern gallery, shouting to his secretary for pen, ink and paper, and forthwith composed a note to the Crown Prince of Denmark:

To the brothers of the Englishmen, the Danes: Lord Nelson has directions to spare Denmark, when no longer resisting; but if the firing is continued on the part of Denmark, Lord Nelson will be obliged to set on fire all the floating batteries he has taken, without having the power of saving the brave Danes who have defended them.

He sent the note ashore on a truce boat. Two hours later, both sides flew truce flags. Not a gun sounded. The Danes had agreed to a temporary cessation of hostilities during which they could talk things over with the British.

Jubilant, Nelson drove his exhausted force unremittingly throughout the rest of the day. By dusk, he had taken possession of his

Danish prizes and prisoners, his most severely damaged vessels had been removed from the scene of action, and he had placed his bomb vessels in strategic positions from which they could bombard the city if and when hostilities resumed.

Both sides counted their dead. Nelson reckoned almost a thousand men killed or wounded. Six thousand Danes were dead, wounded or prisoners. Nelson made arrangements to go ashore and interview the Danish Crown Prince. Then he went to his bed and fell instantly into a deep sleep. For a time, at least, the butchery was over.

Hardy and Fremantle accompanied Nelson in the barge. As they neared shore, they saw that the entire Copenhagen waterfront where they would land was packed with mobs of Danes. Nearer still, they heard the ugly murmurs of this crowd that blocked their path. Nervously, Fremantle suggested that they row back to pick up a guard of English marines. Nelson, his face amiable and interested, looked at the nearing faces and did not answer. He was the first one to leap from the barge to the shore.

The crowd surged around the English officers, staring, muttering among themselves. A few voices were raised angrily. Nelson asked Fremantle what they were saying. Fremantle told him they were trying to guess if one of them were really Nelson, whereupon Nelson smiled broadly at the close-pressing faces, seized the greatcoat that covered him, and swept it off his shoulders, revealing his decorations and his famous stump.

As he stepped forward toward the carriage that awaited him, the crowd parted, making a path for him. There were still murmurs and some angry faces, but most of the Danes just gaped at Nelson as they would have at any legendary figure suddenly come to life in their midst. Nelson climbed into the carriage. Before closing the door, he turned and waved to the crowd, smiling. Dozens of them waved back, their proper emotions thrown completely out of joint by his outrageous friendliness.

At the palace, the Crown Prince greeted Nelson and the two of them were soon exchanging compliments. The Prince said that many of his people believed Nelson was so brave because he was Danish in origin—Nelson being a Danish name.

But many of the Crown Prince's advisors and diplomats did not accept Nelson so pleasantly. In the long, stubborn negotiations that followed, they fought against giving in to Nelson. The British fleet had no business in Danish waters, they argued; the Danish navy had done very well against Nelson, might do even better if hostilities were resumed.

"Renew hostilities!" Nelson cried back hotly. "We are ready at a moment! Ready to bombard you this very night!"

Then Nelson glanced significantly around the huge palace room and leaned back toward Hardy with a stage whisper that carried to every man in the room: "Though I have only one eye, Hardy, I see that all this will burn very well."

Denmark signed the armistice, by the terms of which they resigned from the Northern Armed Neutrality Confederation.

The news of Nelson's naval and diplomatic victory reached England swiftly—and with it the story of how Nelson had deliberately turned his blind eye toward Sir Hyde Parker's signal to retreat. The nation's wild acclaim for Nelson forced the government to act: Sir Hyde Parker was recalled. Nelson was made a Viscount and named the new commander-in-chief of the Baltic fleet.

But there was no one left to fight. Russia's Czar had been murdered, and its new ruler was friendly toward England. With Denmark already out of the Northern Confederation, only Sweden was left—and Sweden decided to forget the whole thing.

Now that there was nothing more active to do than maintain the fleet, Nelson suddenly became aware that the cold damp of the Baltic did not agree with him. He resigned his position and sailed home—to England, to Emma Hamilton, to his baby daughter.

18

The Nelson Touch

Nelson had only a short time with Emma Hamilton after he returned from the Baltic. Bonaparte seemed to be preparing for an invasion of England. To reassure the British people, the Admiralty appointed Nelson to the Channel Fleet. Then England and Bonaparte signed a treaty, and an uneasy peace set in. Nelson considered it a foolish treaty, certain as he was that Bonaparte was only bargaining for time in which to build up his forces.

Nevertheless Nelson accepted the peace gratefully. He was sick of cruising the cold Channel, and eager for Emma Hamilton. Back in England, he purchased Merton, a lovely rustic estate. Then, briefly, Nelson, Emma and Sir William Hamilton moved into it, resuming their strange Mediterranean relationship—until on a cool spring morning in 1803, Nelson and Emma buried the body of her husband. Sir William's attitude toward the love of his friend and his wife remained odd to the end. In his will, he left a prized painting of Emma to "my dearest friend Lord Nelson . . . the most virtuous, loyal and truly brave character I ever met with. God bless him, and shame fall on those who do not say Amen."

274

After Sir William died, Nelson and Emma brought their daughter, Horatia, to Merton to live with them. These were golden days for Nelson, the happiest of his life till then. But they were numbered. One month after Sir William Hamilton died, England declared war against Bonaparte again.

Soon after the declaration of war, at the Admiralty in London, Nelson received his orders. Whatever Bonaparte's plans, he would need ships to get at England. And most of his ships were in the Mediterranean. Nelson was appointed commander-in-chief of the Mediterranean Fleet.

Two days later, Nelson and Hardy climbed up onto the wide, busy deck of the largest ship Nelson had ever commanded. It had been Jervis' ship at the Battle of Cape St. Vincent: the *Victory,* with an 840-man crew and three gun decks to help carry the tremendous weight of its one hundred and ten cannons. For a long, prideful moment, Nelson stood on deck gazing about his ship. Then he took Hardy below to his big, freshly painted cabin, and began issuing his orders.

On July 8, 1803, Nelson arrived at his Mediterranean station south of Toulon and set his squadron to the first part of their task: watching the French harbor and waiting for Bonaparte's ships to make a try for the open sea.

A year and a half later, Nelson was still there, waiting. Then, on January 19, 1805, two of his frigates came sailing over the horizon from the north, flying the signals: "The Enemy Is at Sea."

What followed was a long, frustrating search and chase much like the one that had worn Nelson down before the Battle of the Nile. For the French fleet, commanded by Admiral Villeneuve, sailed south from Toulon and vanished. Nelson sailed to Sicily. Villeneuve's fleet had not been seen there. He sailed to Egypt. The French were not there. He turned around and sailed north again. It was March before Nelson learned that the French fleet had run into the teeth of a gale and scurried back into Toulon. Nelson had had almost two months of worry for nothing.

In April, Villeneuve's French fleet slipped out of Toulon again —and again vanished. Nelson stretched his fleet from Sardinia to the coast of North Africa. The *Victory* prowled incessantly, day and night, her captain in a fever of anxiety, squinting at the horizon, marking time for news that did not come. When it rained, Nelson stayed on deck until he was soaked through. Then he went inside his cabin, yanked off his boots, and paced in his soggy stockings, back and forth like a caged tiger, until his clothes dried to dampness. Then he went out on deck again.

The bitter memory of two long, time-wasting searches for French fleets across this sea rankled deep: "I shall neither go to the eastward of Sicily or to the westward of Sardinia, until I know something positive."

News came at last: a neutral merchant ship had sighted the French fleet sailing toward the Straits of Gibraltar—two weeks before. And Nelson had his fleet on the move before the merchant vessel got under way again. He headed for Gibraltar. But now the wind, which had been fair for Gibraltar for weeks, turned around and beat dead against his fleet. Nelson scratched in his report: "I cannot get a fair wind, or even a side wind. Dead foul! Dead foul!" It was the fifth of May before he reached Gibraltar—to find that Villeneuve's French fleet had sailed past into the Atlantic a whole month before. Where was he headed? No one knew.

Three days later, when he anchored in Lagos Bay to provision his ships, a Scotsman in the employ of the Portuguese navy got word to Nelson: Villeneuve had sailed to the West Indies, supposedly to wait there for the fleet of Spain—which was united with Bonaparte against England—to join him. Nelson set out across the Atlantic toward the West Indies.

The pursuit continued through that entire summer. Nelson sailed his fleet across the Atlantic in twenty-four days. It had taken Villeneuve thirty-four. For two weeks Nelson combed through the islands for Villeneuve. The French admiral knew he was being followed—and by whom. With twenty ships to Nelson's ten, he avoided a fight, kept on the move.

In the middle of June, Nelson learned that Villeneuve, harried by his pursuit, had given up waiting for the Spanish reinforcements —and sailed east. Back across the Atlantic went Nelson after Villeneuve. He reached Gibraltar on July eighteenth, and there was soon news: The French fleet had gotten through another British squadron, and safe into the Spanish port of Ferrol. Villeneuve showed every indication of staying put there for a while.

Worn out from the long chase, Nelson took advantage of a sick leave that had been granted him months before. He reached England in the middle of August. Two years had passed since he had set foot on land, two years since he had seen Emma Hamilton

and their daughter. He rode straight for Merton, knowing he would
have to leave again at the first sign that Villeneuve might stir out
of port. He suspected that he hadn't much time. He had just
twenty-five days.

Nelson was summoned from Merton to London again and again
to confer with the heads of the government. Cabinet officials, wary
of the temper of the people and knowing the fantastic faith the
country had in Nelson, treated him now with a deference that
surprised him at first, then amused him. "They want my opinion on
each little thing," he told Emma. "I am now set up for a conjuror.
God knows they'll soon find out I am far from one. If I make one
wrong guess, the charm will be broken."

In a final conference with the Prime Minister, William Pitt,
Nelson learned that Villeneuve had managed to get his fleet out
of Ferrol and into the harbor of Cadiz. There, the combined fleets
of France and Spain were joined: thirty-three ships-of-the-line.
And Bonaparte had issued orders to Villeneuve to sail out and
fight the English fleet.

England was in real danger. Bonaparte had 150,000 troops
with 400 cannons drawn up along the French coast. He had over
2,000 small boats ready to carry this invasion force across the
Channel against England. If such a force landed, England would
have the greatest difficulty withstanding it.

Bonaparte had handed Villeneuve's combined fleet of Spanish
and French warships the jobs of clearing a path across the English
Channel for this invasion force to cross, of pushing the English
fleet out of the way just long enough for the French troops to reach
England. Said Bonaparte: "Let us be masters of the Strait for six
hours, and we shall be masters of the world."

It was Nelson's job to deny Bonaparte those six hours.

On the morning of September 29, 1805 Nelson walked out of
an inn in the coast town of Portsmouth with Hardy and three other
officers, and down the cobbled streets toward the wharf where his
barge waited to take him out to the anchored *Victory*. The entire
population of Portsmouth seemed to be assembled to cheer him.
He had become used to such crowds during his twenty-five days
in England. He smiled at them and waved, shaking some of their
hands as he strode through them.

But as he reached the wharf, an astounding thing happened. A few men in the crowd dropped to their knees and pulled off their hats. Within seconds, every man, woman and child was following their example—all were kneeling and baring their heads as though in prayer, their eyes turned to the slight one-eyed, one-armed, white-haired figure in the medal-bedecked uniform.

Nelson stopped in his tracks for a moment, staring at them. The crowd was silent now.

"God bless you, Nel," one of the kneeling women said softly.

"Lord love you," said a man, also softly.

"God bless you, Nel! . . . God protect you, Nel . . ."

Nelson had never held a command as heavy as this one. His step was slow as he moved through the kneeling people to his waiting barge. He balanced as the coxswain pushed off. The oars dipped into the water and pulled the boat away, toward the *Victory*. Nelson turned and looked back at the wharf. The crowd was still there, still kneeling, watching him go. He took off his hat to them.

Thirty-three French and Spanish warships, commanded by Admiral Villeneuve, were cutting through a heavily swelling Atlantic sea south past Cape Trafalgar on the early morning of October 21, 1805. Twenty-seven British warships could be seen far off to windward, sailing before a westerly wind in two lines toward them.

The chief officer aboard each of those British ships carried with him a copy of Nelson's plan of attack:

The business of an English Commander-in-Chief being first to bring an Enemy's Fleet to Battle, on the most advantageous terms to himself (I mean that of laying his ships close on board the enemy, as expeditiously as possible) and to continue them there, without separating, until the business is decided. . . .

. . . I being fully assured that the Admirals and the Captains of the Fleet I have the honour to command, will, knowing my precise object, that of a close and decisive battle, supply any deficiency in my not making signals. . . .

In short, Nelson wanted each of his ships to get in close, to fight, and keep fighting until the enemy surrendered. And he trusted the officers under him to do so without any moment-by-moment nudging from him.

Each officer carried a sharp memory of Nelson explaining his plan of attack in his cabin: The enemy being stronger by six ships, the British fleet would form two lines of battle—one led by Nelson's *Victory,* the other by Collingwood's *Royal Sovereign*—to slice through the enemy line at two points, separate it into three parts, and devour each of these parts with a superior concentration of ships. "That, gentlemen," he told them, "is the Nelson touch!" And: "Something must be left to chance. . . . But . . . no captain can do very wrong if he places his ship alongside that of an enemy."

At the first sign of dawn, Nelson rose from his prayers and stood alone for a moment in his dim cabin. His signal lieutenant found him standing that way, pensive, shrunken inside his undress-uniform coat, the one with the four bright stars of Knighthood sewn on its left breast. Nelson told Lieutenant Pasco that when Blackwood, captain of the frigates detailed to watch the enemy's movements, came aboard, he would receive him and Hardy in his cabin.

Alone again, he sat at his desk and began writing by the light of a candle:

. . . I leave Emma Lady Hamilton a Legacy to my King and Country, that they will give her an ample provision to maintain her rank in life. I also leave to the beneficence of my Country my adopted daughter, Horatia Nelson Thompson; and I desire she will use in future the name of Nelson only.

These are the only favours I ask of my King and Country at this moment when I am going to fight their Battle. May God Bless my King and Country, and all those who I hold dear. . . .

He finished as Blackwood and Hardy presented themselves, greeted them pleasantly and held out his pen. "Gentlemen, I have written a last Codicil to my will. Would you do me the honor to witness it."

Solemnly, the two captains signed the document. Then they followed him up onto the poop deck, where the marines were drawn up stiffly at attention in their scarlet coats.

The cold air seemed to brace him. He smiled strongly and took in the positions of the ships dotting the circle of sea. Ten miles ahead, the combined fleets of the enemy were going through a complicated maneuver in a clumsy manner that twisted their long line into a knot.

"They seem to be wearing in succession," Blackwood informed Nelson.

Nelson nodded. The enemy would soon be pointing north, instead of south. If the day went badly for them, Villeneuve undoubtedly hoped to escape back to Cadiz. But Nelson was determined that none should escape. He turned abruptly to Lieutenant Pasco, ordered him to make signal for his fleet to form the order of sailing in two columns, bear up, and steer east. Then, glancing at Blackwood, he gestured toward the enemy fleet. "Captain Blackwood, what would you consider a victory?"

Blackwood hesitated. "I think if fourteen ships are captured, it would be a glorious result."

"Fourteen? No!" Nelson turned eagerly toward the enemy. "Twenty," he said emphatically. "We must take twenty of them at the very least. I mean to annihilate them."

He stared ahead for a long time, lost in his planning. Then he glanced behind the stern of the *Victory* at the sinuous line of his ships trailing its wake. To the leeward, another column was forming up in a line behind Collingwood's *Royal Sovereign*.

"Twenty," he insisted again.

But then the wind began to fail. Soon there was hardly enough breeze to stir the full sails all ships carried. At that snail's pace, Nelson's tactics could prove fatal. For as his ships moved head-on into the side of the enemy line, the hostile fleet could rake his bows with all their broadsides. Propelled by a good wind, the British ships would be into them before many such broadsides could do any great damage. But creeping before that listless breeze, there might be a full hour during which the enemy could continuously rake the bows of the approaching English. If the enemy gunnery was good, they would blow Nelson's lead ships to splinters.

Still, his only other choice was to let Villeneuve escape back to Cadiz, without a fight. And this he was not willing to do. He put his faith in the enemy's inept gunnery, and let his orders stand.

By ten o'clock, the heaviness of the air began to oppress Nelson. He glanced at the clear sky, then at Hardy. "There'll be a storm before this day is done," he commented. Then he called for his signal lieutenant, ordered him to make signals for all ships to anchor after action.

As Pasco hurried away, Nelson looked back toward the enemy,

now a straggling line pointed north. The British were drifting nearer to them—but so very slowly. . . .

He left the poop and took a walk through his ship, nodding at the seamen who grinned widely at the sight of him. He warned the gun crews in the bowels of the ship to save their fire until they had a close target. He had each of the *Victory's* guns double-shotted, and he didn't intend to waste a single load. He reached the spot where his cabin had been. Now the bulkheads had been removed for battle, and what had been his cabin was part of a great open gun deck. Seamen were carrying off his furniture. Two of them held the portrait of Emma Hamilton.

"Take care of my guardian angel," he told them, smiling tightly.

The chaplain, Reverend Scott, was on the poop deck when he got there. He hurried up to Nelson anxiously. "Sir! Your stars will make you too much of a target!"

There would be Tyrolean marksmen in the French masts, and Scott was afraid they might recognize Nelson with his decorations. But Nelson laughed and shook his head. It was no time to be shifting coats.

He paced to the rail and watched Collingwood's lead ship forge ahead with the other column. The *Royal Sovereign's* bottom was newly coppered, and she slipped easily through the seas. The *Victory,* slowed down by two years of continuous sea duty, would be beaten into the fight. As Collingwood's ships drew near the enemy up ahead, dark clouds appeared along the sides of the two enemy ships nearest Collingwood. A hundred fountains of water shot up into the air around the *Royal Sovereign.* Then the low thunder of the cannons reached Nelson. "That Collingwood is sailing into them like an angel!" he muttered.

Blackwood appeared beside him, nervously glancing at Hardy and Scott as though for support. With that wind, the enemy was sure to make mincemeat of the lead ships, he pointed out. Nelson nodded matter-of-factly: He would be patient and repay the enemy in kind when he reached them.

Blackwood asked if it might not be better for Nelson to shift his command to one of the center ships back in his column. Nelson looked away without replying. The enemy, firing regularly at the *Royal Sovereign* now, was breaking out its flags. He picked up his spyglass.

Blackwood persisted: The *Victory* would be terribly exposed.

Might some of the other ships in the column forge ahead? Nelson put the spyglass to his eye and began focusing it. Absently he answered: "Let them go faster if they are able."

One of the enemy ships swam into sharp view through his glass. He raised his glass to its flags. He shifted from ship to ship until he found the one he was seeking: a three-decker that flew the pennant of the admiral of the hostile fleet. For two years Villeneuve had evaded and outwitted him. Now Nelson meant to finish him.

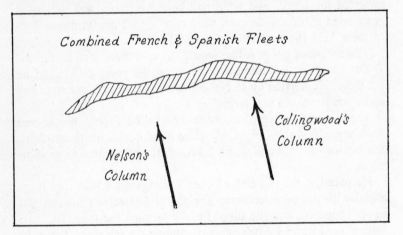

BATTLE OF TRAFALGAR

Nelson suddenly became aware that the bow of another ship was coming up alongside his quarter. Startled, he looked aside and saw that one of his three-deckers, the *Temeraire,* was about to pass the *Victory.* He shot a glance around at his rigging, saw that the *Victory's* lee lower studding sail was down. Enraged, he charged onto the forecastle and shouted at the lieutenant to get the sail back up, quickly. Then he strode back to the stern, snatching up a speaking trumpet as he went.

"Captain Harvey!" he shrilled toward the *Temeraire.* "I'll thank you to keep in your proper station, which is astern of the *Victory!*"

A few minutes later, the *Temeraire* began to drop back. Satisfied, Nelson went back up onto the poop deck, where his officers held their faces carefully expressionless. None could remember Nelson ever having given way to a fit of nerves during a battle before.

Nelson's column was about a mile and a quarter from the enemy line, crawling toward it with maddening slowness. At that moment, a puff of smoke appeared from the hull of Villeneuve's flagship. A few moments later, a single iron ball whistled through the sky and plummeted into the sea ahead of the *Victory*.

"Hands to quarters, Captain Hardy." The shot seemed to have suddenly restored Nelson's good humor. He smiled eagerly at his officers and the stiffness vanished from their features.

The thundering of the enemy cannons increased to leeward. Looking in that direction, Nelson saw the *Royal Sovereign* two miles to the south, receiving the blows of the section of enemy ships which Collingwood was about to enter. Nelson moved his shoulders back and forth to loosen his bunched nerves.

"Lieutenant Pasco!"

"Yes, sir!"

"I will now amuse the fleet with a signal."

The officers aboard twenty-seven British ships watched the signal flags go up on the *Victory*. The signal was read, and then relayed to those for whom it was intended: up the masts to the men in the rigging, down through the holds to the gun crews and powder boys—"England expects that every man will do his duty."

A few minutes later, a little after noon, the *Royal Sovereign* —its deck smashed and two hundred of its crew dead after a steady half-hour's pounding by enemy guns—drove through the enemy line. It let go a raking broadside from its starboard that smashed the bow of one enemy, and a port broadside that demolished the stern of another. Collingwood, having succeeded in being the first to break the enemy line, turned to his flag captain and exulted through the ear-shattering roar of cannons: "Rotherham, what would Nelson give to be here!"

Villeneuve's flagship was now trying shot after shot at the on-coming *Victory*. The balls fell on either side of Nelson's flagship. As Nelson sent Blackwood back to his frigate, the younger man reached out impulsively and shook his single hand. "I trust, my Lord, that on my return to the *Victory* I shall find your Lordship well and in possession of your twenty prizes."

A shot from Villeneuve's flagship tore through the main-top-gallant sail overhead with a loud ripping sound. Nelson squeezed Blackwood's hand. "God bless you, Blackwood. I shall never speak to you again."

Nelson watched Blackwood go down the side into his boat. He waved to him and turned back to the business of the day. There was a roar from across the water ahead. The hulls of eight enemy ships nearest the *Victory* disappeared in billowing black smoke. Nelson saw the mass of spinning death fly at him, felt the shocks against the hull under him, heard the splintering of wood, rending of sails. Near him, someone began a scream that stopped abruptly in a gasp.

Nelson and Hardy looked at each other.

"Warm work, Hardy."

"Yes, sir."

From then on, for forty long, horrible minutes, the *Victory* crept forward into a steady barrage of cannon balls and chain shot. Nelson and Hardy paced the deck together through the rising wreckage and carnage. Not a gun was fired back by the *Victory*. Its rigging melted away under the iron hail. Its studding-sail booms broke off one by one. Its canvas came apart in flapping shreds. Its crew were cut down steadily: fifty men dead or wounded.

Hardy halted for a second to speak to Nelson's secretary. An iron ball, rushing low over the deck, whirled Hardy completely around and dropped him to his knees. He regained his feet quickly. Nelson's secretary lay dead on the deck, his torso twenty feet away from the rest of him. Hardy saw to throwing the remains overboard, out of the way, and another officer was rushed up on deck to take his place. But as he hurried over to Nelson, a cannon ball whistled past his head—so close that the concussion killed him instantly.

Nelson kept staring at Villeneuve's flagship. Nearer. Nearer. Less than a quarter of a mile away now. The *Victory's* mizzen topmast came crashing down onto the deck, crushing three men under it. Their dying screams made Nelson whirl in time to see the ship's wheel torn from the quartermaster's grasp and hurled out into the foaming water. Hardy rushed men below to steer the ship by the tiller in the gun room.

Nelson looked past the bow. The *Victory* was nearing three enemy ships packed together almost bow-to-stern. The mouths of a hundred cannons spewed death at the oncoming English flagship. The center ship of the three was Villeneuve's.

Hardy informed Nelson that the three ships were too close together for the *Victory* to get through at that point and round-to alongside Villeneuve's flagship. The best he could do was to take the *Victory* past close under Villeneuve's stern. Nelson shrugged. It could not be helped. Hardy could take the ship alongside whichever ship he pleased. But first, he wanted the *Victory* to pass close to Villeneuve.

Hardy stalked away to tend to the sailing. Nelson stood where he was, watching. The bow of the *Victory* crossed Villeneuve's wake. Seconds later the *Victory* was slipping past the French admiral's stern, so close that the yardarms of the two ships brushed. Nelson's voice shrilled across the deck of the *Victory*: "Fire as your guns bear!"

The *Victory* shuddered. Roar after roar filled Nelson's ears as, one by one, each of fifty carefully aimed port guns let go its double load of destruction at point-blank range. In that one, long-held-back raking broadside, one hundred cannon balls demolished the structure of Villeneuve's flagship, knocked twenty of its cannons across its wrenched-apart decks, and killed four hundred of its men. What had once been Bonaparte's flagship was now floating wreckage.

"I can do no more," Nelson murmured. "The rest is in the hands of the Almighty."

The impetus of the *Victory* carried it two ships astern of Villeneuve's destroyed flagship, until it crashed into a French seventy-four with a force that shook both ships and threw Nelson against the hatch ladder. Quickly back on his feet, he saw that the *Victory's* yardarm was caught in the enemy's rigging. Locked together, the two ships drifted before the wind, wallowing drunkenly. The *Victory's* deck quaked steadily under Nelson's pacing feet. Its starboard guns rammed broadsides into the French ship's side while its port guns fired at a huge Spanish three-decker, drilling huge holes in its waterline.

Riflemen in the French tops, hanging fifty feet over Nelson's quarter-deck, began to fire down through the *Victory's* rigging, and the British marines on deck replied. But the two locked ships lurched so badly that neither French nor British could hope to aim with any degree of accuracy. Chance alone directed the destinations of the hundreds of musket balls tearing upward into the French masts and pattering down onto the *Victory's* decks.

Hardy joined Nelson, began pacing by his side. For with the ships caught together, there was no more directing to be done. It was up to the gun crews from now on.

Nelson anxiously watched ship after ship from his column crash through the enemy line around him. Each found an opponent and engaged it yardarm to yardarm. A mile to the south, half of Collingwood's column was already wreaking havoc among the French and Spanish ships. The enemy line, ragged to start with, no longer existed. The fleets were milling around in separated bunches, crashing broadsides into each other. It was becoming exactly the sort of pell-mell fight Nelson desired. The confusion would destroy any preconceived tactics. It put each ship's captain on his own, with his own separate battle to direct. In this situation the enemy officers were likely to panic and make fatal errors. The British officers had years of experience to steady them.

What Nelson's strategy had done—as it had at the Nile and Copenhagen—was to bring down the odds against his officers, to give them a better-than-even fight. His fleet no longer had to fight a superior number of ships. By breaking the enemy line apart in two places, Nelson had given his ships separated clusters of the enemy to concentrate on.

Nelson, pacing beside the ponderous Hardy, was completely satisfied. He would win. He was certain of it. Now it was the proportions of the victory that possessed his thoughts and directed his anxious glances across the smoke-hung sea to each group of dueling ships. He was unaware of the metal pellets hailing down on the deck around his pacing feet.

Nelson was halfway between the demolished wheel and the hatchway to his cabin when a terrible shock ripped through him. It started at his left shoulder, burned through his lung, and ended abruptly when it reached into his back. He knew instantly. For after that first shock, there was no pain.

Hardy took a few more steps before he suddenly realized that he was alone. He whirled, saw Nelson fall forward onto his knees on the gouged-up deck. Nelson's hand reached out to stop his fall. His fingertips touched the wood of the deck for a second before his arm crumpled under him. He fell on his face, helpless. Before Hardy could reach him, a roll of the ship flopped Nelson over on his back. He stared up at the jungle of torn rigging and sails between himself and the sky.

A marine and two seamen reached the fallen admiral an instant before Hardy. They dropped to their knees and started to lift him up. Their faces were torn with shock. Hardy trembled as he leaned over Nelson. Nelson looked up at him and smiled gently. "Hardy,

I believe they have done it at last." Despite his smile, Nelson's face was ghastly.

"I hope not, sir." Hardy choked on the stiffly formal words.

"Yes," Nelson told him softly. "My backbone's shot through."

Hardy watched the men carry Nelson below. He shook himself and turned away. For the moment, he was in command of Nelson's fleet. He went through the motions in a daze.

Nelson felt no pain as arms lifted and carried him. He saw everything quite clearly, sharply. A seaman stopped suddenly and stared openmouthed. With tremendous concentration, Nelson managed to get out his handkerchief, raise it, and hide his face with it. The battle was in a crucial stage. His men must not be panicked by news that he had fallen. He closed his eyes under the handkerchief and listened to his life draining away somewhere inside him. An artery was severed; he was weaker each second.

Below, in the surgeon's cockpit, Nelson was placed on a cot. Pain had returned, wrenching his spine. He was beginning to have difficulty breathing. When the handkerchief was removed from his face, it took him a moment to recognize the harried face of Beatty, the chief surgeon. His sight was dimming. "You can do nothing for me, Beatty," he gasped. "I've only a short time to live."

Beatty's hands removed Nelson's clothing with swift skill. He studied Nelson's wound. "Tell me what you feel, sir."

"There's a gush of blood every minute within my breast, Beatty." Nelson drew a shuddering breath. "I felt it break my back."

Beatty's face was a mask as he pulled a sheet over Nelson's thin body. "Rest easy, sir," he told him softly. "I'll put you through no more pain."

"I understand, Beatty." Nelson turned his head to one side. He saw Reverend Scott kneeling beside him, sobbing hysterically, his forehead pressed hard against the side of the cot. Nelson touched the chaplain with his forefinger. Scott's head jerked up. Tears streamed down his cheeks. Nelson forced a small smile.

"Pray for me, Doctor," he said wistfully. "I have not been a *great* sinner."

"Sir! You must not . . . Your dear country and friends . . ."

"Ah! It is all over. . . . I can't breathe. Lift me up. . . ."

Scott and the purser raised Nelson's head and torso a bit.

"Better! Thank you . . . Doctor!"

"Yes, sir?" Scott sobbed.

"I have to leave Lady Hamilton, and my adopted daughter Horatia, as a legacy to my country."

He moaned as a thundering noise twisted his brain. Moaned again. "What is that? What . . ."

"The *Victory's* cannons, sir."

"Oh yes. . . . Broadsides . . ." He moaned again. "Oh, *Victory! Victory!* How you distract my poor brain!"

He could hardly see now.

"Beatty?"

"I am here, my Lord."

"You know I am gone."

"My Lord, unhappily for our country, nothing further can be done for you."

"I know. God be praised I have done my duty. . . . Hardy! Hardy!"

"He is above, sir."

"I must know how the battle goes. . . . Ah! My head!"

"Is the pain still very great, sir?"

"So very severe I wish I was dead. . . . Yet, one would like to live a little longer, too. . . . How dear is life to all men. . . . Will no one send me Hardy? Is he killed?"

"No, my lord. The business of the battle . . ."

"What will become of my poor Emma. . . . I am hot . . . thirsty."

"Sir!"

A hazy red figure that loomed larger than the others appeared.

"Who is that? Oh! Hardy."

Nelson held out his hand. Hardy, his big features twisted with grief, shook it.

"Well, Hardy," his voice whispered raggedly, "how goes the battle? How goes the day with us?"

"Very well, my Lord. We have got twelve or fourteen of the enemy's ships in our possession. But five of their van have tacked and show an intention of bearing down on the *Victory*. I've called three of our fresh ships round us. Have no doubt we will give them a drubbing, sir."

"I hope none of *our* ships have struck, Hardy?"

"No, my Lord. There is no fear of that."

"I am a dead man, Hardy. It will be all over with me soon. Come nearer, Hardy."

Hardy lowered his head.

"Pray let Lady Hamilton have my hair, Hardy, and all other things belonging to me."

"You may come through it yet, sir."

"Oh, no. It is impossible. Beatty will tell you."

Nelson seemed to sleep awhile. When he opened his eyes his vision was almost gone.

"Hardy?"

"He is gone back up on deck, sir."

"Is that you, Dr. Scott?"

"Yes, my Lord."

A short time later, Nelson's hand was seized in two huge palms.

"Hardy?"

"Yes, my Lord. It is a brilliant victory, sir!"

"How many ships?"

"Eighteen have struck to us, sir!"

"I bargained for twenty. . . . The storm. . . . Anchor, Hardy! Anchor!"

"Shall we make the signal, sir?"

"Yes. For if I live, I'll anchor. . . . Don't throw me overboard, Hardy."

"Oh, no! Certainly not."

"Then you know what to do. And take care of my dear Lady Hamilton. . . . Take care of poor Emma. . . . Kiss me, Hardy. . . ."

Hardy, his eyes swimming, hesitated. Awkwardly, he bent over and kissed Nelson's scarred forehead.

A whisper: "Who is that?"

"Hardy, my Lord."

"God bless you, Hardy! . . . Remember I leave Lady Hamilton and my daughter. . . . Thank God I have done. . . ."

The report of the battle sped home. England learned that its fleet had smashed the French and Spanish fleets beyond recovery, that Bonaparte's chances of invasion were demolished. England received the news of its victory and went into mourning. Nelson was dead.

PART SIX

A Few Fir-built Things

As a result of Nelson's victories, England became the undisputed lord of all the oceans of the world. By 1812, England could look back on about two hundred ocean victories, in actions great and small. Against these could be counted only a few actions in which lone ships had been defeated by superior forces; for, in the great majority of cases, English ships prevailed even over enemies with superior numbers of guns, men and ships.

No other European nation any longer was in a position to challenge the English sea might. The young United States of America showed less discretion. The moment it gained its independence from England, the United States had launched itself on the seas: shipbuilding, trading around the world, fishing, whaling, slaving. By 1812, the new nation possessed one of the world's most active commercial fleets, and was well on its way to becoming rich in consequence.

The restrictions that England, which considered the sea its own property, placed upon the trade of other nations did not sit well with America's commercial families. And when England's navy began to impress large numbers of seamen from American ships into its service, the flame of American anger was fanned to a hearty blaze.

Thus, with the cry for "Free trade and sailors' rights!" began the War of 1812 between England and the United States. On land

291

the Americans, who had neglected to build an army of any sort, were usually beaten—until the very close of the war. But on the water the situation took a surprising turn: The Americans proved to be superb seamen and canny fighters.

The government of the United States had little faith in the effectiveness of its fledgling navy—and with some reason. In 1812, England had over 680 warships under sail. Besides smaller craft, she had 124 two- and three-decked ships-of-the-line, and 116 frigates. Against this, the United States could oppose just seven frigates and nine little war sloops, schooners and brigs. She had no ships-of-the-line. There seemed little sense in pitting a 16-ship navy against one of 680 ships.

But what actually happened confounded the numerical odds: The American navy was too small to bring out a full fleet in a group for the British to destroy in a single fleet battle. Instead, the English navy had to deal with the U. S. warships one at a time. The results of these single-ship actions—and two odd small fleet battles on American lakes—astounded the world.

The best three ships in the American navy were frigates of a large new type conceived by Yankee shipbuilders. Though no match for two-deckers or three-deckers, they were bigger and carried more guns than any other frigates afloat, including those of the English. British officers, who had inspected these new types of frigates just before the war broke out, declared them to be clumsy, and generally worthless in any fight against smaller standard British frigates. The British Secretary of State for Foreign Affairs contemptuously called them "a few fir-built things with bits of striped bunting at their mast-heads." And the London Statesman declared: "America certainly cannot pretend to wage war with us; she has not the navy to do it with."

For, ships aside, what could Americans, virtually untried in sea warfare, do against officers and crewmen and gunners who had learned their jobs fighting under Nelson? As English Captain Carden explained to U. S. Commodore Decatur after carefully examining one of the big new American frigates: "Though your ships may be good enough, and you are a clever set of fellows, what practice have you had in war? There's the rub."

The President of the United States agreed so completely with all these English opinions that he almost decided that the best service the U. S. frigates could give would be if they were deliberately sunk at harbor entrances to prevent British ships from getting in. Almost, but not quite. The frigates were allowed to remain afloat—and as a result, the world was shocked to see the doughty English navy suffer a series of humiliating defeats at their hands.

19

A Half-Hour's Hard Work

THE UNBEATABLE "CONSTITUTION"

Isaac Hull, the plump, florid, thirty-nine-year-old captain of the *Constitution*, lowered his spyglass and glanced anxiously upward. Every sail was set, but the canvas flapped sporadically before the on-and-off breeze. His ship rolled under him sluggishly on the sea swell, making hardly any headway at all. The frigate *Constitution*, making its way along the New Jersey coast beyond sight of land on its way to New York, was trapped.

Those six warships just beyond range off her stern in the first dim light of the day were English: one ship-of-the-line, four frigates, a brig and a schooner. And they were giving chase under all sail.

Hull didn't waste many seconds looking at them. Tucking away his spyglass, he once more began to jog to all parts of the *Constitution*—repeatedly altering the trim of the sails to catch the light, teasing puffs of wind, reassuring himself that the men kept the sails soaked with water to shrink the texture of the canvas, so that less of the precious breeze would slip through.

The pursuing frigates, being slightly smaller, were, the British felt, faster. And they were handled by captains who knew every trick of navigation, in any kind of wind. But Isaac Hull had so far managed to keep them from gaining on him. A man who had devoted himself to learning his profession from the time he ran away to sea at fourteen, Hull was one of the best seamen in America.

He knew this ship of his almost as well as he knew his own body. After eleven years in the merchant service, he had come aboard the *Constitution* as fourth lieutenant and risen by degrees to the position of captain.

Suddenly, as the sun rose over the watery horizon, Hull felt the fitful breaths of wind die out entirely. He waited, tensely. Above him, the sails hung limp, without a flutter. The *Constitution* was becalmed. Quickly, Hull looked aft. The British squadron back there still had some kind of breeze, was creeping up on him with three frigates leading, the big ship-of-the-line bringing up the rear.

Puffs of smoke abruptly blossomed from the three lead frigates. With the muffled booms of the cannons came the shots. Hull watched them arc high and wide, some sending up geysers of water far to port and starboard, others passing over the masts and plunging into the sea beyond. The three lead English frigates were still too far away for any kind of accurate shooting. But they'd be close enough soon, if the *Constitution* just sat here motionless and waited for them.

Hull shouted orders for the *Constitution's* boats to be hoisted out. When each was secured to a line from the ship, the oarsmen rowed their boats out ahead of the *Constitution's* bows and began the back-breaking work of towing the dead weight of the becalmed ship through the water.

The time it took those straining, sweating oarsmen to drag the *Constitution* just a few feet was heartbreakingly long. But the English ships a few miles astern, Hull saw with relief, had also reached the point where they hadn't enough wind to make headway. They were putting out their boats to tow after him. Now, with the English squadron and his own ship entirely dependent on the toil of the oarsmen, the distance between them would again remain even. But Hull took little joy from that. Unless he got farther away from his pursuers, there was always a chance that a strong puff of wind would hit them—and not him—just long enough to bring them up within accurate gunnery range.

To lighten the ship, Hull had the *Constitution's* drinking water

—thousands of gallons of it—pumped overboard into the ocean. It reduced the total weight of his big frigate infinitesimally—but enough so that the *Constitution* began to increase the distance between itself and its pursuers by slow inches.

By eight in the morning, the slight gain became apparent to the English squadron's commander. Hull felt a lurch of despair as he saw the English ships change their tactics: All the boats of the squadron rowed out to the bows of a single English frigate and joined in towing it. The towed frigate, furling all its sails to decrease wind resistance, left the rest of its squadron behind and rapidly began to overtake the *Constitution*.

Hull considered furling his own sails, but realized it would not in the long run help. His few boats could not possibly tow the *Constitution* as fast as all those English boats were able to pull the gaining English frigate. Hull's only hope was a sudden wind. He let every inch of canvas remain set.

Hull was more than willing to fight another frigate. The *Constitution* carried rows of 24-pounders on its gun deck; the standard English frigates weren't built to carry more than 18-pounders. English officers with whom he had talked before the war didn't think that would affect the outcome much. Hull did. But this wasn't a matter of fighting just another frigate. Once that English frigate caught up and engaged him, it would delay him long enough for the rest of the English squadron to come up and smother him into surrender.

The English frigate had cut a half mile off the distance between them and was almost within accurate gunnery range, when the wind came. A good, stiff blast of it. The *Constitution* shot ahead, grabbing up its boats on the run.

Hull, exultant, in a matter of minutes saw the pursuing frigate lose the half mile it had gained with an hour of hard rowing. For the English frigate's sails, being furled, could not catch the wind. By the time they were hastily let out and set, the wind had vanished —as abruptly as it had come. And the *Constitution* had more than regained its lead.

Again the towing chase began. And again, the English frigate, pulled by all the boats from its squadron, began to gain on the *Constitution* by steady inches.

Hull, glancing up at the few clouds scattered in the blue morning sky, saw not a trace of another breeze. He began to have a sinking feeling that before nightfall the *Constitution* would be a sunk wreck or the property of the British navy.

Charles Morris, his first lieutenant, came up beside him with a suggestion: They had sounded the bottom the evening before. It was twenty-six fathoms. Deep, but not too deep for kedging. Hull stared at Morris as though he were an angel sent him from heaven.

A light kedge anchor was brought up on deck. Every hawser and unused length of rope that could be found on the ship was knotted together to form the longest line possible. One end of the line was secured to the kedge anchor, which was now placed in one of the ship's boats. The boat was swiftly rowed out beyond the *Constitution* as far as the line would stretch—a full mile. There, the anchor was dropped into the sea, and the rowers watched it sink out of sight toward the bottom.

The other end of the line, on the *Constitution's* forecastle, was grasped by as many of Hull's men as could get a hold on it. Bracing their legs and backs, they began to struggle toward the ship's stern with the line. As room was made at the bows, other men kept seizing the line and walking it to the stern. When the first men reached the stern, they dropped the line and raced up to the forecastle to begin pulling it back again. There was soon a close-packed line of men, from one end of the ship to the other, hauling away on the line. The *Constitution* was thus pulled toward the anchor, which had taken hold of the ocean bottom, a mile ahead. The ship moved slowly at first, then faster as it gained momentum. By the time it reached the end of the line—the place where the anchor was dropped—it had covered the mile more than twice as fast as it could have been towed.

The anchor was hauled up, placed in a boat, rowed out ahead for the full mile-length of the line, and dropped again. And again the ship was kedged forward a mile to the anchor. And again.

Together with the steady kedging, Hull kept the boats towing. Rowers and kedgers were soon working in a daze of fatigue. But they went on working. No one slacked, no one grumbled. They didn't fancy spending the rest of the war as prisoners.

It went on all day, this fantastic snail's-pace chase. The *Constitution* couldn't get away from the English squadron, which in turn was unable to close the distance. All that night pursuer and pursued crept across the surface of the sea, only rarely and for short periods getting a breeze to sail on. By dawn of the next day, the winds of night had brought the ships of the English squadron together again. But they were no nearer the *Constitution*.

The chase continued. All day long. Hull knew the English must wear out his men eventually. Having more men to draw on, they could change their rowers more often than he could relieve his kedgers and towers. He whistled for a wind, had a set of skysails made and added to the *Constitution's* spread of limp, waiting canvas.

The calm broke toward the second evening. First there was a breath of moving air, then a breeze, then a light squall hit the area. The *Constitution* felt it first. Hull, realizing that the English a few miles back could judge the force of the storm only by what *he* did for the moment, began slowly to take in his sails. From the decks of the English ships, it would look as though the *Constitution* was furling its sails in the face of a fierce gale.

All the English ships, heeding the *Constitution's* example, hastened to furl their own sails, snugging them down tight in anticipation of weathering a bad storm. As soon as they did, Hull quickly set his sails to the wind again. The *Constitution* shot forward on the wings of the squall and was far ahead by the time the English captains realized they had been outfoxed, and began to set their own sails again.

Now Hull was able to show them what Yankee ship designing could accomplish. For the new American frigates, though bigger, wider-decked and heavier than standard frigates, had been given carefully sharpened underwater lines and balance by way of compensation. The English frigate captains, as soon as they set their own canvas and gave chase in a pure sailing race, found to their surprise that though they sailed as cleverly as they knew how, they dropped farther and farther astern of the flying *Constitution*— which by now was setting an incredible 12½-knot pace.

They followed Hull all night, and at dawn saw that he had added miles to the distance between them. They set every inch of sail they had and chased him all the third day. By nightfall, they had lost him over the horizon ahead.

The orders from Washington that had sent Isaac Hull sailing up the New Jersey coast for New York originally, had contained this message from the Navy Secretary: "You are not to understand me as impelling you to battle unless attacked." In addition, they had specified: "On your arrival in New York, you will report yourself to Commodore Rodgers. If he should not be in that port you will remain there till further orders."

But Hull had never arrived at New York. Instead, his race against the British squadron had carried him north, to Boston. There, of course, waited neither Commodore Rodgers nor any orders. Hull was aware that he should remain in port until new orders arrived. But he was burning to test his *Constitution* in a fight, and so he sailed out again without orders, in search of prey.

When the Navy got word that Hull had left Boston on his own initiative, it immediately removed him from command of the *Constitution*. It was a career-smashing reprimand. But Hull, far out at sea by then, sailed blissfully on in search of a fight, unaware that he was no longer the captain of the *Constitution*.

A little before two on the hot afternoon of August 19, the lookout spotted another frigate to the southeast, 750 miles off Boston. Having the wind, Hull immediately broke out the American flag and raced toward the stranger. He had spent a fruitless two hours the day before, chasing what turned out to be an American privateer. Thinking him a British warship, the privateer had even thrown all its guns overboard to get more speed. Hull didn't want a repetition of that.

Within two hours it could be seen that the frigate was flying English colors. It was apparently as anxious to fight as he was. Lying to leeward, it could not sail toward him; but it had been hauled upon the wind with its main topsail backed to await him. Its light sails were being taken in to clear for action. It was the frigate *Guerrière*. Hull couldn't have chanced upon a more perfect opponent for the first frigate engagement of the war.

He knew both the *Guerrière* and her captain, James Dacres. Dacres was as swaggering as Hull was modest, as tall as Hull was short, as lean as Hull was plump. And he happened to be Hull's friend. They had met many times before the war, and the extreme opposites had been attracted to each other. Now, Hull had cause to remember the time he had had Captain Dacres aboard the *Constitution* to compare it with his own *Guerrière*. Dacres had ridiculed the *Constitution's* extra length and width, her outlandishly heavy timbers above the waterline, her long spars, the guns that were too big for her class. As far as Dacres was concerned, the *Constitution* was a freak—and no match for his own battle-proven *Guerrière*.

Jokingly, Hull and Dacres had bet their hats on the outcome of a fight between the two ships.

Now the bet was no longer a joke. If the fight took on something of the aspect of a sporting contest because the two men knew and respected each other, this would not prevent either from killing his friend.

Hull remembered something else: It was Dacres who had sent in a challenge to Commodore Rodgers of the *President,* saying that he would "be very happy to meet him or any other American frigate of equal force . . . for the purpose of having a few minutes *tête-à-tête*."

Well, here was his chance.

Trying to contain his excitement, Hull ordered the *Constitution* cleared for action, her guns loaded with two shots apiece. There was a clamor of running feet, drums-and-bugles sounding the call to battle stations, yells, rumbling gun carriages, boatswains' whistles and creaking lines as four hundred and sixty men rushed to their duties. The guns were run out and sand spread across the decks to soak up the blood that would soon be running across it. The *Constitution* drove in toward the *Guerrière*.

They were barely within range of each other when the *Guerrière* slipped across the *Constitution's* path and hurled a broadside at its oncoming bows. The shots fell short and to either side. The *Constitution* bore on. The *Guerrière* wore, came around across Hull's path again, and thundered out its other broadside.

This time some of the shot pierced Hull's sails and ripped across his forecastle deck. First Lieutenant Morris ran up onto the quarter-deck to report. "The enemy fire has killed two of our men, sir. Shall we return it?"

Hull screwed down his excitement and shook his head. "Not yet, sir." To send in an answering broadside meant yawing away from his course and slowing the ship's progress. He wanted to be in close, very close, when he let Dacres have that first load of double-shotted 24-pounders. Ordering the gunners to hold their fire till he gave the word himself, he set the main-topgallant sail for more speed.

Up ahead, the enemy wore again, turned its side to Hull's bow, and began raking the *Constitution* steadily as the guns bore and reloaded. The shots smashed harder and harder against the *Constitution* as she came on. But the extra-heavy timbers at which the

English captains had sneered were proving themselves. The shots that hit the hull did damage, but they did not break through. "Old Ironsides" was what the men aboard her nicknamed the *Constitution*.

But the shot that came whistling over the bulwarks downed men, slashed away rigging, ruined the spanker and mizzen-topsails. Twice more Lieutenant Morris anxiously asked his captain if he was ready to fire back. And each time Hull replied: "Not yet, sir."

They were very close now. Hull gripped the quarter-deck rail tightly, watched the *Guerrière* start to wear for another rake, slowing so much in doing so that the speeding *Constitution,* with a final lunge, drew close alongside its enemy. The excitement bottled up in Hull burst forth. Leaning over the rail so suddenly and energetically that the seat of his breeches split all the way down the seam, he screamed at his gunners: "Now, boys! Pour it into them!"

The *Constitution* lifted and quaked as its first broadside of heavy iron balls and lethal grapeshot swept across the enemy's main deck. The *Guerrière* reeled with the shock, its masts shaking, its sails and rigging riddled, its main yard torn away, several of its guns overturned with their carriages.

Both ships staggered on, side by side, their guns roaring at each other individually, as fast as they could be reloaded and run out again after they recoiled against their breechings. The English 18-pounders, as the English officers had predicted, being lighter, were handled faster—firing four shots to every three of the *Constitution*. But the heavy American 24-pounders hit harder, smashing English oak to splinters, driving all the way across Dacres' decks, tearing their way into the *Guerrière's* sides and through its vitals.

Both ships tried to wear and rake each other. Instead, they found themselves side by side again. But now almost every gun on the *Constitution* had been reloaded in the pause occasioned by the maneuvering. Another full broadside thundered high across the English ship's decks.

Hull watched the mass of iron demolish sails and rigging, saw the *Guerrière's* mizzenmast go crashing down. The English frigate sagged under the first impact of its fallen weight, then rolled. The mast slid across the deck and plunged over the starboard side, still attached to its ship by a vast tangle of snarled rigging, sails and spars.

Hull leaped for joy, caring not one bit at the moment that even in the heat of the fight men around him grinned when they glanced at his ventilated breeches. "We've made a brig of her!" he yelled down to his gunners. "Now, hull her, boys! Hull 'er!"

There was no need to smash at the *Guerrière's* sailing power any more. The weight of the mizzenmast dragging along her side made the ship almost impossible to maneuver. She wallowed and waited, while her men hacked desperately at the wreckage in an attempt to cast loose the dragging mizzenmast. Before they could succeed, Hull had his ship luffing short across Dacres' bows.

While Hull's forecastle and quarter-deck 32-pounder carronades belched showers of scattering grapeshot along the length of the *Guerrière's* upper decks, the crews of his gun-deck 24-pounders punched their shots low into the enemy frigate's hull. The *Constitution* swept past, wore around, then drove back across the *Guerrière's* mashed bows on the opposite tack for another rake, her guns firing as they bore. The English frigate began to take in water at an alarming rate through a number of big holes below her waterline. "The decks," said a man aboard her, "had the appearance of a butcher's slaughterhouse."

Hull started to wear for another rake as the waist of his ship passed the *Guerrière's* bows. But the English shots had torn away more of his rigging. The *Constitution,* failing to respond properly, suddenly lost headway. The *Guerrière,* lurching forward, snagged its big bowsprit over Hull's quarter-deck and into the mizzen rigging.

The simultaneous yells of Hull and Dacres reached each other through the masses of armed men rushing up from both sides to the point of contact: "Boarders!"

A hail of musket fire from marksmen in the masts of the two ships met both parties of boarders. On one side of Hull, Marine Lieutenant Bush fell dead. On the other, First Lieutenant Morris crumpled, badly wounded.

Before either boarding attempt could succeed, the wind filled the *Constitution's* sails again and wrenched her loose, still firing her heavy guns into the enemy. Hull swung his ship away. Before he could bring her back in again, the fight was all over.

The wrench as the ships parted had slacked the *Guerrière's* forestay, which had been about the only thing left holding the foremast up. As the foremast toppled, it fell on the mainstay, and the mainmast, splintered by 24-pounders, came thundering down.

The dismasted frigate wallowed so badly in the heavy swells that its guns dipped into the sea with each roll. Several gun carriages had been broken loose from their securing tackle and were smashing their way back and forth across the deck with each dip and tilt. Captain Dacres had a musket-ball wound in his shoulder, and seventy-eight of his men were down, dead or wounded. The sides of his ship were riddled with holes.

In a daze, Dacres had the flag nailed to the stump of the main-mast. But when he saw the *Constitution* coming back to rake his bows again, he took the flag down and fired a signal shot to leeward to acknowledge surrender. It was the only thing he could do. The *Guerrière* was so close to sinking that her men were hastily shifted to the *Constitution*—and Hull, finding that she couldn't be saved, set her afire and left her.

Hull, watching Captain Dacres struggling up the side of the *Constitution* from his boat—a little more than half an hour after the fight had begun—saw his bloody shoulder and rushed over to help him aboard. "Give me your hand," he said softly. "I know you are hurt."

On the deck, they stared at each other, remembering a great deal. Dacres drew his sword from its scabbard and held it out to Hull in silent surrender.

Hull shook his head. "No, I won't take a sword from one who knows so well how to use it, Captain." But he couldn't refrain from glancing up at the taller man's head and adding: "But I *will* trouble you for that hat."

The completeness and speed of the American victory sent U. S. spirits soaring dizzily, and shocked the British navy. Henry Adams later summed up the reaction with: "A small affair it might appear among the world's battles. It took but half an hour, but in that one-half hour the United States of America rose to the rank of a first-class power."

England just couldn't believe it. Of course, the American frigate was slightly bigger and threw a heavier broadside, but *no* English ship of frigate size had ever struck to an American before. Instead of seeing what had really happened—that Dacres had been out-sailed and outfought—the English looked everywhere else for something to blame, and missed what could have been an instruc-tive lesson. They blamed the ship: The *Guerrière* was after all not English made; it had been captured from France, and was probably a defective vessel to begin with. When Dacres was tried by a court-martial after having been returned to England in a prisoner exchange, the court agreed that he had been forced to surrender after the collapse of his masts—which, the court decided, "was occasioned more by their defective state than the fire of the enemy." The masts had been poorly set in by the French, that was the answer to this unexpected defeat. It was a freak accident, and wouldn't happen again.

Even Dacres failed to understand what had happened. "It is my earnest wish," he said, "to be once more opposed to the *Constitution,* with the same officers and crew under my command, in a frigate of similar force to the *Guerrière.*" That, at the moment, was also the wish of every frigate captain in the English navy.

The *Constitution* became target number one for every British seagoing officer. It was to Captain Henry Lambert and his frigate, the *Java,* that fate awarded the great honor—and bad luck—of trying to purify the honor of his navy by taking on the *Constitution.*

It happened just four months after the destruction of the *Guerrière.* Isaac Hull was no longer captain of "Old Ironsides." The slap-in-the-face order removing him from command of the ship had been turned quickly into promotion when word reached Washington of his victory. He was appointed to an important naval post ashore.

The new captain of the *Constitution* was William Bainbridge, a cultured, serious, charming man with the strength of any three sailors in his crew—as he had proved in a number of brawls while in the merchant service. He was a splendid seaman, but he had a record of bad luck. In the short sea war with France in 1798, while commanding the 14-gun schooner *Retaliation,* he had mistaken two French frigates for ships of a friendly nation and had been captured and made prisoner. As captain of the frigate *Philadelphia* during the 1803 campaign against the Barbary pirates, he was engaged in blockading Tripoli when he ran his ship aground; Tripolitan gunboats captured his helpless frigate and made him a prisoner.

So, in two wars it had been William Bainbridge's ill luck to strike the flags of both ships he commanded and be taken captive. It was with this dismal record that Bainbridge—who had the look of a man much older than his thirty-seven years—sailed out in command of the *Constitution* in his third war.

His opponent, Henry Lambert, captain of the English frigate,

Java, was a lucky man with a happy record. The fact that the *Constitution* carried 52 guns to the *Java's* 49 (and hurled a total weight of 654 pounds of shot to his 574) meant even less to Lambert than it had to Dacres. For Lambert had a great victory to his credit: In 1804 he had taken on a Frenchman whose ship threw a total of 240 pounds of shot to Lambert's meager 99 pounds and had beaten the big French ship into fleeing for its life.

The two captains met on December 29, 1812, off the Atlantic coast of South America. For three and a half hours they fought. The *Java* proved to be a far quicker sailer than the *Constitution.* But Bainbridge proved himself a far better seaman than Lambert. A dozen times, each captain tried for the weather gauge, got it, and lost it. Darting in and out and around each other, the *Java* raked the *Constitution's* bows, only to have its stern raked in turn minutes later. And it went on that way—the two ships weaving intricate, tight designs across the ocean—through the whole battle, with their guns thundering at each other most of the time across distances short enough for effective pistol shooting.

Lambert was so confident in his gunners, many of whom had served under Nelson, that he had given them only one day of practice since leaving England. Bainbridge, on the other hand, had been practicing his gunners daily since coming aboard the *Constitution.* Drilled to a keen edge of performance, these American gunners soon showed themselves more than a match for the more experienced, but rusty, English gun crews.

Hour after hour the two frigates circled each other, firing all the while. They fought so close that Bainbridge got an English musket ball in his hip early in the fight. But he continued to stand and command in the smoke and roar of the slugging-and-sailing match.

An 18-pound ball smashed the *Constitution's* wheel, sending a shower of splinters over Bainbridge and punching a torn copper bolt into his thigh. Afire with pain, Bainbridge refused to leave his quarter-deck. Clinging to the taffrail to hold himself upright, the big captain shouted orders for his men to steer the ship with the tiller lines below deck, kept his cannons battering at the *Java's* masts and hull.

Slowly, as the *Java's* sails and rigging gave way bit by bit, as its sides began to cave in, Captain Lambert realized that he was fighting a ship that sailed as well as his own, and gunnery that was heavier and more accurate. But there was one more weight he could throw into this fight: boarders. Gathering his marines on the fore-castle, Lambert drove the *Java's* bow against the *Constitution's* quarter and grappled. The British marines surged forward, only to be driven back by the fire of the American riflemen. Captain Lambert dropped with a musket ball through his middle. Before the English could mount another boarding attempt, the big guns of the *Constitution* roared, knocking the *Java* loose from it and smash-ing over its foremast.

With the foremast gone, First Lieutenant Chads, who now had charge of the *Java,* found that his ship could no longer be easily maneuvered. Bainbridge, enduring agony from the wounds in his hip and thigh, was quick to see his advantage. He swung the *Constitution*—now the faster ship by far—across the *Java's* bows for a rake, then came back and raked again, and again.

The *Java's* mizzenmast went over. And then the upper half of her mainmast. With all her sails now part of the wreckage smother-ing her decks, the *Java* rolled helplessly in the ocean, unable to sail at all, her hull filling with water, most of her guns silenced by the smashing blows of American shot. Lieutenant Chads gave up the fight.

Bainbridge collapsed as soon as he saw the *Java* strike to him, and was carried below to his cabin half-fainting from loss of blood and pain. Under the ministrations of the ship's surgeon, he recovered enough to hear the results of his fight: The *Constitution* had nine men killed, twenty-five wounded. The *Java* had sixty dead, 170 wounded—and there was not enough left of her to do anything with except set afire. Bainbridge's luck had changed at last.

Captain Lambert, dying from his wound, had to be carried aboard the *Constitution.* Stretched out on a cot on the quarter-deck, he gave his sword to an American lieutenant in token of his surrender. The sword was brought down to the cabin where Bainbridge lay. Unable to rise, Bainbridge took the sword and ordered some of his men to carry him, cot and all, up onto the quarter-deck. There, beside the dying Lambert, Bainbridge reached over and gave the English captain back his sword.

Another single-ship frigate duel had been fought—and won by the Americans—between these two fights of the *Constitution.* Now, when England heard the news of the loss of the *Java,* it was aghast. Its naval publication, the *Pilot,* cried out: "The public will learn, with sentiments which we shall not presume to anticipate, that a third British frigate has struck to an American. . . . Yet down to this moment not a single American frigate has struck her flag." "Good God!" howled the London *Times,* "that a few short months should have so altered the tone of British sentiments! Is it true, or is it not, that our navy was accustomed to hold the Americans in utter contempt? . . . an American frigate was an object of ridicule to our honest tars. Now the prejudice is actually setting the other way."

Having learned at last to fear American frigates in single-ship encounters, the English countered with a big blockading fleet that bottled up these frigates in their ports. So effective was this blockade that the *Constitution* did not manage to get out to sea again for two years. It sailed into its final sea fight in this war on February 20, 1815—under a new captain named Charles Stewart, a thin, redheaded Irishman from Philadelphia.

The *Constitution* this time ran into a pair of British vessels sent out to tackle lone frigates. They were the *Cyane,* a 32-gun frigate, and the *Levant,* a 20-gun war sloop. Their officers' idea was that these two ships could dance all around the heavy *Constitution,* rake it fore and aft at will, and cut down its sails, while easily dodging its return fire.

But due to Stewart's seamanship, the *Constitution* outmaneuvered the faster *Cyane* just long enough to smash it into surrender, then devoted itself to catching and capturing the smaller *Levant.*

These three sea fights of the *Constitution,* all victories at the expense of the proud British navy, lowered the prestige of the English lion as drastically as a full fleet defeat would have. England finally had to admit that the American frigates were superior to theirs. They pointed to the American frigates' 24-pounders, extra size and heavier superstructure, however, and declared that they were actually line-of-battle ships in disguise.

The Americans lost only one of the single-ship frigate actions fought in the War of 1812. Of the eight main fights that occurred between United States and English war sloops equally matched, the Americans won seven, lost only one. American privateers—many of their officers trained in the United States navy—slipped easily through the British blockade, raided enemy shipping, out-fought English warships their own size, outran anything too strong for them.

The depredations of the navy and privateer raiders sent British insurance rates soaring to the skies. Halfway through the war, a group of the most powerful businessmen in Glasgow demanded an end to the war, pointing out that American raiders "have proved ruinous to our commerce, humbling to our pride and discreditable to the British navy . . . 800 vessels have been taken by that Power, whose maritime strength we have impolitically held in contempt."

America had given birth to new ships, new men and a new naval spirit that were a match for a veteran navy whose tradition of victory stretched all the way back to Drake and his *Revenge*. How had the American navy, so new and untried that other nations scarcely realized it existed, managed to ready itself for such sudden glory? The answer can be found by tracing the career of one of its officers: handsome, strong-willed Stephen Decatur.

20

"What practice have you had in war?"

The first Stephen Decatur—the first name was Étienne before he Americanized it—was a French naval lieutenant until failing health forced him to settle down in Philadelphia with his American bride. The second Stephen Decatur was a merchant skipper who joined the Continental navy during the American Revolution. He was among the small, exclusive group of Revolutionary naval officers who did not disgrace themselves in action— and he was fighting the British on the seas at the moment that the third Stephen Decatur was born on January 5, 1779.

The child saw little of his far-voyaging father during the first eight years of his life—but he kept him in his thoughts. For his father was a man for any boy to hero-worship: tall, fashioned like a Greek statue, handsome, and with a springy strength. His record in the Revolutionary War was something to boast to other boys about: He had served so well that he had risen steadily from his first command, a six-gun galley, until—with a 22-gun ship under him—he captured a British war sloop of equal strength in fair fight. And now that the elder Stephen Decatur was back in the merchant trade, he came home with marvelous tales for his son's ears of foreign lands and storms at sea.

When he was eight, young Stephen's father, disturbed by the fact that the boy looked more sickly each time he came home, decided his health would improve if he got some of the sea air his blood demanded. Overriding his wife's objections, he took his son off on his next trip, to France. The boy loved the ship and the sea, and his hero worship increased as he watched his father command the vessel and crew with firm authority leavened by good humor. And his father was right: Young Stephen's sickliness vanished with that one voyage; never to return.

As far as Stephen could see, the men who ruled ships were a new kind of Knights of the Round Table, and he meant to be one of those knights some day. On his return to Philadelphia, he was sent to the Reverend Mr. Abercrombie's school for boys, but he proved strongly resistant to any kind of learning that didn't seem to him to have any application to the future he planned for himself. The only enduring thing he got out of his years at school was the friendship he formed with two other Philadelphia boys of his own age: Charles Stewart (who, as we have seen, was one day to command the *Constitution* in her last fight) and Dick Somers (who was among the first of the American navy's heroes killed in action).

Even as a child, Stephen Decatur's dreams of his destined role in life were forming in him a code of honor peculiarly his own. Once, when a younger, smaller schoolmate with whom he had had words asked him to step out to the graveyard to fight it out, Decatur told him he would accept only if he could also fight the boy's older brother at the same time.

After graduating from Abercrombie's boys' school, Stephen Decatur followed his mother's wishes and entered the University of Pennsylvania. He did so poorly, however, that before a year was out his mother admitted her defeat, and his father got him a clerk's job with Gurney and Smith, shipping agents.

While he was in the employ of Gurney and Smith, they were appointed government agents in charge of the new frigate *United States,* which was to be built in the Philadelphia shipyards of Joshua Humphreys. The firm knew that Humphreys needed no supervision. But since they were required to place a representative in the shipyard they sent a token one: young Stephen Decatur. He spent every day there, watching the *United States* grow. When it was finished, no one knew more about every nail and timber in the ship than he. When it was launched, he slid down the ways into the water on it. In his daydreams, he was already her captain.

The *United States* was not only built by Joshua Humphreys, but had also been designed by him. It was Humphreys' belief that America needed a warship slightly different from any possessed by the navies of other nations.

For America was having its hands full maintaining its merchant fleet on the seas. "The Revolution has been won," Franklin had warned, "but the war of independence is still to be fought." That was turning out to be all too accurate. England and France, being constantly in a state of war, each assumed the right to prevent the United States from trading with the other. England seized American ships headed for France. France seized American ships headed for England. And the Barbary pirates seized American ships, cargoes and seamen unlucky enough to be caught by them in the Mediterranean.

No one feared America's powers of retaliation. After all, its navy had proved so useless that it had been done away with by its own government after the Revolution. And there was still no navy. The government, however, had at last decided that it needed a few real warships, if only for show.

Shipbuilder Joshua Humphreys wrote a letter to Pennsylvania's Senator Robert Morris, in which he strongly urged a revolutionary idea. In retrospect, it seems hardly an exaggeration to say that this single letter kept the United States from losing the War of 1812.

Since America could not hope to build a navy equal in size to those of older nations, Humphreys said, it should instead concentrate on building as many ships as it could that were stronger than other ships of their own class, and fast enough to escape ships of a larger class.

The government decided that the largest class of ships it could afford to build were frigates—which, in addition to the guns on its forecastle and quarter-deck, carried just one main gun deck below. And it decided that six frigates were the largest number that could be built.

Humphreys then suggested that instead of the 18-pounders

carried by standard frigates, these ships should carry long 24-pounders—and more of them than other frigates carried. Experienced sea officers objected, pointing out that the weight of these guns (24-pounders weighed about 5,000 pounds, as contrasted with the 4,200 pounds of an 18-pounder) would unbalance a ship of frigate size when fired all together from one broadside. They were too heavy for a frigate's construction, might break its back in a storm, couldn't be handled and fired as fast as the lighter 18-pounders.

To all these objections, Humphreys had an answer: The upper structure of the frigate he had in mind would be built longer, wider and heavier than usual to carry the greater number of heavier guns. To prevent the additional weight from making the ship slower than standard frigates, the spars would be longer to carry more sail, and the vessel's underwater lines would be cut finer, narrower, to slip more easily through the ocean. With the underwater lines slimmer, the upper structure wider, and the spars longer, Humphreys admitted, the resulting vessel required extremely careful designing for proper balance. He had such a design ready, and had complete faith in it.

So few others had faith in it that it was surprising that he had his way at all. But he did. Of the six new frigates to be built, three were to be smaller and carry fewer guns than Humphreys envisioned: the *Chesapeake, Constellation* and *Congress.* But the other three were to be built in full accordance with Humphreys' design. Of these three heavier frigates, the *President* was to be built in New York, the *Constitution* in Boston, the *United States* in Humphreys' own Philadelphia shipyard.

While Stephen Decatur was watching the *United States* take shape day by day, trouble came up with France. France had once been America's best friend, but since its own revolution, the new French government had seized over three hundred American merchant ships and their cargoes to help its own finances. When American envoys arrived to try to settle matters peacefully, they were met with the demand that, before France would discuss the problem, America must hand over a large amount of money—some of it as a "loan" to France, the rest as a bribe to three of its officials, who came to be referred to as X, Y, and Z. Howling "Millions for defense, but not one cent for tribute!" the Americans prepared to fight the short, undeclared sea war with France which was called the XYZ Affair.

At the time, three of the six new frigates had been built, but there was still no official navy. As America prepared to create one in a hurry, it suddenly realized that the only officers available for it were a handful of old men left over from the Revolution. New officers had to be raised quickly.

Twenty-year-old Stephen Decatur's warrant as a midshipman was issued on April 30, 1798, on the same day that the government created its new Department of the Navy. Assigned to the frigate he knew so well—the *United States*—he found among the other young officers the two boys who were his closest friends at Abercrombie's: Midshipman Dick Somers and Fourth Lieutenant Charles Stewart.

It was on this ship, also, that the shadow of James Barron first fell across Decatur's path (or Decatur's shadow fell upon Barron; it depends from whose side you view what followed). James Barron, a proud, strong young man from Virginia, was third lieutenant on the *United States*. It was his seamanship and sharp thinking that saved the ship from foundering in a bad storm on its first trip, when even the captain thought they were lost. He was rewarded with a promotion to post captain. From that time on, the naval careers of Barron and Decatur were to crisscross several times—fatefully for both, fatally for one.

The XYZ Affair wasn't much of a war, and didn't last long. Young Decatur's father, commanding a 20-gun converted merchant vessel, achieved the first victory of the fight, capturing a 20-gun French schooner. The *United States,* like most of the U. S. warships, had to be content with mopping up a few French privateers apiece. Only Tom Truxtun, commanding the frigate *Constellation,* had been lucky enough to meet, and beat, two sizable French warships. It was enough. France quickly agreed to discuss matters with America in the future reasonably and honorably.

But what was accomplished during the XYZ Affair went far beyond this as far as America's future was concerned. From it, the beginnings of a real navy began to emerge.

The old men who commanded the American ships were really merchant men for whom wartime naval duty was an interruption of their normal activity. Relics of the Revolution—men like the elder Decatur, Truxtun, Richard Dale (who had been John Paul Jones' first lieutenant on the *Bon Homme Richard*), Morris and John Barry, who was in command of the *United States* and ranking officer of the entire small war fleet.

But Truxtun, the elder Decatur and Barry—if they were not pure navy men and hadn't many more years of service left in them—had the vision to see that the future lay in the hands of the raw, spirited, undisciplined officers under them. Out at sea during the XYZ Affair, they began training these puppies with a vengeance.

Under these "old captains" the idea grew that a young man might actually make a full-time career for himself in the American navy. Even a noncommissioned seaman; and this was the newest idea of all. England and the other older countries obtained the majority of their seamen by impressment—forcefully snatching them aboard navy ships, where they were poorly paid, lived in sullen squalor, and did their duty in order to avoid brutal punishments. Only a rare leader such as Nelson could extract wholehearted enthusiasm from such seamen.

But the American seamen had a tradition of independence behind them. They could make a fair living in the merchant service or on privateers. To lure such men into the navy—for impressment would not be tolerated by America—real inducements were offered: decent pay, a discipline that tempered sternness with consideration of the seamen as human beings. They responded by joining the warships and entering into the constant drilling and training aboard with a willingness unknown in any other navy. This was later to become one cause of the War of 1812; for English seamen began deserting the British navy to sign aboard American warships, where they believed they would be treated like men, not animals.

Gunnery, seamanship, navigation, ship handling, manners, discipline, naval formalities—Decatur and the other junior officers were drilled in these things unremittingly. Gunnery was given special emphasis on the new frigates, since the 24-pounders were harder to handle than the 18-pounders of standard frigates. The fledgling officers and gun crews practiced for hours every single day at the heavy guns. Other navies depended on the total effect of broadsides: the whole enemy ship was usually the target. But the "old captains" of this new navy trained their young officers and gun crews to aim every single gun at a specific target aboard an enemy ship, even in a full broadside—as though every cannon were a musket. Daily contests were held with each cannon in turn firing at floating targets. The men were even taught to handle ship and guns in total darkness, by quick feel.

For the fledgling officers, there was also daily practice with swords, pistols, knives, pikes, grenades. . . . They lived, talked, thought and dreamed their new roles.

They had no tradition to be proud of; instead, it was they who were creating a tradition for those to follow, and they were kept constantly aware of it. From the XYZ Affair on, they became increasingly sensitive about the honor of the navy depending on their every word and gesture. And whenever any of them forgot to be touchy about their honor as naval officers, the old captains were there to remind them.

The elder Stephen Decatur, as one of those "old captains," was shocked and disappointed in his son. Young Decatur was surprised; he thought the story he had just told his father was amusing, and reflected some credit on his determination. He had been sent ashore to recruit some more seamen for the *United States*. He had signed up the required men, but before he could take them aboard, a merchant ship in port offered them more pay. When young Decatur found his men had slipped away, he followed them quickly. Reminding them that they had already signed as crewmen of a warship—and would be in serious trouble if they now deserted —he forced them to leave the merchant ship with him. The mate of the merchant ship had been so chagrined that he had howled curses at the departing Decatur and vanishing crewmen.

Decatur thought it was funny. His father did not: His son was an officer of the United States Navy, was he not? The mate had cursed at him, had he not? That was showing a lack of respect for the entire navy, was it not? Would an officer in any other navy in the world allow such an insult to his navy's authority and reputation? He would not!

Young Decatur withered before his father's disgust and disappointment. Against his own good-humored instincts, he went back to the merchant ship and challenged the mate to a duel. Then he went to the *United States* and got his pistols. To Dick Somers and Charles Stewart, who accompanied him as seconds, he expressed his unhappiness: He was a good shot and the mate probably wasn't; he intended to shoot for the mate's hip, in order not to kill him.

The mate's shot missed. Decatur's shot dropped the mate to the ground with a bullet in his hip. Badly upset, Decatur was consoled by Somers and Stewart: He had done the right thing; the navy's honor must be upheld, and every officer was a living representative of that navy.

Soon it didn't take the prodding of the old captains. The young officers became super-sensitive about the duties due to their honor as officers of the navy.

When Decatur called Dick Somers a "fool" for dressing sloppily, Somers understood he was joking. But the other midshipmen aboard the *United States* did not regard the word "fool" as something a naval officer could accept as a joke. They felt that it was Somers' duty to challenge Decatur to a duel, openly doubted his courage, and began giving him the silent treatment. Somers, infuriated, did issue his challenge—to the midshipmen who doubted his courage. He named Decatur as his second, and prepared to shoot it out with all of them, one at a time, one hour apart.

Somers and his opponent were both slightly wounded in the first duel, Somers' arm being cut by the other's pistol ball. In the second duel, Somers was wounded in the leg. Decatur offered to fight the rest of the duelists in his place. Somers refused, though he had to sit in a chair to face his next opponent. Decatur kneeled beside Somers with his arm around him, his hand supporting his shooting arm. Somers put his bullet in his third opponent's shoulder. The rest of the challenged men offered their sincere apologies. Somers had proved his courage to them, and the honor of the navy was vindicated.

This sort of bravura seems silly to us today. But understandable. Since no other nation respected the honor of this young navy, its officers had to respect themselves and their service with a fierceness that was sometimes ridiculous.

By the time young Stephen Decatur was twenty-two, he had risen to the rank of first lieutenant. It was while he was serving on the *New York,* anchored at Malta, that he became involved in another—and more serious—"affair of honor."

Midshipman Joseph Bainbridge (younger brother of Captain William Bainbridge, who would later command the *Constitution* in its second victory) and some other midshipmen had been in a theater ashore when some English officers sitting nearby had made jokes at their expense. They loudly remarked that the Americans, who were in the Mediterranean to try to force the

Barbary States to stop seizing U. S. merchant ships and enslaving American seamen, would run at the first smell of enemy gunpowder. Young Bainbridge and the other midshipmen left the theater to discuss what they should do about it.

The English officers followed them out. One of them deliberately bumped into Midshipman Bainbridge, who promptly punched the Englishman, knocking him down. The Englishman had challenged Bainbridge to a duel—and it turned out that this Englishman was one of the deadliest men with swords or pistols on Malta.

The duel must be fought, Decatur told him, even though Midshipman Bainbridge was not very expert with either swords or pistols. The honor of the navy demanded it. But Decatur said he would act as the midshipman's second. . . .

The duelists and their seconds met in a secluded spot. Since the Englishman was the challenger, the choice of weapons and conditions was up to Midshipman Bainbridge. His second made the choice for him. "Pistols," Decatur said. The Englishman and his seconds were agreeable to that.

"At four paces," Decatur added. The Englishmen were horrified; the standard distance was ten paces. At the distance Decatur demanded, no one could miss.

"Four paces!" one of the English seconds protested. "That looks like murder, sir."

"No, sir," Decatur told him coldly. "It looks like death. Your friend is a duelist. Mine is wholly inexperienced. If you insist upon ten paces, I will fight your friend at that distance."

"We have no quarrel with you, sir," the second objected.

"Then, sir, I must insist upon our terms."

The duelists took their places. The short distance unnerved the Englishman. Decatur—who, as the challenged man's second, was supposed to give the order to fire—unnerved him more by the deliberate slowness with which he gave the order.

The Englishman missed completely. Bainbridge's shot took off his hat.

The guns were reloaded. "Aim lower if you wish to live," Decatur told Bainbridge softly. The two men faced each other again, took aim. The Englishman was even more shaky this time because he had missed with his first shot. And again Decatur tormented him by delaying his order to fire. The Englishman missed again, went down with a bullet hole between his eyes.

First Lieutenant Decatur and Midshipman Bainbridge were sent back to America to explain what had happened and take their punishment. Instead of being reprimanded Decatur was sent back to the Mediterranean and given command (still as a lieutenant) of the 12-gun schooner, *Enterprise*. And Midshipman Bainbridge was made a junior lieutenant.

The government had decided that it would be a mistake to dampen the ardor of young officers such as these. The United States intended to teach the piratical Barbary States some respect for the new flag—and the navy that would have to do the teaching was through training its fledgling officers; it was time for them to take wing and lead.

For after the end of the XYZ Affair, the United States had cut down its number of officers drastically. Most of those to go were the "old men"—the elder Decatur, Barry and the men of their vintage. Only a few remained. The bulk of the navy's officers were the new, navy-bred breed: young captains like Isaac Hull, William Bainbridge and James Barron, none of them yet thirty; still younger lieutenants like Decatur, Somers, and Stewart; and, youngest of all, midshipmen like Thomas Macdonough (destined to achieve immortality eight years later on Lake Champlain) and Stephen Decatur's brother, James (doomed, like Somers, to early death in his duty). The navy was now in their hands.

"A pack of boys!" Captain Edward Preble called them, with contempt and despair. For he had been handed the job of heading a squadron that was to bring the Barbary States to heel. Preble had not been given the appointment as any special honor; there had been three commanders before him who had failed to produce any results. He was simply the government's latest try at finding someone who might possibly get anything done.

If Preble had contempt for the fact that not one of his officers was less than twenty years younger than himself, they returned his scorn and hatred. He had never accomplished anything much, not even in the Revolution. He was uncouth, loud, irritable. His young officers were sure they wanted to learn nothing from him, and that there was nothing in him to learn. They were wrong.

Preble's flagship, the *Constitution,* was sailing past the Mediterranean coast of Spain one night in August of 1803, headed for Tripoli, when another ship was glimpsed through the darkness, sailing along beside it. The night was so thick that it was impossible

to make out the size, shape or much of anything else about the
stranger that had suddenly drawn near them. Preble took up
his speaking trumpet and hailed the vaguely seen ship from his
quarter-deck. There was no answer.

Quietly, Preble ordered all men to battle quarters on the double.
As the crews saw to their big guns, Preble hailed again: "What ship
is that?"

There was no answer from the strange ship. Preble softly sent
word to open the gunports, load, and get matches ready. When the
gun crews were set, matches in hand, Preble put the trumpet to
his mouth again. "I hail you for the last time!" he yelled. "If you do
not answer I'll fire a shot into you!"

Out of the darkness came an answering shout, in an un-
mistakably British accent: "If you fire, I will return a broadside!"

"I'd like to see you do it!" Preble screamed back in a voice his
junior officers had come to know and fear. "I now hail you for an
answer. What ship is that?"

"This is His Majesty's ship *Donegal*. Eighty-four guns. Sir
Richard Stranahan, an English Commodore. Send your boat on
board!"

Preble leaped up into the shrouds to roar back his own answer:
"This is the United States ship *Constitution*. Forty-four guns.
Edward Preble, an American Commodore—who will be damned
before he sends his boat on board any vessel!" And, turning to his
gunners, Preble yelled: "Blow your matches, boys!"

Within moments, while the American subofficers and gun crews
waited Preble's order to fire on a ship twice their size, a boat
appeared alongside. It was from the other ship—which turned out
to be not the *Donegal* but the 32-gun frigate *Maidstone*. The
English officer who came up onto the deck to pay his respects was
very respectful.

The officers of the squadron, when they heard the story of
Preble's challenge, had to admit that though he might be a dis-
agreeable old codger, a man with his courage had something to
teach them after all. They absorbed the lesson with relish. Along
with new respect for their commander, it put new steel in each
of them.

They were soon to need it.

The seventy-five armed men packed around Stephen Decatur
in the little ketch were as quiet as death as they stole through the

night of February 16, 1804, into the harbor of Tripoli. Decatur was at the helm with Salvadore Catalano, a Sicilian sailor, the only man aboard who knew Tripoli harbor well enough to maneuver it in the dark.

Over the shadowed mass of Tripoli, the slim minarets rose against the stars. The ketch sailed deeper into the harbor, slowly, past batteries that could have sunk it with a shot if the enemy officers behind those guns had suspected what it was.

That was where Preble had showed a flash of genius. Decatur had wanted to use his own schooner, the *Enterprise,* but Preble had vetoed him. The watchful eyes in Tripoli harbor knew an American warship when they saw it, even in the dark. This ketch was a native vessel that had been captured while trying to run through the American blockade. It was well known in this harbor. No one knew yet that it had been caught and renamed the *Intrepid.* Its appearance would excite no one behind those harbor guns.

Decatur's heart gave a painful lurch as he recognized at last in the darkness ahead a shape—the largest vessel in the harbor: the *Philadelphia,* one of Humphrey's new frigates. Decatur's father had been her first captain, briefly, just before he retired from the service. Now it was Decatur's job to destroy the *Philadelphia.*

Though the success of America's negotiations with the Barbary pirates rested on Decatur's success on this cold February night, it was a mission to make any man's heart hurt. For to succeed meant to wipe out a ship that represented about 10 per cent of the total effective strength of the U. S. Navy. The *Philadelphia,* commanded by young William Bainbridge, had sailed so proudly into the Mediterranean with its sister frigate, the *Constitution,* and the squadron of smaller vessels.

The Barbary States had long ago forgotten the lesson taught them by an English fleet commander named Blake. From Tunis, Morocco, Algiers and Tripoli, pirates sallied out and snatched merchant vessels of all nations, sold their cargoes, sent their crews into slavery or held them for high ransoms. The great nations of the world could avoid their raids only by paying the various Barbary rulers regular bribes. Even mighty England found it less troublesome to pay them the tribute they demanded than to send warships to convoy every merchant vessel passing through the Mediterranean. America paid them their bribes along with the rest. Bainbridge had once been sent to carry one of these bribes to the Dey of Algiers—who had taken it and then demanded that Bainbridge carry out an errand for him with his navy ship. When Bainbridge protested, the Dey pointed out, quite logically: "You pay me tribute, by which you become my slaves. I have a right to order my slaves as I please."

Bainbridge did the Dey's errand, and America went on paying. But it went against America's grain. And once the United States succeeded in showing France that it would pay "Millions for defense, but not one cent for tribute," it turned a more confident eye on the situation in North Africa. At the same time, the Barbary pirate rulers became more demanding, seized a number of American vessels, demanded $1,000-per-man ransoms for their crews.

America sent Preble with his squadron to do the job no other nation was willing to tackle: making the Barbary rulers behave out of fear, not because of bribes. At first, Preble and his "boys" did well. Preble sent Isaac Hull cruising up and down the North African coast in his little *Argus,* capturing Barbary merchant vessels and letting the people along the shores have a look at an American warship. Preble himself started with the Sherif of Morocco, going ashore personally to beard that ruler in his palace.

The Sherif smiled at him and pointed out that by coming ashore he had placed himself in the Sherif's power. What was to prevent him from throwing Preble in a dungeon and demanding ransom for him? Preble pointed out the window. Out beyond the harbor lay the *Constitution,* Decatur's *Enterprise,* Stewart's *Siren,* Somers' *Nautilus,* and two other smaller warships—all with their guns run out and pointing at the city of Tangier.

"If you do," snapped Preble, "my squadron will lay your castle, your batteries, and your city in ruins in an hour!"

The Sherif signed a treaty, agreed to leave American ships alone from then on, and agreed he could get along without bribes. Preble went back to the *Constitution* in triumph. But his exaltation was quickly snuffed out by terrible news.

While Preble was at Tangier, Bainbridge's *Philadelphia* had been blockading Tripoli, another Barbary power in need of strong persuasion. Since none of the Barbary rulers had any ship as powerful as the frigate, Bainbridge was having no difficulty when the *Philadelphia* suddenly grounded on an uncharted shoal.

Bainbridge hacked down the mainmast to lighten the ship enough to float off. No use; the frigate was caught fast. As it heeled over on the shoal, helpless even to defend itself, swarms of gunboats sailed out from Tripoli to surround it. Bainbridge knocked holes in the frigate's hull to sink it. No use; the shoal held it up. Bainbridge was forced to surrender. He and his officers and crew became prisoners of the Bashaw, ruler of Tripoli.

But even worse, a few days after Bainbridge surrendered, high water enabled the Tripoli pirates to float the *Philadelphia* off the shoal and drag it into Tripoli harbor. By the time spring came, they would have it repaired and ready to sail out under the flag of Tripoli—a ship that could easily wipe out all of Preble's smaller warships, and was strong enough to take on the *Constitution* itself in an equal battle.

There was only one hope. While the squadron kept out of sight of Tripoli, a small vessel must go in and try to set fire to the *Philadelphia* and blow it up. Decatur, not content with his plan, suggested that he try, instead, to sail the *Philadelphia* out of its captivity. But Preble had pointed out that even if Decatur managed to take the ship, with the mainmast missing the *Philadelphia* would be very slow and difficult to maneuver; the gunboats of Tripoli would recapture it before it even managed to crawl out of the harbor. As it was, the odds were against the Americans even being able to destroy the *Philadelphia,* still more against their being able to get out of the harbor alive afterwards.

The ketch *Intrepid* slipped through the darkness of the harbor toward the looming bulk of the *Philadelphia,* on which a few lights winked. Decatur sent most of his men below deck. Decatur, Catalano and the few others remaining in sight on deck all wore turbans and dress common to North African seamen. Decatur had his sword and pistols hidden under a ragged coat.

The side of the big frigate hung directly overhead now. A voice called down from the *Philadelphia's* deck suddenly, asking what they wanted. But there wasn't a trace of alarm in that voice. Preble had been right; this ketch was too well-known in the harbor to upset anyone.

The Sicilian, Catalano, answered the hail loudly, as he had been rehearsed by Decatur: The ketch had managed to slip through the American warships' blockade, but had lost its anchor in a storm. Could they warp to the frigate for the night, instead of having to drift around the harbor till dawn?

Other voices sounded up on the frigate's deck. It would be all right for the ketch to tie up to the big ship. Lines were thrown down to them. Decatur whispered to his men, who began crowding up out of the hold of the ketch, their weapons ready. Inevitably, there was a clang of metal—a sword knocking against a pike, perhaps. A lantern was suddenly held out over the *Philadelphia's* bulwarks. Its light shone down on the men crowding the ketch.

The alarm was given and abruptly the sounds of racing feet and excited voices filled the *Philadelphia*. Above Decatur's head, gun-ports banged open, cannons were being moved. . . .

Decatur flung aside his coat, snatched at his sword. "Boarders!" he yelled, and sprang up the side of the *Philadelphia* with his men.

The Barbary corsairs were at their best in a hand-to-hand struggle. But this time they were taken by surprise by a perfectly organized force. The sword-slashing Decatur drove into them with his brawlers, slaughtering his way across the decks. The surviving Tripoli seamen dropped their weapons and leaped overboard. In five minutes there wasn't a live Tripolitan aboard the *Philadelphia*. It was over so fast that Decatur couldn't believe it. But already his men, each drilled for days in his specific job, were at work. Lieu-tenant Thorn and gunner Hook were hauling up gunpower and combustibles from the *Intrepid*. Midshipman Charlie Morris had his men setting fire to the cockpit and after storeroom. Lieutenant James Lawrence and Midshipman Macdonough were directing the firing of the forward storeroom. Lieutenant Joseph Bainbridge and his group were setting the steerage and wardroom afire.

In minutes, the whole inside of the *Philadelphia* was ablaze, the roaring flames driving the firing parties up onto the quarter-deck, where Decatur stood watching anxiously the vague shapes of anchored Tripoli warships. None of them showed signs of alarm yet. But they soon would, Decatur knew. The deck under his boots was getting hot. Flames suddenly licked up out of open hatches, tasted the lower rigging, and went racing up the masts. The Americans were about to lose the miraculous invisibility that had preserved them till now.

Decatur yelled for his men to get back down onto the *Intrepid*. He waited, counting them as they went over the side, as across the water came the sounds of shouting on other ships.

He counted the last man over—every single one still on his feet, only one of them wounded slightly. Decatur swung over the side, climbed quickly down to the deck of the ketch. The *Intrepid* shoved away from the frigate.

Decatur worked his way through the jam of his men to where Catalano stood by the helm, directing the ketch as it sailed back across the harbor. No need to feel their way this time. The whole harbor was bathed in firelight. The *Intrepid* was a sharply outlined target as cannons began to thunder at it from anchored warships and shore batteries. Heavy shots whistled overhead, plunged into the water on either side, sent up fountains astern. An iron ball ripped through a sail over Decatur's head.

Decatur turned and looked back. The *Philadelphia* was one enormous torch, completely enveloped in a cocoon of flame that rose high above its two masts. Suddenly the guns of the *Philadelphia* —kept loaded with double shot—began to go off like claps of thunder. Some of the shots plunged into the water near the fleeing *Intrepid*. But more of them arced high over the harbor, crashed down into the buildings of Tripoli. The flames ate through the *Philadelphia's* anchor cables. The blazing frigate drifted toward shore, still firing its cannons into the city of the enemy that had captured it. Then, as Decatur watched, the whole ship suddenly rose a bit in the water and blew itself apart with a harbor-shaking explosion, hurling its parts far and wide. The fire had reached its powder stores.

Decatur turned away from the sight. Every gun in the harbor was firing at the *Intrepid* now. But the ketch was very small, and sailing very fast, zigzagging all the way. Before long, the ketch was beyond accurate range. And by the time some of the warships in the harbor were ready to give chase, the *Intrepid* had reached Stewart's waiting *Siren*. Together, the two little vessels raced away across the Mediterranean to rejoin Preble.

Later, Nelson, hearing of what Lieutenant Decatur had done, called it "the most bold and daring act of the age." Naples toasted Decatur as "Terror of the Foe." Preble was gruff as ever. Obviously, his "pack of boys" were up to man's work after all. But all he would admit was that their performance was "quite satisfactory." Decatur had no way of knowing that Preble had written the Secretary of the Navy that "Lieutenant Decatur is an officer of too much value to be neglected," and recommended him for an immediate promotion to Captain.

It was summer when Lieutenant Decatur once again found himself sailing into Tripoli harbor in a small boat. This time there was no possibility of surprise. It was one o'clock in the afternoon, under a high, blazing sun.

This time his vessel was even smaller than the *Intrepid*: a little, flat-bottomed gunboat barely large enough to carry its single cannon and crew of twenty-five men. Decatur looked around at the five similar gunboats driving into the harbor with him. Then he looked toward the harbor defenses. Fourteen Tripoli gunboats, bigger than the Americans', each carrying three guns and overflowing with crews of up to fifty, were streaming out to meet them.

Outside the harbor, Decatur heard the big guns on Preble's warships suddenly let loose. The shots arced over the harbor and crashed into the palace of the Bashaw of Tripoli and buildings surrounding it. The shore batteries opened up, answering the anchored American squadron. Under the arcing cannon balls, the American and Tripolitan gunboats sped toward each other, firing their guns as they closed in for a hand-to-hand clash.

The Americans drove toward the fourteen enemy gunboats in two groups of three boats each. Decatur led one group, followed by the boats of Joseph Bainbridge and Lieutenant Trippe. Somers led the other, followed by Lieutenant Blake and a boat commanded by Decatur's younger brother, now Lieutenant James Decatur.

Decatur picked out the nearest Tripolitan gunboat and told his helmsman to ram it, shouted for his men to stand ready for the crash. The next moment, the two boats slammed into each other. The Tripoli pirates had centuries of this kind of fighting behind them. Yet it was Decatur and his Americans who moved first. They leaped into the crowd aboard the other gunboat, Decatur in the lead, straight ahead across its short deck. Decatur plunged on through a mass of screaming, shouting men, clashing cutlasses and scimitars, crackling small arms. Reaching the other side of the deck, he turned quickly and fought his way back—more carefully this time because the boat was a tangle of enemies and friends; picking his foes, parrying thrusts, driving home with his own bloodied blade.

In ten minutes it was over. Every Tripolitan was either dead or in the water. The enemy boat was Decatur's.

Panting, wiping the blood from his sword, Decatur quickly looked for the rest of the American boats. Joseph Bainbridge's boat had lost its lateen yard. Unable to sail in and come to grips, it was firing its single cannon accurately at enemy gunboats, doing them severe damage. Off to the west, two of the boats had been forced away from the point of battle by a fluke of wind, and were doing what they could against the enemy with the two cannons.

But Lieutenant Trippe's boat had rammed one of the enemy gunboats, boarded it. Trippe, wounded eleven times by scimitar slashes, reached the enemy captain and cut him down with one thrust of his cutlass, then forced the surviving Tripoli seamen to strike to him.

And off to one side, Decatur saw with pride, his brother James had managed to reach the battle, pounding his adversary so accurately with his cannon that its flag was lowered just as he was preparing to board it.

The commanders of the other Tripoli gunboats, shocked by the speed with which three of their fellows had been taken, suddenly turned their boats around and raced back toward the harbor defenses. As they neared shore, however, they ran into the downpour of heavy shot from Preble's squadron. Three of them were hit and sunk within minutes.

Decatur turned back to his own immediate job. Leaving half his crew to take the surrendered gunboat outside the habor, he prepared to return to his own boat with his wounded and eleven sound men. As his prize crew took the captured gunboat away, Decatur heard a hail from across the water. Looking up, he saw his brother's boat racing past him, away from the battle. The gunboat that had struck its flag to his brother was flying it again, turning to sail away in the opposite direction.

His brother's boat swung in close to him. Decatur scanned it quickly; James was not in sight. Midshipman Brown stood by the tiller, shouting at him, his face red with rage and dismay.

As James had boarded the surrendered enemy boat to take possession, its captain had shot him in the head, fired his guns into the American boat, and raised his flag again. James had fallen back into his own boat, his wound mortal.

For a moment, Decatur could only stare at his dying brother's boat, stunned. Then he turned his boat in pursuit of the fleeing gunboat whose captain had shot his brother.

The fleeing enemy boat, loaded with twice as many men as Decatur's, was slower, could not escape him. Decatur closed in, rammed it, leaped aboard before any of his men. In a split second, he spotted the captain who had shot James: a huge, bearded man brandishing a pike in his massive hand. For a moment, a mass of enemy crewmen barred Decatur's way. Then his own Americans were up beside him, hacking and thrusting with a fury nearly matching his own. They knew what he wanted. They cleared a path for him.

Decatur fought through the opening. The hulking enemy captain thrust with his pike at the same time that Decatur swung his sword. The two weapons crashed together. Decatur's sword snapped at the hilt. The enemy captain drove in with the pike again.

Decatur felt a searing pain as the pike ripped through the muscles of his arm, tore into his side. Reeling, he grabbed the shaft of the pike, twisted it with all his strength, wrenching it out of his side and his enemy's grasp. The pike clattered to the deck.

The next instant, the enemy captain was upon him, his greater weight and strength hurling him backward to the deck. Decatur struggled wildly to throw off the pinning weight, could not. Just in time, he saw the flash of a knife in the huge man's hand. Decatur's left hand caught the knife wrist, held it away from him just long enough for him to be able to reach into his own pocket with his right hand. He got his finger across the trigger, cocked the pistol; but he could not pull it out of his pocket. The knife moved slowly toward his throat under the more powerful pressure of the bigger man's arm. Decatur twisted the pistol and fired upward through the material of his pocket. The enemy captain fell away from him, rolled on his back on the deck. He was dead. And his gunboat was surrendered—this time with no chance of treachery.

When Decatur later wearily climbed up the side of the *Constitution* outside the harbor, he found Preble pacing the deck in a fit of near-hysterical disappointment. Decatur, his clothes torn and bloody, his face dark with thoughts of his brother, presented himself and saluted. "I have brought you out three enemy gunboats, Commodore."

Preble, who had hoped to wipe out the enemy's gunboat squadron entirely, looked at his lieutenant with eyes red with anger. Grabbing Decatur's torn collar, he shook him furiously. "Aye, sir! And why did you not bring me out more?"

Decatur fell back a step, his hand instinctively reaching for the knife at his belt, his face flaming. But Preble had already turned away, was stalking into his cabin. Decatur stood where he was, as though frozen. A moment later, word came from Preble's cabin. The Commodore wanted to see Decatur.

The other officers on the quarter-deck watched Decatur disappear into Preble's cabin. They waited. Long minutes passed. There was no sound. Thinking of the way Decatur had clapped his hand to his knife, the officers moved fearfully to the cabin door and peeked inside.

Preble and Decatur were sitting together at the Commodore's table, talking softly, both with tears running down their faces. And Preble was addressing Decatur as "Captain."

"The United States," the Pope announced in Rome, "although in their infancy, have done more to humble the anti-Christian barbarians on the African coast than all the European states had done for a long period of time."

The American navy had reason to be proud. And so did Stephen Decatur, now officially a captain, who back home was already considered "the flower of the navy."

But the fight against the Barbary pirates had been costly for him: James was dead—and so was Somers. Dick Somers, whose close friendship with Stewart and Decatur had begun back at Abercrombie's boys' school in Philadelphia, had taken the *Intrepid* into Tripoli harbor one night, loaded with gunpowder. Somers was to try to get to the harbor shore and blow up the Bashaw's castle. But he had been spotted, fired on. The *Intrepid* had blown up, destroying itself and every man aboard.

It was over now. America was coming to be known as a power to be reckoned with. And Decatur at last had Preble's real opinion of him; had it in black and white—in an order from Preble, who was leaving his command: "You will please . . . take command of the United States ship *Constitution*. . . . I feel a peculiar pleasure in leaving the *Constitution* under the command of an officer, whose enterprise and manly conduct in battle I have so often witnessed. . . . May you ever continue in the pursuit of glory and be crowned with success."

Preble, returning to the United States and fading from the stage of history, left his job to his "pack of boys"—who were, he finally admitted, "good boys."

The fledgling officers of the XYZ Affair, the pack of boys of the campaign against the Barbary pirates, were now the men in control of the navy that had raised them. In 1808, a number of these men—including Decatur, William Bainbridge, Jacob Jones, David Porter, James Lawrence and Charles Stewart—sat as judges in a court-martial, solemnly considering what should be done with another member of their group of young captains: James Barron.

Decatur had offered to remove himself as a judge. He had boarded Barron's frigate, the *Chesapeake,* when it returned to port in its damaged condition; had listened to the charges made by Barron's junior officers. He was convinced of Barron's guilt, and had said so, openly. But Barron had proudly refused to ask that Decatur be removed. He felt he had done nothing wrong.

There was no state of war existing between England and America when Barron took the frigate *Chesapeake* out to sea—but there was much tension. While the *Chesapeake* was still in port, the British navy had listed three of its crew as deserters from an English warship, and demanded their return. The matter was investigated. The three men were found to be Americans who had been impressed into the British navy. The demand was refused.

The American government should have known that the English navy would not be content to let the matter drop. Though English officers usually impressed men from American merchant ships, they had also, on a few occasions, taken them from American navy ships. With Nelson's victories only a few years behind it, the English navy was at its most arrogant. Admiral Collingwood had calmly snatched three members of an American gunboat crew in the Mediterranean. Fifty-five men were just as calmly taken off the 20-gun warship *Baltimore* in the Caribbean by an English squadron short of crews. It was easy, the British officers said, to see the difference between Englishmen and Americans among an American ship's crew: An English seaman had an alert look to him; an American had "a degenerate, hangdog air quite different."

The American government should have alerted Captain Barron to expect trouble. He took the *Chesapeake* to sea with her decks still cluttered with stores that he intended to stow below later. The *Chesapeake* was just nine miles offshore when the 50-gun English warship *Leopard* cruised up alongside. Its guns were run out with their tampions off, ready for action. But this did not alert Barron, who was aware only of the fact that America and England were not at war.

From the *Leopard* came a demand for Barron to deliver up the three "English deserters." Barron refused. The *Leopard* immediately smashed a broadside into the *Chesapeake*. Only then did Barron awake. He ordered his ship cleared for action. Too late. The *Chesapeake's* gun wads and charges, rammers, and matches were under the tangle of cables, timbers and supplies cluttering her decks. Her ports were closed, her powder horns empty, her guns neither primed nor run out. In fifteen minutes, the *Leopard* poured three broadsides into the *Chesapeake*. Only one gun was fired back: Lieutenant Allen managed to run out the single gun, fired it with a red-hot coal he rushed up from the galley in his bare hand.

The *Chesapeake* was badly damaged; three of its men were dead, eighteen wounded, including Captain Barron. Barron struck his flag. The English took off the three men they claimed as deserters—plus one other who had "the alert look" of an English tar. One of the "deserters" was promptly hanged, the other three given five hundred lashes apiece—which killed one of them and left the other two maimed cripples for the rest of their lives.

The verdict of Decatur and his fellow captains was unanimous. Captain James Barron was one of the best seamen in the navy, perhaps *the* best. But as a military man, in the court's opinion, he was lacking: he had sailed out in a year filled with warnings of a coming war, and had been caught unaware, completely unprepared for an emergency fight. Barron was suspended from the navy for a period of five years, and missed whatever chance he would have had to redeem his name in the War of 1812.

Barron placed the whole blame for the verdict on the shoulders of Decatur, who had made the first investigation of the tragedy, had openly admitted his opinion before the court-martial, and who now took Barron's place as commander of the *Chesapeake*. His hatred was to rankle for years before its final violent end.

Coincidence again—one of the many startling ones in the sea war that erupted between England and America in 1812: Captain John Carden of the English frigate *Macedonian,* carrying 49 guns, had inspected the frigate *United States,* carrying 54 guns, just before the war. He told Decatur—who was now captain of the frigate he had watched abuilding, and on which he had first served as a midshipman—that the brand-new *Macedonian* would certainly beat the *United States* in a fight. In short, he said that "though your ships may be good enough, and you are a clever set of fellows, what practice have you had in war? There's the rub."

On Sunday morning of October 25, 1812, Decatur stood on the quarter-deck of the *United States,* discussing the day's work with First Lieutenant Allen—the officer who had carried the live coal that fired the *Chesapeake's* single shot against the *Leopard.* They were seventeen days out of port, off the Canary Islands, looking for a frigate to fight.

A hail came from the masthead: A square-rigged vessel was in sight. Decatur sent Allen up into the rigging to study the stranger. It was an English frigate, bearing toward them with the weather gauge—Captain Carden's *Macedonian.* Decatur calmly ordered: "All hands clear the ship for action."

When the ships were a mile apart, the *Macedonian* suddenly hauled up and began to fire at the *United States.* Carden, certain that British gunners were the best on the seas, had decided to teach the Americans a lesson in accurate long-distance gunnery. He did not know that Decatur had come to believe that gunnery alone should be able to settle a contest—without the necessity of boarding—and had drilled his gun crews every single day for the three years he had been in command of the *United States.*

Backing his mizzen-topsail, Decatur accepted Carden's long-distance duel conditions. The shots from the *Macedonian* were striking his hull and falling all around his ship when the big guns of the *United States* began to crash out their answer. Decatur walked through his frigate, quietly making sure every gun was carefully aimed before firing, coolly looking up to watch the results.

The results were described by a seaman aboard the *Macedonian:* "The large shot crashed against the sides of the ship like monstrous sledge hammers, shaking her to the very keel, or passing through her timbers scattered terrific splinters which did more appalling work . . . the whole scene grew indescribably confused and horrible. It was like some awfully tremendous thunder storm . . . streaks of lightning carrying death in every flash . . . torrents of blood dyed our decks. . . . The cries of the wounded now rang through all parts of the ship. These were carried to the cockpit as fast as they fell, while those more fortunate men who were killed outright were immediately thrown overboard."

Carden endured less than half an hour of Decatur's long-range gunnery. He could see that his English gunners were doing relatively minor damage to the rigging and sails of the *United States,* while their 18-pound balls, which bounced off the American frigate's sides at that distance, did practically no damage at all. His own frigate was breaking apart under him as a result of the fantastically accurate fire of the American cannons.

Carden decided to change the game. He drove his ship toward the *United States* to try to win by boarding.

But Decatur was satisfied with the game the way the British captain had started it. He let the *Macedonian* get just so close, and no closer. As Carden tried to close in, Decatur kept the *United States* swinging away from the English frigate, hitting it with alternating starboard and port broadsides.

The American gunners were now firing their 24-pounders with such incredible speed that their gunports seemed to belch continuous sheets of flame and the whole *United States* was wreathed in rising gun smoke. The English seamen, seeing the smoke, thought the American ship was on fire, and began to cheer.

Their cheers were chopped short. The *Macedonian's* fore-top-mast was torn away and flung into the sea. Its head braces were hacked away. The main-topmast crashed down. The mizzenmast fell and trailed over the stern. The *Macedonian* was a helpless, dismasted wreck, its hull riddled with over one hundred shot holes, rolling in the swells like a log. But Captain Carden, unable to believe what had happened, refused to surrender.

If Carden did not know he was beaten, however, Decatur knew he had won. As he saw it, there was no need for any more men to be killed. With the utmost coolness, he swung the *United States* into position to rake the *Macedonian's* stern, and then held his fire and waited, content to merely demonstrate to Carden that the *Macedonian* was helpless to avoid anything the American frigate now chose to do.

Carden, shaken, saw reason at last, and hauled down his flag in surrender. "I am an undone man," he told Decatur upon coming aboard the *United States.* "I am the first British naval officer that has struck his flag to an American."

Decatur waved aside Carden's offered sword and consoled him with the news of the recent loss of the *Guerrière* to the *Constitution.*

The *United States* had 12 casualties; the *Macedonian* had 104— but she was not too badly damaged to be patched up and taken back for a proud America to look at. The British frigate became the U.S.S. *Macedonian.*

The British blockade of the United States coast closed down hard, locking in the American frigates. It was a long time before Decatur managed to get out of port again. This time he was on the frigate *President* when he tried to dodge through the blockade on a stormy night.

The *President* grounded. By the time Decatur managed to get it off, two hours later, his ship was leaking badly, its masts were strained, its speed was slowed to a crawl. Before the *President* could limp back into port for repairs, it was sighted by four big British warships.

Decatur ran for it, the four English ships after him. The British frigate *Endymion* was the first to get within range. Decatur turned and fought. Realizing that he must shake loose this English frigate if he hoped to escape the rest of its squadron, he loaded his guns with chains and iron bars linked together, fired high to shred the *Endymion's* sails and rigging.

The dismantling shots tore the *Endymion's* rigging apart, brought down every one of its sails. But by the time the *Endymion* had been stopped, the other British ships had closed in on Decatur's badly wounded frigate. A fifth of Decatur's crew were casualties: Three of his lieutenants were dead and a fourth crippled; and Decatur himself, with a metal splinter in his chest and a torn forehead, was in a daze of exhaustion after thirty hours of flight and battle when he surrendered.

This time it was an English captain's turn to refuse an American's sword. Decatur, a prisoner, was treated as if he were a distinguished guest of honor. The English were open in their admiration for him.

But Decatur was in the depths of gloom. What must America think of him? He was soon to find out, for the war quickly ended after his surrender. He went home nervously, expecting the worst —arrived to find himself greeted by noisy bands, cheering mobs, honor banquets. America, which had won the respect it demanded from the world with this war, was in a mood to go on considering Decatur "the flower of the navy."

Life as Commissioner of the Navy—exalted as that post might be—was little to Stephen Decatur's taste. He hated spending day after day ashore, doing nothing more active than arguing with shipbuilders and uniform makers and politicians. "What shall I do?" he wrote to a friend in 1818. "We have no war, nor sign of a war, and I shall feel ashamed to die in bed."

He need not have worried. James Barron entered his life again. For the last time.

In 1818, Barron applied for command of a new navy vessel, one of the first American ships-of-the-line to be built. His term of suspension from the navy after the *Chesapeake* fiasco had ended in 1813. But he had not applied for a warship until five years later, when the war was over—perhaps feeling that he would not be accepted, perhaps proudly waiting to be asked.

Whatever the reason, Commissioner Decatur thought he should have applied during the war, not after it. He took this into consideration—as much as the fact that he still considered Barron's unpreparedness with the *Chesapeake* inexcusable—when he recommended that Barron not be given the appointment to the ship he requested. Barron was turned down by the Secretary of the Navy.

There followed a note from James Barron to Stephen Decatur: "Sir, I have been informed that you have said you could insult me with impunity. If you have said so, you will, no doubt avow it, and I shall expect to hear from you."

Decatur answered: "Sir, I do not think that fighting duels, under any circumstances, can raise the reputation of any man, and have long since discovered that it is not even an unerring criterion of personal courage. . . . From your manner of proceeding, it appears to me, that you have come to the determination to fight some one, and that you have selected me for that purpose . . . your object would have been better attained, had you made this decision during our late war, when your fighting might have benefitted your country, as well as yourself."

A series of letters, each more angry, passed between them— until there was no turning back. When the inevitable duel took place, William Bainbridge acted as Decatur's second. Decatur told him he would shoot only to wound.

Decatur and Barron confronted each other, the faces of each drawn and full of misery. "I hope," said Barron in a choked, trembling voice, "that on meeting in another world we will be better friends than we have been in this."

And Decatur answered with emotion: "I have never been your enemy, sir."

They fired at the same time. Barron crumpled with a ball in his right thigh, as Decatur had intended. Barron's shot plunged into Decatur's abdomen. He died that night in terrible pain.

Poor Barron had gained nothing from the duel. He recovered from his wound to find himself in worse disgrace than ever. He lived out his life under the shadow of it, and died forgotten.

Decatur was carried to his grave by coffin bearers who were the most distinguished officers in the navy. He was buried with flowery speeches in the presence of the President, the Chief Justice of the Supreme Court, the heads of Congress and representatives from all the great nations of the world. And his name lives on to this day.

21

"To windward or leeward, they shall fight today"

TWO STUBBORN MEN

The single-ship actions of the War of 1812 established a reputation for the American navy and won the United States the recognition and respect of the rest of the world. But these fights left unanswered the question of how the Americans would do in a battle between fleets.

This question was answered on Lake Erie and Lake Champlain, where the two miniature fleet actions of this war were fought.

So far, neither the navy nor the war had brought twenty-seven-year-old Oliver Hazard Perry the glorious adventure he longed for. He was a romantic, softly good-looking young man, capable of startling bursts of constructive energy followed with depressing regularity by bouts of incapacitating sickness. His sea captain father had made a sailor of him at an early age in hopes that it would cure his tendency toward sickliness. It didn't. Perry had joined the navy as a midshipman expecting to find an outlet for his flair for the dramatic. But though he served during the campaign against Tripoli, he never got a chance to distinguish himself.

A lieutenant at the start of the War of 1812, his dreams of romantic glory were again stifled. Promoted to master commandant, he was assigned to the boring task of commanding eight harbor-defense gunboats in Newport, Rhode Island, the city of his birth. Since he had just finished over a year of superintending the building of gunboats, which never went anywhere or did anything, he begged the Navy Department for a chance at something else.

In February of 1813, the Navy obliged. The romantic, relatively inexperienced young Perry was handed the job of tackling the English fleet on Lake Erie—a fleet commanded by Captain Barclay, a veteran sea-fighter who had lost an arm following Nelson at Trafalgar eight years before.

It was the job of the English fleet to keep Lake Erie open as a supply route to the British army occupying Detroit and controlling that whole western section of the United States. It was an easy job. For there was no American fleet on the lake to cause trouble—not until young Perry arrived.

Perry knew that he had been given his new job because the government was building vessels on Lake Erie, and Perry was an available officer with the right kind of experience to hurry the construction along. American troops were waging a campaign to win back Detroit and the whole huge territory that had earlier been surrendered to the British.

On the Canadian side of the lake, the English quickly got wind of the new American fleet abuilding. In the British port of Malden, work began on new ships to increase the size of their fleet. But they couldn't match the fiery drive of Perry's enthusiasm-driven energies.

By July, Perry had his hastily thrown-together vessels ready. When he had arrived at the port of Erie, the American fleet waiting for him was composed of a 1-gun sloop, two 1-gun schooners, a 2-gun schooner, and a 3-gun brig. These were under the command of Lieutenant Elliot—whose resentment when Perry suddenly was placed over him was to have a marked effect on the subsequent battle.

Using wooden pegs in place of nonexistent nails and fresh-cut trees in place of seasoned timbers, Perry added to this fleet two more schooners, and two 20-gun brigs, the vessels upon which his success would depend. He named one of them the *Niagara,* and placed Lieutenant Elliot in command of it. The other was named in memory of a setback that occurred on the high seas:

Captain James Lawrence had become the only man in the war to lose a single-ship frigate action to the British. His *Chesapeake* —that ill-fated ship on which James Barron had disgraced himself—was one of the smaller, less well built American frigates. The English ship it met, the *Shannon,* was the biggest and best of the British frigates. It outgunned the *Chesapeake* and outsailed it. And its captain, Broke, outthought and outfought Lawrence. But Lawrence had resisted to the end. His dying order, impossible to carry out, was: "Don't give up the ship!"

Lawrence's courage had fired Perry's imagination. Now he named the brig which he would personally command, *Lawrence.* And he had a special blue pennant to fly from its masthead cut and sewn with the words DON'T GIVE UP THE SHIP in white letters.

Now Perry's fleet was ready to sail out of Erie. But he had no sailors, marines or gun crews to man it. The government had sent no men. Desperately, Perry appealed to his superior, Commodore Chauncey, who was busy building a fleet of his own on Lake Ontario.

Chauncey sent him only sixty men, none of whom knew anything about sailing or gunnery, half of them too ill with fever even to work. In despair, Perry began training those well enough to walk, and sent a plea to General Harrison, leader of the American army waging the land campaign for this territory.

Harrison didn't have any seamen, but he did send a group that proved as valuable as any sailors would have been: one hundred musket-toting Kentucky woodsmen. Still, Perry needed seamen. He appealed to Chauncey again, got another seventy men so near-to-useless that his temper broke its bounds and he wrote to his superior officer: ". . . a motley set . . . I cannot think you saw them after they were selected."

One hundred real navy seamen finally arrived, plus a number of men Perry personally recruited from the area. This brought his force of able-bodied men to about four hundred. He was still three hundred men short of the force he felt was necessary to man his nine vessels; but Washington was insisting that he sail out and fight. He could wait no longer.

There was one last obstacle: Barclay's English fleet was blockad-

ing Perry's fleet inside the harbor of Erie. As long as Captain
Barclay stayed out there and watched him, Perry could not
possibly get out. For there was a sand bar across the mouth of
Erie harbor. Even Perry's schooners would have to have their
guns taken off so that they could ride high enough in the water to
be worked across that bar. And Barclay could destroy each of
them in turn as they came out slowly and defenseless.

Then, on August 2, 1813, Barclay suddenly gave Perry his
chance when he sailed his fleet away to the Canadian side of the
lake to attend a dinner being given in honor of him and his officers.

Barclay reasoned that he didn't mind if the smaller American
vessels did work across the bar while he was gone. His fleet far
outnumbered and outgunned them. The only ships Perry had that
he had any reason to fear were those two 20-gun brigs, the *Lawrence*
and the *Niagara*. But Barclay knew ships, and he knew that those
two brigs could not get across the bar blocking the mouth of the
harbor. Perry could take everything movable off them, and they
would still ride far too deep, their keels far below the top of that
bar.

Barclay's estimate of the depth of the brigs' keels and the height
of the bar was correct. But he did not understand Perry's energy
or Perry's mind.

Perry worked like a beaver possessed of genius and driven by
the sudden unexpected approach of winter. Removing the guns
from the *Lawrence* to lighten her as much as possible, he towed
her to the bar. Then he brought up two big scows, one on either
side of the brig. He cut holes in the hulls of the scows, sinking
them. Submerged, their decks were about on a level with the
bottom of the *Lawrence*.

Getting the longest, strongest logs he could find, Perry jammed
them into the gunports on both sides of the *Lawrence,* fore and aft,
so that half of each log was inside the ship, half projected out from
its side over the decks of the submerged scows.

Then he took plugs that had been cut especially for this purpose, and used them to seal the holes he had cut in the submerged
scows. At the same time, the ends of the long logs projecting from
the sides of the *Lawrence* were bolstered underneath by timbers
reaching down to rest on the decks of the submerged scows. The
water was pumped out of the scows, and as they rose, they took
the *Lawrence* up with them. The *Lawrence,* supported on the

logs sticking out from its gunports and resting on the decks of the scows on both sides of her, rose a full two feet higher out of the water—just enough. The flat-bottomed scows were dragged across the bar carrying the *Lawrence* with them. The bottom of the ship's keel passed over the bar with less than an inch to spare.

It was a stroke of genius on Perry's part. But without his amazing energy, it would never have been accomplished on time. For two days and two nights he worked without sleep, driving his men until they dropped, waking them up and driving them again. At eight o'clock on the morning of August 5, the *Lawrence* floated in the waters of Lake Erie, on the other side of the bar.

Captain Barclay had expected Perry to try to get his big ships across that bar while he was gone. But he hadn't expected him to succeed. At that dinner across the lake, he told his other officers: "I expect to find the Yankee brigs hard and fast on the bar at Erie when I return, in which predicament it will be but a small job to destroy them." Returning about nine o'clock on that morning of the fifth, he was stunned to see the *Lawrence* outside Erie harbor, riding free and easy on the lake.

Captain Barclay was not prepared to meet a brig carrying 20 guns. The largest vessel in his own squadron at the moment was the 17-gun *Queen Charlotte*. And from the distance, it looked to him as though the other American brig, *Niagara*—which had been towed up to the bar by that time—was actually already across it.

Barclay had a new ship, the 19-gun *Detroit,* almost ready for him across the lake at his Malden harbor. He turned his fleet around and raced back to get it.

If Barclay had only known, he could have attacked Perry without fear and destroyed the *Lawrence,* at least, without opposition. Not only was the *Niagara* still stuck inside Erie harbor, but Perry hadn't managed to get even one of his guns back onto the *Lawrence* before Barclay showed up.

Now Perry had time to get out his smaller ships, and work the brig *Niagara* across the bar as he had the *Lawrence.* It took a long time. But by the twelfth of August, Perry had his fleet out and was sailing across the lake in search of Barclay.

Perry's tremendous exertion took its predictable toll on his frail strength, however. He fell into an exhausted stuporlike sleep and awoke to find himself too ill to rise from his ship's cot. His fleet had to anchor and wait while Perry remained in bed, slowly regaining his strength.

By the beginning of September, he was up again, bursting with excitement and restored health. The fleet moved once more.

On the night of September 9, anchored off Malden, Perry gathered the officers of his fleet and gave them their battle instructions —the strongest point of which was that each of them was to do his best to drive in for a close-range duel.

At dawn of the next morning, as he watched Barclay's fleet coming out to do battle, Perry raised the American flag, and then the big square blue pennant bearing the white motto DON'T GIVE UP THE SHIP.

Perry studied the English ships coming on in a single-file line. He had to shade his eyes with both hands against the dazzling reflections of morning sunlight that danced on the rippled surface of the water. Sailing master Taylor came up beside him, disturbed by the light, changeable wind. At the moment, he pointed out, the wind was blowing toward them from the enemy, putting the Americans to leeward and giving Barclay the weather gauge. But Perry was too excited to care: "To windward or leeward, they shall fight today."

The two fleets were fairly evenly matched. Perry had seven minor vessels carrying one to four guns; Barclay had only two of these. But in bigger, more heavily armed ships, Barclay had the advantage: the 19-gun *Detroit,* the 17-gun *Queen Charlotte,* the 13-gun *Lady Prevost,* the 10-gun *Prevost*—a total of 59 guns to the 40 guns of Perry's only sizable vessels, the *Lawrence* and *Niagara,* combined. In all, Perry's nine vessels carried 54 guns to the 63 guns carried by Barclay's six vessels.

But Perry's thick-barreled, short guns threw a much heavier total weight of shot at short range. The English had mostly long, light guns designed for long-distance gunnery.

If Perry's fleet took its time maneuvering, Barclay's long-guns would riddle it from far off. So Perry had instructed his officers to drive their ships straight in against the English as fast as they could sail, to fight it out at short range. Once in close, his heavier weight of cannon shot would eat up the English vessels and the Kentucky riflemen now climbing up the masts of the American ships would do a murderous job on the English decks.

Sailing master Taylor hurried up again: The wind had shifted;

now Perry had the weather gauge, was being blown toward the enemy. But the wind was light; the *Lawrence,* leading the way, was barely doing three knots. The two fleets were now a mile apart. From Barclay's flagship, *Detroit,* the music of a band playing "Rule, Britannia" drifted across the water to Perry.

A gun boomed from Barclay's *Detroit.* Perry watched the shot arc high over the water, pass above his masts and plummet into the water behind. That would be one of Barclay's light long-guns.

Perry wished the wind would stiffen. But it didn't. The American ships glided in with nerve-wracking slowness.

A gun spoke from the *Detroit* again. The shot smashed through the *Lawrence's* bulwarks, wounding several gunners in a shower of jagged splinters. Perry clamped his jaws together hard and glanced back at his own ships.

The 4-gun schooner *Ariel* and 2-gun schooner *Scorpion* were pulling up beside the *Lawrence,* using their greater speed to move ahead and lead the way into battle. Astern—too far astern—came the 3-gun brig *Caledonia.* And behind that came Elliot's 20-gun *Niagara* and the rest of the much smaller vessels.

Perry shook his head in exasperation. They should be closing up faster than that. Elliot should be seeing to it, knowing Perry's battle plan: Perry's *Lawrence,* together with *Scorpion, Ariel* and *Caledonia,* were to concentrate on Barclay's 19-gun *Detroit* and 10-gun *Hunter.* The rest of the smaller American vessels were to combine against the 13-gun *Lady Prevost* and 3-gun *Little Belt.* The other 1-gun English schooner was to be taken on by anyone who got near it.

Elliot was to pit his 20-gun *Niagara* against the 17-gun *Queen Charlotte.* The night before, Elliot had been quite boastful about what his much heavier broadsides would do to that English ship. But to do it, he had to get in close where his short-range carronades would be effective. Instead, Elliot seemed to be falling farther behind every minute.

Splintering crashes fore and aft suddenly shook the *Lawrence* to its keel. Barclay's ships, now stretched out in a line-ahead with their broadsides toward the oncoming Americans, were firing every long-gun they had. And every single one of them was aimed at the *Lawrence.* The English guns were sounding steadily now. Shot whistled over Perry's head, thudded into the hull under his feet. Barclay obviously intended to wreck Perry's flagship before it could get in close. With the *Lawrence* out of the way, the English could then take on the rest of the Americans at a great numerical advantage.

The *Scorpion* and *Ariel* sped ahead of Perry and began to fire their six combined guns into the English ships. Perry let loose with his few long-guns. But they could scarcely be heard against the thundering of all those English cannons. And the *Lawrence* still wasn't close enough for the carronades which made up most of his battery to hit anything.

Perry begged Taylor for more speed. The sailing master shook his head. The *Lawrence*, crawling before the weak breeze, was being slowed even more by those English long shots, which were ripping away rigging and sails.

Perry began to move through the ship, consoling the dozens of men who already lay wounded or dying in the blood-soaked sand that covered the decks. He encouraged the men who stood waiting at their guns and the Kentucky woodsmen who clung in the masts, telling them that their time would soon come.

It did come, at last. Perry drove his *Lawrence* in through the point-blank fire of all the English ships and laid himself alongside Barclay's *Detroit*. An instant later, the *Detroit* quaked as Perry's first massive broadside crushed into it. Up in the *Lawrence's* masts, the Kentucky backwoodsmen began to pick off man after man exposed on the *Detroit's* decks and masts. Perry poured broadside after broadside into the *Detroit,* tearing it apart. The one-armed Captain Barclay was shot down on his deck by a musket ball, staggered back to his feet only to be knocked down again by a spinning chunk of bulwark, rose again, refusing to be taken below. For a few minutes it seemed that his *Detroit* was doomed under the crushing power of Perry's blows. Then Perry's broadsides began to slacken noticeably, became ragged and less effective.

For Perry was still fighting almost alone against Barclay's whole force. His only support came from the meager six guns of the *Scorpion* and *Ariel,* ahead, and the three guns of the *Caledonia,* astern. The rest of the smaller American vessels had failed to close in near enough to fire at the English.

Neither had Elliot's *Niagara.* Perry had his bugler sound a clear call for Elliot to come up to help him. The *Niagara* remained far astern. Nineteen of its guns were silent, useless at that long range. Elliot went on firing his single long-gun at the enemy.

The *Lawrence* was being torn apart by the full weight of fire from Barclay's *Detroit, Queen Charlotte* and *Hunter.* Slowly, the American *Caledonia* moved up in response to Perry's bugler, began to absorb the shots from the *Hunter* and some of the stern fire of the *Queen Charlotte.* But it was too late. By then, Perry's flagship had been taking all the broadsides of most of the English ships for almost two and a half horrible hours.

Perry, pale as a ghost, found himself commanding a shattered, blood-soaked jumble of wreckage. All of his guns except one had been smashed out of action. The *Lawrence,* without a shred of sail left to her, drifted helplessly under the relentless pounding from three English ships. More than half of Perry's crew were dead or too badly wounded to rise from the splintered decks. There was no one left to tend the fallen: the surgeon and all his helpers were dead in the cockpit below. Perry, untouched himself through all this, was soaked from the soles of his boots to his knees with the blood of others.

Perry was forced to admit it: The *Lawrence* must surrender quickly or sink taking all the wounded under with her. He looked up at the shot-ripped pennant fluttering in the breeze: DON'T GIVE UP THE SHIP. Well, after all, giving up a ship did not mean giving up the whole battle—not in a fleet action. Perry hauled down the ragged pennant and rolled it up under his arm. He hurried to Lieutenant Yarnell and informed him that he was about to get command of the *Lawrence.* He told Yarnell not to haul down the United States flag till after he was gone. When a ship struck its flag, it officially surrendered itself and every man aboard it. Perry didn't intend to be aboard when the *Lawrence* struck.

Lowering a boat over the side, he climbed down to it, told the oarsmen: "Row me to the *Niagara.*" They bent to their oars with all their strength and speed, in a frenzy to get out of the storm of cannon balls, grapeshot and musket balls suddenly being spat at the boat from every English vessel. For the English had spotted Perry, standing up erect in the stern of the boat, carefully balanced, proudly carrying his blue banner through the deadly hail.

One of the oarsmen abruptly reached out and yanked Perry down into the boat. Perry started to rise again. Another of his boat crew grabbed him with a strong hand. Perry sat.

Elliot had placed the *Niagara* on the other side of the *Lawrence* by this time, so that Perry's now-surrendered flagship shielded

Elliot from the English fire. And he was so far away from the battle that it took fifteen minutes of hard rowing to reach the *Niagara.*

Perry climbed the Jacob's ladder. Elliot, his face pale, met him on the deck. Perry stared at him, waiting for an explanation. Elliot said nothing. It was Perry who spoke at last, gazing straight into Elliot's eyes: "I've been betrayed."

Then he turned on his heel, telling Elliot over his shoulder to leave the *Niagara* at once and tend to the schooners. Elliot left without a word. Perry raised his pennant, DON'T GIVE UP THE SHIP, and took the *Niagara* into the battle.

Barclay's *Detroit,* and his 17-gun *Queen Charlotte,* had taken a savage beating on their port sides from the *Lawrence* in the process of smashing it into surrender. Now they saw Perry coming back toward them in a fresh 20-gun flagship. Both of the English ships tried to wear around at the same time so that they could present their untouched starboard broadsides to the oncoming *Niagara.* In their hurry—awkward from the damage done their sails and rigging by the *Lawrence*—they fouled each other. Caught together, unmanageable, the two biggest English ships began to drift away from the already ragged English line.

Perry saw the opening instantly. Making sure every one of the twenty guns aboard the *Niagara* was packed with double loads of heavy shot, he drove his new flagship in through the hole. He waited until he had the fouled *Detroit* and *Queen Charlotte* at half-pistol-shot distance on his starboard, the 13-gun *Lady Prevost,* 3-gun *Little Belt* and 1-gun *Chippewa* on his port. Then he gave the order: Fire!

The *Niagara's* guns roared together out of both sides, smashing into English ships right and left. Perry was down among his gunners, infecting them with his own wild excitement, driving them to the limits of their speed in reloading and refiring. He kept it up, raking his broadsides into the *Detroit* and *Queen Charlotte* on his starboard, pounding the English vessels trying to get away on his port.

The *Queen Charlotte* lowered its flag eight minutes later. Now Perry concentrated all his fire on Barclay's flagship. The *Detroit* had been badly maimed before by the carronades of the *Lawrence.* The *Niagara* completed Perry's job of destruction.

Barclay, flat on his back with five wounds now, his flagship shorn of its braces, most of its rigging, its mizzen-topmast and gaff, and its sides caved in from stem to stern, "was under the painful necessity of answering the enemy to say we had surrendered."

By then, Perry's smaller vessels had swept in and smothered all but two of the other English vessels into surrender. Those two, the 1-gun *Chippewa* and the 3-gun *Little Belt,* were running for it, trying to escape. But their rigging had been so hacked apart by then that they were slow. Caught by two of Perry's smallest vessels, they struck their flags.

Perry had himself rowed back to the wreck of the *Lawrence,* raised his pennant in it once more, and sat down on an overturned cannon in the midst of the wreckage to compose a hasty report to General Harrison. Taking off his bullet-ripped navy cap, using it for support, he wrote on the back of an envelope: "Dear General— We have met the enemy, and they are ours. Two ships, two brigs, one schooner, and one sloop."

And then, his burst of energy spent, he slumped back and let exhaustion have its way with him.

The British army, its route of food and supplies cut off, could do nothing but retreat when the American troops attacked on receiving Perry's message. Detroit, and the whole British-held territory, returned to American hands.

Stephen Decatur had called Thomas Macdonough "my favorite midshipman." He hadn't chosen the navy as a career. It had been chosen for him by his father, who had been a major in the American army during the Revolution and believed in having a military man in every generation of the family.

As a youth Thomas Macdonough had intended to make religion his profession. His father had not interfered, since Thomas' older brother, James, was already a midshipman aboard the U.S.S. *Constellation,* under Captain Truxtun. Then came the XYZ Affair, and the *Constellation* fought the French *Insurgente,* tore the French ship apart at a cost of only four casualties to itself. One of these casualties, James Macdonough, lost his foot and was retired from the navy. It was decided by the family that sixteen-year-old Thomas Macdonough should take his brother's place. Thomas believed in honoring his father's authority and went without a murmur.

His fellow midshipmen found him a pious boy, given to prayerful moods. It was a piety he never lost. But with the campaign against the Barbary pirates, Macdonough revealed another side of himself: He absorbed every technique of sea fighting and gun handling and he fought with a rigidly controlled passion that was overwhelming.

He fought beside Lieutenant Decatur when they burned the *Philadelphia* in Tripoli harbor. He was with Decatur when they went into Tripoli harbor again and fought the enemy gunboats. Young Tom Macdonough, everyone said, was a fellow you could depend upon to stick to his guns, no matter what. He proved it soon after his promotion to lieutenant at the end of the campaign.

Anchored in the British harbor of Gibraltar aboard his 16-gun war sloop, *Siren,* Macdonough saw a press boat from an English frigate seize a seaman from an American merchant vessel. Macdonough lowered a boat, armed his oarsmen, and gave chase. He caught up to the press boat as it reached the English warship, demanded the English turn over the man they had taken. The officer of the press boat refused, said the man was a British deserter. Macdonough told his men to cock their muskets and pistols. The seaman was quickly turned over to him, and Macdonough returned the man to the American merchant ship.

Shortly thereafter, the captain of the English frigate came aboard the *Siren.* Was Lieutenant Macdonough aware, he asked pointedly, that his frigate hurled a broadside more than four times as powerful as the little *Siren's,* that this was an English harbor and all the guns in the shore batteries were English, that there were quite a number of other English warships in the harbor at the moment? Unless Macdonough wanted his sloop sunk in a very few minutes, he'd better turn that seaman over to his press boat again, and be quick about it.

"As long as the *Siren* swims," Macdonough told him without raising his voice, "you shall not have that man."

Furious, the English captain snapped back: "Suppose *I* impress men from that American brig? Would you attempt to stop *me*?"

"You have only to try," said twenty-year-old Thomas Macdonough firmly, "to find out."

The English captain declined the invitation to create an international incident.

Then came the War of 1812, and crushing boredom for Macdonough. For almost two years he sat with his small squadron of tiny gunboats on the American end of Lake Champlain and looked across the water toward the Canadian end, where the English commander was sitting with a similar little squadron. He thought wistfully of luckier navy officers, his friends from midshipmen days, who were out fighting on the high seas in their frigates and sloops. As for himself, twenty-eight-year-old Lieutenant Macdonough fully expected to go on sitting for the duration of the war.

The British high command decided otherwise. Early in 1814, they conceived a plan to win the war with one long stroke: an army advance from Canada, down past Lake Champlain and into New York to the Atlantic coast, which would sever New England completely from the rest of the country. Ten thousand of the best, most experienced fighting troops that England had were landed in Canada for this purpose. If this thrust succeeded, the United States would be brought to its knees in short order. And there was no reason why it shouldn't succeed; America had nothing that could stand against such a force.

Only one item was needed before the thrust could begin: Lake Champlain, the only practical route over which enough food and supplies could be transported down to the advancing army, must first be taken.

The British began building up their Lake Champlain fleet. But Washington learned of the plans, and suddenly Macdonough found his own fleet in Plattsburg Bay growing.

The British built four sailing warships. The Americans built four sailing warships. The three smaller American warships, plus ten little gunboats, were a pretty even match for the three smaller British warships and thirteen galleys.

But the largest English warship was a frigate carrying 38 guns. The English commander, Captain George Downie, considered this frigate, the *Confiance,* strong enough to tackle the whole American fleet alone. Against it was the largest American vessel, Macdonough's flagship, the *Saratoga,* with only 26 guns.

While ten thousand British troops stood ready to begin their thrust to the Atlantic as soon as Lake Champlain was taken, Captain Downie sailed his fleet down to take it. On the dawn of September 11, 1814, the English ships appeared outside Plattsburg Bay.

Macdonough had just come out onto the quarter-deck of the *Saratoga* in his full-dress uniform to conduct the Sunday-morning religious service when the news of the British approach reached him.

Macdonough nodded. There was no need for impious haste. He was ready; his fleet was in station, everyone had their orders, and all the guns were loaded and run out. Since the wind was light and chancy, he had decided not to depend on it. His four sailing ships were at anchor off the town of Plattsburg in a single-file line-ahead, their starboard broadsides toward the approaching enemy. At the head of his line was the 20-gun *Eagle.* Behind it was the *Saratoga.* Astern of the *Saratoga* was the 17-gun *Ticonderoga.* The rear vessel in his line was the 7-gun *Preble.* His ten tiny gunboats—near-useless little fragile-sided creatures—were between the four sailing ships and the shore, ready to dive in where the battle demanded their presence. Macdonough was ready. The rest was in the hands of God.

He knelt before his assembled crew and raised his eyes to the cloudless heavens, prayed aloud for the Lord's strength in what was to follow. Then he rose, sent the men to battle quarters, and strode across the deck to one of his long 24-pounders to set them an example.

Standing with the gun's crew, Macdonough gazed across the water at the approaching enemy fleet. The four English sailing ships came on side by side: the 11-gun *Chubb,* the 16-gun *Linnet,* the massive *Confiance,* the 11-gun *Finch.* The thirteen English gunboats scurried along behind the *Finch,* aiming toward the rear of the American line.

It was Captain Downie's flagship, the *Confiance,* that Macdonough selected. Carefully, expertly, he aimed the long-24 at the English flagship's oncoming bows, gave the word for the crew captain to touch it off. The cannon roared and recoiled. The heavy iron ball spun across the water, smashed through the *Confiance's* bulwarks. It ploughed its way down Captain Downie's deck from bow to stern, sending up showers of splinters that killed four men outright, and demolished the wheel together with the helmsman.

Macdonough, having set the example, stepped back. His gunners went to work on the four American ships. The English fired their few bow guns as they came on slowly with a light wind against the deadly raking fire of the American broadsides. One English shot, bounding across the *Saratoga's* deck, bashed open a chicken coop in which some of the seamen kept a fighting cock. The cock, unhurt but angered, flapped up onto one of the guns and crowed its fighting challenge. The sweating gunners of the *Saratoga* laughed and let out a cheer for the cock's pugnacious spirit. Macdonough smiled and kept his eyes on the enemy.

They were at point-blank distance now, swinging to present their own broadsides to the Americans'. The battle was locked in earnest.

Early in the battle, Macdonough saw the power of the two American ships astern of the *Saratoga* lost to him: The *Preble* was smashed out of line and crawled away to the shore; the *Ticonderoga* became completely embroiled in a tangle of enemy gunboats. On the British side, Macdonough was relieved to see, the *Finch,* knocked out of action before it reached the American line, went aground on Crab Island; the *Chubb* was dismasted and drifting aimlessly.

That left just two effective ships on each side: the American *Saratoga* and *Eagle,* the English *Confiance* and *Linnet.* Before long, Macdonough realized that his 20-gun *Eagle,* up ahead, was being outfought completely by the 16-gun English brig, *Linnet.*

Lieutenant Macdonough tensely watched Captain Downie's *Confiance* drive toward him with the stolid assurance of a 38-gun ship tackling a 26-gun ship. The *Confiance* had more on its side than superior weight of shot: It was much bigger, higher, had thicker-armored sides, carried many more men. Macdonough poured his starboard broadsides into its bows, but still it shoved in to point-blank range. Then it swung slowly to show Macdonough the out-thrust teeth of its high port broadside, and dropped its anchors.

Aboard the *Confiance,* Captain Downie had waited patiently for this moment, every gun stuffed with two full-sized iron balls. As his anchors rattled down, he snapped the order: Fire! Plattsburg Bay reverberated with the concussion of his double-shotted broadside.

The *Saratoga* rose in the water and heeled over violently. Macdonough felt himself twirled around in the midst of a massive explosion and hurled to the deck, his sight blurring, his brain jammed with crashes, screams, roaring guns and snapping timbers. He shook his head to clear it, staggered to his feet. All around him men were pulling themselves up off the deck, their faces blank with shock as was his.

But one-fifth of his entire crew did not get up off the deck. One-fifth! With a single broadside! Gunners stood motionless, stunned by the detonation that had engulfed them, numbed by the sight of all those mangled corpses strewn through the wreckage.

Macdonough shook off his astonishment, leaped down to the gun deck, ran to one of the idle cannons. Its crew, seeing him lay his hands on the gun, moved again, drew in to take over the gun. Macdonough worked it with them, loaded it, shoved it out, aimed and fired it himself. He stayed there, working as part of the gun crew. All along the gun deck, the sight of their captain working that gun stirred the other crews, brought them back to their guns. Another double-shotted broadside from the *Confiance* thundered into the *Saratoga,* dismantling guns, killing men, ripping out the mainmast. Macdonough and the remaining gunners went on firing their guns.

One of the American 24-pound shots clanged head-on against the mouth of a cannon on the *Confiance's* quarter-deck, breaking it and its carriage loose from the breechings, flinging its gun crew aside. The cannon raced backward across the quarter-deck, driving into Captain Downie and over him, leaving him dead in its wake. His first lieutenant assumed command, kept the *Confiance's* guns punching at the *Saratoga's* torn-apart side.

Macdonough was aiming his cannon when the spanker boom, cut by a whirling iron ball, fell, giving his head a glancing blow that knocked him unconscious. When he slowly came to, he found himself lying in the scuppers. Dragging himself up on his knees, he waited till his head cleared, and staggered to his feet.

He found himself another gun to fire. It was not just a matter of setting an example now. There weren't enough men left to fire all the guns. But soon, under the smashing blows of the *Confiance's* guns, the situation was reversed. Gun after gun aboard the *Saratoga* was broken or dismantled or exploded. There weren't enough guns for his remaining gunners to man.

A heavy shot smashed through the port at which Macdonough was toiling, tore off the head of one of the gun crew and hurled it in his face, drove the weight of the gun back against him with such force that he fell senseless to the deck for a second time. He lay there a long time before regaining consciousness. Dazed, agony-wracked, he picked himself up at last to find only a few of the guns in his shattered starboard battery still firing. He looked wearily across the water. The *Confiance,* big as she was, was in almost as bad shape. Her port side was so caved in that the ship had been heeled over to starboard to keep from sinking. Some of her remaining guns were firing too high, their shots arcing harmlessly over the stumps of the *Saratoga's* masts. But not all of them.

Two hours of giving and taking steady barrages finally had their net effect. The last of the *Saratoga's* starboard guns was silenced. Across the water, four of the *Confiance's* guns still fired, but were shooting high.

Neither ship could hit the other now, and neither had surrendered. But up ahead, the balance suddenly swung against the American side. The American *Eagle* was finally completely disabled by the 16-gun English *Linnet* and drifted toward the shore. The *Linnet* swung down to rake the helpless *Saratoga* into submission.

Macdonough, however, had one chance. The day before the battle, he had prepared for this emergency by running cables from his bow to his stern, and having kedge anchors ready at either end. Now, he cut his bow anchor, dropped his stern anchor with the cable attached from it along the length of his ship to the bows. Then he heaved on this cable, throwing out kedges from the bow to help, and turned the *Saratoga* around by brute force.

When the turn was completed, the *Saratoga* presented its undamaged port side to the smashed side of the *Confiance*. The acting commander of the English frigate hastily tried to run out a cable and follow suit. But it was too late. Before the English flagship could be turned around, Macdonough's *Saratoga* was pounding full broadsides into it from his fresh side.

The *Confiance* was torn apart; its men were dying in batches. At last, one of her officers reported, the English survivors "declared they would no longer stand to their quarters nor could the officers with their utmost exertions rally them."

The *Confiance* surrendered. Macdonough turned his fresh broadsides on the 16-gun *Linnet,* which could endure only fifteen minutes of his murderous fire. The *Linnet* struck its flag—and the whole English sailing fleet was in Macdonough's hands. Lake Champlain was still American.

Unable to advance, now that there would be no way for food and supplies to reach them, the ten thousand picked English troops could do nothing but retreat back up into Canada, beaten by a fighter they never saw: Lieutenant Macdonough. The English plan of a northern invasion was ended before it began.

As the war ended, the London *Times* laid out what had happened in black and white: "We have retired from the combat with the stripes yet bleeding on our backs. . . . Scarcely is there an

American ship of war which has not to boast a victory over the British flag; scarcely one British ship in thirty or forty that has beaten an American. With the bravest seamen and the most powerful navy in the world, we retire from the contest when the balance of defeat is so heavy against us."

So the Americans came out of the War of 1812 with a young new navy respected the world over; with free reign on the high seas that in the years that followed made the United States one of the great ocean-going powers.

Farewell

With the end of the War of 1812, our history of wooden-hulled warships under sails draws to a close. The greatest era of commercial sailing ships was just beginning, but their fighting days were numbered. The big sailing battles were retreating swiftly into the past, and the great sailing-navy captains were no more.

In fighting ships, steam was soon to replace sails, ironclad sides to replace wooden hulls, explosive shells to replace solid round shot. With the American Civil War, sailing navies were left to moulder while all attention was turned to steam-and-armor construction.

But if the days of fighting ships of sail were short and done with, their glory was not. The spirit of the men who ruled those ships lives on, not only in the navies that followed them, but as a precious, proud heritage for men of courage now and in the future.

BIBLIOGRAPHY: GENERAL

BOWEN, FRANK C., *Wooden Walls in Action*. London: Halton & Company, 1951

MAHAN, CAPT. ALFRED THAYER, *Naval Strategy*. Boston: Little, Brown & Company, 1911

ROBERTSON, FREDERICK L., *The Evolution of Naval Armament*. London: Constable & Company, 1921

ROBISON, S. S., and ROBISON, M. L. C., *A History of Naval Tactics from 1530 to 1930*. Newport, R.I.: United States Naval Institute, 1942

STEVENS, W. O., and WESTCOTT, A. F., *A History of Sea Power*. New York: Doubleday, Doran & Company, 1942

VAN LOON, HENDRIK WILLEM, *Ships and How They Sailed the Seven Seas*. New York: Simon & Schuster, 1935

PART ONE

(My special thanks for the assistance of Ann Buurman and Henrietta Van Nierop of the Netherlands Information Service)

GEYL, PIETER, *The Revolt of the Netherlands against Spain, 1555–1609*. London: Williams & Norgate, 1932

FRUIN, ROBERT J., *The Siege and Relief of Leyden in 1574*. The Hague: M. Nijhoff, 1927

METS, JAMES ANDREW, *Naval Heroes of Holland*. New York: Abbey Press, 1902

MOTLEY, JOHN LOTHROP, *The Rise of the Dutch Republic*. London: John Murray, 1904

PONCELET, ÉDOUARD, "Guillaume de la Marck." Brussels Academie Royale de Belgique; Commission Royale d'Histoire. Bulletin, Tome 100, 1936

VERE, FRANCIS, *Salt in Their Blood; the Lives of the Famous Dutch Admirals*. London: Cassell & Company, 1955

VERSTEEG, DINGMAN, *The Sea Beggars*. New York: Continental Publishing Company, 1901

VLEKKE, BERNARD, *Evolution of the Dutch Nation*. New York: Roy Publishers, 1945

PART TWO

BARROW, JOHN, *The Life, Voyages, and Exploits of Sir Francis Drake*. London: John Murray, 1844

CORBETT, JULIAN, *Drake and the Tudor Navy*. London: Longmans, Green & Company, 1898

COXERE, EDWARD, *Adventures by Sea.* New York: Oxford University Press, 1946

LAUGHTON, JOHN KNOX, EDITOR, *From Howard to Nelson: Twelve Sailors.* London: Lawrence & Bullen, Ltd., 1899

MASON, A. E. W., *The Life of Francis Drake.* New York: Doubleday, Doran & Company, 1942

UPCOTT, J. D., *Sir Francis Drake and the Beginnings of English Sea Power.* New York: G. P. Putnam's Sons, 1927

WILLIAMSON, JAMES A., *Sir Francis Drake.* London: Collins, Sons & Company, 1951

WOOD, WILLIAM C. H., *Elizabethan Sea-Dogs; A Chronicle of Drake and His Companions.* New Haven, Conn.: Yale University Press, 1921

PART THREE

ADAMS, W. H. DAVENPORT, *Records of Noble Lives.* London: T. Nelson & Sons, 1869

ANDERSON, R. C., EDITOR, *Journals and Narratives of the Third Dutch War.* London: Navy Records Society, 1946

BEADON, ROGER, *Robert Blake.* London: Edward Arnold & Company, 1935

BLOK, PETRUS, *The Life of Admiral De Ruyter.* London: Ernest Benn, Ltd., 1933

BOXER, C. R., EDITOR, *The Journal of Maarten Harpertszoon Tromp, anno 1639.* London: Cambridge University Press, 1930

CORBETT, JULIAN, *Monk.* London: Macmillan & Company, 1889

CURTIS, C. D., *Blake: General-At-Sea.* London: Williams & Norgate, 1934

GRINNELL-MILNE, G., *Life of Lieut.-Admiral De Ruyter.* London: Kegan Paul, Trench, Trubner & Company, 1896

GUIZOT, FRANÇOIS P. G., *Memoirs of George Monk, Duke of Albemarle.* London: R. Bentley, 1838

—— *Monk and Washington; Historical Studies.* London: G. Routledge & Company, 1851

HANNAY, DAVID, *Admiral Blake.* New York: D. Appleton and Company, 1886

MAHAN, CAPT. ALFRED THAYER, *The Influence of Sea Power Upon History, 1660–1783.* Boston: Little, Brown & Company, 1898

METS, JAMES A., *Naval Heroes of Holland.* New York: Abbey Press, 1902

SKINNER, THOMAS, *The Life of General Monk from an original manuscript by T. Skinner . . . edited by W. Webster.* London: Bowyer, 1723

The Life of Cornelius Van Tromp. London: J. Orme, 1697

VERE, FRANCIS, *Salt in Their Blood; the Lives of the Famous Dutch Admirals.* Cassell & Company, 1955

WARNER, OLIVER, *Hero of the Restoration; A Life of General George Monck, First Duke of Albemarle.* London: Jarrolds Publishers Ltd., 1936

PART FOUR

BURROWS, MONTAGU, *The Life of Edward, Lord Hawke.* London: W. H. Allen & Company, 1883

CUNAT, CHARLES M., *Histoire du Bailli de Suffren.* Rennes: A. Marteville et Lefas, 1852

DE KOVEN, A., *Life and Letters of John Paul Jones.* New York: Charles Scribner's Sons, 1913

DUVIC, G. O., *Suffren et al Campagne des Indes.* Paris: Larousse, 1952

JOHNSON, GERALD W., *The First Captain; the Story of John Paul Jones.* New York: Coward-McCann, Inc., 1947

LAUGHTON, JOHN KNOX, *Studies in Naval History. Biographies.* Longmans, Green & Company, 1887

LOCKER, EDWARD HAWKE, *Memoirs of Celebrated Naval Commanders.* London, Harding & Lepard, 1832

LORENZ, LINCOLN, *John Paul Jones.* Newport, R.I.: United States Naval Institute, 1943

MAHAN, CAPT. ALFRED THAYER, *The Influence of Sea Power Upon History, 1660–1783.* Boston: Little, Brown & Company, 1898

——— *Types of Naval Officers,* Boston: Little, Brown & Company, 1901

——— *Major Operations of the Navies in the War of American Independence.* Boston: Little, Brown & Company, 1901

RUSSELL, PHILLIPS, *John Paul Jones, Man of Action.* New York: Brentano's Inc., 1927

PART FIVE

BERRY, EDWARD, *An Authentic Narrative . . . of the Proceedings of His Majesty's Squadron under the command of Rear-Admiral Sir Horatio Nelson. . . .* Edinburgh: J. Simpson, 1798

BROWNE, G. LATHOM, *Nelson.* London: T. F. Unwin, 1891

CLARKE, J. S., and MC ARTHUR, J., *The Life of Admiral Lord Nelson.* London: T. Cadell & W. Davies, 1809

FITCHETT, W. H., *Nelson and His Captains.* London: Smith, Elder & Company, 1902

GORE, J., *Nelson's Hardy and His Wife.* London: John Murray, 1935

GRENFELL, RUSSELL, *Nelson, the Sailor.* London: Faber & Faber, 1949

JAMES, W. M., *Durable Monument: A Life of Nelson.* London: Longmans, Green & Company, 1948

KERR, M. E. F., *The Sailor's Nelson.* London: Hurst & Blackett, Ltd., 1932

MAHAN, CAPT. ALFRED THAYER, *The Life of Nelson.* London: Sampson Low, Marston & Company, 1897

MURRAY, GEOFFREY, *The Life of Admiral Collingwood*. London: Hutchinson & Company, 1936.

NELSON, HORATIO, *The Letters of Lord Nelson to Lady Hamilton*. London: T. Lovewell, 1814.

NICOLAS, N. H., EDITOR, *The Dispatches and Letters of Vice Admiral Lord Viscount Nelson*. London: H. Colburn, 1846.

OMAN, CAROLA, *Nelson*. New York: Doubleday & Company, 1946.

SOUTHEY, ROBERT, *The Life of Nelson*. London: John Murray, 1813

PART SIX

ALDEN, C. S., and WESTCOTT, A. F., *The United States Navy*. Philadelphia: J. B. Lippincott Company, 1943

ANTHONY, IRVIN, *Decatur*. New York: Charles Scribner's Sons, 1931

CLARK, GEORGE R., STEVENS, WILLIAM O., ALDEN, CARROLL S., and KRAFFT, HERMAN F., *A Short History of the United States Navy*. Philadelphia: J. B. Lippincott Company, 1911

FROST, JOHN, EDITOR, *The Book of the Navy*. New York: D. Appleton and Company, 1842

LAING, ALEXANDER, *Clipper Ship Men*. New York: Duell, Sloan & Pearce, Inc., 1944

MACLAY, EDGAR STANTON, *A Youthful Man-O'-Warsman*. Greenlawn, N. Y.: Navy Blue Company, 1910

MAHAN, CAPT. ALFRED THAYER, *Sea Power in Its Relation to the War of 1812*. London: Sampson Low, Marston & Company, 1905

NICOLAY, HELEN, *Decatur of the Old Navy*. New York: D. Appleton-Century Company, 1942

PAINE, RALPH D., *The Fight for a Free Sea: A Chronicle of the War of 1812*. New Haven, Conn.: Yale University Press, 1921

PRATT, FLETCHER, *Preble's Boys*. New York: William Sloane Associates, 1950

ROOSEVELT, THEODORE, *The Naval War of 1812*. New York: G. P. Putnam's Sons, 1902

TUCKER, GLENN, *Poltroons and Patriots*. Indianapolis: The Bobbs-Merrill Company, 1954

INDEX